LEGALIZED GAMBLING
For and Against

LEGALIZED GAMBLING
For and Against

Edited by Rod L. Evans and Mark Hance

Foreword by Senator Paul Simon

OPEN COURT
Chicago and La Salle, Illinois

Open Court Publishing Company is a division of Carus Publishing Company.

Copyright © 1998 by Carus Publishing Company

First printing 1998

Printed and bound in the United States of America.

Library of Congress Cataloging-in-Publication Data

Legalized gambling : For and against / edited by Rod L. Evans and Mark
    E. Hance.
        p.   cm. —(For and against : v. 2)
    Includes bibliographical references and index.
    ISBN 0-8126-9353-1 (alk. paper). — ISBN 0-8126-9354-X (pbk. :
alk. paper)
        1. Gambling—United States.   I. Evans, Rod L., 1956–   .
II. Hance, Mark E., 1963–   .   III. Series.
HV6715.L44   1998
363.4'2'0973—dc21   97-36501
                                                                CIP

Contents

About the Contributors

VICKI ABT is an associate professor of sociology at Pennsylvania State University and co-author of *The Business of Risk: Commercial Gambling in Mainstream America.*

GARY S. BECKER won the Nobel prize for economics in 1992. Since 1985 he has written a monthly column for *Business Week.* He is a professor of economics and sociology at the University of Chicago and a Fellow of the Hoover Institution. His books include *The Economics of Discrimination* and *A Treatise on the Family.*

REUVEN BRENNER is a professor of economics at McGill University in Canada known for his studies of gambling, risk-taking, and speculation. Before joining McGill, he was a professor at the University of Montreal. With his wife, Gabrielle, he wrote *Gambling and Speculation.* He has previously authored *History: The Human Gamble* and *Betting on Ideas,* both published by the University of Chicago Press.

EUGENE MARTIN CHRISTIANSEN was Special Assistant to the New York City Off-Track Betting Corporation during the 1980s. He is a co-author of *The Business of Risk: Commercial Gambling in Mainstream America.*

MARC COOPER is a contributing editor to *The Nation* and host of *RadioNation, The Nation*'s syndicated weekly radio show. He has been an international as well as a domestic correspondent for NBC, CBC, and Monitor Radio, as well as for a wide range of publications. He has also been a reporter and a producer of news documentaries for CBS news, *The*

Christian Science Monitor, and *PBS Frontline*. An anthology of Cooper's work, *Roll Over Che Guevara: Travels of a Radical Reporter*, was published by Verso in 1994.

PAUL D. DELVA is an attorney practicing in Philadelphia. He received a J.D. degree from Temple University School of Law in 1996.

ROD L. EVANS has a doctorate in philosophy from the University of Virginia. With Irwin Berent he has written *Fundamentalism, The Right Words, Getting Your Words' Worth, Weird Words, More Weird Words, The ABC of Cat Trivia*, and has edited *Drug Legalization: For and Against* as well as *The Quotable Conservative*. He has also written the script for "Drugs and Alcohol," two audio cassette tapes containing a historical and philosophical analysis of drug policy for Knowledge Products.

NICK GILLESPIE is a senior editor of *Reason*, a monthly magazine that covers politics, culture, and ideas from a broadly libertarian perspective. His articles and editorials have appeared in the *Washington Post*, the *Los Angeles Times*, and *The Utne Reader* among others. He holds master's degrees from SUNY-Buffalo and Temple University.

ROBERT GOODMAN is Lemelson Professor of Environmental Design at Hampshire College and a former columnist for the *Boston Globe*. He is the author of *After the Planners* and *The Last Entrepreneurs: America's Regional Wars for Jobs and Dollars* as well as numerous articles on legalized gambling and urban planning.

MARK HANCE is a graduate student at Eastern Virginia Medical School who has studied biology, psychiatry, and biochemistry.

THOMAS JEFFERSON was the third president of the United States, principal author of the Declaration of Independence, and founder of the University of Virginia.

JOHN WARREN KINDT is a professor of commerce and legal policy at the University of Illinois. He is especially known for his numerous articles on gambling.

HENRY LESIEUR is the editor of the *Journal of Gambling Studies* and president of the Institute for Problem Gambling in Pawtucket, Rhode Island. He is the author of *The Chase: Career of the Compulsive Gambler* (1984).

LEAH L. LORBER is a former law school student at Indiana University School of Law.

RICHARD LUGAR has been a senator of Indiana since 1977. From 1968–1974 he was mayor of Indianapolis and was the president of the National League of Citizens from 1970–1971. He has chaired important committees in the Senate, is a former Republican candidate for president, and is the author of *Letters to the Next President* (1988).

PAUL PASQUARETTA completed his doctoral studies at the State University of New York at Stony Brook. His dissertation, "Tricksters at Large: Pequots, Gamblers, and the Emergence of Crossblood Culture in North America," examines native responses to European colonialism in North America and the role of traditional Indian culture in the modern world.

RONALD RENO is a research associate in the public-policy division of Focus on the Family, based in Colorado Springs, Colorado.

DAVID SEGAL is a Washington writer.

PAUL SIMON was a member of Congress from the 24th and 22nd districts in Illinois from 1975–1985 and from 1985 until his retirement in 1996 was a Democratic senator of Illinois. He was a Democratic presidential candidate in the 1987–1988 election. Senator Simon served on the

Judiciary, Labor, and Human Resources Committee, and on the Budget and Indian Affairs Committee. He is also a prolific writer whose books include: *The Politics of World Hunger* (1973), *The Tongue-Tied American* (1980), *The Once and Future Democrats* (1982), *The Glass House: Politics and Morality in the Nation's Capital* (1984), *Advice and Consent* (1992), *Freedom's Champion, Elijah Lovejoy* (1994), and *We Can Do Better* (1994). Senator Simon was named Best Legislator by independent voters of Illinois seven times.

JAMES F. SMITH is associate professor of English and American studies at Pennsylvania State University. He is a co-author of *The Business of Risk: Commercial Gambling in Mainstream America*.

DAVID RAMSAY STEELE is a writer whose articles have appeared in a wide range of magazines and journals, both scholarly and popular. His detailed argument that election to political office by voting should be replaced with a system of selecting office-holders by lottery appeared in *National Review* (September 11, 1995) and provoked intense controversy. Dr. Steele is the author of *From Marx to Mises* (Open Court, 1992) and co-author with Michael R. Edelstein of *Three Minute Therapy* (Glenbridge, 1997).

R. EMMETT TYRRELL, JR. is the founder and editor-in-chief of *The American Spectator*. He is the author of several books, including *The Liberal Crack-Up* and *The Conservative Crack-Up*.

RICHARD VATZ is a professor of rhetoric and communication at Towson State University in Maryland. He is known for his study of psychiatrist Dr. Thomas Szasz, whose writings have influenced him. He is co-author, along with Lee Weinberg, of the book *Thomas Szasz: Primary Values and Major Contentions*, published in 1982 by Prometheus.

LEE S. WEINBERG is an associate professor at the University of Pittsburgh's Graduate School of Public and International Affairs. He is co-author, with Richard Vatz, of the book *Thomas Szasz: Primary Values and Major Contentions*, published by Prometheus in 1982.

JOY WOLFE is a former student at University of Mississippi School of Law.

JOHN ZIPPERER is a writer and editor living in Chicago working in both print and Internet publications. He is a graduate of the University of Wisconsin.

Foreword

Rod Evans and Mark Hance have compiled an impressive array of authors who shed light on the nation's most recent plunge into legalized gambling.

There are financial interests who want no change.

There are moral leaders who want a total ban.

And there are concerned citizens who see the problems of addiction and corruption growing who want to do something, but they are not sure what to do.

This is not a simple "how to" guide.

But for the policy maker, editorial writer, academician, and responsible leader in any field, here are valuable insights into a complex field.

Indifference does not solve problems. And we have gambling-related problems.

Passion without knowledge rarely solves problems. The passion the reader must provide, whichever side of the issue he or she may lean toward. And this book provides a great deal of information.

I hope that a combination of actions can lead us to a more prudent response to the present craze. Today's response by those addicted and those fostering the addiction is the answer of all addictions: more.

This book helps to bring balance to serious consideration of this issue. I am grateful to the authors for that.

Paul Simon
Southern Illinois University
March 27, 1997

Preface

This collection of writings for and against legalized gambling captures all the main arguments on both sides; in a long-running controversy like this, it is unlikely that any fundamentally new arguments will appear in the future. We have tried in each part to balance at least one forceful statement on one side with at least one equally persuasive statement to the contrary. We were able to do this in most cases, but not all.

We hope that the selection will be used in classes to stimulate debate, and will also appeal to general readers interested in this highly controversial topic. Most of the sub-headings were not part of the original articles or excerpts, but were added by the editors.

We want to thank Open Court Publishing Company for its support in publishing insightful and important work in legal, social, and political issues. We also want to thank Elaine Dawson from Old Dominion University's Arts and Letters Office of Research Services. She is without doubt one of the best and most gracious typesetters on the planet, with a remarkable eye for detail.

Rod Evans

Mark Hance

The Background to the Debate

Making up Our Minds on a Complex Issue

Thomas Jefferson once recommended state-sponsored gambling as a tax assessed "only on the willing." He thought that gambling activities might create useful public revenue for governments that could not levy direct taxes for certain purposes. He believed that the purchase of a lottery ticket need not be painful, since its price does not produce any "sensible injury." Yet Jefferson was not altogether happy about the popularity of gambling in young America and tension of the sort he felt is evident in current public policy discussions of gambling.

Many people who defend legal gambling conducted either by private businesses or by governments argue that legal gambling is a fairly painless way for governments to generate revenue. Echoing Jefferson, they may argue that money government can get from gambling is often more desirable than money from taxes because the former is normally voluntarily given while the latter is usually coercively extracted.

Recently, state governments have come either to liberalize gambling laws or to sponsor gambling because of economic pressures resulting from less federal revenue and Americans' increasingly strong aversion to tax increases. In fact, 48 states now permit legalized gambling of some form. Legalized gambling has grown rapidly, especially since the mid-1980s. Although in 1986 only Nevada and New Jersey had casinos, in 1997 there were about two dozen states with casinos, including betting houses run by 126 different Indian tribes. By 1997, 37 states ran lotteries, and bingo houses were legal in 47 states as well as the District of Columbia. More than a dozen states allow dog race wagering. Over 20 million tourists visit Las Vegas yearly, and Americans wager over $300 billion annually in legal gambling.

Although many Americans enjoy gambling and see it as harmless recreation, other Americans, including many social conservatives, see gambling as a socially destructive temptation that ought not to be indulged by private citizens, much less sponsored by government. The National Coalition Against Legalized Gambling has stymied casino and slot-machine plans in 23 states, and its former leader, Methodist minister Tom Grey, has described the gambling industry as a "predator." Social conservative Pat Buchanan has said that "gambling should return to the swamp whence it came." Former director of the Christian Coalition Ralph Reed has called gambling "a cancer on the body politic, destroying families, stealing food from the mouths of children, turning wives into widows."

Against the conception of gambling as a relentless disease, other people have argued that most gamblers are responsible citizens who prudently budget their expenditures. They argue that while relatively poorer people spend more proportionally on wagers and bets, most people who gamble do so responsibly.

At the center of many discussions of gambling policy, especially since 1987, are American Indians. In that year, in the case *California v. Cabazon* the United States Supreme Court upheld the rights of Indian tribes to offer unregulated gambling enterprises, provided that those operations do not violate state criminal policy. In 1988, Congress passed the Indian Gaming Regulatory Act (IGRA) in response to the Cabazon decision. The Act authorizes federal and tribal regulation of bingo games and Indian-state government agreements for regulating casinos on reservations.

Today dozens of tribes operate casinos, and their members argue that they have a right to operate casinos because of legitimate Indian sovereignty. Many state governments and commercial gaming interests, however, see things differently, arguing that the IGRA gives Indians an unfair—and perhaps even an unconstitutional—commercial advantage. For the Act, in recognizing Indian sovereignty, exempts tribes from state taxes while allowing them to sue states that refuse to negotiate in good faith on gaming agreements. Several states have objected to the IGRA by appeal to the Tenth Amendment, which prohibits Congress from forcing state governments to do anything not spelled out in state law. The states have also argued that the IGRA violates the Eleventh Amendment, which in effect bans states from suing other states. Indian tribes respond by arguing that they are not asking for unfair preferential treatment but rather political sovereignty—the right to run their own internal affairs. They argue further that, because of cooperation between tribes and states, Indian casinos and bingo halls have created thousands of taxpaying jobs in such states as Minnesota, Wisconsin, Michigan, California, and Washington.

But some opponents of Indian control of gambling argue that the question should not be framed as one of Indian sovereignty but one of the moral, social, and cultural consequences of gaming on Indian communities. Many Indians respond by holding that Indians, and not state or federal officials, should decide the degree to which Indians control gambling.

In discussing gambling policy it is important to examine a wide variety of empirical and philosophical questions. Some relevant empirical questions: How has gambling been regulated historically? What are the social and economic costs of legalized gambling? (For example, will legalized gambling drain much money from retail sales?) Roughly how many more citizens might be encouraged to gamble irresponsibly if gambling becomes increasingly permissible? Some relevant philosophical questions: What are the legitimate purposes of law? Are there areas of conduct that are none of the law's business? Are American Indians morally entitled to any special consideration in running gaming houses? Should casinos ever be legally responsible for gambling losses of people who claim to be "compulsive gamblers"? Or, what is perhaps more fundamental, are conceptions of pathological gambling incompatible with a belief in personal responsibility?

A Historical Overview of Gambling in America

As early as the 1620s many New England colonists viewed gambling as a dangerous though popular vice. In 1682, the Quaker government of

Pennsylvania colony passed anti-gambling legislation, though it was less than effective. Indeed, Benjamin Franklin, Pennsylvania's leading citizen, was a frequent lottery player throughout his adult life. In 1776, Thomas Jefferson and his wife gambled at backgammon and lotto. After American Independence, the first wave of gambling hit, as lotteries funded war activities. In 1777, the Continental Congress initiated a lottery game, after which legislative bodies in Massachusetts, New York, and Rhode Island followed suit.

A major economic tool for financing civic projects, lotteries in the 1790s helped build the District of Columbia and many college buildings, as at Harvard, Yale, Columbia, and Dartmouth. Other schools and even churches used lotteries for the same purpose. Indeed, from 1790 to 1830, 21 state governments issued licenses for nearly 200 lottery schemes.

In the early 1800s riverboat gambling became popular, and in 1832 early lottery play was at its height, with 420 lottery games in eight states, often attended by scandals and mismanagement. In 1833, the Jacksonian Era's call for governmental reform included a demand for ending gambling. After Pennsylvania and Maryland prohibited lotteries, most other states followed suit. By the end of the Civil War all legal lotteries had been stopped, marking the end of America's first major wave of legal gambling.

Nineteenth-century American gambling in other forms, however, went west, especially during the 1840s, when the gold strike in California marked a new trend—mining camp gambling halls, as in San Francisco. In 1860, riverboat gambling reached its apex, as more than 500 boats operated, holding many dishonest card sharps. In 1868, Louisiana instituted a lottery to generate revenue for the war-torn, bankrupt state, and New York entrepreneurs sustained it by bribing state officials. That lottery, though, was successful, and its tickets were sold by mail across the continent. In 1890, Congress banned the sale of lottery tickets through the mail in an attack on the Louisiana Lottery. Within two years the Louisiana Lottery was voted out of existence.

In 1891, a private board of control in New York state began licensing jockeys and trainers. So began the first organized regulation of horse racecourses, as track activity was monitored by neutral parties. In 1906, as Kentucky became the first state to establish a government-run state racing commission, Tennessee closed its tracks. California closed its tracks in 1909, and New York followed in 1911.

In 1907, the Arizona and New Mexico territorial governments outlawed all gambling so that they could qualify for statehood. By 1910, the era of anti-gambling reform was nearly complete, as Nevada closed its casinos; legalized gambling, except for a few race tracks, was quiet.

To generate public revenue during the Great Depression, Nevada, in 1931, legalized wide-open casino gambling. Originally gaming was regulated by counties and confined to small saloons and taverns and local and state governments shared the taxes. In 1935, new horse-race betting legislation was enacted in several states: New Hampshire, Massachusetts, Rhode Island, Michigan, Illinois, Ohio, West Virginia, Delaware, and Florida. California legalized horse-race betting in 1938, and New York did likewise in 1940. In the 1940s Las Vegas began to earn its reputation as the world's foremost casino location. In 1945, Nevada began to license casinos for the first time, and, in 1946, gangster Benjamin (Bugsy) Siegel, financed by Meyer Lansky, opened the Flamingo Casino, which featured a showroom with Hollywood entertainment.

Siegel was murdered in 1947, sensationalizing the Strip and fortifying Las Vegas's reputation as a naughty place where ordinary citizens could come into contact with gangsters. In 1950, the United States Senate investigated organized crime and gambling casinos. Heading the committee was Tennessee Senator Estes Kefauver, who described Las Vegas as a "den of evil" controlled by "the Mob." While the investigation speeded up the closing of illegal gambling establishments in jurisdictions other than Las Vegas, it encouraged gambling operators to move to that city.

The beginning of the third wave of legalized gambling in 1963 was marked by the New Hampshire Lottery, the first government lottery since the closing of the Louisiana Lottery in 1892. The first ticket was sold in 1964. In 1967, New York began a lottery, which failed to meet state officials' budget expectations. In 1970, New Jersey began sales of weekly lottery tickets using mass-marketing techniques. That lottery has been successful, presumably at least partly because the ticket prices are low and games occur regularly. Other states noticed New Jersey's success, and lotteries began to spread quickly.

In 1974, Massachusetts became the first North American jurisdiction to introduce an instant lottery game, which became the most popular game of the decade. Between 1975 and 1976 the Commission on the National Policy Toward Gambling affirmed that gambling should be subject to control by state governments. After an unsuccessful campaign for casinos in 1974, New Jersey voters authorized casino gambling for Atlantic City in 1976 by 56 to 44 percent. The 1976 campaign was well financed by the Resorts International Casino organization of the Bahamas, which encountered only minor and unorganized opposition from some religious officials.

In 1977, New Jersey created regulatory bodies for casino gambling, and, in 1978, Atlantic City saw casino gaming with the opening of Resorts International. That same year the Seminole Indian reservations in Hollywood, Florida, began high-stakes bingo, marking a new period of Indian gambling. In later litigation in federal court the Indians retained the right to conduct games unregulated by the state.

During 1985–1986 the President's Commission on Organized Crime did not issue a report on gambling because it considered gambling to be a generally legitimate industry. In 1987, the United States Supreme Court upheld the rights of Indian tribes to offer unregulated gambling enterprises, provided that the operators do not violate state criminal policy. The case *Cabazon v. California* determined that regulation of noncriminal matters must come from the federal government or be explicitly authorized by Congress. In 1988, the Indian Gaming Regulatory Act was passed as a response to the Cabazon decision. The Act provides for federal and tribal regulation of bingo games and allows Indian-state agreements for regulating casinos on reservations. In 1989, the Iowa state legislature approved riverboat casino gambling with $5 stakes. Also in that year the state of Oregon began the first sports-game-based lottery in the United States, awarding prizes to players selecting four out of five winners of football or basketball games and giving the proceeds to support college athletics in the state.

In 1990, riverboat casinos began in Iowa and were also approved by the Illinois state legislature, and Colorado voters approved limited casino gaming for the historic mountain towns of Blackhawk, Cripple Creek, and Central City. The following year, the Mississippi legislature approved riverboat casinos, allowing them to be permanently docked. In 1992, Congress prohibited the spread of sports betting beyond the four states then authorizing it: Nevada, Oregon, Montana, and Delaware. In 1993, the Indian legislature approved boat casinos.

By 1996, there were, as mentioned earlier, about two dozen states with casinos, including betting houses run by over 100 different Indian tribes. There are now (in 1997) 37 states that run lotteries and 47 that run bingo games. There are also more than a dozen states that allow dog race wagering. It is estimated that more than $300 billion is legally wagered each year in America, with gamblers losing about $30 billion. In 1990, it was estimated that state revenues from gambling exceeded death taxes, severance taxes, property taxes, and tobacco and alcohol taxes, though they were less than revenue generated by general sales taxes, individual income taxes, corporate taxes, gasoline taxes, and license fees.

I

OPENING
SHOTS

INTRODUCTION TO PART I

The gambling debate raises questions about the degree to which gambling should be regulated as against prohibited. The debate also raises philosophical questions about the proper role of government and raises factual questions about the degree to which gambling is socially harmful. In many respects the gambling debate resembles the drug debate. Just as many drug prohibitionists argue that recreational drug use poses a significant enough social threat to warrant prohibition, so many anti-gambling activists argue that gambling poses a significant enough social threat to warrant prohibition. And, just as drug legalizers or decriminalizers often argue that the effects of drug prohibition are worse than the effects of drug use in a largely free market, so gambling legalizers and decriminalizers often argue similarly about the effects of gambling.

Editor-in-chief of *The American Spectator*, R. Emmett Tyrrell, Jr., sees gambling as often socially undesirable but also views it as an ineradicable vice that needs to be regulated and contained but not encouraged by government.

Journalist Nick Gillespie sees the organized reaction against legalized gambling (as by the National Coalition Against Legalized Gambling) as rejecting personal freedom and responsibility. According to him, most people who gamble act responsibly, so that gambling prohibitionists must exaggerate the evils of gambling to try to justify their position.

John Zipperer, in an article for *Christianity Today*, asserts that religious anti-gambling activists are well justified in their position. For he believes that gambling, even when legal, harms individuals and society. He agrees with the religious activists but laments that the activists are not more popular within religious communities.

Economist Gary S. Becker approves of the trend toward legalized gambling as respecting the freedom and choices of large numbers of usually responsible citizens. He favors a freer market in gambling, friendlier toward the private sector. Becker maintains that freer markets would favor consumers, who receive about 95 percent of the revenues in privately-run casinos but sometimes as little as 50 percent of the revenues from state-run lotteries.

1. The Government Should Not Promote Vice

R. Emmett Tyrrell, Jr.

R. Emmett Tyrrell, Jr., the founder and editor-in-chief of The American Spectator, *views state-run gambling as both hypocritical and destructive. He sees it as hypocritical because much if not most private-sector gambling is illegal and as destructive because it to some degree legitimizes gambling, which has "ruined families, imperiled and destroyed children, bankrupted thousands, and opened vast opportunities" for members of organized crime.*

Taxpayers of New York, rejoice! The law enforcement agencies of your great state, in league with educators, gamblers, and a couple of shrinks, are once again providing you with plenty of entertainment value for every nickel you cough up to live in the Empire State. Recently a fourth-grade teacher (male), celebrated as inspirational in the classroom, was hauled off to the slammer for participating in a gambling ring. In America state and local government can conduct gambling on a vast scale, but not the Genovese family or the Bruno Scarfo crime family. Our fourth-grade Socrates allegedly had links to both.

New York's Westchester County District Attorney is certainly not anti-family. Yet she is vexed that when police arrived at the alleged gambler's home, sledgehammer in hand, they found him with gambling slips. The slips of paper contained forty bets totaling $10,000. He also had

This short piece first appeared as "Quick Draw McGraws," in *The American Spectator* (February 1996), pp. 14, 16. Used by permission.

$8,000 in cash. And the television was tuned to a football game. Well, what is wrong with sports enthusiasts putting down money in private transactions over football games? Few people holler when large numbers of New Yorkers put their money down on one of the state lottery's gaming ventures. I suppose the concern of the state here is that when one loses to the Genovese family, one pays up or bad things happen. Furthermore, gamblers of the Genovese variety might be tempted to approach athletes with a get-rich-quick scheme involving missing a few blocks or fumbling a few balls or otherwise adversely affecting a game's outcome.

The gambling lobby in New York would rather have gambling regulated by the state. It promises revenue from state-regulated casinos. It promises still more revenue when the state controls the gambling, for instance, New York's new casino-style game, "Quick Draw." In an era in which the citizenry has been taxed to the outer limits of the tolerable, state lotteries and state-regulated casinos can pick up the tab for still more government spending. Thus states with lotteries advertise to encourage still more people to gamble. The Genovese family is restrained from advertising, but not the New York state lottery.

Actually my guess is that the Genoveses are delighted that the state advertises its lottery game. Any encouragement to gambling has got to mean more customers in the long run for the Genovese football betting ring. Perhaps the day will come when this distinguished family can set up betting rings for the truly affluent who follow tennis and polo. Now you know there are some tennis fans whose interest in the game would only be heightened if they could put a little wager on Pete Sampras's performance on a given day, say $1,000, perhaps more.

As I say, this story is abundant with the nonsense of our age. After their gifted teacher was arrested, the twenty fourth-graders suddenly bereft of his presence were rounded up by the school's "crisis intervention" team. Composed of at least one psychologist and a social worker, the team is trained to cope with what the *New York Times* report of the arrest called "the kind of unplanned lesson that has become more common as arrests of teachers have made the news." Basically, the team tells the students their teacher is "innocent until proven guilty." If found guilty the team will, according to its psychologist, stress that "it was a mistake in judgment on his part."

But how can the adroit members of this "crisis intervention" team come down even that hard on a man who merely gambled? The governor and other state luminaries lure the citizenry to gamble every day. Several months ago, after the state unveiled "Quick Draw," it began placing the game in more than 2,000 bars, bowling alleys, delis, and restaurants. New York state lottery officials purr that they raise over a billion dollars a year for education from such officially sanctioned gambling.

What the state's gambling officials do not point out is that, for many, gambling is an addiction like drugs or alcohol. It has ruined families, imperiled and destroyed children, bankrupted thousands, and opened vast opportunities for people like the Genoveses. Gambling is a breeding swamp for crime. Sure, some can enjoy it in moderation just as many enjoy booze in moderation. That is why we allow Las Vegas and the neighborhood pub. But the state ought not to champion gambling any more than it champions alcohol. And it ought not to be surprised when gambling spreads to fourth-grade teachers. If the government wants to spend money, let it tax the citizenry in a straightforward way. That it resorts to a vice to pay its exorbitant bills should remind us that government is frequently not so virtuous.

2. Most Gamblers Are Responsible Adults, Not Victims

Nick Gillespie

Nick Gillespie holds that opponents of legalized gambling, in the name of morality, try to "strip individuals of the right to make moral decisions." He asserts further that people providing gaming are not predators, and most of their customers are not "passive victims." Rather, most gamblers, according to Gillespie, are almost indistinguishable from non-gamblers. He maintains that public policy should be based not on worst cases but on the actual (and usually responsible) behavior of most citizens. Accordingly, he argues for a free market for adult gamblers.

It is common these days to chatter about smaller government and individual responsibility, but we are actually living in increasingly prohibitionary times. Choices properly decided by private individuals are instead being limited or abolished through restrictive public policy. Hence, the V-Chip, government-mandated ratings of television programs, and attempts to regulate information flow on the Internet; federal- and state-level attempts to regulate cigarettes as "nicotine-delivery devices"; and a reinvigorated War on Drugs, which finally has a bona fide general in command.

This appeared originally as "Wagers of Sin: Dealing with the Anti-Gambling Backlash," in *Reason* (June 1996), p. 8. Used by permission.

The latest target of prohibitionists is legalized gambling, which has enjoyed a decade or so of rapid growth. Ten years ago, only Nevada and New Jersey boasted casinos. Nowadays, there are two dozen states with casinos, including betting houses run by 126 different American Indian tribes. Thirty-seven states run lotteries and some have either allowed or are considering slot machines at existing gambling sites such as horse- and dog-racing tracks. Last year, Americans spent more than $40 billion on legalized gambling, up from about $10 billion in 1982.

The anti-gambling backlash is here, there, and everywhere. Over the past two years, the National Coalition Against Legalized Gambling (NCALG) has stymied casino and slot-machine plans in 23 states. The backlash is worth pausing over not only because it threatens yet another personal liberty but because it also allows insight into the prohibitionist mindset.

Prohibitionists are in the difficult position of telling people that certain choices are so misguided that they simply can no longer be allowed. But since the targeted behavior is usually highly popular and widespread, pro-hibitionists must redefine it as an unconditional evil that cannot be resisted, even by men and women of character. Ironically, in the name of morality, prohibitionists must strip individuals of the right to make moral decisions.

This is certainly the case with gambling, where opponents traffic in metaphors of invasion and addiction that define bettors as passive victims. The Rev. Tom Grey, the Methodist minister who heads the NCALG, describes himself as "a man committed to all-out war" against the "preda-tor" gambling industry. The middle Americans who fill the casinos, you see, don't *really* want to spin the wheel, throw the dice, or take the chance. Pat Buchanan rails that "gambling should return to the swamp whence it came," ignoring the fact that 125 million Americans willingly choose to go to casinos every year.

The Christian Coalition's Ralph Reed pronounces gambling a "cancer on the body politic, destroying families, stealing food from the mouths of children, turning wives into widows." Betting as rapacious disease? That would have been news to the folks I used to ride with on infrequent trips to Atlantic City during the '80s. We gambled because it's fun to do, every

once in a while. Forty or fifty people—college kids, vacationers, re-
tirees—would pile in a bus in midtown Manhattan and ride a couple of
hours to play slots and cheap blackjack. When it came time to leave, no
one, to my knowledge, ever had to be pried away from the roulette table
or the slot machines.

Indeed, the social scientific literature, including studies done for the
Swedish, British, and U.S. governments, tends to characterize gamblers as
virtually indistinguishable from non-gamblers—except that gamblers are
more sociable, more involved in community activities, and bigger opera,
theater, and museum buffs. While it is true relatively poorer people
spend more proportionally on wagers and bets, the overwhelming majority of gamblers responsibly budget their expenditures and use their winnings for "home-centered items."

The profile of gamblers as normal people, however, is unlikely to
work its way into many stories about anti-gambling activism. Rather, the
media showcase the dark side of gambling. A recent *Time* story, for
instance, recounts the fate of a 40-year-old school teacher and mother of
two who shot herself in the head after racking up huge gambling debts.
"The day she died," writes *Time*, "sheriff's deputies were on their way to
her home with an eviction order. . . . [H]er husband . . . knew nothing of
their financial problems, although she had pawned their wedding rings and
skipped making the house payments for 17 months."

Such a story is, of course, undeniably tragic—and undeniably rare.
Time itself mentions in passing that Harvard University's Center for
Addiction Studies estimates that "between 3.5 percent and 5 percent of all
adults exposed to gaming can be expected to develop into pathological
gamblers." Other estimates are lower still.

Horror stories, however bleak, should not guide public policy.
"Gambling," note Reuven and Gabrielle A. Brenner in their 1990 history
Gambling and Speculation, "is a mass phenomenon, and its study must not
be confused with that of a pathological minority of compulsive gamblers,
just as the examination of a few workaholics, alcoholics, obese people,
womanizers, addicted TV watchers, and addicted exercisers is irrelevant
for a social judgment on the behavior of the billions who work, drink, eat,

love and/or have sex, watch TV or enjoy exercising with customary frequency."

For prohibitionists, of course, the self-regulation evinced by better than 95 percent of gamblers is a logical impossibility or, perhaps, a logical improbability. The world confounds prohibitionists, as do people who believe they should decide how to live their own lives.

3. Christians Agree That Gambling Is a Sin

John Zipperer

Writing from a Christian perspective, John Zipperer asserts that traditional criticisms of gambling are warranted. He contends, for example, that crime has risen as a result of casino gambling in Las Vegas and Atlantic City. He also holds that the gambling critics who warned that poor people would disproportionately gamble their money have been correct, and he writes approvingly of efforts by Christians to oppose expansion of legalized gambling. Finally, he implies that church groups should consistently oppose casinos, even after they are in place.

When gambling broke out of the glitter ghettos of Las Vegas and Atlantic City in the late 1970s, it began a long and successful march into nearly every state and many local communities, racking up surprising victories and cowing opponents.

Gambling has advanced so swiftly that until recently there were few national organizations devoted to opposing it. Instead, anti-gambling activists have toiled in isolation and with little national fundraising to combat the gambling industry's estimated $35 billion in revenues.

Now, however, the sparkle has worn off some of the early promises made by gambling industry promoters, and Christians are attempting to bear witness to the failed predictions for gambling's abilities to bring true

---

This article first appeared as "Against All Odds: Will Christians Reclaim the High Ground in a Battle to Fight America's 'Recreational Pastime'?" in *Christianity Today*, November 14, 1994, pp. 58–60, 62. Used by permission.

prosperity: Anti-gambling leaders had predicted crime would rise due to casino gambling, and it has. Las Vegas and Atlantic City have two of the nation's highest crime rates. In Biloxi, Mississippi, a regional casino hot spot, armed robberies doubled from 1992 to 1993.

Christians warned that underage gamblers would be insufficiently policed. A 1992 report by Chicago's Better Government Association (BGA) estimates that 7 million juveniles gamble in the United States. In the northeastern part of the country, as many as 80 percent of high-school students reported gambling for money in a one-year period.

Anti-gambling activists cautioned that the burden of lotteries and other gambling methods would fall disproportionately on the poor. Low-income households have quickly become heavier users of state lotteries than the wealthy. The gambling industry is developing new ways to attract the moderate-income gambler with entertainment and by installing easy-to-use slot machines.

Nevertheless, gambling, once roundly condemned not only by church leaders, but by societal leaders as well, is now widely accepted and available, often with state governments promoting and benefiting from lotteries. Today, Utah and Hawaii are the only states that do not permit gambling of any kind.

The proliferation and acceptance of gambling has been explosive:

- The amount Americans wager each year has grown from $17.3 billion in 1976 to $329.9 billion in 1992, according to the National Council on Problem Gambling.
- Organized gambling has crossed over into "family-oriented" entertainment. Las Vegas has been in the forefront, hoping to gain new customers as it loses its dominance in gambling. At the MGM Grand, billed as the world's largest "hotel, casino, and theme park," parents and children can visit 33 acres of rides, shows, themed streets, restaurants, shops, and casinos.
- The race to conquer new markets for gambling is shifting into high gear as the gaming industry saturates markets. Through much of 1994, as many as two casinos were opening each month in Mississippi. (Yet Gannett News Service reports that half of the

casinos in Atlantic City are bankrupt, and half of the casinos in Nevada are operating with a 3 percent profit margin.)

- Gaming Entertainment television (GETV), a Pittsburgh-based cable television network, offers viewers a broad range of gambling activities. The network hopes to have nearly 3 million subscribers by the end of the century.

In some cases, social problems have already been dogging the footsteps of gambling operations. There are unemployment and money woes, for example: The closing of Mhoon Landing casino in Mississippi, only one year after it opened, will throw almost 1,000 people out of work. It is the second casino operated by the same company to close this year. From a survey of its callers, the Texas Council on Problem and Compulsive Gambling reports 59 percent of compulsive gamblers have financial problems, 29 percent are addicted to alcohol, and 25 percent are unemployed.

Opposition to Gambling Unites Churches

In some ways, gambling is the last agreed-upon sin for many Christians. Denominations that disagree vehemently over abortion, female pastors, and capital punishment nonetheless unite to oppose betting. The reason may be straightforward—people work together to rebuff attacks on their community—but some observers see the unusual unanimity as a sign of the deterioration of the culture.

"That's the terrifying part of it for me," says Eugene Winkler, senior pastor of downtown Chicago's First United Methodist Church/Chicago Temple. "When you trace the history of just the Methodist part of this, we have stood against all of these immoral forms throughout our history, and we have yielded over and over again, and we've just acquiesced. I think this is kind of the last moral crusade for us."

In the long run, he believes the pendulum will swing back toward outlawing gambling when its negative effects become too large to ignore. "I don't think there's any doubt we are in a state of moral decay that is growing, eating away at the body politic in America," says Winkler.

The current struggle between gambling entrepreneurs and religious leaders reprises a similar struggle in the nineteenth century, which had its own fights over gambling and lotteries.

Marvin Olasky, professor of journalism at the University of Texas at Austin and a senior fellow at the Capital Research Center in Washington, D.C., notes that the *Boston Recorder* did more than just run sermons against gambling in the nineteenth century. "It [covered] particular people who had gambled and lost everything. They gave a face to the issue." Politicians of early America also tried to dissuade gamblers.

"Now, probably the opposite is the case," Olasky says, "because we have our government leaders promoting state lotteries, and you have journalists very often winking at it."

Though churches may have fairly broad agreement that gambling is harmful to individuals and to society, few place it at the top of their church's crowded agendas. Nonetheless, Olasky suggests that people from different denominations who represent different theologies can work together against gambling without compromising doctrinal stands.

Winkler agrees. "The church cannot keep yielding moral ground and expect to be any force for good in society." He says gambling foes must "make the government do what it promises to do when it licenses [casinos], and that is to control them."

To Tom Grey, [former] spokesman for the National Coalition Against Legalized Gambling, the mix of big money politics suggests a disgrace of major proportions is coming. "You think the savings and loan was a scandal," he says. "Wait until the gambling thing hits on how government sold us to Las Vegas."

Anti-Gambling Activists Are Fighting Back

Determination is increasing on both sides of the battle lines as the gambling industry undergoes severe growing pains.

In this mix of events, wartime terminology comes easily to gambling opponents. Not content to be on the defensive, they have initiated an aggressive offense. Grey, a United Methodist minister from Galena,

Illinois, recounts a meeting he had with a gambling industry leader who told him, "'We have Las Vegas in the west, Atlantic City in the east, New Orleans in the south, now we want Chicago for the head of the cross.' I'm sitting there, saying, 'We'll deny you Chicago.'"

"This thing dies in the Midwest," Grey vows. "Ten years from now, they'll write the story that in the heartland of America, it got turned back."

As a longtime anti-gambling activist, Grey has had the opportunity to view the tactics of gambling proponents, who promise cash-strapped cities easy money.

Gambling companies "used to come in in parades, with governors cutting ribbons. Now they have to fight their way in, they have to bribe their way in," Grey says. "We are breaking the invincibility of their advance."

Fresh from a handful of recent successes . . ., Grey is taking his fight nationwide through the National Coalition Against Legalized Gambling.

The coalition formed in May, following the successful rebuff of a lottery referendum in Oklahoma. A group of anti-gambling activists, members of a wide range of faith groups—from Unitarians to Christian Coalition activists to United Methodists to Muslims—met in Chicago to create the organization. The group shares tactics and information, helping to transform a series of local skirmishes into a nationwide movement.

Two years ago, Missouri voters overwhelmingly approved riverboat gambling, but, due to a mistake in the wording of the bill, games of chance were not allowed. Pro-gambling forces pushed through another referendum, this time to be decided two days after Easter this year. Grey saw a chance to "steal" a victory and traveled to Missouri, where he hooked up with conservative businessman Mark Andrews. Grey then put together a coalition of conservative and liberal Christians to defeat the referendum.

"We had no money; we generated a movement," says Grey. "The Right already had phone banks and was already working on this. The mainline churches hadn't really done a thing. So what happened was that God gave us this incredible victory." Out of a million votes, the referendum failed by 1,261.

Native American Reservations Need
Other Economic Opportunities

Despite those recent victories, anti-gambling activists are facing a battle zone with dozens of front lines. The 1988 passage of the Indian Gaming Regulatory Act made it possible for Native American groups to run reservation-based gambling operations, which have become extremely profitable and are spread nationwide.

Paul G. Jones, executive director of the Christian Action Commission of the Mississippi Baptist Convention, reports that one local Native American tribe in his state already has a 24-hour casino on its reservation and is trying to buy land along the Mississippi River shoreline. This bid is leading some to challenge whether land purchased by a tribe becomes part of the reservation—and thus open to gambling—or is merely tribal-owned land, one of many new questions raised by gaming's spread.

"In a period of twelve-and-a-half years, it's gone from no legalized gambling in the state to all kinds of legalized gambling," Jones says. He says charitable bingo, legalized in 1987, "has been a total disaster," requiring the state to change the law several times to fix loopholes. "There are still some groups out there that have some of the strangest reasons for operating as a charitable organization."

For many Native American groups, faced with high rates of alcoholism, unemployment, and suicide, the promise of big profits from gambling has been quickly embraced. Native American activists suggest that the way to dissuade tribes from pursuing reservation gaming is to offer economic alternatives. Huron Claus, a Mohawk and discipleship coordinator for Christian Hope Indian Eskimo Fellowship (CHIEF) in Phoenix, says Christians need to examine why Native Americans are attracted to gambling's profits. Gambling has caused some tribes to grapple with the cultural impact of sudden wealth and the presence of casino workers from outside the tribe, sometimes outnumbering the entire tribe.

"The real issue is: How do we deal with the gambling?" Claus says. "There needs to be a call to the Christian leadership on a tribal level and a church level. There are few Christians in tribal leadership; they need to be role models in their tribes." Claus does not support reservation gambling and he urges Christians to develop businesses that offer healthy alternatives to Indians. Claus also notes that it is an opportunity to share the gospel: of the 2 million Native Americans in about 500 different tribes, he says fewer than 8 percent are professing Christians.

Riverboat Gambling Is a Subterfuge

Perhaps the nation's most-watched gambling skirmish is in Chicago, where Mayor Richard M. Daley has sought for years to introduce casino gambling, first in land-based form and now on riverboats. Casino gambling remains stalled in the state government, not so much because of church pressure but because of the strength of the racing industry, which fears the loss of gaming dollars to 24-hour casinos.

After rural horseracing interests teamed up with state Republican lawmakers—as well as some religious activists—to defeat land-based casinos in 1992, gambling forces came back with a proposal for a downtown entertainment complex with a riverboat casino.

"It'll be essentially what they tried to get land-based," says Winkler. "The riverboat is just going to go about 100 yards and come back. It's subterfuge."

One of the greatest fears of casino opponents has been the corruption of public officials. J.T. Brunner, staff director of the Chicago Metro Ethics Coalition Project, charged in 1992 that his organization's investigation of the effort to bring casino gambling to Chicago "was complicated by a high degree of misinformation filtered to the general public by individuals and organizations which had already taken a position on the issue. . . . Our academic research confirmed that many of the proponents' claims were highly questionable."

In its 1992 white paper, "Casino Gambling in Chicago," the BGA claimed that irregularities had occurred in the city's study and promotion of casino gambling. In his introduction to the study, Brunner, who also serves as BGA's executive director, wrote, "The accounting firm who supposedly ran objective projections for the Mayor's Committee has joined them, appearing as an advocate at the Mayor's press conferences."

In discussing the proposed job gains caused by casinos, Brunner writes: "It is interesting that the proponents didn't suggest the alternate sales pitch, social gains from additional revenues. One may understand this by examining their public-relation documents, 'Jewel in the Crown' and 'P.R. Battle Plan,' in which they found that Chicagoans simply don't believe that additional money will effectively cure social problems because of the Atlantic City experience and our own experience with the lottery."

Christians Can Resist Casinos Locally

Weston Ware, associate director of the Texas Baptist Christian Life Commission, believes Christians need to be more vocal about the spread of gambling. "When you look at Atlantic City, their success is still very questionable," says Ware, who estimates that he has testified on every piece of gambling legislation before the Texas legislature since 1982. "It was a slum by the sea. And now, it's a slum by the sea with casinos."

Ware says the clout of churches and individual Christians is in their ability to deal with the issue locally. "The power that we have in lobbying the legislature has to do not with some individual that's recognized as representing the churches," Ware says. "The power has to do with the persons back home who know and supported or have worked with legislators over time. That legislator has to feel that he is being held accountable and responsible by individuals at the local level."

Texas, which does not have casino gambling, does have a state lottery, charitable bingo, and dog- and horse-racing tracks. When Texas adopted the lottery, it also agreed to print on every lottery ticket the number for a hotline for compulsive gamblers. The state gives the hotline—run by the Texas Council on Problem Gambling—$575,000 to spread awareness of problem gambling.

If proponents succeed in legalizing casino gambling, Texas may have as many as 25 casinos, says Sue Cox, executive director of the council and a former activist against gambling. She fears that if casinos are legalized, the total number of problem gamblers may not grow dramatically, but people playing bingo will shift to slot machines, and those who are betting on sports will also patronize casinos. "Because casinos offer the opportunity to lose money more quickly on a 24-hour basis than do other games, the degree of the problem will grow."

To Cox, the problem with churches is that they do not continue their activism once the casinos are in place. As a resource person who has only received one call from a church for assistance, she says, churches have failed to show compassion and offer help to compulsive gamblers and their family members. Cox recommends that churches gather information on gambling—stocking their libraries with books on compulsive gambling—and minister to problem gamblers either through small groups on compulsive gambling or at least an all-purpose addiction support group.

"It's easy to have sympathy with the family," Cox says. "It's very difficult for many believers to have sympathy with the gambler."

4. There Are Worse Sins Than Gambling

Gary S. Becker

Nobel Prize-winning economist Gary Becker approves of the trend toward legalized gambling—but not because he thinks that legalized gambling will enable governments to solve fiscal crises. He does not believe that it will. Rather, he holds that opponents of gambling are motivated by overblown fears, which lead them to calls for frustrating people's fairly harmless desires while unintentionally strengthening the influence of organized crime and unnecessarily abridging the freedom of usually responsible citizens.

Many state and local governments face even greater fiscal pressure to raise taxes than Washington does. In the scramble for additional revenue, Mississippi and Indiana, along with Boston, Chicago, New Orleans, and the District of Columbia, among other localities, already allow or are seriously considering the enfranchisement of casino gambling and other gaming devices such as lotteries. I support this trend toward legalized gambling, although my reasoning has little to do with revenues.

Mayors and governors drool in anticipation of what gambling taxes can do for their budgets. Nevada, for example, collects more than $200 million a year from its casinos, the state's largest employer, and New Jersey better than $314 million. Several Indian reservations—notably in

---

Originally one of Professor Becker's monthly *Business Week* columns, "Gambling's Advocates Are Right—But for the Wrong Reasons," was reprinted in *The Economics of Life* (New York: McGraw-Hill, 1997), a collection of his columns edited by Professor Becker and by Guity Nashat Becker, pp. 45–46. Used by permission.

Connecticut and South Dakota—have become rich from slot machines, poker, and blackjack tables, and other gaming devices. The U.S. Supreme Court ruled in 1987 that reservations could operate gambling facilities comparable to any others permitted in their states.

As casinos spread across the country, however, the number of communities competing for the limited tax revenues from gambling will increase. They won't be able to duplicate the financial success of Nevada, Atlantic City, or the Indian reservations.

State and local governments must forget about gambling as a fail-safe jackpot. There is no way gambling is going to solve their fiscal crises. It would only add a modest amount of tax revenue. But there is this to be said for legalizing gambling. It would enable the many people who wish to place a bet to do so without patronizing illegal establishments and facilities controlled by criminals.

There's No Good Reason to Deny People the Pleasures of Moderate Gambling

For me, the issue comes down to this: The arguments against legalized gambling are specious, so why not allow it? The assertion by religious and civic groups that gambling is sinful and hence shouldn't be encouraged is of dubious validity. Gambling is surely less sinful than smoking and drinking, since smoking damages health, and drunkenness causes automobile and job accidents and domestic violence. And assuming so-called sin taxes should be proportionate to the degree of sin, the sin component of gaming taxes should be below the sin tax rates on smoking and drinking. Federal and state governments together tax about 20 percent of cigarette and beer sales, while Nevada collects about 6 percent of net casino revenues in that state.

More than 30 states already encourage gambling by running enticing advertisements for state lotteries. The poor bet on these lotteries—as well as on illegal gaming such as numbers and card games. The rich can speculate as recklessly as they wish through buying and selling equities, options, real estate, and other highly risky assets. It is principally the middle classes that are affected by present restrictions on casinos and other forms of gambling. But few families in this group bet much of their income and assets in the attempt to hit it big.

Some opponents paint a picture of gambling addicts frittering away their life savings in pursuit of the big killing of their fantasies. Analysis of the betting patterns of lottery and casino patrons, however, shows that addictive gambling is not common—surely much less so than addiction to tobacco and alcohol. Few people buy so many lottery tickets that they jeopardize their funds for food and other necessities. Most casino visitors are middle-aged folks having a good time with friends. Why deny them the pleasures—thrills, even—they get from modest betting on lotteries and other gaming devices?

Legalization Reduces Criminal Involvement

Many of those opposed to legalized gambling don't care a fig whether the patrons would commit a sin or risk addiction. Their concern is with organized crime, which did, after all, create Las Vegas. But that was long ago, and nowadays reputable companies such as Hilton, Hyatt, Bally's, and Grand Casinos control most of the gambling facilities and hotel rooms in Las Vegas and Atlantic City and run the newly legalized casinos along the Mississippi River.

Organized crime thrives on illegal activities such as drugs and betting on numbers. Criminals have an advantage over honest businesspeople in bribing law-enforcement officials—and in using force to collect their debts. The influence of criminals on gaming would be reduced, not raised, if companies were able to operate casinos and other facilities on riverboats or anyplace else that is zoned for gaming. Many legitimate companies are eager to enter this industry as soon as it becomes a legal activity.

The fear of organized crime has encouraged state and local governments to operate state lotteries, the Off-Track Betting shops in New York City, and other facilities. But governments have been no more successful at these activities than they are at providing other services: New York's OTB offices are among the few unprofitable gaming establishments in the world. State lotteries have been slow to innovate, and they rip off their mainly less-educated clientele by paying out only 50 percent of their revenue. By contrast, privately run casinos in Las Vegas and elsewhere are forced by competition to pay out about 95 percent of the amount wagered.

II

EXCESSIVE
GAMBLING:
A MORAL OR
A MEDICAL
PROBLEM?

INTRODUCTION TO PART II

Everyone agrees that some gamblers are habitually reckless, sometimes even to the point of ruining their relationships, finances, and health. But not everyone agrees on the best way to describe such reckless behavior. Are the people who gamble recklessly "mentally ill"? Are they suffering from some psychiatric disorder? Or do such people have weak characters and bad judgment? In short, are they suffering from some disorienting condition or are they exercising—and perhaps misusing—their free will?

Henry Lesieur, formerly professor in the department of criminal justice at Illinois State University, and now president of the Institute for Problem Gambling in Pawtucket, Rhode Island, defends the proposition that reckless gambling, in certain circumstances, is a distinct and definable psychiatric disorder, characterized by a preoccupation with gambling, a desire to increase the stakes for excitement, a feeling of restlessness or irritability when attempting to cut down or stop gambling, the tendency to deceive people about the degree of one's involvement in gambling, a willingness to jeopardize or lose a significant relationship, job, or educational or career opportunity, and an inability to control one's gambling.

Richard Vatz, professor of rhetoric and communications at Towson State University (Maryland), and Lee Weinberg, an associate professor at the University of Pittsburgh's Graduate School of Public and International Affairs, believe that heavy or even reckless gambling is not a disease but a behavior, within the control of people. Both men think that viewing reckless gambling as a disease undermines efforts to hold people accountable for their actions.

Joy Wolfe, a law student writing for the *Indiana Law Journal*, argues that most legal cases for casinos' compensating compulsive gamblers for their losses are weak because the courts have ruled that it is unreasonable to require casinos to be able to identify compulsive gamblers and to determine the precise level of loss destructive to a given gambler.

5. Pathological Gambling Is a Psychiatric Disorder

Henry R. Lesieur

Dr. Henry Lesieur, editor of the Journal of Gambling Studies *and president of the Institute for Problem Gambling, believes that some forms of habitually reckless gambling are pathological and constitute a distinctly definable psychiatric disorder. When gambling is the focus of people's lives, when gambling is habitually used by people to escape from problems and to relieve dysphoria, when gambling so dominates people's lives that gamblers lie, cheat, or jeopardize their relationships or careers or finances, it is, according to Lesieur, pathological.*

After defining pathological gambling according to a cluster of symptoms, Lesieur discusses the costs of pathological gambling to individuals, families, insurance providers, and society generally. He outlines actions he believes the government should take and calls for a heightened awareness of what he believes is a growing problem.

In 1974, the number of Americans who gambled was 61 percent of the total population. They wagered 17.4 billion dollars legally. In 1989, the Gallup organization reported that 71 percent of the public gambled, while the gross legal gaming handle was 246.9 billion dollars for the year. This represents a 1,400 percent increase in dollar volume in just 15 years. Currently, 48 states (all but Utah and Hawaii) have some form of

---

This appeared under the title, "Compulsive Gambling," in *Society* (May–June 1992), pp. 43–50. Used here by permission.

legalized gambling. The California lottery alone is a 2.5-billion-dollar-a-year operation.

Not only did the number of states involved increase, but the variety of gaming offered has moved up as well. In addition to the state of Nevada and Atlantic City, New Jersey, local casinos have opened in Deadwood, South Dakota, and were approved for three mining towns in Colorado, and on the Mashantucket Pequot reservation in Connecticut. Iowa, Illinois, and Mississippi authorized riverboat or dockside casinos; video lottery terminals (VLTs), similar to slot machines, have been approved for Iowa, South Dakota, and West Virginia; charitable gambling has increased at a similar rate. For example, Minnesota with bingo run by charities and recently legalized pull tabs (called "paper slot machines") had gross sales of 1.2 billion dollars a year in charitable gaming in 1989.

Evidence suggests that in areas where more forms of gambling are legal, the incidence of problem and pathological (compulsive) gambling is also higher. In 1974 fewer than 1 percent of the adult population in the United States were recognized as compulsive gamblers while the comparable rate for Nevada was 2.5 percent. Recent surveys done in New York, New Jersey, Maryland, and Iowa and in Quebec, Canada, revealed that problem and pathological gambling in Iowa, where there is less legalized gambling, was about half that in other states and Quebec, where the studies were made.

Given the recent increase in legalized gambling, it is important to determine the potential impact [of] such legalization on the segment of the population prone to developing problems. So far, no systematic analysis of the costs of pathological gambling has been made.

What is pathological gambling? The American Psychiatric Association defines it as chronic and progressive failure to resist impulses to gamble, and gambling behavior that compromises, disrupts, or damages personal, family, or vocational pursuits. While the terms "pathological" and "compulsive" are technically not synonymous—for psychiatrists a compulsion is a behavior that is involuntary and in gambling this does not occur until quite late in the problem gambler's career—professionals and lay persons use them interchangeably.

Pathological Gambling Is Similar to Addictions

While pathological gambling does not involve the use of a substance, research conducted by numerous scholars has noted similarity with other addictive behaviors. For example, pathological gamblers state that they seek "action" as well as money or a means of escaping from problems—an aroused, euphoric state comparable to the "high" derived from cocaine or other drugs. Action means excitement, thrills and tension—"when the adrenalin is flowing." The desire to remain in action is so intense that many gamblers will go for days without sleep, without eating, and even without going to the bathroom. Being in action pushes out all other concerns. During the period of anticipation, there is also a "rush," usually characterized by sweaty palms, rapid heart beat, and nausea.

Pathological gamblers, like alcoholics and drug addicts, are preoccupied with seeking out gambling; they gamble longer than intended and with more money than intended. There is also the equivalent of "tolerance" when gamblers have to increase the size of their bets or the odds against them in order to create the desired amount of excitement.

Researchers in Australia, Germany and the United States have noted "withdrawal-like symptoms" in pathological gamblers who stop gambling. Hence, while not physiologically addicting, gambling has addictive qualities. Because of this, excessive dependence on gambling is often called an "addiction." Like substance abusers, pathological gamblers make frequent unsuccessful attempts at cutting down and quitting. While gambling does not produce intoxication or physical impairment and consequently does not have an impact on social, educational or occupational obligations in that way, the obsession with gambling has been noted to impair performance in these spheres.

The American Psychiatric Association is proposing new diagnostic criteria for pathological gambling for inclusion in its *Diagnostic and Statistical Manual*. Maladaptive behavior is indicated by at least four of the following: 1) preoccupied with gambling—preoccupied with relieving past gambling experiences, handicapping or planning the next venture, or thinking of ways to get money with which to gamble; 2) needs to gamble with increasing amounts of money in order to achieve the desired excitement; 3) is restless or irritable when attempting to cut down or stop gambling; 4) gambles as a way of escaping from problems or reliving dysphoric mood—feelings of helplessness, guilt, anxiety, depression; 5) often returns another day in order to get even ("chasing" one's money) after losing; 6) lies to family or others to conceal the extent of involvement with gambling; 7) engages in illegal acts such as forgery, fraud, theft, or embezzlement, committed in order to finance gambling; 8) has jeopardized or lost a significant relationship, job, educational or career opportunity because of gambling; 9) relies on others to provide money to relieve a desperate financial situation caused by gambling (a "bailout"); 10) repeats unsuccessful efforts to control, cut back, or stop gambling. "Dimensions" for each of the criteria are: preoccupation, tolerance, withdrawal, escape, chasing, lies/deception, illegal acts, relationship/job disruption, financial bailout, and loss of control.

Most gambling is merely a reshuffling of resources from one player to another with no net loss to the system as a whole. However, there is a redistribution of resources from losers to winners and from losers to the operators of the gambling activities. In some instances the operators are illegal bookmakers, people who run card rooms illegally, and so on. More recently, with the increasing legalization of gambling, the operator has been the state. State (as well as charity or corporate) profits therefore represent player losses.

Pathological Gamblers Often Get into Debt

Some people gamble more than others. These people, including pathological gamblers, account for a greater share of the state profits than the typical player. Most of this money comes out of paychecks and savings and is difficult to measure, particularly since the average gambler does not always lose but experiences a roller-coaster relationship with wins, losses and breaking even. Because losses outweigh wins in the long run for pathological gamblers, they typically borrow in order to finance continued play or to recover past losses. This debt can be examined.

Researchers have reported on different rates of indebtedness of pathological gamblers in treatment. The mean gambling-related debt (excluding auto loans, mortgages, and other "legitimate" debts) of individuals in treatment ranges from 53 thousand dollars to 92 thousand dollars. Female Gamblers Anonymous (GA) members have a lower level of gambling-related debt, averaging almost 15 thousand dollars. This is only the debt they accumulate and does not include the debt they pay off. For an estimated 18 percent of males and 8 percent of females in studies of treatment samples and members of Gamblers Anonymous, this eventually led to bankruptcy. Other defaults on indebtedness and civil suits also need to be added to the costs.

Since the data are limited, it is not possible to estimate the total debt, bankruptcy, and other civil problems produced by pathological gambling in the United States per year. Using a twenty-year gambling history and estimates of the number of probable pathological gamblers in New Jersey, I estimate that over 514 million dollars are accumulated in debt by compulsive gamblers in that state alone per year. This, however, is based on the assumption that pathological gamblers not in treatment are similar to those in treatment. Yet, it does not include the costs of bankruptcy proceedings, attempts to garnish paychecks, and other civil actions related to indebtedness.

Gambling-related debts appear to be a reflection of easy credit and check-cashing politics of the casino and the racing industry in New Jersey. Based on a review of the literature as well as discussions with members of Gamblers Anonymous, the following policies by gambling establishments appear to exacerbate the debt of pathological gamblers: 1) check-cashing services at gambling facilities; 2) holding a check for months or allowing gamblers to "buy back" their checks at a later date rather than cashing them right away; 3) cash machines at the gambling location or within easy walking distance from the casinos; 4) credit in any form associated with gambling; 5) one-time credit checks on the gamblers rather than a periodic review of credit required; 6) no total review of credit when a payment for a marker has "bounced" or is overdue; 7) loan sharks operating in or near the gambling facility; 8) drinking in association with gambling, which produces irrational play and increases debt. This is based on overall assessments of debt-related problems of GA members and those in treatment. A review of the interaction of these policies in other states and the gambling patterns of the broader gambling public would prove useful in guiding public policy.

Pathological Gambling Has High Medical and Emotional Costs

Pathological gamblers also borrow from life insurance policies, surrender their policies, and allow them to lapse or be revoked. This is costly for the insurance companies and the insurance-buying public as well as the gamblers' families. Gamblers operate uninsured automobiles, get into accidents, and become disabled or die without insurance. While these costs have not yet been calculated, one study of (primarily male) GA members found that 47 percent had engaged in insurance-related fraud or thefts where insurance companies had to pay the victims. The average amount of fraud was 65 thousand dollars. Pathological gamblers engage in an estimated 1.3 billion dollars in insurance-related fraud per year.

Pathological gambling has adverse health and emotional consequences. In the later stages of their gambling, pathological gamblers experience depression, insomnia, intestinal disorders, migraines, and other stress-related diseases. In a study done at Taylor Manor Hospital in Maryland, researchers compared chemically dependent patients with chemically dependent patients who were also pathological gamblers. They found that the chemically dependent gamblers reported more chronic medical problems, conflicts with family members, and more psychiatric symptoms than the non-gambling chemically dependent patients. In addition, studies have reported rates of suicide attempts by GA and hospitalized pathological gamblers that range from 15 to 24 percent—five to ten times higher than for the general population.

terns of exploitation of family finances, lies, distrust as a consequence of the lies, periodic arguments, separation and divorce threats, all related to excessive gambling. Valerie Lorenz of the National Center for Pathological Gambling in Baltimore has conducted most of the systematic research in this area.

The bulk of Lorenz's subjects were wives of compulsive gamblers attending Gamblers Anonymous/Gam-Anon Conclaves (regional conferences). Her data show serious problems within the family including harassment by bill collectors (experienced by 62 percent of the spouses in Lorenz's 1981 study), insomnia related to gambling-produced difficulties (78 percent), physical violence by the spouse against the gambler (62 percent), and suicide attempts by the spouse. The suicide attempt rates of 11 to 14 percent she has reported are three times higher than the reported rate of suicide attempts in the general population.

In more recent research, Lorenz and her colleague Robert Yaffee examined the psychosomatic, emotional, and marital difficulties of pathological gamblers and their spouses. Five hundred questionnaires were filled out at Gamblers Anonymous/Gam-Anon conclaves. Of these, 215 were completed by spouses. They found very high incidence of the following illnesses when compared with studies of female hospital patients: chronic or severe headache, bowel disorders (excessive constipation or diarrhea), asthma, depression, and suicide attempts. Aside from Gam-Anon, present resources to help families cope with gambling-related problems are nearly nonexistent in most states. While there is a growing body of literature on pathological gambling itself, relatively little is known about the children of compulsive gamblers. What is known tends to point to serious problems in the children as well as their parents.

The children of compulsive gamblers are caught in a situation of extreme behavior by their parents. At times the gambler dotes on them, then ignores them. This seesaw relationship has been portrayed in the few accounts of the dynamics of the family of pathological gamblers. The children feel angry, hurt, lonely, guilty, abandoned, and rejected. According to Robert Custer and Harry Milt,[1] their teen years are troubled, they run away from home, use drugs, become depressed, and experience psychosomatic illnesses. However, when they asked in their study of spouses of pathological gamblers about psychosomatic illnesses of the children, Lorenz and Yaffee did not find a statistically significant difference between the rates of these children and the general juvenile population. More systematic research of this issue is needed.

Some studies have found serious psychosocial maladjustment in the children of pathological gamblers. Durand Jacobs, in a study of California high school students, found compulsive gambling in the parents of students [who] were abusing stimulant drugs and tended to overeat. These students were also more likely to report having an unhappy childhood, having a legal action pending, being depressed and suicidal, and showing other signs of psychosocial maladjustment than children without troubled parents. Studies done in New Jersey and Quebec found that high-school students whose parents had a gambling problem were more likely to have a gambling problem themselves than those whose parents were not reported to have a gambling problem. These studies reinforce the need for state-mandated education about pathological gambling in the schools.

In her studies of spouses of compulsive gamblers, Lorenz asked about the parents' relationship with their children. Eight percent of the gamblers and 37 percent of spouses of gamblers physically abused their children. A more recent study has shown that children of Gamblers Anonymous members in the United States are more likely to be abused than children in studies of the national population.

Pathological Gamblers Have Problems at Work

Little systematic study has been done on the pathological gambler in the workplace. Previously, I have described differences between supervised, less supervised, and self-employed male compulsive gamblers. The lower the level of supervision on the job, the more likely the compulsive gambler is to exploit the time and finances the position grants. This has been found to be the case with female compulsive gamblers as well.

Extended card games and casino venture cause lateness and absences from work; lunch hours are lengthened for off-track betting (OTB); the gambler's mind may not be at work because of heavy losses, indebtedness, and intense preoccupation with getting even; irritability, moodiness, and poor concentration on work are added consequences. Many gamble on company time including card playing, betting on numbers, and acting as runners, writers, or bookmakers for a gambling operation at work. Money is borrowed from fellow employees; advances are taken on paychecks; paychecks are garnished. As a last resort, the employee may steal from the company or engage in illegal activities on company time. Those who own a business exploit it and drain its assets as well as those of suppliers and other creditors. The exact cost of these activities to employers, employees and fellow employees is not known, but it appears to be rather extensive. This aspect too needs further research.

In spite of these problems, very few employee assistance programs are actively screening troubled employees for a gambling problem. Systematic education is sorely needed.

Pathological Gambling Leads to Crime

Ultimately, pathological gambling results in crime. Studies conducted to date uncovered a wide variety of illegal behaviors among compulsive gamblers we interviewed. Jay Livingston found compulsive gamblers involved in check forgery, embezzlement, theft, larceny, armed robbery, bookmaking, hustling, running con games, and fencing stolen goods. My research uncovered similar patterns. In addition, I found gamblers engaged in systematic loan fraud, tax evasion, burglary, pimping, prostitution, selling drugs, and hustling at pool, golf, bowling, cards, and dice. Compulsive gamblers are engaged in a spiral of options and involvements wherein legal avenues for funding are utilized until they are closed off. Dependent on personal value systems, legitimate and illegitimate opportunity, perceptions of risk, the existence of threats (for example, loan sharks) and chance, gamblers become involved in more and more serious illegal activity. For some, the amount of money involved runs into the millions of dollars.

Studies of prisoners, alcohol- and drug-abusing inpatients, female members of Gamblers Anonymous, and a study of Veteran's Administration inpatients and Gamblers Anonymous members provide useful comparative information. In all four studies, the subjects were asked if they had engaged in a range of financially motivated crimes in order to gamble or to pay gambling debts.

Approximately two-thirds of non-incarcerated and 97 percent of incarcerated pathological gamblers admit engaging in illegal behavior to finance gambling or pay gambling-related debts. White-collar crimes predominate among treatment samples while street crimes and drug sales are more frequent among imprisoned compulsive gamblers. The total cost of this crime is unknown at present. An estimated 10 to 30 percent of prisoners are probably pathological gamblers. Most are also addicted to alcohol and/or other drugs. We need to find out what percent of their drug-related crimes are actually produced by gambling in combination with drug use. Treatment programs that address multiple dependencies are vitally needed in prisons and diversion programs, and halfway houses are needed for individuals on probation and parole.

Given the high level of property crime among pathological gamblers, to what extent do they engage in violent behavior? In a study examining nonviolence among pathological gamblers, Iain Brown surveyed 107 Gamblers Anonymous members in England and Scotland and found that 35 of them (33 percent) had criminal convictions. He examined these convictions to find out whether pathological gamblers had patterns of crime which were more similar to alcoholics (with a mix of violence and property offenses) or drug addicts (primarily property offenders). Theft and fraud offenses accounted for 94 percent of all criminal convictions. An additional 4 percent of convictions were for armed robbery. Fewer than 1 percent of convictions were for non-property violence offenses. Brown concluded that pathological gamblers are primarily nonviolent and their crime patterns are closer to those of heroin addicts, who exhibit primarily property-oriented crimes, than to alcoholics, who have high rates of violent crime.

The Social Cost of Pathological Gambling Is Difficult to Measure, but Is Enormous

Estimates of the percentage of probationers and inmates who are pathological gamblers range from 14 to 30 percent. There is no accurate estimate of how many got there as a result of gambling-related offenses. In one study, 13 percent of both male and female prisoners stated they were in prison as a result of gambling-related debt. The cost of arrest, prosecution, probation, parole, and imprisonment must also be figured into the total cost of pathological gambling to the general society.

The relatively high rate of illegal activity among pathological gamblers and its obvious social cost makes it imperative that probationers, parolees, and inmates be screened. Treatment for gambling should be provided along with treatment for alcoholism and for drug addiction.

How does one measure the cost of pathological gambling? The financial costs seem fairly straightforward. If the 514 million-dollars-a-year figure for New Jersey can be believed, even one-third of this figure extrapolated to the United States would mean billions of dollars in loans every year. If the 1.3 billion dollars in insurance fraud is accurate, this must also be added to other theft and fraud engaged in by pathological gamblers. The cost to employers is also immense and has not yet been measured. Similarly, the expense of prosecution, probation, prison, and parole for pathological gamblers driven to crime to support their obsession has not been studied. However, if the 13 percent figure arrived at in New Jersey (or even half of it) is accurate, these costs are enormous as well.

While financial costs can be assessed, how does one measure the cost of a suicide attempt, an ulcer, a child filled with anger and hatred for a parent or using drugs to obliterate painful memories? We could conceivably measure these in terms of cost of medical care, psychiatric care, marriage counseling, suicide prevention, drug prevention and other counseling. The greatest difficulty lies in measuring the intangible. Loss of trust in a marriage, divorce and separation, heart-wrenching tears, burning anger, shame, resentment and guilt, all leave emotional scars wrought by gambling-related problems.

No statistical evidence exists that confirms that the legalization of gambling increases the rate of pathological gambling. However, as noted above, there is an association between legalization and the extent of gambling problems. Calls to hotlines in Maryland, New Jersey, and New York reveal that the majority of callers are dependent on legalized forms of gambling. In New Jersey, for example, 62 percent of the callers mention problems with casino gambling, 33 percent with horse racing, 38 percent with state-run lotteries, 10 percent with bingo, and 8 percent with stocks and commodities. (These figures add up to more than 100 percent because many pathological gamblers have problems with more than one type of gambling.)

States Should Provide Help to Problem Gamblers

Gambling problems are not evenly distributed across the general population. Epidemiological surveys indicate that the problem is greater among the poor and minorities than other segments of the population. There is also evidence that the poor, minorities, and women are grossly underserved by available treatment resources. There are long waiting lists (up to six months) in states with some treatment services to pathological gamblers and their families. In spite of enormous gaming revenues the states receive and the enormous expenditures for advertising to attract new customers or repeat business, these same states devote nothing or only meager resources to education and training of professionals and the general public about problem gambling.

At present, only Massachusetts, Connecticut, New York, New Jersey, Maryland, Iowa, Minnesota and Delaware parcel out money to deal with problem gambling. Connecticut, Maryland, and Delaware spend less than 100 thousand dollars per year each. Massachusetts and Iowa recently cut the budget devoted to the issue and the governor of New York proposed wiping it out altogether while floating plans to legalize sports gambling to ease the fiscal crisis. In the 1990/91 fiscal year, the New Jersey state treasury took in a net sum of 783 million dollars from various sources (after winners were paid out and other expenses), yet the state spent only

260 thousand dollars for all compulsive-gambling-related programs combined—in other words, only 3/100th of a percent of its gambling revenues—this in a state where compulsive gamblers accumulate an estimated 514 million dollars in gambling-related debts per year. The irony is that New Jersey is one of the most generous states. Nevada, for example, contributes nothing to education, training, research, or treatment of problem gambling.

Surveys indicate that approximately 1 to 2 percent of the adult population are probably pathological gamblers and 2 to 3 percent are problem gamblers. We have *no* estimates of what percentage of total gaming revenues are produced by problem gamblers. Given that they expend much more money than the typical player, it would not be unreasonable to estimate that at least 10 percent (and possibly as much as 50 percent) of gaming revenues are produced by problem gamblers.

Given this simple reality, I propose the following steps to be taken:

1) No new forms of gambling should be legalized without first providing treatment on demand for gambling-related problems in all localities of a state. A no-waiting-list policy should be adopted whereby all costs of treatment should be derived from gambling revenues. This does not mean that the state should be responsible for the gamblers' debts, but it should be responsible for providing adequate treatment programs for the gamblers and their families.

2) No promotion of gambling should be allowed without a warning label and an 800 help line number to call for those with gambling problems. The full cost of the help line would be derived from gaming revenues or specific gambling fees (possible sources include but are not limited to unclaimed prizes, taxes on gaming machines, entree fees, and so on).

3) Careful epidemiological studies of all gamblers should be conducted to gain an estimate of what percentage of the money wagered is being wagered by problem gamblers.

4) A percentage of the revenues lost by problem gamblers (and hence, added to state coffers through state gambling taxes) should be devoted to education, treatment, and research.

We Need a Federal Program for
Problem Gambling

Gambling has national implications and consequences. Gamblers from Minnesota, Illinois, and Florida travel to Las Vegas, Atlantic City, Deadwood, and other gambling heavens. People from the Dakotas, Iowa, and Wisconsin venture to race tracks in neighboring states and vice versa. In some instances the local lottery ticket agent in an adjoining state is closer than the one from your own state. Players win money in one state only to lose it in another. They also lose money and make cash transfers from their home state to the host. In some cases they lose money in one state and steal in another in order to repay their debts. The common feature of interstate gambling is that most benefits, such as increased jobs and the "voluntary tax" revenues, appear to be local while some (though by no means all) of the problems are exported. Pathological gambling is clearly a problem with costs that cross state boundaries.

Gambling is not just an interstate problem. It also has implications for one of America's most poverty-stricken and oppressed minorities— Native Americans. On the federal level, the Indian Gaming Regulatory Act of 1988 has allowed Indian tribes to operate any form of gambling currently legalized in the state in which the tribe resides. Ironically, this opportunity for entrepreneurship and self-reliance has improved the lot of some tribes—which now have their own unemployment insurance and poverty relief programs funded by gambling proceeds—and has the potential of reducing federal aid to the tribes involved. On the other hand, Indian gambling has its victims as well. Like the states with neighbors who gamble, most of the benefits appear to be localized while the problems are exported. The major question then becomes, how can we allow people who want to gamble, and groups that need the economic benefits that can accrue from operating gambling operations, to pursue their goals with a minimum amount of disruption to potential pathological gamblers and their families?

A national commission on compulsive gambling is needed to investigate the issues discussed. Short of this, federal legislation is needed to provide education, treatment and research into pathological gambling. Ideally, the

National Institute on Drug Abuse and the National Institute on Alcoholism and Alcohol Abuse would have another counterpart, a National Institute on Problem Gambling. If governments benefit from gambling revenues, they have an obligation to help those who are hurt by their actions.

Suggested Readings

Abt, Vicki, James F. Smith, and Eugene M. Christiansen, *The Business of Risk: Commercial Gambling in Mainstream America* (Lawrence, Kansas.: University of Kansas Press, 1985).

Custer, Robert L. and Harry Milt, *When Luck Runs Out* (New York: Facts on File Publications, 1985).

Eadington, William R. and Judy Cornelius, eds., *Gambling and Public Policy: International Perspectives* (Reno: University of Nevada Press, 1991).

Lesieur, Henry R. *The Chase: Career of the Compulsive Gambler* (Cambridge, Massachusetts: Schenkman Books, 1984).

Shaffer, Howard J., Sharon A. Stein, Blase Gambino, and Thomas N. Cummings, *Compulsive Gambling: Theory, Research, and Practice* (Lexington, Massachusetts: Lexington Books, 1989.)

Note

1.   Robert L. Custer and Harry Milt, *When Luck Runs Out* (New York: Facts on File Publications, 1985).

6. Heavy Gambling Is Not a Disease

Richard E. Vatz and Lee S. Weinberg

Richard Vatz, professor of rhetoric and communication at Towson State University, Maryland, and Lee Weinberg, an associate professor at the University of Pittsburgh's Graduate School of Public and International Affairs, believe that the concept of compulsive gambling embodies a psychiatric myth used to relieve gamblers of personal responsibility for failing to exercise self-control. They reject the definition of compulsive gambling as a "disorder of impulse control." Many researchers, according to Vatz and Weinberg, want people to view reckless gambling as a disorder to help generate sympathy for self-destructive gamblers and acquire third-party payments and grants for mental health professionals and researchers. Arguing against those researchers, they assert that accepting gambling as addictive and uncontrollable not only falsifies reality but also may make it more difficult for gamblers to resist their urges.

They assert further that psychiatry's diagnostic manual lists no medical criteria for defining pathological gambling, only criteria referring to frequency of wagering and its social, financial, and legal consequences. What's more, no one, according to Vatz and Weinberg, has produced any neurochemical or neurophysiological correlates specific to heavy gambling, only changes common to many exciting actions, such as increased adrenaline or palpitations. The authors also reject the idea that gamblers would not willfully destroy their families or waste money. For they argue that many gamblers simply don't care

This first appeared as "Refuting the Myths of Compulsive Gambling," in the monthly magazine *USA Today* (November 1993), pp. 54–56. Used here by permission.

much about their families and enjoy taking substantial risks for the excitement of "big wins."

The authors are especially concerned that, when gamblers are told that they are powerless to change their habits, they will be discouraged from exercising self-control. Finally, Vatz and Weinberg worry that, if self-destructive gambling is regarded as a medical problem, many gamblers will lose a sense of personal responsibility for their actions.

Robert Terry, the *Philadelphia Inquirer*'s chief police reporter, borrowed money from that city's police commissioner and other department officials. Despite the fact that such borrowing creates a blatant conflict of interest, Terry was suspended *with pay*, with no decision made on a final disciplinary action. His managing editor, James Naughton, accepted Terry's explanation that it was a "disease" of gambling that put him in such dire straits. Naughton stated that he would await the outcome of a therapy program intended to cure Terry's "disease" before rendering final judgment.

In 1992, former *ABC Monday Night Football* producer Chet Forte was given a suspended sentence for bank fraud and income tax irregularities after Gamblers Anonymous testified at his sentencing hearing.

Former Baltimore Colt quarterback Art Schlichter went from object of scorn to one of pity in 1983 when it was claimed that his wagering, which had cost him hundreds of thousands of dollars, was the result of the "disease of compulsive gambling" (sometimes called "pathological gambling"). The late psychiatrist Robert Custer, often referred to as the father of compulsive gambling, stated, "Art has suffered the full effects of his disease."

In mid-1989, it was revealed that baseball hero Pete Rose dropped more than $500,000 through heavy gambling. It also was reported that he had to sell treasured memorabilia because of his debts. After weeks of bad press following a denial that he had a problem with gambling, Rose made a public statement that he had what his recently acquired psychiatrist called "a clinically significant gambling disorder" that rendered him powerless over his gambling. He then went on a media tour, during which he was greeted by a lengthy standing ovation from Phil Donahue's television audience and congratulations for his "admission" from Barbara Walters. Rose had gone from miscreant to courageous victim.

Since then, press attention to compulsive gambling—with uncritical acceptance of its being an illness and uncontrollable—has abounded. It has been heralded as the "Addiction of the 1990s." In the *Journal of Gambling Studies (JGS)*, the major academic journal on gambling and social issues, editor Henry Lesieur wrote quite accurately in 1992 that "Not a day goes by . . . without something appearing in the professional literature or mass media about compulsive gambling."

The groundwork for the successful promotion of the disease model for heavy gambling was laid firmly more than a decade ago. After years of what *JGS* called his "unflagging advocacy," Custer persuaded the American Psychiatric Association in its 1980 update of the *Diagnostic and Statistical Manual (DSM-III)* to elevate gambling to one of its categories of impulse disorders or, more specifically, a "Disorder of Impulse Control not Elsewhere Classified." This act was heralded in articles and media appearances by prominent gambling researchers as establishing that heavy, self-destructive gambling was a disease, the medical identity that was seen as necessary for sympathy for heavy bettors, and status and financial support (third-party payments, grants, etc.) for the researchers themselves, of whom few were—or are—medical doctors. If such gambling were a disease (the manual uses the term "disorder," but its "nomenclature" specialist, Robert Spitzer, claims that it may be considered the same as disease), it was axiomatic that it was beyond the individual's control.

There's No Evidence That Problem Gambling Is a Disease

The problem is that there is no evidence that compulsive gambling is a disease (a point psychiatrist Thomas Szasz has made for decades) or uncontrollable. Revealingly, there are indications that, at least as far as the disease claim is concerned, many gambling researchers don't believe it either. Moreover, the consequences of accepting compulsive gambling as addictive or uncontrollable may be to hinder efforts of heavy gamblers to resist their urges.

Psychiatry's diagnostic manual lists no medical criteria in its "diagnostic criteria" for pathological gambling, only those referring to frequency of wagering and its social, financial, and legal consequences. Put simply, heavy gambling is not an illness in the sense that most people think of one. There is no credible evidence whatsoever of any neurochemical or neurophysiological status causally linked to heavy gambling, only changes such as increased adrenaline or palpitations caused by the excitement of the action. No study has found any neurobiological status specific to compulsive gamblers as contrasted with other excitable people. Yet, the finding of neurobiological correlates—especially if they were specific to heavy gambling—would constitute a Holy Grail for researchers, providing a basis for maintaining that it is a disease and uncontrollable.

Thus, it was discouraging to gambling researchers in the late 1980s (and confirmed in recent follow-ups) when a year-long study at the National Institute of Alcoholism and Alcohol Abuse showed no differences in serotonin levels between compulsive gamblers and normal men. A positive finding could have been used to argue that such gamblers lacked impulse control.

In 1989, however, gambling researchers argued that they finally had their "proof." A study published in *The Archives of General Psychiatry* found that 17 heavy gamblers had neurochemical elevations correlated with their "extroversion." The article was—and continues to be—heralded by gambling researchers and the popular press as evidence that gamblers' biology is destiny. The *New York Times* headline read: "Gambling: Biology May Hold Key," and a piece in the February 1992 *Harvard Mental Health Letter* argued that the 1989 study demonstrates that "The gambling addiction may even have a physiological basis."

Even this study, the gambling researchers' best evidence that chronic gambling is compulsive and a disease, proved little beyond what one would expect—namely, that gamblers are excitable personalities who evidence heightened neurological measures of excitement. It demonstrates neither that such biological differences are causal nor that they are specific to compulsive gamblers or even gamblers at all. As the study's senior researcher, psychiatrist Alec Roy concedes, the gamblers "were not compared to other groups, so we cannot answer the question with regard to specificity." He adds that no follow-up studies have been done or currently are being done to his knowledge.

Responsible gambling researchers do not maintain that there is any proof of biological causation in compulsive gambling. Sirgay Sanger, president of the National Council on Problem Gambling, admits in the *Journal of the American Medical Association* what one rarely, if ever, reads in gambling researchers' quotes in the popular press: Pathological gambling "has the smell of a biochemical addiction in it," but, he admits, "there is no research proof."

The most prominent medical doctor promoting the gambling-as-disease concept is psychiatrist Sheila Blume, the medical director for the alcoholism, chemical dependency, and compulsive gambling programs at South Oaks Hospital, Amityville, N.Y. She often talks about heavy gambling as an illness, but there is reason to believe she doubts the claim herself and uses medical language only for strategic purposes.

In an article in *JGS*, Blume makes a remarkably frank recommendation that, regardless of objections to the medical model, heavy gambling should be considered an illness for practical benefits for gamblers and their doctors: "It is concluded that the many individual and social advantages of the medical model make it the preferred conceptualization of our present state of knowledge." Lesieur also has cited the strategic importance of public acceptance of pathological gambling as an illness, arguing that, without it, the gamblers themselves are less likely to accept the disease model, an acceptance he views as crucial to successful treatment.

Valerie Lorenz is executive director of the National Center for Pathological Gambling and one of the most vocal promoters of the illness model for gambling in her constant beseechings for governmental and other source funding. She sees the acceptance of gambling as illness as crucial to legal exculpation and counsels that "the expert witness for the compulsive gambler facing legal charges" must "educate" judges and others as to the "illness" of the "compulsive gambler" in legal trouble; in order to avoid the unfair punishing of those who are "seriously disturbed" and "out of control."

Significantly, Norman Rose, a professor of law and vice-president of the California Council on Compulsive Gambling, who, according to *JGS*, is the "nation's leading authority on gambling and the law," disputes the medical model for compulsive gambling. In an interview, he expressed skepticism regarding the notion that heavy gambling can be a disease: "I have a lot of trouble with that idea, especially within the law, where it is used as an excuse." In terms of insanity-like defenses, wherein people are found not guilt of crimes by virtue of suffering from pathological gambling, Rose says, "It just doesn't work anymore," even though the plea is still attempted. What does work to some degree—and probably is increasing in usage—is its employment in criminal cases to provide alternative sentencing programs comparable to alcohol treatment programs, as well as in divorces, tax problems, and bankruptcy.

Regardless of questions of validity, the public appears conditioned to call any deviant behavior disease if the situation entails sufficient poignancy. In an article in *Good Housekeeping* titled "When Gambling Becomes a Disease," the magazine asserts that "It is only when gambling overtakes a person's life that it moves from recreation to an illness." However, does gambling *really* overtake people's lives?

There's No Evidence Compulsive Gamblers *Cannot* Control Their Actions

In the wake of the claim of the astronomical prevalence (almost six percent of all adults in Maryland—more than one in every 20) of problem or pathological gambling, legislation was passed in Maryland to require all state lottery tickets to carry the following warning: "Compulsive gambling is a treatable illness." Those six words concede all three of the major disputable claims of the gambling researchers: that heavy, self-destructive gambling is an illness, is uncontrollable, and is treatable, which implies that treatment programs have been shown to be significantly helpful to those who seek aid to resist the urges. (The study was fueled by a National Institute of Mental Health study using a broad definition of pathological gambling, nearly guaranteeing a large claim.)

Researchers who argue that compulsive gambling is beyond control believe the proof to be self-evident by virtue of the devastating consequences of such activity and confirmed by the participants' claims that they cannot stop. How, they wonder, could people willfully gamble themselves into such financial, legal, and family problems, consequences that define for the most part gamblers' "chronic and progressive failure to resist impulses to gamble" as required for psychiatry's current diagnostic manual (*DSM-III-R*)? This is, of course, a circular definition, as no one can verify a person's ability to control his or her behavior. Let us look at that assertion with reason as a guide.

When we wrote an article several years ago that "control" is not accessible or measurable except through the potentially self-serving claims of gamblers, Blume responded by accusing us of saying that gamblers could not be believed. Leaving aside that researchers invariably insist that lying is one of the cardinal signs of the compulsive gambler, the point is that a claim of inability to control one's gambling—even if made sincerely—cannot logically confirm such inability. At most, the statement might reveal his or her honest belief.

Chet Forte, who gambled himself into millions of dollars of losses, has asked rhetorically how anyone could think he willfully would have "gone through the money" or "destroyed my family"? The answer is twofold. First, his stated concern for his family notwithstanding, many heavy gamblers—including, perhaps, Forte, according to a letter written to us by his first cousin, Anne Perrin, and her husband—simply don't care so much about their families.

Gambling researchers themselves are aware that the image of the heavy gambler whose actions destroy what otherwise would be a great family man (most heavy gamblers are men) is simply a myth. Most compulsive gamblers are not committed family men, with or without their gambling. Perrin stated that Forte defrauded her family, despite his being "someone my mother helped put through college and whose parents were constantly helped financially by my parents!" She adds that Forte has no real remorse and quotes him as saying that he learned that, "when you are stealing, steal big." Along a similar line, gambling researchers who attribute great social costs to gambling, such as those to businesses due to lost productivity, do not consider the possibility that a compulsive gambler who wasn't gambling would not be very productive or might have high absenteeism regardless.

Second, gambling is exciting for many reasons, including the risks and opportunities it provides for "big wins," as well as extensive losses. Heavy gamblers often engage in "chasing," which involves a type of exponentially increasing betting that can win back losses quickly, even substantial ones. Gamblers don't expect to lose.

So Far, There's No Evidence That "Treatment" for Compulsive Gambling Works

The assumption that they cannot control their urges figures largely in gambling treatment programs, as it does with those for other behavioral "addictions." In fact, the first in the well-known Twelve Steps of Recovery common to such programs is that the addict must admit that he or she has a problem (or illness) and is powerless to resist it. Despite the exaggerated claims of the promoters of groups like Gamblers Anonymous (GA) and Alcoholics Anonymous, there is little or no evidence of their widespread success. With respect to compulsive gamblers, anecdotes exist in abundance, but there are few studies available on the outcomes of such group-oriented treatment.

What studies there are reveal very limited success in achieving gambling abstinence. The astronomical dropout rate of 70 percent and more in GA and other groups makes it appear that whatever success there is—and sometimes high rates are claimed—is due largely to the high level of commitment of those who stay in the program, rather than the program itself. Neither is abstinence verifiable.

It is time for at least some skepticism regarding the unquestioned need for addicts to admit powerlessness over their own behavior. It is worth considering whether such admissions constitute a self-fulfilling prophecy—that is to say, the belief that a habit is uncontrollable actually may discourage people from trying to stop behaving in a self-destructive manner since it is beyond their control.

Assertions that heavy, destructive gambling is a disease, uncontrollable, and treatable simply do not withstand close scrutiny. Questionable research, reasoning, and evidence are used to criticize the existence of state lotteries, exculpate irresponsible behavior of heavy gamblers, and, in the case of treatment, perhaps undermine efforts to help people resist the urge to gamble. That the unique excitement and risk-taking motivates some people to neglect many important aspects of their lives is intriguing, but not overly surprising. It is the medicalizing of heavy gambling that makes it seem so utterly mysterious.

The debate about compulsive gambling, like that about other self-destructive or socially unacceptable behaviors ranging from compulsive drinking to compulsive shopping (a supposed new disorder whose advocates urge its inclusion in the next revision of psychiatry's diagnostic manual), ultimately comes down to a single question: Should individuals who engage in these behaviors be excused on the grounds that they suffer from a disorder that produces urges they are unable to resist? Without further evidence, we believe the answer to be no.

Whether talking about newspaper employees who have a conflict of interest due to borrowing to pay off gambling debts, people who defraud banks and associates, or athletes who bet on games in violation of league rules, there should be no general moral or legal recognition of compulsive gambling disorder as a valid reason for such behavior. The practical effect of recognizing disorders is to make these excuses significant because they are alleged disorders while rejecting other exculpatory claims.

The implication of this position, however, is not that no differences exist among individual cases of misconduct or self-destructive conduct. Quite the contrary. For instance, the employee who embezzles money to pay for a child's medical care may be entitled to more consideration than the one who pleads compulsive gambling. While both should be made to repay the stolen money, perhaps the former, not the latter, is entitled to a second chance. This much is clear: it is time to stop all special consideration for those whose excuses are sympathy-provoking only because they bear the unscientific "disorder" imprimatur of psychiatry.

7. It Won't Be Easy to Hold Casinos Legally Responsible for Patrons' Losses

Joy Wolfe

In a law review comment, law student Joy Wolfe examines the issue whether casinos should be legally responsible for claims against them made by compulsive gamblers, who, according to Wolfe, lack the capacity consistently to withstand the urge to gamble. She describes the claims arising from the relationship between the casinos and compulsive gamblers. Commonly, gamblers present claims against casinos to recover their losses, asserting that the gamblers should not be liable for the debts because of their lack of self-control.

According to Wolfe, the gamblers' claims may be either tort claims or contract-based claims. In this context tort claims would allege that the casino breached a duty to the gambler, owed because of the gambler's alleged disorder. After examining a number of torts, she holds that they have favored casinos against compulsive gamblers, whose conditions have been viewed as having no right to be identified by casinos and whose behavior, according to judicial decisions, has not been entitled to paternalistic monitoring.

Wolfe asserts that a gambler's potential for recovery seems strongest when casino employees know of the gambler's compulsion. She notes though that the casino would argue that the gambler should bear the responsibility for his or her own actions. She contends that it is unclear how courts would respond to that

---

This first appeared as "Casinos and the Compulsive Gambler: Is There a Duty to Monitor the Gambler's Wagers?" in the *Mississippi Law Journal* 64 (1995), pp. 687–701. Used here by permission.

complaint, since no compulsive gamblers have yet produced evidence of their compulsions' being known by casino operators.

A gambler bringing a tort claim might, according to Wolfe, try to argue from analogy to "dram-shop" laws, under which tavern owners can be held liable for serving alcohol to an obviously intoxicated patron who later harms others. But there are, she argues, two critical differences between dram-shop liability and what would be necessary in the gambling case. First, while the intoxicated patron might endanger others, the gambler's actions are presumably harmful principally or only to himself or herself. Second, while tavern owners may be able to know when someone is obviously intoxicated, casino operators cannot reasonably be expected to know the precise level of debt destructive to a given gambler. "Thus, although the analogy to 'dram-shop' liability appears to provide support for the imposition of a duty on casinos to monitor compulsive gamblers, there are fundamental differences which make the extension of such liability to the gaming industry impossible."

Wolfe also briefly examines common-law contract defenses, such as incapacity and duress, as a basis for canceling gambling debts. She discusses a 1992 New Jersey state court decision in which it was held that compulsive gambling, by itself, cannot invalidate contracts but that a particular compulsive gambler might theoretically be able to demonstrate, in some circumstance, a lack of free will, which would invalidate a contract. A particular gambler would have to show, on this theory, that he or she was taken advantage of while negotiating a contract.

The Mississippi Legislature legalized dockside gambling on the waters of the Mississippi River and the Mississippi Gulf Coast in 1990.[1] Since that time, the growth of the industry has been phenomenal, with thirty casinos now operating in the state.[2] These new businesses create jobs, increase tax revenues and improve tourism for the state; however, in addition to the much-extolled economic benefits, there appears to be a less positive aspect of legalized gambling—compulsive gambling.

As the number of compulsive gamblers increases, the industry, the practicing bar of Mississippi and the courts will be forced to examine and define the legal relationship between the casino and the compulsive gambler. This comment will explore this relationship through a discussion of the potential claims against casinos by compulsive gamblers and related parties. It will also seek to assess the validity of such claims in light of general legal principles and judicial rulings from foreign jurisdictions.[3]

Compulsive Gambling Is an Identifiable Disease

Compulsive gamblers lack the capacity to consistently withstand the urge to gamble.[4] Persons affected by the disease are controlled by an irresistible impulse to gamble which, over time, drains the victim financially, emotionally and physically, often destroying all meaning in his life.[5] Estimates indicate that between five and ten percent of those regularly participating in gaming activities are compulsive gamblers.[6]

Although compulsive gambling is an identifiable disease, the presence of other problems, such as drug or alcohol addiction, often masks its presence.[7] The exact number of compulsive gamblers in Mississippi is unknown; however, reports from various sources indicate that the number has grown substantially since the casinos arrived. For example, Gamblers Anonymous, a self-help group for problem gamblers, reports increased attendance at existing groups, as well as the founding of new groups in areas most affected by the casinos.[8] The number of cases treated by the state's Mental Health Services has also increased,[9] and a national hotline reports receiving between 100 and 200 calls per month from Mississippi since the introduction of legalized gambling.[10] Concern over these statistics, and the problems they represent, has led to calls for industrial and governmental involvement in compulsive gambling treatment programs in the state.[11]

However, implementation of a full-scale treatment program will not eliminate the problem, since many compulsive gamblers will not avail themselves of treatment.[12] Therefore, the issue of potential casino liability in connection with compulsive gamblers remains a viable one, even as the state and the industry attempt to alleviate the problem.

Claims arising from the relationship between casinos and compulsive gamblers fall generally into two categories: 1) claims brought by the compulsive gambler to recover losses; and 2) claims brought by a representative of the compulsive gambler under the applicable wrongful death statute.

Compulsive Gamblers Claim They Should Not Be Liable for Debts

The most common claim of the compulsive gambler is that he should not be liable for his gambling debts because of his disorder. These claims, often raised as counterclaims in actions commenced by casinos to collect past-due debts, are primarily tort claims which allege that the casino breached a duty to the gambler. However, a gambler might choose to advance a contract-based claim as well.

A. Tort Claims

Any claimant bringing an action based on negligence principles must establish four elements in order to be successful.[13] The compulsive gambler faces a tremendous hurdle in establishing the first of these elements, that of a duty owed to the gambler by the casino.

1. Claims Distinguished from "Dram-shop" Claims. Prior to a discussion of possible factors giving rise to an enforceable duty on the part of a casino toward a compulsive gambler, it is important to note that these claims are not based on excessive alcohol consumption nor an extension of "dram-shop" liability per se.[14] Claims alleging that a casino allowed an obviously intoxicated gambler to continue to wager have met with some success in the courts.[15] However, regardless of the validity of such claims, they may be distinguished from the claims which are the subject of this comment. The claims involved here allege that a duty to the compulsive gambler arises as a result of his mental condition. This distinction does not negate the potential usefulness of an analogy between the rationale underlying "dram-shop" laws and the proposed rationale for creating a duty requiring casinos to monitor the behavior of compulsive gamblers. Instead, the distinction clarifies the scope of this comment.

2. Case Law. In 1983, a compulsive gambler sought debt cancellation and restitution of losses from a casino which allegedly had "preyed on [the gambler's] sickness" and caused him to incur losses beyond his financial resources.[16] The complaint did not specify the precise duty which it claimed a casino owed its patrons, but the case appears to have been based on a presumed duty to look after the best interests of the player. The case settled, so a jury never examined the existence or non-existence of such a duty.[17] Despite the settlement of the claim, the case generated considerable attention in the gaming industry. Casino officials claimed that saddling them with the two-fold burden of identifying problem gamblers and controlling their activities would be unjust and would be a virtually impossible standard to satisfy.[18] A casino spokesperson, reflecting the general response of the industry, noted that, "There is not, and there should not be, any duty imposed on the casino to ensure that plaintiff and other patrons do not lose their money. Gambling by definition is a risky business. It is also a legal one."[19]

In 1984, it was alleged that a casino granted credit and thereby encouraged the gaming activity of a person whom the casino knew, either actually or constructively, to be a compulsive gambler.[20] The judge held that the casino followed state regulations in extending credit to the gambler and could not be punished for losses resulting from the player's subsequent wagers.[21]

In 1989, a compulsive gambler initiated an action in the United States District Court for the Eastern District of Pennsylvania, asserting the same claim raised in the 1983 action discussed above.[22] The defendant casino countered with an action in state court to recover past-due debts.[23] The state court judge ruled that the gambler's defense to the debt, which was his claim in federal court, was without merit and observed that to accept the position advanced by the gambler would place an impossible burden on the casino industry to identify and control compulsive gamblers.[24] The district court ruled that the doctrine of *res judicata* prevented relitigation of the issues and granted the casino's motion for judgment as a matter of law.[25]

Harrah's Club v. Van Blitter[26] involved a claim similar to those discussed above.[27] The gambler in *Van Blitter* explicitly stated that the casino breached its duty to conduct a "fair game" by its failure to control her wagers once it was apparent that she was losing. The plaintiff alleged that the breach was aggravated by the complimentary lodging and meals she received from the casino. The United States District Court for the District of Nevada rejected Van Blitter's argument and held that there was no support for imposing tort liability on the casino.[28] In its opinion, the court stated that casinos did not have a duty to force unsuccessful players to stop betting. The court also observed that if such a duty existed, the industry would soon fail because there would be no potential for economic success.[29] Although this decision appears almost identical to the cases mentioned earlier, a statement by the court regarding the casino's awareness of Van Blitter's mental status warrants particular attention. In absolving the casino of liability, the court noted that the casino had no knowledge of those problems which caused Van Blitter to begin gambling, and evidenced no intent to take advantage of a "demonstrable psychological weakness."[30]

3. Potential Success of Future Claims. The previously discussed cases favor casinos in actions for restitution brought by compulsive gamblers. The courts which have addressed the issue have uniformly held that the gambler cannot recover under tort law because of the absence of a duty on the part of the casino to recognize a compulsive gambler and, thereafter, monitor his betting activity. These cases clearly demonstrate that a gambler will not prevail on his claim unless he can show exigent circumstances which impose upon the casino an enforceable duty.[31]

The gambler's potential for recovery seems strongest in a situation where a casino, with actual knowledge of the gambler's compulsive disorder, ignores such knowledge and permits on-going gambling. In such a situation, the gambler might persuasively argue that the casino's

knowledge gave rise to a duty which the casino subsequently breached by
failing to bar the gambler from the gaming tables. However, casinos will
undoubtedly point out that if they possess actual knowledge of the
player's problem, then the player also possesses that knowledge and
should bear the responsibility for controlling his own actions.[32] In sum, a
compulsive gambler could invoke the dicta in *Van Blitter* to argue that a
casino actually knew of his disorder and, by allowing continued gambling,
failed to act as a reasonably prudent party in response to that knowledge.
The actual merit of this complain is unclear, since no gambler has yet
produced evidence of actual knowledge on the part of a casino.

A compulsive gambler bringing a tort claim for recovery of losses will
probably claim that the public policy arguments underlying the imposition of liability on tavern owners under "dram-shop" laws apply equally
to support imposing a duty on the casino industry to monitor compulsive
gamblers.[33] "Dram-shop" legislation creates a duty precluding tavern
owners from serving alcohol to an obviously intoxicated patron and holds
an owner liable for injuries proximately caused by the patron if the duty
is breached.[34] The justification underlying this liability is that the bartender is in the best position to avoid the foreseeable harm by refusing to
serve the intoxicated patron. It is conceivable to argue that the same
rationale applies to a compulsive gambler and a casino employee. However, there are two important distinctions between these situations. First,
the compulsive gambler's actions are presumably harmful only to the
gambler himself. Many true "dram-shop" laws, as well as Mississippi's
legislation,[35] impose liability only when a third party is injured by the
intoxicated person.[36] Secondly, the application of this principle to
compulsive gamblers raises a problem of foreseeability. "Dram-shop"
liability attaches when a bartender serves alcohol to an obviously
intoxicated customer. Therefore, there is a reasonably objective standard,
that of visible intoxication, by which a bar owner may judge his actions.
No such standard exists to distinguish between a casual gambler on a
losing streak and compulsive gambler in debt beyond his financial means.
If the law required casinos to make such a distinction, one could argue
that the only way to avoid liability would be to establish a limit on the

losses which a gambler could incur before asking him to cease gambling.[37] The flawed nature of such a provision is obvious. Because of the varying economic levels of patrons it would be impossible to establish a level which would protect all players while still allowing the casual gambler to push his luck to the limit. Thus, although the analogy to "dram-shop" liability appears to provide support for the imposition of a duty on casinos to monitor compulsive gamblers, there are fundamental differences which make the extension of such liability to the gaming industry essentially impossible.

B. Claims Based on Contract Law

Common-law contract defenses, such as incapacity, duress and un-conscionability, provide compulsive gamblers with another arguable basis for cancellation of their gambling debts. For a compulsive gambler's contract claim to succeed, the courts must accept the proposition that the markers representing gaming debts, which the casino seeks to enforce and the gambler seeks to have rescinded, are contracts between the parties.

In 1992, a New Jersey state court held that common-law defenses were available to a compulsive gambler seeking to avoid paying obligations represented by casino markers.[38] The court carefully drafted its opinion to ensure that the scope would not be too far-reaching. Specifically, the court held that compulsive gambling, in and of itself, would not suffice to invalidate the contracts.[39] Instead, the court noted that the compulsive gambler might have demonstrated, through his words and actions, a lack of free will to contract which would subsequently void the markers.[40] The court recognized that the New Jersey Casino Control Act did not preclude the assertion of common-law contract defenses, but simultaneously rejected the argument that compulsive gambling should be an independent basis for voiding contracts.[41]

Thus, a compulsive gambler may successfully assert a common-law contract defense in order to avoid his gaming obligations. However, recovery in such actions would not be premised on the gambler's compulsive disorder; instead, the result would flow from the application of established legal principles which prohibit one party from taking advantage of another when negotiating a contract. In order to successfully pursue such a claim, the compulsive gambler must demonstrate that all elements of the common-law defense are present, a burden which the *Lomonaco* court clearly indicated is not necessarily satisfied by simply being a compulsive gambler.[42]

Relatives Claim Casinos Are Responsible for Gamblers' Suicides

The second category of complaints against casinos arising from their involvement with compulsive gamblers consists of complaints asserted under wrongful death statutes following the suicide of the gambler.

A. Wrongful Death Actions

At common-law, death did not give rise to a viable tort claim for recovery of damages resulting from the death; however, wrongful death statutes alter this rule.[43] Under Mississippi's wrongful death statute, an action may be brought in situations where death resulted from "any real, wrongful or negligent act or omission" which would have given the decedent a cause of action had he survived.[44] An action may be initiated by a surviving spouse, a surviving child or other person as described in the statute.[45] A plaintiff in a wrongful death action may recover monetary damages to compensate for the death of the represented party[46] provided that the act of the defendant is shown to have been the proximate cause of death.

B. Case Law

A California state court rejected a wrongful death claim alleging that a casino breached a contractual duty to the decedent.[47] The court held that the contracts on which the plaintiffs relied, check-cashing agreements establishing a monetary limit, were insufficient to create a duty since the decedent necessarily rescinded the contracts when he requested that the casino cash checks exceeding the limit.[48] Characterizing the plaintiffs' argument as nothing more than an effort to impose a duty on the casino not to allow the decedent to rescind the contract, the court rejected the claim summarily.[49]

C. Application of Wrongful Death Claims to Casinos

Since wrongful death statutes allow actions only when the decedent would have been able to pursue a claim had he survived, the plaintiff asserting a wrongful death claim faces many of the same obstacles which confront a compulsive gambler bringing a tort action. The plaintiff must show that the casino owed a duty to the gambler, breached that duty and proximately caused the suicide of the bettor. With respect to establishing a duty, the plaintiff occupies a position identical to that of a compulsive gambler seeking to recover his losses.[50] However, even if a wrongful death plaintiff succeeds in establishing the existence and breach of such a duty, there is an additional problem which must be overcome before recovery will be forthcoming. The statutes require the plaintiff to show that the defendant's actions proximately caused the death of the gambler. This will [most] likely be a difficult burden to bear, since tort principles ordinarily treat suicide as an unforeseeable intervening cause breaking the causal chain.[51]

Casinos Are Not Obliged to Monitor Gamblers' Bets

Based upon a survey of existing case law and the application of general legal principles, it appears that the compulsive gambler seeking to recoup his losses will face a bitter struggle in establishing his claim. Case law supporting his position is tenuous, and arguments for the imposition of a statutory duty on casinos fail to demonstrate the advisability of such an extension of "dram-shop" liability.

However, despite the uniform rulings of the earlier cases, there is language which could support an argument that a casino has a duty to monitor a compulsive gambler when it has actual knowledge of his condition. Additionally, as the gaming industry experiences new growth, more claims are sure to emerge. Absent legislative action which explicitly precludes the advancement of claims of this nature, the determination of the validity of these claims will fall to the judiciary. At the present time, it appears that casinos bear no legal obligation to monitor or control the wagers of patrons; however, as these new claims arise and are pursued, the scope of the relationship between the gambler and the casino will necessarily be fully examined. The cases and legal principles discussed herein provide a beginning point for such an examination.

Notes

1.　*Miss. Code Ann.* § 97–33–1 (Supp. 1994). The statute exempts "vessels" and "cruise vessels" which meet certain criteria from the general prohibition against gambling in the state. Ibid.

2.　Telephone interview with Stacy Hammond, Mississippi Gaming Commission (February 3, 1995).

3.　The courts have yet to decide firmly whether floating casinos qualify as "vessels" and meet other requirements necessary to fall within federal admiralty jurisdiction. See, e.g., Steven E. Psarellis et al., "Bet Your Lien and Roll the Dice: Maritime Liens and Riverboat Gambling," *U.S.F. Mar. L.J.* 6 (1993), pp. 49, 61 (presenting argument that riverboat casinos do not fall within bounds of admiralty jurisdiction). For the remainder of this comment, the potential claims against riverboat casinos will be treated as though they fall within the realm of state tort law.

4.　Sarah C. Campbell, "Miss. Council Wants Casinos to Help Compulsive Gamblers," *Com. Appeal* (Memphis), October 28, 1994, p. B1. Recovering compulsive gamblers allege that the disorder robs them of the ability to control their wagers. Jon Schmitz and Tom Barnes, "Some Bettors Play Too Long and Wager Too Much," Pittsburgh *Post-Gazette*, August 23, 1994, p. A5. For example, one woman reports that she routinely lost in excess of $5,000 per night gambling. Ibid.

5.　Robert Custer and Harry Milt, *When Luck Runs Out* (1985), p. 35. The World Health Organization and the American Psychiatric Association recognize compulsive gambling as an illness. Ibid., p. 36. Victims of the disorder often attribute their losses to bad luck and claim that they possess the ability to control their actions. Ibid., p. 37. This attitude mirrors the "denial" stage observed in other addictions, including alcoholism. Ibid.

6.   Campbell, "Miss. Council," p. B1. Other studies indicate that the disorder afflicts between two and six percent of American adults. Schmitz and Barnes, "Some Bettors," p. A5. Some experts assert that only approximately 4 percent of gamblers are compulsive gamblers, but these same sources indicate that an additional 10–15 percent of gamblers wager beyond their means. Chris Welles, "America's Gambling Fever: Everybody Wants a Piece of the Action—But Is It Good for Us?" *Business Week*, April 24, 1989, p. 120. This 20 percent of the gambling population reportedly accounts for 50 percent of all money wagered. Ibid.

7.   Charles Bernsen, "Miss., Tenn. Keep Their Distance from Gambling Addict Problems," *Com. Appeal* (Memphis), April 5, 1994, p. A1.

8.   Schmitz and Barnes, "Some Bettors," p. A5. A Gamblers Anonymous group in Memphis, Tennessee, attributes its membership increase to the legalization of gambling in Mississippi. Ibid. Additionally, Gamblers Anonymous has organized eight new support groups in southern Mississippi to combat the impact of the casinos. Ibid.

9.   Ibid. Counselors at the Warren-Yazoo Mental Health Service, which serves the city of Vicksburg, report that the opening of the Vicksburg casinos resulted in approximately 20 cases of compulsive gambling within six months. Ibid. Officials of the mental health district encompassing Tunica County are unsure as to the number of compulsive gamblers that are present in the area, since many of the cases are handled in conjunction with treatment for alcohol or drug abuse. Bernsen, "Miss., Tenn. Keep Their Distance," p. A1. However, the executive director of the district acknowledges that the number is significant and predicts that the issue will "become a very public problem very soon." Ibid.

10.   Schmitz and Barnes, "Some Bettors," A5. According to officials with the Council on Compulsive Gambling, the hotline received only 10 calls each month from Mississippi prior to the legalization of gambling. Ibid.

11.   Campbell, "Miss. Council," p. B1. In late 1994, supporters of the creation of a Mississippi Council on Compulsive Gambling approached casinos to suggest that such an organization should be financed by voluntary contributions from the casinos. Ibid. The proposed council would provide counseling and other services to compulsive gamblers and would presumably relieve some of the burden currently resting on self-help groups, private therapists and private hospitals. Bernsen, "Miss., Tenn. Keep Their Distance," p. A1. However, no action was taken on the matter. Campbell, "Miss. Council," p. B1. A bill which would have imposed a .1 percent tax on gross casino revenues to be used to fund treatment programs failed in the Mississippi House Ways and Means Committee in 1994. Bernsen, "Miss., Tenn. Keep Their Distance," p. A1.

Approximately 15 states fund compulsive gambling treatment programs. Campbell, "Miss. Council," p. B1. A 3 percent tax on gambling supports treatment programs in Iowa. Bernsen, "Miss., Tenn. Keep Their Distance," p. A1. In New Jersey, the initial $500,000 in fines imposed on casinos goes to support the Compulsive Gambling

Council. Ibid. However, neither of the two largest riverboat gambling states, Mississippi and Illinois, have provided for any of the gaming revenue to be set aside for treatment programs. Schmitz and Barnes, "Some Bettors," p. A5.

Casinos claim to address the problem through posting hotline numbers, funding educational programs aimed at curbing underage gaming, contributing to existing programs and advising patrons to gamble responsibly. Bernsen, "Miss., Tenn. Keep Their Distance," p. A1; see also Schmitz and Barnes, "Some Bettors," p. A5 (noting casinos' involvement with compulsive gambling programs).

12. See Custer and Milt, *When Luck Runs Out*, p. 37 (observing that denial prevents individuals from recognizing that they suffer from compulsive disorders and therefore prevents them from seeking help).

13. W. Page Keeton et al., *Prosser and Keeton on the Law of Torts* (5th ed., 1984), § 30, pp. 164–65. A successful negligence action requires that the plaintiff show: (1) the defendant owed to the plaintiff a legally recognized duty or obligation; (2) the defendant breached the duty; (3) the breach was the proximate cause of plaintiff's injury; and (4) the plaintiff suffered actual damages. Ibid.

14. "Dram-shop" liability is the common name for liability imposed upon tavern owners for injuries resulting from the owner's service of alcohol to a visibly intoxicated patron. Jeffrey C. Hallam, Comment, "Rolling the Dice: Should Intoxicated Gamblers Recover Their Losses?" *Nw. U. L. Rev.* 85 (1990), pp. 240, 244. Claims brought by gamblers seeking to recoup losses due to intoxication while wagering are merely claims arguing that casinos should be included in the establishments affected by "dram-shop" liability.

15. See, e.g., *GNOC Corp. v. Aboud*, 715 F. Supp. (D.N.J. 1989), pp. 644, 655 (stating that casino has duty to prevent wagering by visibly intoxicated player); *Great Bay Hotel & Casino, Inc., v. Tose*, No. 91-600, 1991 WL 639131 (D.N.J. December 16, 1991), *6 (noting that *Aboud* allows gambler to assert negligence claim against casino which allowed gambler to wager while obviously intoxicated). But see Barbara Gottheld, "Casinos Not Subject to Dram-Shop Suits, Judge Rules," *N.J.L.J.*, April 18, 1994, p. 3 (reporting that casinos were not liable for losses incurred by intoxicated persons).

16. Fen Montaigne, "High Stakes: Compulsive Gamblers Taking Casinos to Court," Philadelphia *Inquirer*, March 9, 1986, p. A1. The claim, filed by John Heymann in New Jersey state court, stated that the casino "recklessly and negligently" granted him credit and permitted him to imbibe excessive amounts of complimentary alcohol as part of "an elaborate scheme" to cause compulsive gamblers to continue their gambling activities. Ibid.

17. Ibid. Officials in the gaming industry observed that the settlement probably resulted from the casino's unwillingness to risk allowing the case to go to trial due to the potentially devastating effect on the entire industry if the gambler prevailed. Ibid.

18. Ibid. Gambling officials maintained that allowing a compulsive gambler to recover on Heymann's theory would be equivalent to allowing a compulsive overeater to recover from a restaurant or permitting a compulsive shopper to bring an action against a department store. Ibid.

19. Ibid. The spokesperson also claimed that the casino bore no obligation to recognize a compulsive gambler and treat him differently from an ordinary patron. Ibid.

20. Ibid. The claim arose after the casino sought to enforce an unpaid debt. Ibid. The gambler responded with the counterclaim seeking to recover her losses. Ibid. The counterclaimant alleged that the more she lost, the more credit the casino extended, even after it was apparent that she suffered from a gambling addiction. Ibid.

21. Montaigne, "High Stakes," p. A1. The judge ruled that the practice of extending credit was authorized by state law and could not be the justification for allowing a losing player to recover. Ibid. The judge also noted that legislative action on the issue had made it apparent that the state favored gambling as a matter of public policy. Ibid.

Much of the betting which takes place on casino floors involves chips obtained through credit extended by the casino. Michele DiGirolamo, "Compulsive Gambler Challenges Casinos' Credit Policy," UPI, July 16, 1989, available in LEXIS, Nexis Lib., UPI File. According to an official with the New Jersey Casino Control Commission, the economic viability of the gaming industry would be threatened if credit could not be extended to patrons. Ibid. For sample credit regulations bearing upon casinos see *Ill. Ann. Stat*, ch. 230, para. 10 (Smith-Hurd, 1993) (allowing extension of credit for use on riverboat casinos); *Nev. Rev. Stat. Ann.* § 463.368 (Michie, 1994) (outlining credit procedures for Nevada casinos under Nevada Gaming Control Act); *N.J. Stat. Ann.* § 5:12–101 (West Supp., 1994) (establishing credit guidelines for casinos under state's Casino Control Act).

22. DiGirolamo, "Compulsive Gambler." The gambler, Sheldon Karabell, alleged that the casinos took advantage of his compulsive gambling disorder by providing him with complimentary accommodations, alcohol and extending large amounts of credit to him. Ibid.

23. Michele DiGirolamo, "Compulsive Gambler Loses A.C. Casino Suit," *Philadelphia Inquirer*, March 31, 1990, p. B1. The casinos filed their action in Atlantic County Superior Court just two months after Karabell filed his action. Ibid.

24. Ibid. The judge opined that the duty which the player wished to establish would essentially require casinos to perform a mental exam of all credit applicants before extending credit. Ibid. The judge dismissed such a duty as absurd. Ibid. An important aspect of this case for future claimants is that the gambler neither gave notice of his disorder, nor requested that the casino cease extending him credit. Ibid.

25. *Karabell v. Caesar's on the Boardwalk*, No. 89–2885, 1990 WL 59359, *3 (E.D. Pa. May 4, 1990).

26. Nos. Civil R–85–267 BRT, Civil R–86–21 BRT, 1988 U.S. Dist. LEXIS 18348 (D. Nev. February 16, 1988).

27. Van Blitter alleged that the casino encouraged her to continue to wager even though she was a terribly inept blackjack player. *Van Blitter*, 1988 U.S. Dist. LEXIS 18348, *4–5.

28. Ibid., *6. The court pointed out that Van Blitter failed to provide any authority supporting her claim that the casino owed the alleged duty to her as a patron. Ibid., *5.

29. Ibid., *6. The court also held that the efforts of the casino to attract business through complimentary services did not establish tort liability. Ibid.

30. Ibid.

31. The Nevada Legislature took direct action on the issue of claims by compulsive gamblers by enacting a provision within its Gaming Control Act which states that "[a] patron's claim of having a mental or behavioral disorder involving gambling" does not constitute a defense to an action to collect on a credit instrument and is not a valid counterclaim in a collection action. *Nev. Rev. Stat. Ann.* § 463.368(6) (Michie, 1994). This provision precludes a claim by a compulsive gambler regardless of the surrounding circumstances.

32. This argument by the casinos is particularly persuasive in those states which have mechanisms allowing the compulsive gambler to place his name on a "no-credit" list with the casinos. See, e.g., *N.J. Stat. Ann.* § 5:12–101(j) (West Supp., 1994) (providing that compulsive gambler may request that casinos not extend him credit by placing his name on list distributed to credit departments). Even without such a provision, however, the casinos may base the argument on a theory of personal responsibility.

33. Cf. Bartholomew Sullivan, "Woman Sues Splash Casino on Suicide of Estranged Husband," *Com. Appeal* (Memphis), December 14, 1994, p. B1 (noting that attorney for gambler's wife borrowed his theory of liability from "dram-shop" legislation).

34. Hallam, Comment, p. 244.

35. *Miss. Code Ann.* § 67–1–83 (1991). This section imposes criminal liability on persons selling alcohol to a member of the proscribed class. Ibid. Thus, it is not a true "dram-shop" act which would impose civil liability on bar owners for injuries to third parties. *Cuevas v. Royal D'Iberville Hotel*, 498 So. 2d (Miss., 1986), pp. 346, 348.

36. See, e.g., *Cuevas*, 498 So. 2d, p. 348 (holding that adult who voluntarily consumed alcohol and sustained injuries could not recover under § 67–1–83); *National Alcoholic Beverage Control Association, A Compilation of Dram Shop Statutes and Judicial Rulings* (4th ed., 1984), p. 3 (stating that purpose of dram-shop legislation is to protect third parties injured due to actions of intoxicated patron served by tavern owner).

37. Neither Illinois nor Mississippi, the states most involved in riverboat gambling, imposes ceilings on betting or losing. Schmitz and Barnes, "Some Bettors," p. A5.

38. *Lomonaco v. Sands Hotel Casino and Country Club*, 614 A.2d (N.J. Super. Ct. Law Div. 1992), pp. 634, 638. The plaintiff alleged that his behavior during the visit to the casino put the casino on notice that he suffered from a gambling addiction, and that casino employees exerted sufficient psychological pressure to override his free will. Ibid., p. 634. The behavior which plaintiff alluded to consisted of being loud,

obnoxious and causing a disruptive scene while losing large sums of money at the gaming tables. Ibid.

39. *Lomonaco*, 614 A.2nd, p. 639.

40. Ibid., pp. 638–39.

41. Ibid., pp. 637–39.

42. Ibid., pp. 638–39. The *Lomonaco* court held that the facts in the case *might* support a defense of duress or unconscionability, but held the validity of the defenses to be a question of fact, thereby establishing that the disorder of compulsive gambling does not necessarily encompass the elements of the defenses. Ibid. Additionally, the court held that the elements of the common-law defense of incapacity had not been demonstrated, again indicating that the disorder alone does not create a defense. Ibid., p. 638.

43. Keeton, et al., *Prosser and Keeton on the Law of Torts*, § 127, pp. 945–46.

44. *Miss. Code Ann.* § 11–7–13 (Supp., 1994).

45. Ibid. A wrongful death action may be pursued by a surviving spouse, child, parent, sibling or by the decedent's personal representative on behalf of the beneficiaries under the wrongful death statute. Ibid.

46. Ibid. Plaintiff's recovery may include, but is not limited to, property damages, medical expenses and funeral expenses. Ibid.

47. *Duff v. Harrah S. Shore Corp.*, 125 Cal. Rptr. 259 (Cal. Dist. Ct. App. 1975).

48. *Duff*, 125 Cal. Rptr., p. 261. The court reasoned that the agreements probably were not contracts in the legal sense because of the supposed inability of the casino to claim a breach if the gambler refused to submit checks for cashing. Ibid., n.2. However, the court pointed out that its decision was not grounded in this assumption, since the agreements might have contained terms, unknown to the court, with the effect of creating a binding contract. Ibid. The court instead premised its ruling on the fact that any contract which might have existed ceased to exist either "prior to or concurrently with its alleged breach," since the gambler explicitly requested that checks in excess of the limit be cashed. Ibid., p. 261. Therefore, the court found that, regardless of any previous contractual duty, there was no duty at the time the casino cashed the checks which exceeded the agreement's limit and allegedly resulted in the gambler's suicide. Ibid.

49. Ibid. The court stated that holding the casino to such a duty would be as unreasonable as holding that the casino had a "duty not to let him kill himself." Ibid.

50. For a discussion of the potential methods of establishing a duty to the compulsive gambler, see above nn. 31–39 and accompanying text.

51. Keeton et al., *Prosser and Keeton on the Law of Torts*, § 44, pp. 310–11. The general rule with regard to the effect of suicide on the causation element of a tort claim is that if the decedent's suicide was not due to any mental deficiency, then the choice to take one's life is viewed as abnormal and is considered a superseding cause relieving the defendant of liability. Ibid., p. 311.

III

STATE-SPONSORED GAMBLING: PAINLESS MONEY-RAISER OR DESTROYER OF COMMUNITIES?

INTRODUCTION TO PART III

Americans have always been ambivalent toward gambling and taxes. Commonly, both have been considered evils—but unavoidable ones—and their more realistic opponents have tried more to contain than to eliminate them. Lotteries came to the New World as an import from the Old. The Virginia Company, for example, used them to finance the early settlers. Lotteries were also used in colonial America to sell property in the absence of a banking system. But ordinary lotteries with customary monetary prizes also existed and they too had their critics, including the Quakers of Pennsylvania, who prompted laws against them. Despite some criticism, colonial governments used lotteries to attract revenue from citizens who resisted increased taxes. In fact, lottery-generated revenue was used to protect the Massachusetts seacoast against the French in 1744, pay for fortifications in New York City in 1746, build Yale, Harvard, and Princeton, and construct Pennsylvania churches in 1765.

What's more, the financially pressed Continental Congress used a lottery to finance the Revolutionary War, and after the war the independent United States used lotteries to finance county and municipal buildings, repair streets, and build roads. Thomas Jefferson, as readers will see in this section, called the lottery "wonderful" because it "lays taxation only on the willing." And George Washington, Benjamin Franklin, and John Hancock all, at one time or other, supported lotteries for public works.

Despite their widespread use in eighteenth-century America, lotteries still had their critics, whose principal objection to lotteries is echoed today: Lotteries attract poor people's money and energy, which might be more productively spent in other ways.

Marc Cooper, a contributing editor for *The Nation*, argues that state-run lotteries exploit the poor by tempting them to spend their money on false hopes instead of on manufacturing, which produces real goods.

Journalist Peter Keating, in an article for *Money* magazine, also criticizes lotteries for wasting too much money on administration and not either reducing taxes or increasing revenue for education.

Founding father Thomas Jefferson defends lotteries against charges of immorality and argues that they are a useful device for raising money.

8. Casinos Destroy Industry and Rob the Poor

Marc Cooper

Marc Cooper, a contributing editor of The Nation, *sees gambling not as an issue of temperance or free choice but one of social class and public economic policy. Writing from the political left, he sees legalized gambling as exploiting the poor and "sucking away millions of dollars from whatever is left of the rest of local economies."*

He submits that gaming establishments have often replaced industries in such urban areas as Gary, Indiana, and East St. Louis, that the number of compulsive gamblers goes up with the increased availability of gambling, and that those gamblers cost taxpayers because of treatment, law enforcement, divorce, spousal battering, and absenteeism.

He is particularly concerned that poor people are more likely to spend a higher percentage of their income on gambling than people in the middle class. While many poor people, according to Marc Cooper, gamble to get rich, most gamblers lose money.

He agrees with the traditional criticism of gambling: "The casinos produce no wealth (except for the owners, of course). No goods are manufactured or exchanged. Almost every dollar lost in the casino is cannibalized, sucked out of the community and not spent somewhere else or, God forbid, socked away in a savings account."

This article appeared as "America's House of Cards," in *The Nation* (February 19, 1996), pp. 11–19. Used here by permission.

"I'm a man on a mission, a man committed to all-out war," the Rev. Tom Grey tells me as we stand on the hill overlooking his Mississippi River town of Galena, Illinois. Grey may be a Methodist minister, but it's his experience as a Vietnam infantry vet and his ongoing work as a lieutenant colonel in the Army Reserve that shape his speech. "This time around we're the ones who have the guerrillas among the people, we're the ones winning the hearts and minds. The enemy is being surrounded."

The enemy, "the predator" that Grey wants to "hunt down and destroy," is the burgeoning national gambling industry. And Grey's adversaries are just as visible as the behemoth U.S. choppers that rattled over the Indochinese jungle like giant floating targets. Whereas just ten years ago casino gambling was found only in Nevada and Atlantic City, Americans now lose some $40 billion a year in hundreds of casinos spread over twenty-seven states. Gambling is the new American pastime. Seventy million go to pro baseball games each year; 125 million visit casinos.

Gambling Is Not Economic Development

"I'm not a prohibitionist," says Grey, [now former] field coordinator of the National Coalition Against Legalized Gambling. "This isn't an issue of personal morality. This is about social morality, about an issue of social justice, a battle for who we are in America." Growing more angry as he speaks, he adds, "And this is about pure greed. Either we decide as a country to build a future on solid economic foundations that mean something for our kids and our grandchildren, or we build a casino economy where we say it doesn't matter. America isn't gonna be here so go try and hit a jackpot; a casino economy where you have a mass sell-out, where you empty out the middle, making the rich richer and the poor poorer. Let's call gambling what it is, not pass it off as economic development."

Grey's grass-roots organizing efforts have halted the building of any new American casino since 1994. So successful has his counterinsurgency been—defeating pro-gambling referendums about 90 percent of the time in twenty-three contests—that one top gambling consultant has likened the 55-year-old minister to Adolf Hitler. But Grey draws from a long past of liberal social activism, pastoring an inner-city congregation, protesting the invasions of Grenada and Panama, even publicly questioning the Gulf War while in the active Army Reserve. And while he uses the left's language to decry gambling—denouncing the "greedy wedding of bottom-line entrepreneurs and cynical politicians who have given up on America"—most of his volunteer foot soldiers are from the right.

Leftists Have Been Slow to Join the Fight Against Gambling

Grey's tactical alliances include the Christian Coalition and the fundamentalist Traditional Values Coalition. Except for some anti-gambling statements from California State Senator Tom Hayden and U.S. Representative John Conyers, Grey doesn't hear as much as boo from progressives. "This is a natural issue for the left, but it is nowhere to be found," Grey tells me. "When I went up before Congress to testify, Barney Frank told me gambling was an issue of personal choice. Well, Barney Frank just doesn't get it. And frankly, I don't get how in hell the left is so slow to come around to this issue."

Grey's befuddlement is legitimate. Gambling in today's United States—repackaged, sanitized, video-ized, down-marketed and ubiquitous—is not an issue of temperance or free choice but rather one of social class and public economic policy. Here we have an industry popping up in areas devastated by Reaganomics (under any of its names) and imposing the most regressive of taxes on the most vulnerable part of the population, while simultaneously sucking away millions of dollars from whatever is left of the rest of local economies. But in this election year, in this uncertain economic climate, the issue has so far been ceded—by default—to pseudo-moralists like Richard Lugar, Pat Buchanan, and the Christian Coalition's Ralph Reed, who have been the only major political voices to speak out against the proliferation of legalized gambling.

You could have gone to the G.O.P. presidential debate in Des Moines last month, as I did, and strained to hear some allusion to the plight of working Iowans as they struggle with poverty-level wages. The only candidate who even mentioned creating something as grudging as $10-an-hour manufacturing jobs was businessman Morry Taylor, who, upon acquiring a wheel company, stripped his workers of their pensions and retirement health benefits. Or you could, like the rest of the chattering classes, obsessively speculate on the emergence of Steve Forbes as Bob Dole's leading challenger. While the pundits spill tons of ink over the implausible prospect that Forbes's flat tax might ever be enacted, much more about the future of ordinary Americans can be learned by looking at the riverboat gambling casinos twinkling just a few yards outside the Iowa hotel rooms of the traveling White House press corps. For if Lenin once summed up Communism as "Soviet power plus electrification," the highest formulaic expression of the New American Economy might just be "casinos plus part-time jobs."

Casinos Have Replaced Steel Mills and Factories

Quad Cities meet where Davenport and Bettendorf, Iowa, shake hands with Moline and Rock Island, Illinois, across the muddy Mississippi. It's no accident that this is where America's gambling fever has incubated and spread over the past half-decade. To look at the clumps of casinos now clogging the heartland is to look at a map of every place that once had a booming industry—or had none at all. Like a toadstool blooming on rotted wood, a casino will be replacing the steel industry in Gary, Indiana, America's murder capital in 1993. The most lucrative of Illinois's nine riverboats, Harrah's, rakes in a royal take of $210 million a year from its berth in Joliet, where it has replaced the Caterpillar tractor plant as the town's biggest employer. East St. Louis, described by the *St. Louis Post-Dispatch* as "American's Soweto," with no obstetric services, no regular trash collection and 75 percent of its almost all-black population on welfare, is now saddled with casino gambling. Other boats jostle for space downriver in poverty-stricken Tunica, Mississippi, traditionally known as the "Ethiopia of America."

And here in the Quad Cities, three riverboats now compete within a five-minute drive of one another, two on the Iowa side of the river, one on the Illinois side. Such a concentration is a sad spectacle in this area, once known as the "Detroit of the farm belt" for its headquartering of mighty John Deere and International Harvester, which produced the heavy machinery that plowed and harvested the fields of the world. I.H. cranked out fleets of the legendary Big Red tractors, which became an icon of rural and prosperous America. Nearby, Alcoa ran the biggest aluminum-rolling mill in the world. "Those industrial jobs were so good that I remember back in the sixties college kids buying overalls and working in those factories at night knowing they'd make more money that way than when after they'd graduate," says local historian Ronald Tweet.

If downtown Davenport and Rock Island look postnuclear now, you can date the holocaust to the early eighties. "The reason we have these riverboats today is because of the economic crisis of the last decade," says Tom Fennelly, who as director of Davenport's Eastern Iowa Center for Problem Gambling has seen his client list "jump tenfold" since the local boats opened in 1991. "Case tractors left, I.H. closed down, Cat left, Deere laid off thousands. It was literally 'last man leaving please turn out the lights.'" The farm crisis, the Reagan recession of 1981–82, the overall shifts in the economy and the disastrous results of a couple of marathon strikes against intractable managements hit this area like the apocalypse.

By the end of 1984, 35,000 jobs in a metropolitan community of 400,000 had been cut. Unemployment, fluttering between 17 percent and 22 percent, was the highest in the country after Flint, Michigan. Between 1980 and 1985, Iowa lost a higher percentage of its population to internal migration than any other state in the Union. Eight million square feet of industrial floor space lay empty. "We waited and waited for two, three, four years for someone, anyone to come in and take up the slack, something like maybe a Saturn plant," says Professor Tweet. "Who would have guessed it would have been riverboats?"

Promoters of Riverboat Gambling Won
Support by Rosy Promises

In 1989, two Iowa state legislators—both Democrats, by the way—
took on the formidable task of convincing this puritanical state, one that
owned all liquor stores and was known to raid church bingo games, to lay
its chips on the table. This followed five years of dogged lobbying by the
gambling industry, which had been looking precisely for some busted-out
place like Davenport as a site to break the national tradition of casino
bans.

The political strategy they used promised kinder, gentler gaming—not
wicked gambling. Promotional materials pictured a neat fleet of noble
paddle-wheelers steaming on the Mississippi while curious out-of-towners
sipped wine, munched Brie and, oh yes, laid a few bucks down on the
green felt. The gambling stakes would be kept small, to attract wholesome families and not urban gambling junkies. Gaming would take place
only during limited two-hour cruises. Maximum bets would be $5. A limit
of a $200 loss per day would be imposed. "It's a fool's game. It's enter-
tainment-style gaming," said one of the two sponsors of the measure at
the time. "We're selling the lore of Mark Twain," said Robert Arnould,
then Democratic majority leader of the Iowa House. Opposition to the
gambling proposal was countered with assurances that a healthy portion
of casino revenues would be gathered up in new taxes and that another
portion would be earmarked for social improvement projects.

This political soft-shoe turned the trick. Even organized labor signed
on, knowing full well that the new casino jobs would be nonunion. "We
were deeply involved in and strongly supported bringing in the riverboats," says Jerry Messer, president of the Quad City Labor Federation.
"You know, the lesser of two evils. Either work on a boat or be unemployed. I believe in everybody making a paycheck."

After a popular referendum to seal the deal, the first of the new
generation of riverboat casinos—the Diamond Lady docked in Bettendorf
and the President in Davenport—opened their tables and slots on April 1,
1991. Disneyland's Columbia is much closer to a real paddle-wheeler, the

new casinos being little more than glorified barges with a thin film of Mississippi riverboat gloss. But that was of little concern to the endless caravan of buses from wealthy Chicago and the surrounding states that brought in hundreds of thousands of gamblers for one-day turnarounds. Indeed, in the year the President opened, a full 40 percent of its patrons came from Chicago ZIP codes.

States Compete for Gambling Revenues

A panic immediately gripped the neighboring states. Soon, Mississippi legalized its own casinos and—unlike Iowa—did away with all pretenses, allowing patrons to lose as much as they liked and, in addition, not actually have to go out and cruise the river. Illinois followed suit, eliminating the $200 loss limit while maintaining the cruise requirement. The prairie wildfire had been touched off, and casino lights began to blaze from impoverished ports and Indian reservations throughout the heartland.

The competition devastated Iowa's boats (their owners, in the meantime, had built exactly *none* of the land-based tourist developments they'd promised in the lobbying campaign). Within two years, out-of-town visits fell to less than 15 percent of casino business. The Diamond Lady in Bettendorf lifted anchor and floated down to the more liberal no-cruise/no-limit state of Mississippi; the Emerald Lady in Fort Madison, Iowa, also weighed anchor for Mississippi. These departures dumped 600 workers out of their jobs and left the town holding the bag for a $2.6 million tax-dollar investment in a municipal dock.

"'Chasin' the losses' is what we call it when compulsive gamblers up the stakes trying to recoup previous losses," says treatment counselor Fennelly. "When the other states took away part of the casino traffic, Iowa, by now itself an addict, started chasin' its losses." In fact, as competition among the river states surpassed any back-alley cutthroat game of Texas Hold 'Em, Iowa threw Tom and Huck overboard and went instead for the Meyer Lansky approach.

By 1994, Iowa was dependent on gambling revenue and answerable to a new constituency of riverboat owners, workers and gambling addicts. Responding to a vigorous lobbying campaign led by a prominent G.O.P. lawyer, the state dropped its quaint $200 loss limit, loosened the requirement that casinos actually cruise the river and went for full-bore, round-the-clock dockside gambling. To fight off the out-of-state competition, Iowa also *reduced* gambling taxes, expanded off-track betting and actually took over ownership of a collapsing racetrack in Des Moines, turning it profitable by legalizing the installation of hundreds of slot machines. The state had moved from regulator to pit boss. "With each liberalization, from the allowing of more A.T.M.s, to the lifting of limits, to the end of cruising requirements, our client base would incrementally jump," says Fennelly.

No matter that each compulsive gambler costs the taxpayers between $13,000 and $35,000 a year in treatment, law enforcement, divorce, spousal battering and absenteeism. No matter that Iowa's compulsive-gambling population has more than tripled since the boats opened, from 1.7 percent to 5.4 percent. "Before the boats came I used to gamble a maximum of once a year in Las Vegas and limit myself to maybe a $500 loss," says Linda Edwards, a 45-year-old single mother who drives a forklift for John Deere. "When the President opened in 1991 it was like a new adventure. I went the second night it opened and I lost the $200 limit." Soon Edwards was back, at first once a month or so, then once a week, then every night. As the limits were lifted, she fell deeper into debt. "I'd play one slot machine at a time, mostly quarter slots. At first I could go through the $200 limit in fifteen minutes. When the limit was lifted I could stay all night." Eventually she was maxing out credit cards, taking out personal loans, even bouncing checks in the casino itself. Last year, when she was $75,000 in the hole and thinking of suicide, she sought treatment. "I came on the boats to escape my problems. I was already behind in my bills, [had] problems with my boyfriend and my daughter, so what the heck? It was the excitement. There's not much to do around here, and the boat was like a candy store."

Casinos Take Money from the Poor

The Saturday afternoon of the Iowa presidential debate the pit manager of Davenport's President swears casino attendance is abnormally high. "Maybe that debate brought more people in," he laughs as he signs a credit voucher for one bearded gambler in a Harley T-shirt. Any daily attendance bump would be hard to figure, as casino patronage in Iowa has been climbing astronomically since the liberalization of 1994—up nearly 100 percent in 1994 to 3.1 million visits; the state now has nine riverboats.

The President is the largest of them, but on this day there is standing room only at the crap, roulette, and 21 tables. (In part because there are proportionally fewer gaming tables than in Vegas, the riverboats' more downscale clientele favor the slots and video poker machines.) The dress is strictly jeans, workboots, flannel shirts and baseball caps. The gnarled hands of workers and farmers snap up cards dealt from across the table by the equally gnarled hands of former factory workers now making the average $19,000 a year paid to those 60 percent of casino employees who are full time—or by recent high school graduates whose career aspiration is to graduate to Reno or Las Vegas.

These floating casinos are what Professor Robert Goodman calls "convenience gambling" in his just-published book, *The Luck Business*. The 7-Elevens of the industry, they are to the Vegas mega-casinos what crack cocaine is to pure Colombian snow. This is like the town carnival that never closes and never leaves. Always open to empty your pockets, the casinos endlessly recycle desperate and now mostly local day-trippers. One doesn't have to stay long at any table to see the visible pain that comes with the loss of a $5 or $10 bet, the high number of "players" digging deep into their purses or pockets for that ciggy money they'll put down to chase the loss.

Statistics show that the poor are likely to spend two-and-a-half times the percentage of their income on gambling as the middle class. And with the stock market and limited-partnership opportunities not much of a draw among K-Mart workers, gambling is the only "investment" many of the working poor think they can afford. A full 27 percent of lower-income gamblers polled in one study said they were in the casino "to get rich." Yet the average result of each gambling visit is a loss of between $25 and $100.

Of the total casino take, a city like Davenport gets about $1 per gambler head in tax revenue. A similar amount—more than $2 million a year—flows into a local development fund that is then doled out in dozens of grants to schools, police forces, homeless shelters, charities and so on. In Davenport in 1992 the biggest grant, $750,000, went directly to the business elite in the form of an expansion of the city's convention center. Another 15 percent of the take goes to the state. The other 80 percent of the casino revenue, hundreds of millions of dollars, is transferred from the pockets of the gamblers into the pockets of the owners—some local, some based in Las Vegas.

Casinos Produce No Wealth

It's a chilling experience to stand in front of any one of these riverboat casinos and realize that each year a million or more people flock to it and yet there is, apart from parking lots, nothing, absolutely nothing—not a bar, a cafe, a hamburger shop, a souvenir stand—that has sprung up near it. Gamblers want to gamble, not shop. And no restaurant can compete with the casinos' $6 all-you-can-eat buffets of prime rib and seafood. Those few who still come on buses from out of town apparently see no reason to stay overnight in the Quad Cities.

The casinos produce no wealth (except for the owners, of course). No goods are manufactured or exchanged. Almost every dollar lost in the casino is "cannibalized," sucked out of the community and not spent somewhere else or, God forbid, socked away in a savings account. Last year in Iowa and Illinois alone more than $4 billion was lost on one form or another of legal gambling. That's about *three times* the revenue earned from gambling by cities and states in the entire rest of the country. A just-completed review by *U.S. News and World Report* of fifty-five counties that got casinos between 1990 and 1992 shows they had no more growth than similar counties without casinos, and in some cases they lost local businesses.

"Since the boats have come in, all we see is more people needing help of more kinds," says Chuck Landon of Churches United of the Quad City Area. "And things are supposed to be getting better! The gambling appeals to the very people who can least afford it." I talk with Landon in the Martin Luther King Community Center, which is surrounded on four sides by sprawling empty lots. On those fields used to prosper the commercial heart of Rock Island's black community. Now little business is left even in the white-dominated downtown. Landon helps coordinate a network of church-run food pantries that serve more than 30,000 people a year in the Quad Cities. But surely, I ask him, you can't blame all that need on just the introduction of casinos?

"Of course not," he answers. "Let me say we do see a lot of people gambling their food money away. But we served food to 11,000 families last year. That's one out of ten in the Quad Cities. That's families, not homeless or vagrants. These are largely unemployed or, more likely, underemployed. Despite the official version that we are in a period of rebuilding, more and more people just aren't making it. A state study shows that by the year 2000, 70 percent of the jobs in this area will pay less than $20,000 a year. That's the problem." Indeed, unemployment levels hover at a reasonable 5 percent, but Quad Cities wages run 10 percent or more below the national average.

Legalized Gambling Is No Panacea for Depressed Areas

Later that afternoon, a few blocks away, Vince Thomas, who runs Project Now, one of Rock Island's largest nonprofit social service agencies, pulls out a file of state reports and statistics. One set of numbers tells it all: Though the overall population has decreased, there were nearly twice as many residents of Rock Island County on food stamps and/or public assistance in March 1995—a time of "recovery" with roughly 5 percent unemployment—than there were in the summer of 1982, when the local economy was flattening out and joblessness was in the high double digits. "If you had kidnapped me in 1982 when the economy collapsed, held me incommunicado on Mars and dropped me back here last week, I would tell you that nothing has changed," says Thomas. "The only difference is, where we once served the unemployed, we increasingly serve more of the working poor who need help with clothing, energy bills, food bills and, most of all, rent and housing assistance." Five years after the panacea of legalized gambling, 47 percent of Rock Island County residents are classified as "low, very low or extremely low income," though 95 percent of them are employed.

And starting this year, Rock Islanders are being saddled with the extra burden of *directly* subsidizing their one casino riverboat. Squeezed by Iowa's more liberal dockside, no-cruise gambling, the Rock Island Casino has seen its receipts plummet; even so, 14 percent of the city's operating funds derived from casino revenues as late as 1994. Rock Island has had to factor out that income from its budget for this coming fiscal year, so jobs have been cut and taxes have been raised to make up the shortfall. And now the city is rebating all casino taxes owed it if the riverboat's revenue is less than its monthly cash losses. So far, this city of 40,000 has returned nearly half a million dollars in tax money to the casino owners. "We can't get the city to give us a $15,000 grant for minority businesses and a job search program," says John Carroll of the Alliance for Justice. "But it gives hundreds of thousands of dollars in tax abatements to the riverboats and then raises our water bills to pay for it."

The most jarring thing about the Quad Cities is the fact that their overall economic situation is now considered absolutely normal in America's new postindustrial era. Except for a handful of activists like Landon and Thomas, no one in the establishment dares speak of crisis. All you hear about is the low unemployment rate.

"Our economy is very, very rosy. Robust and diversified," says Larry Reed of Davenport's Chamber of Commerce. "The local economy is healthy and growing," concurs Republican Mayor Patrick Gibbs, sitting beneath a signed photo of Newt Gingrich. The riverboats, he says, are economic development. As proof of revival, he points to the arrival of a telemarketing firm providing a few hundred jobs at $16,000 a year. When I ask what sort of business boom the boats have brought, the Mayor boasts of a downtown Starbucks-like coffee bar, one that seats maybe six or eight people and certainly employs fewer.

These two officials are no different from thousands of others across the country, at both the local and national levels. The scene in Davenport is repeated in hundreds of other American communities. Local industry collapses in the global market. Local commerce goes with it, leaving downtown boarded up and joblessness in the stratosphere. Service industries move in to exploit the battered work force and national retail chains open up on the fringe strip malls, driving the final stake into Main Street, while local banks and TV stations are snapped up by out-of-town networks. Jobs reappear—albeit at subsistence wages. Victory is declared. The only problem for local officials is finding an adequate tax base. Along the Mississippi River that dilemma has been solved by the riverboats. Now the poor can throw their money on the table—and get new convention centers in return.

The day I receive Larry Reed's "rosy" economic forecast there's a near-riot at the Moline Holiday Inn. America's twenty-ninth Farm and Fleet store—a retail outlet like K-Mart or Sears—is soon to open out on John Deere Road. A ten-day "Job Fair" has been scheduled at the hotel to fill the 200 open positions—40 percent of them part time, average starting wage less than $6 an hour. A thousand applications have been printed for the week-and-a-half event. But within the first five hours they are gone and the swelling throng of job seekers, packed elbow to elbow in the Holiday Inn banquet room, is angry. "My God, to see this kind of turnout for something like this, it's sad," says 41-year-old Betty VanEck-houette, out of a full-time job for the past four years. "They're scraping to get these $6-an-hour jobs. How can you sustain a family on $6 an hour?"

The War over Legalized Gambling
Will Go National

With new casino construction stalled by growing local backlashes, the next battle over gambling will take place at the national level. Partisans on both sides are readying to fight over a measure proposed by Senator Paul Simon and Representative John Conyers that would create a national commission to study the effects of widespread gambling.

The commission bill will most likely be approved. But any proposed rollback or ban on gambling will meet a wall of resistance from the industry lobby, which is aggressively buying its political standing [see "Vegas Bob," February 12]. Meanwhile, the industry's full-time foe, Tom Grey, hopes that before this political season is over, legalized gambling will surface in the national debate. "What an opportunity for us," says Grey of the '96 campaign. "Where else in America could we catch all the bad guys together at the feeding trough? We could really clean house. The right, the left, all of America has to come together and ask what we want as an economic foundation for the next century." And Grey continues to believe his eventual success depends on bringing the left on board. "Liberals tend to look at 'isms.' They don't see the little battles that open the door to the big battles," he laments. "The left keeps closing the door, withdrawing, giving up on the people in the middle. They'd rather attack the right than talk to ordinary folks in between. Unfortunately for the left, it's the right which is doing a much better job of talking to the middle."

While Grey is waiting for the left to come around, the gambling industry is forging ahead with plans for expansion. At a recent gambling industry summit in Las Vegas, Melvin Simon, whose company helped build the mammoth Mall of America in Bloomington, Minnesota, said he envisions the day when casinos, not department stores, will be the anchor of the country's malls. "It will take a lot of legislation," said Simon. "But believe me, it's a possibility."

9. Lotteries Cannot Resolve the States' Fiscal Crisis

Peter Keating

Peter Keating holds that economic arguments for state-run lotteries are based on false premises. According to him, lotteries are an inefficient way to raise revenue. He contends that states with lotteries have not lowered taxes but "typically rely on lottery revenues to plug ever-widening budget holes rather than using the cash to lower taxes." What's more, states with lotteries, according to Keating, spend, on average, less of their budgets on education than states without lotteries. Nor, he argues, do state lotteries hold down taxes. Indeed, he maintains that taxes in states with lotteries have increased more than in states without lotteries. Finally, he argues that the benefits of the lottery are outweighed by their social costs, since compulsive gamblers, whose numbers have reportedly grown in the last decade, are "more likely than healthy consumers to attempt suicide, destroy their families, write bad checks, embezzle money, go bankrupt and land in court or jail."

It's 9:00 p.m. on a wintry Thursday night as three sweatshirt-clad New York State Lottery agents start working the crowd at a small tavern named Cavanaugh's in Blue Point, N.Y., a Long Island suburb of New York City. From their corner table at Cavanaugh's—one of 3,157 bars, restaurants and delis in which the state of New York has recently installed lottery machines—the officials schmooze with patrons, offering

---

This originally appeared as "Lotto Fever: We All Lose!" in *Money* (May 1996), pp. 142–49. Used here by permission.

them baseball caps and key chains as well as free lottery tickets. They hope to persuade the crowd to play Quick Draw, a video keno—or bingo-type—game so addictive that players call it Lotto Crack.

The lottery agents don't have to do much selling. Quick Draw, displayed on three of the 10 television screens at Cavanaugh's, already has the zombie-like attention of a dozen or so customers. Players fill out cards, choosing as many as 10 numbers from 1 through 80, and then bet as much as $100 per card. When the game starts, 20 electronic balls float across the screens, landing on numbers. Players win prizes according to how many of their choices match. And win or lose, a new game begins *every five minutes*. As is typically the case with lottery games, tonight most players will lose far more than they win. Cavanaugh's Quick Draw winners collect $1,250 on an average night, about half of the $2,500 spent by all the players. "I know I'm probably going to lose," says Joe Doucett, a 29-year-old electrical engineer, "but I keep playing because I might just get lucky."

That, of course, is the idea. Tempted by the possibility of turning $1 into $1 million, Doucett and his fellow gamblers throw more than $88 million every day into lottery games—more than Americans spend on all spectator sports combined. As a result, lottery sales in the District of Columbia and the 36 states that have the games soared 12.2 percent in 1995 to $32.1 billion, up from just $2.9 billion 15 years ago, according to the North American Association of State and Provincial Lotteries in Cleveland. (In 1996, New Mexico became the 37th lottery state.) What the estimated 55 million Americans who play the lottery at least once a month probably don't realize, however, is how big a rip-off the state-run games are for them as taxpayers. A six-month investigation by *Money* reveals that the lotteries have neither lowered taxes for their residents nor boosted funding for education, as their champions have often promised. What's more, by helping turn people into compulsive gamblers, lotteries are adding an estimated $10.9 billion a year to the financial burdens of the states and their taxpayers. Among our findings:

- *Lotteries are an inefficient way to raise public money.* Of the $32.1 billion that states took in from lotteries last year, they kept just $11 billion—

a mere third of sales—after shelling out about $21 billion on administrative costs and prizes (see table at end of chapter).

- *Cash-strapped states typically rely on lottery revenues to plug ever-widening budget holes rather than using the cash to lower taxes.* Indeed, state spending by lottery locales (which make up 84 percent of the U.S. population) is projected to grow more than twice as fast in 1996 as it is in nonlottery states, according to data compiled by the National Conference of State Legislatures (NCSL) in Denver.

- *Despite marketing slogans such as New York's "Supporting education since 1967," lottery states spend less of their budgets on education than do states that go without lotteries, on average.* Some lottery lovers are enticed not only by the prospect of getting rich quick but also by the comforting notion that their money will go to pay for teachers and schoolbooks. But *Money* has learned that states that specifically target lottery dollars to pay for public schools often go on to *decrease* the share of general tax dollars budgeted to pay for education. The result: The proportion of state spending dedicated to education has remained relatively unchanged in the '90s—about 50 percent for lottery states and 60 percent for non-lottery states—despite the growth in lottery revenues.

When you add it all up, the marketing claims by most state lotteries are like losing numbers on instant tickets. They seem promising at first but are disappointing once you scratch beneath the surface. Let's examine some actual marketing pitches.

Lotteries Do Not Keep Taxes Down

"Giving people the choice to raise money by purchasing lottery tickets will let your state hold the line on taxes." So said Governor Thomas Meskill of Connecticut when he successfully proposed a lottery in 1971. But despite strong lottery sales ($670.8 million last year), Connecticut state legislators enacted the state's first income tax in 1991. That's because a lottery does not inoculate a state against higher taxes. To the contrary, most states create lotteries because they need all the income they can possibly

generate. That explains why, although states with lotteries have raked in more than $128 billion in ticket purchases over the past five years, average per capita taxes in those states have increased 21.7 percent anyway, to $1,401 a year. That growth rate is three times as high as in nonlottery states, where annual per capita taxes are now $1,049, up just 7.2 percent since 1990.

Last year, when many state legislatures were in tax-slashing moods, your odds of seeing your taxes go up or down were pretty much the same whether or not your state had a lottery. Of the 36 states with lotteries in 1995 and Washington, D.C., 20 of them (56 percent) cut taxes and nine (25 percent) raised them, for a net tax reduction of $2.8 billion. Similarly, seven of the 14 states without lotteries (50 percent) reduced taxes, while only two (14 percent) passed increases, for an overall savings of $465 million.

According to gambling industry experts, lotteries don't offer much in the way of tax relief for two reasons. First, huge as they appear, lottery sales do little to alleviate state budget problems, because state governments don't get to keep most of the proceeds. Lotteries pay a majority of revenues back to players as prizes—about 54 percent in 1994 (the latest year for which data are available), according to data from *International Gambling and Wagering Business*. Operating costs—including advertising, salaries and commissions to agents and businesses that install ticket machines—gobble up another 12¢ of every sales dollar. That leaves states with only $34.30 in profits for every $100 of lottery tickets sold. By contrast, the typical charity retains $79.80 of every $100 it raises.

What's more, states typically treat lottery revenues as "found money" that they use to close budget gaps rather than to cut taxes or spending. This year, lottery states plan to spend a total of $315 billion, or $11 billion more than they did in 1995. That's a 3.7 percent spending increase and matches exactly the $11 billion in profits that lottery states kept in 1995. Spending in nonlottery states, by contrast, is slated to grow just 1.46 percent this year, to $40.2 billion, according to NCSL. "Voters want states to spend more, and politicians look at lotteries as a way to get tax money for free," says Elizabeth Davis, policy analyst at the Center for the Study of the States in Albany, N.Y.

Lotteries Do Not Boost Spending on Schools

"We are going to need new money if we want to have good schools. Either we have a huge tax bill or we approve a lottery." That's what then Governor Ann Richards told her fellow Texans in a televised address the day before the state voted to establish a lottery in 1991. Money for education is the explicit or implicit promise that most lottery promoters make: 18 states specifically earmark lottery money for education, and most others claim that schools benefit from the games. Says Mary Fulton, a policy analyst at the Education Commission of the States in Denver: "There's a deep and widespread perception among the public that lottery revenues are being used to substantially fund education."

During this decade, however, states with lotteries actually dedicated a declining share of their total spending to schools. In 1994 (the latest year for which data are available), lottery states devoted 49 percent of their total spending to education, down slightly from 50.1 percent in 1990, according to the Center for the Study of the States. Meanwhile, over the same time period, the average budget share for education increased slightly for nonlottery states, from 58.2 percent to 58.9 percent.

Florida, which created its lottery in 1988 to "enhance education," is one of several states that claim to earmark lottery money for schools but in reality mix it with general funds, so it's next to impossible to know where the money goes. This year Florida plans to spend just $114 million, or 14 percent, of its projected $829 million in lottery profits on specific statewide education projects. The other $715 million will be sucked into the general budget. "We've been hurt by our lottery," says Gary Landry, spokesman for the Florida Education Association, the local school employees' union. "The state has simply replaced general revenues with lottery money—at a time when enrollments are increasing. It's a big shell game."

In New York State, lottery profits ($1.24 billion in 1995) are earmarked by law for education, and the phrase "Supporting education since 1967" appears on the back of every Quick Draw play card. The truth: Education funding is set by the state legislature and does not automatically rise with lottery sales. "If they want to use half the money to plug a hole in the budget, there's nothing to say they can't," says Bill Pape, spokesman for the New York State School Boards Association. "Once it's in the general fund, it can be used for anything."

State Lotteries Encourage Gambling Addiction

"The benefits of the lottery far exceed the social costs." These are the words of Jeff Perlee, director of the New York Lottery. Wanna bet? The odds are that you will pick up some of the estimated $10.9 billion tab run by the 1.5 percent to 7 percent of lottery gamblers who lose self-control from compulsive wagering. Robert Goodman, professor of public policy at Hampshire College in Amherst, Massachusetts, and author of *The Luck Business*, conservatively pegs the annual cost to the U.S. economy of each additional problem gambler at $13,200. Reasons for the hefty price tag: Compulsive gamblers are more likely than healthy consumers to attempt suicide, destroy their families, write bad checks, embezzle money, go bankrupt and land in court or jail.

The proportion of callers to the Trenton, N.J.-based Council on Compulsive Gambling's national hotline who say they're addicted to lotteries has risen from 16 to 43 percent over the past decade. And the problem of compulsive lottery gambling seems destined to rise, as states offer more and more quick-action games. "If anyone thinks that putting lotteries and video terminals on every block won't lead to addictive and criminal behavior, they're in outer space," says Dr. Valerie Lorenz, director of the Compulsive Gambling Center in Baltimore. "We saw keno addicts within two weeks after it was introduced in Maryland." Even some state lottery officials agree. "Problem gambling was not apparent in Oregon before the state took video lotteries out of back rooms and turned them into a public experience," admits David Hopper, public affairs manager for that state's lottery.

Currently, state governments are spending more than $350 million a year to market a new wave of especially addictive instant-jackpot lottery games. Oregon, Rhode Island, South Dakota, and West Virginia, for example, have legalized video lottery terminals, which blur the lines between lotteries and slot machines, generating $3.8 billion in sales last year alone. Keno games similar to New York's 12-games-an-hour Quick Draw are now available in 13 states and produced more than $1.6 billion in sales in 1995. "It's a consistent pattern," says public policy professor Robert Goodman. "Revenues are never able to meet the demands of the states over time, so they raise the stakes of the games. The states are the real addicts."

It's Better to Buy Municipal Bonds than to Play the Lottery

Here are three tips for taxpayers:

- *Find out how your state is using its lottery money.* Call your state lottery commission or department of revenue, and ask how lottery revenues are allocated. Inquire whether lottery money is being used to replace general fund spending on schools, and find out if plans exist to expand your state's lottery games. If you don't like what you hear, write to your governor and state legislators and let them know.
- *If you or someone you know is having trouble controlling spending on lotteries, get help.* You can call the National Council on Problem Gambling (800-522-4700), a nonprofit agency whose staffers will refer you to local counselors and meetings.
- *If you live in a state with an income tax and want to help its fiscal health while profiting at the same time, consider investing in your state's tax-free municipal bonds.* Today, such bonds—yielding about 4.65 to 5.75 percent—often pay more after taxes than taxable alternatives such as bank CDs for people in the 28 percent tax bracket or higher (married

couples with taxable incomes above $40,100 and singles with incomes above $24,000). Since the odds of winning a standard lotto jackpot are 1 in 13.8 million, according to James Walsh, author of *True Odds* (Merritt, $19.95), your chances of making money are substantially higher with muni bonds than they are with lottery tickets.

State Lotteries Are Inefficient and Ineffectual

If you think lotteries offer an ingenious way for states to raise extra money for schools, the following table will set you straight. The first surprise: Lotteries are an extremely inefficient way to raise money. In the first columns, we rank states according to the percentage of lottery revenue they keep after spending money on operating costs and prizes. The average state keeps only 34.3 percent of the total proceeds; least efficient Idaho pockets only a fifth, versus most efficient New Jersey and New York at 41.1 percent.

Despite the recent explosive growth in lottery sales, which have soared by 60 percent nationwide in the 1990s, lottery money remains a fraction of most state budgets, as the next four columns show. Partly as a result, lotteries have had little effect in limiting state tax hikes. Since 1990, per capita taxes in lottery states have risen more than three times as fast as in nonlottery states.

The final four columns reveal the states' changing fiscal priorities in the '90s. Contrary to what officials in many lottery states have promised, the average share of their state spending devoted to education has actually declined slightly since 1990, from 50.1 to 49 percent. At the same time, education spending has inched up in states that lack lotteries, from 58.2 to 58.9 percent. Where is the lottery money going? In large part to pay for skyrocketing state Medicaid bills.

How Your State Is Spending Your Lottery Money

State (Year lottery began)	Efficiency (profits as % of lottery sales)	Lottery sales		State tax revenues		Education's share of state spending		Medicaid's share of state spending	
		1995 (in millions)	Growth (or drop) 1990–95	1995 (in millions)	Growth (or drop) 1990–95	1990	1994[6]	1990	1994[6]
New Jersey (1970)	41.1%	$1,576.0	28.8%	$15,022.9	91.8%	39.0%	39.7%	9.3%	12.0%
New York (1967)	41.1	3,028.6	47.2	33,158.0	15.6	42.6	39.8	11.9	18.8
Pennsylvania (1972)	39.7	1,591.8	3.1	15,910.5	38.5	47.3	43.8	10.5	15.2
Oregon (1985)	39.3	670.9	315.7	3,368.9	55.3	43.7	51.5	8.6	12.0
Michigan (1972)	39.2	1,381.4	15.3	7,995.2	11.4	44.6	52.7	11.5	9.8
Florida (1988)	39.1	2,238.1	10.2	14,043.0	40.0	63.2	54.3	7.0	14.0
Delaware (1975)	37.9	114.1	71.8	1,601.6	41.5	49.3	51.5	4.9	8.1
Illinois (1974)	37.4	1,574.4	3.4	17,601.6	32.4	46.1	47.0	11.8	18.5
Connecticut (1972)	37.2	670.8	27.7	8,479.7	38.7	34.8	22.9	8.1	9.6

State (Year lottery began)	Efficiency (profits as % of lottery sales)	Lottery sales		State tax revenues		Education's share of state spending		Medicaid's share of state spending	
		1995 (in millions)	Growth (or drop) 1990–95	1995 (in millions)	Growth (or drop) 1990–95	1990	1994[6]	1990	1994[6]
District of Columbia (1982)	37.1	230.2	54.4	3,247.6	5.2	N.R.	N.R.	N.R.	N.R.
Maryland (1973)	37.0	1,042.0	28.4	7,043.7	22.8	42.1	42.1	10.2	14.7
Georgia[1] (1993)	36.4	1,375.4	29.0	10,244.0	11.0	38.5	48.3	22.2	14.3
Louisiana[2] (1991)	35.7	305.3	(19.7)	4,906.0	(23.9)	31.1	57.8	25.5	6.1
California (1985)	35.5	2,166.2	(12.7)	42,189.0	7.5	51.6	44.6	8.7	14.5
South Dakota (1987)	34.7	161.3	147.8	598.4	36.3	50.9	48.4	10.1	13.7
Virginia (1988)	34.5	902.5	90.1	6,829.5	24.3	53.1	51.8	7.9	13.5
Washington (1982)	33.4	400.9	62.8	8,517.0	35.8	60.8	59.7	9.0	12.8
Texas[3] (1992)	32.9	3,036.5	66.3	21,714.6	7.1	44.1	61.0	21.0	11.7
Arizona (1981)	31.9	286.0	(0.7)	4,406.3	41.3	56.3	56.2	8.7	11.0

State (Year lottery began)	Efficiency (profits as % of lottery sales)	Lottery sales		State tax revenues		Education's share of state spending		Medicaid's share of state spending	
		1995 (in millions)	Growth (or drop) 1990–95	1995 (in millions)	Growth (or drop) 1990–95	1990	1994[6]	1990	1994[6]
Wisconsin (1988)	31.8	518.8	67.4	7,906.5	38.6	46.7	49.1	10.0	11.7
Missouri (1986)	31.4	411.7	84.3	5,241.5	28.9	54.2	54.4	7.1	5.7
Kansas (1987)	31.0	171.9	166.5	3,293.1	44.2	57.5	66.0	7.5	4.7
New Hampshire (1964)	31.0	141.0	44.0	939.8	58.2	23.0	20.6	11.4	17.0
Nebraska[3] (1993)	30.7	79.0	49.3	1,738.0	14.3	40.4	55.7	14.4	12.6
West Virginia (1986)	30.6	180.8	169.9	2,227.5	29.3	68.7	71.2	6.1	6.8
Ohio (1974)	30.0	2,182.3	34.6	12,155.6	5.7	52.0	48.3	11.5	15.2
Indiana (1989)	30.0	610.7	51.5	7,014.7	51.6	59.6	56.1	10.1	16.4
Vermont (1978)	29.6	71.7	67.1	684.8	21.1	46.0	39.5	10.5	17.0
Colorado (1983)	28.6	351.9	151.5	3,911.9	55.6	62.0	56.7	10.5	14.3

State (Year lottery began)	Efficiency (profits as % of lottery sales)	Lottery sales		State tax revenues		Education's share of state spending		Medicaid's share of state spending	
		1995 (in millions)	Growth (or drop) 1990–95	1995 (in millions)	Growth (or drop) 1990–95	1990	1994[6]	1990	1994[6]
Iowa (1985)	28.0	207.6	23.4	3,838.4	33.7	59.0	59.1	6.8	9.1
Kentucky (1989)	27.6	512.6	159.3	5,070.1	41.6	64.0	64.1	7.1	8.3
Maine (1974)	26.9	153.2	59.6	1,671.7	17.9	51.9	43.0	8.2	12.7
Montana (1987)	26.2	32.8	52.6	934.4	114.0	59.7	62.5	6.0	8.2
Minnesota (1990)	25.2	335.9	4.5	8,706.6	26.1	46.7	49.0	10.6	13.0
Massachusetts (1972)	23.0	2,793.2	78.7	16,391.8	39.5	27.4	20.6	12.5	15.3
Rhode Island (1974)	22.9	334.6	408.5	1,665.0	21.3	35.3	36.4	12.8	20.4
Idaho (1989)	21.1	88.0	33.3	1,293.6	54.8	62.9	66.0	4.3	8.3
Lottery States[4] (per capita, in dollars)	34.3	868.1 $145	60.2	8,404.4 $1,401	27.6[5] 21.7%	50.1[5]	49.0[5]	9.1[5]	12.9[5]

State (Year lottery began)	Efficiency (profits as % of lottery sales)	Lottery sales		State tax revenues		Education's share of state spending		Medicaid's share of state spending	
		1995 (in millions)	Growth (or drop) 1990–95	1995 (in millions)	Growth (or drop) 1990–95	1990	1994[6]	1990	1994[6]
Nonlottery States (per capita)	N.A.	N.A.	N.A.	3,190.4 1,049	33.4 7.2	58.2	58.9	5.3	6.9

Notes: All years are fiscal years. N.A.: Not applicable. N.R.: Not reported.
[1] Sales growth, tax and spending data from 1994, the first fiscal year lottery was in effect.
[2] Sales growth, tax and spending data from 1992.
[3] Sales growth, tax and spending data from 1993.
[4] All figures are averages.
[5] Excludes the four states that created lotteries after 1990.
[6] Latest data available.

Sources: State lottery agencies, *La Fleur's 1995 World Lottery Almanac*, North American Association of State and Provincial Lotteries, National Conference of State Legislatures, National Association of State Budget Officers.

10. Lotteries Are a Morally Acceptable and Useful Way to Raise Money

Thomas Jefferson

A strong advocate of limited government and minimal taxation, Thomas Jefferson viewed revenue generated by lotteries as preferable to that generated by taxes because lotteries, unlike taxes, involve only willing participants, whose money is given without coercion. He was wary of a government's power to tax because he believed that such power could, unless carefully checked, easily grow, enabling the government illegitimately to seize wealth to increase its power and serve special interests.

In eighteenth-century Britain and America, it was commonplace to sell a valuable piece of property, such as a house, "by lottery," or by raffling it off. By this method, poor individuals might suddenly come into substantial holdings, and the sellers of the property might get a far higher sum than they could expect through regular sale. This practice had become illegal by 1826, though an exemption could be granted by the state legislature. The following piece, though it may not be obvious at the beginning, is Jefferson's plea to be allowed an exemption so that he could sell his house and lands by lottery. Jefferson, a keen and frequent gambler, especially at backgammon, may be referring here to dice and cards a little more harshly than he might otherwise

---

"Thoughts on Lotteries. February, 1826," Thomas Jefferson, in *The Writings of Thomas Jefferson*, ed. Andrew A. Lipscomb (editor in chief) and Albert Ellery Bergh (managing editor), vol. 17 (Washington, D.C.: The Thomas Jefferson Memorial Association, 1903), "Miscellaneous Papers," XLVIII, pp. 500–511.

have done, to reassure the Virginia legislature that in asking for permission to make a sale by lottery, he is not thereby a friend of vice and debauchery.

It is a common idea that games of chance are immoral. But what is chance? Nothing happens in this world without a cause. If we know the cause, we do not call it chance; but if we do not know it, we say it was produced by chance. If we see a loaded die turn its lightest side up, we know the cause, and that it is not an effect of chance; but whatever side an unloaded die turns up, not knowing the cause, we say it is the effect of chance. Yet the morality of a thing cannot depend on our knowledge or ignorance of its cause. Not knowing why a particular side of an unloaded die turns up, cannot make the act of throwing it, or of betting on it, immoral.

If we consider games of chance immoral, then every pursuit of human industry is immoral; for there is not a single one that is not subject to chance, not one wherein you do not risk a loss for the chance of some gain. The navigator, for example, risks his ship in the hope (if she is not lost in the voyage) of gaining an advantageous freight. The merchant risks his cargo to gain a better price for it. A landholder builds a house on the risk of indemnifying himself by a rent. The hunter hazards his time and trouble in the hope of killing game. In all these pursuits, you stake some one thing against another which you hope to win.

But the greatest of all gamblers is the farmer. He risks the seed he puts into the ground, the rent he pays for the ground itself, the year's labor on it, and the wear and tear of his cattle and gear, to win a crop, which the chances of too much or too little rain, and general uncertainties of weather, insects, waste, &c., often make a total or partial loss.

These, then, are games of chance. Yet so far from being immoral, they are indispensable to the existence of man, and every one has a natural right to choose for his pursuit such one of them as he thinks most likely to furnish him subsistence. Almost all these pursuits of chance produce something useful to society. But there are some which produce nothing, and endanger the well-being of the individuals engaged in them, or of others depending on them. Such are games with cards, dice, billiards,

&c. And although the pursuit of them is a matter of natural right, yet society, perceiving the irresistible bent of some of its members to pursue them, and the ruin produced by them to the families depending on these individuals, consider it as a case of insanity, *quoad hoc*, step in to protect the family and the party himself, as in other cases of insanity, infancy, imbecility, &c., and suppress the pursuit altogether, and the natural right of following it.

There are some other games of chance, useful on certain occasions, and injurious only when carried beyond their useful bounds. Such are insurances, lotteries, raffles, &c. These they do not suppress, but take their regulation under their own discretion. The insurance of ships on voyages is a vocation of chance, yet useful, and the right to exercise it therefore is left free. So of houses against fire, doubtful debts, the continuance of a particular life, and similar cases.

Money is wanting for a useful undertaking, as a school, &c., for which a direct tax would be disapproved. It is raised therefore by a lottery, wherein the tax is laid on the willing only, that is to say, on those who can risk the price of a ticket without sensible injury for the possibility of a higher prize.

Sale by Lottery Is a Useful Procedure

An article of property, unsusceptible of division at all, or not without great diminution of its worth, is sometimes of so large value as that no purchaser can be found while the owner owes debts, has no other means of payment, and his creditors no other chance of obtaining it but by its sale at a full and fair price. The lottery is here a salutary instrument for disposing of it, where many run small risks for the chance of obtaining a high prize. In this way the great estate of the late Colonel Byrd (in 1756) was made competent to pay his debts, which, had the whole been brought into the market at once, would have overdone the demand, would have sold at half or quarter the value, and sacrificed the creditors, half or three-fourths of whom would have lost their debts. This method of selling was formerly very much resorted to, until it was thought to nourish too much a spirit of hazard. The legislature were therefore induced not to suppress it altogether, but to take it under their own special regulation. This they did for the first time by their act of 1769, c. 17, before which time every person exercised the right freely; and since which time it is made unlawful but when approved and authorized by a special act of the legislature.

The Virginia Legislature Has Often Permitted Sale by Lottery

Since then this right of sale, by way of lottery, has been exercised only under the jurisdiction of the legislature. Let us examine the purposes for which they have allowed it in practice, not looking beyond the date of our independence.

1. It was for a long time an item of the standing revenue of the State.
1813. c. 1, § 3. An act imposing taxes for the support of government and
    c. 2, § 10.
1814. Dec. c. 1, § 3.   1814. Feb. c. 1, § 3.   1818. c. 1, § 1.
1819. c. 1.   1820. c. 1.

This, then, is a declaration by the nation, that an act was not immoral, of which they were in the habitual use themselves as a part of the regular means of supporting the government; the tax on the vendor of tickets was their share of the profits, and if their share was innocent, his could not be criminal.

2. It has been abundantly permitted to raise money by lottery for the purposes of schools; and in this, as in many other cases, the lottery has been permitted to retain a part of the money (generally from ten to fifteen per cent.) for the use to which the lottery has been applied. So that while the adventurers paid one hundred dollars for tickets, they received back eighty-five or ninety dollars only in the form of prizes, the remaining ten or fifteen being the tax levied on them, with their own consent. Examples are,
1784. c. 34. Authorizing the city of Williamsburg to raise £2,000 for a
           grammar school.
1789. c. 68. For Randolph Academy, £1,000.

1789. c. 73. For Fauquier Academy, £500.

  c. 74. For the Fredericksburg Academy, £4,000.

1790. c. 46. For the Transylvanian Seminary, £500.

    For the Southampton Academy, £300.

1796. c. 82. For the New London Academy.

1803. c. 49. For the Fredericksburg Charity School.

  c. 50. For finishing the Strasburg Seminary.

  c. 58. For William and Mary College.

  c. 62. For the Bannister Academy.

  c. 79. For the Belfield Academy.

  c. 82. For the Petersburg Academy.

1804. c. 40. For the Hotsprings Seminary.

  c. 76. For the Stevensburg Academy.

  c.100. For William and Mary College.

1805. c. 24. For the Rumford Academy.[1]

1812. c. 10. For the Literary Fund. To sell the privilege for $30,000 annually, for seven years.

1816. c. 80. For Norfolk Academy, $12,000.

    Norfolk Female Society, $2,000.

    Lancastrian School, $6,000.

 3. The next object of lotteries has been rivers.

1790. c. 46. For a bridge between Gosport and Portsmouth, £400.

1796. c. 83. For clearing Roanoke River.

1804. c. 62. For clearing Quantico Creek.

1805. c. 42. For a toll bridge over Cheat River.

1816. c. 49. For the Dismal Swamp, $50,000.

 4. For roads.

1790. c. 46. For a road to Warminster, £200.

    For cutting a road from Rockfish gap to Scott's and Nicholas's landing, £400.

1796. c. 85. To repair certain roads.

1803. c. 60. For improving roads to Snigger's and Ashby's gaps.

  c. 61. For opening a road to Brock's gap.

  c. 65. For opening a road from the town of Monroe to Sweet

Springs and Lewisburg.

c. 71. For improving the road to Brock's gap.

1805. c. 5.   For improving the road to Clarksburg.

c. 26. For opening a road from Monongalia Glades to Fishing Creek.

1813. c. 44. For opening a road from Thornton's gap.

5. Lotteries for the benefit of counties.

1796. c. 78. To authorize a lottery in the county of Shenandoah.

c. 84. To authorize a lottery in the county of Gloucester.

6. Lotteries for the benefit of towns.

1782. c. 31. Richmond, for a bridge over Shockoe, amount not limited.

1789. c. 75. Alexandria, to pave its streets, £1,500.

1790. c. 46.   do.   do.   £5,000.

1796. c. 79. Norfolk, one or more lotteries authorized.

c. 81. Petersburg, a lottery authorized.

1803. c. 12. Woodstock,   do.

c. 48. Fredericksburg, for improving its main street.

c. 73. Harrisonburg, for improving its streets.

7. Lotteries for religious congregations.

1785. c.111. Completing a church in Winchester.

For rebuilding a church in the parish of Elizabeth River.

1791. c. 69. For the benefit of the Episcopal society.

1790. c. 46. For building a church in Warminster, £200.

in Halifax, £200.

in Alexandria, £500.

in Petersburg, £750.

in Shepherdstown, £250.

8. Lotteries for private societies.

1790. c. 46. For the Amicable Society in Richmond, £1,000.

1791. c. 70. For building a Freemason's Hall in Charlotte, £750.

9. Lotteries for the benefit of private individuals. [To raise money for them.]

1796. c. 80. For the sufferers by fire in the town of Lexington.

1781. c. 6.   For completing titles under Byrd's lottery.

1790. c. 46. To erect a paper mill in Staunton, £300.
                To raise £2,000 for Nathaniel Twining.
1791. c. 73. To raise £4,000 for William Tatham, to enable him to
                complete his geographical work.
                To enable ——— to complete a literary work.[2]

We have seen, then, that every vocation in life is subject to the
influence of chance; that so far from being rendered immoral by the ad-
mixture of that ingredient, were they abandoned on that account, man
could no longer subsist; that, among them, every one has a natural right
to choose that which he thinks most likely to give him comfortable subsistence; but that while the greater number of these pursuits are productive of something which adds to the necessaries and comforts of life,
others again, such as cards, dice, &c., are entirely unproductive, doing
good to none, injury to many, yet so easy, and so seducing in practice to
men of a certain constitution of mind, that they cannot resist the temptation, be the consequences what they may; that in this case, as in those of
insanity, idiocy, infancy, &c., it is the duty of society to take them under
its protection, even against their own acts, and to restrain their right of
choice of these pursuits, by suppressing them entirely; that there are
others, as lotteries particularly, which, although liable to chance also, are
useful for many purposes, and are therefore retained and placed under the
discretion of the Legislature, to be permitted or refused according to the
circumstances of every special case, of which they are to judge; that between the years 1782 and 1820, a space of thirty-eight years only, we have
observed seventy cases, where the permission of them has been found
useful by the Legislature, some of which are in progress at this time.
These cases relate to the emolument of the whole State, to local benefits
of education, of navigation, of roads, of counties, towns, religious assem-
blies, private societies, and of individuals under particular circumstances
which may claim indulgence or favor. The latter is the case now submitted to the Legislature, and the question is, whether the individual soliciting
their attention, or his situation, may merit that degree of consideration
which will justify the Legislature in permitting him to avail himself of the
mode of selling by lottery, for the purpose of paying his debts.

Sale by Lottery Is Now the Only Way to Get a Fair Price

That a fair price cannot be obtained by sale in the ordinary way, and in the present depressed state of agricultural industry, is well known. Lands in this State will now sell for more than a third or fourth of what they would have brought a few years ago, perhaps at the very time of the contraction of the debts for which they are now to be sold. The low price in foreign markets, for a series of years past, of agricultural produce, of wheat generally, of tobacco most commonly, and the accumulation of duties on the articles of consumption not produced within our State, not only disable the farmer or planter from adding to his farm by purchase, but reduces him to sell his own, and remove to the western country, glutting the market he leaves, while he lessens the number of bidders. To be protected against this sacrifice is the object of the present application, and whether the applicant has any particular claim to this protection, is the present question.

My Years of Public Service Support My Claim to Be Permitted a Sale by Lottery

Here the answer must be left to others. It is not for me to give it. I may, however, more readily than others, suggest the offices in which I have served. I came of age in 1764, and was soon put into the nomination of justice of the county in which I live, and at the first election following I became one of its representatives in the Legislature.

I was thence sent to the old Congress.

Then employed two years with Mr. Pendleton and Mr. Whyte, on the revisal and reduction to a single code of the whole body of the British statutes, the acts of our Assembly, and certain parts of the common law.

Then elected Governor.

Next to the Legislature, and to Congress again.

Sent to Europe as Minister Plenipotentiary.

Appointed Secretary of State to the new government.

Elected Vice-President, and

President. And lastly, a Visitor and Rector of the University. In these different offices, with scarcely any interval between them, I have been in the public service now sixty-one years; and during the far greater part of the time, in foreign countries or in other States. Every one knows how inevitably a Virginia estate goes to ruin, when the owner is so far distant as to be unable to pay attention to it himself; and the more especially, when the line of his employment is of a character to abstract and alienate his mind entirely from the knowledge necessary to good, and even to saving management.

If it were thought worth while to specify any particular services rendered, I would refer to the specification of them made by the Legislature itself in their Farewell Address, on my retiring from the Presidency, February, 1809. . . . There is one, however, not therein specified, the most important in its consequences, of any transaction in any portion of my life; to wit, the head I personally made against the federal principles and proceedings, during the administration of Mr. Adams. Their usurpations and violations of the constitution at that period, and their majority in both Houses of Congress, were so great, so decided, and so daring, that after combating their aggressions, inch by inch, without being able in the least to check their career, the republican leaders thought it would be best for them to give up their useless efforts there, go home, get into their respective Legislatures, embody whatever of resistance they could be formed into, and if ineffectual, to perish there as in the last ditch. All, therefore, retired, leaving Mr. Gallatin alone in the House of Representatives, and myself in the Senate, where I then presided as Vice-President. Remaining at our posts, and bidding defiance to the brow beatings and insults by which they endeavored to drive us off also, we kept the mass of republicans in phalanx together, until the Legislature could be brought up to the charge; and nothing on earth is more certain, than that if myself particularly, placed by my office of Vice-President at the head of the republicans, had given way and withdrawn from my post, the republicans throughout the Union would have given up in despair, and the cause would have been lost forever. By holding on, we obtained time for the Legislature to come up with their weight; and those of

Virginia and Kentucky particularly, but more especially the former, by their celebrated resolutions, saved the constitution at its last gasp. No person who was not a witness of the scenes of that gloomy period, can form any idea of the afflicting persecutions and personal indignities we had to brook. They saved our country however. The spirits of the people were so much subdued and reduced to despair by the X Y Z imposture, and other stratagems and machinations, that they would have sunk into apathy and monarchy, as the only form of government which could maintain itself.

If Legislative services are worth mentioning, and the stamp of liberality and equality, which was necessary to be imposed on our laws in the first crisis of our birth as a nation, was of any value, they will find that the leading and most important laws of that day were prepared by myself, and carried chiefly by my efforts; supported, indeed, by able and faithful coadjutors from the ranks of the House, very effective as seconds, but who would not have taken the field as leaders.

The prohibition of the further importation of slaves was the first of these measures in time.

This was followed by the abolition of entails, which broke up the hereditary and high-handed aristocracy, which, by accumulating immense masses of property in single lines of families, had divided our country into two distinct orders, of nobles and plebeians.

But further to complete the equality among our citizens so essential to the maintenance of republican government, it was necessary to abolish the principle of primogeniture. I drew the law of descents, giving equal inheritance to sons and daughters, which made a part of the revised code.

The attack on the establishment of a dominant religion, was first made by myself. It could be carried at first only by a suspension of salaries for one year, by battling it again at the next session for another year, and so from year to year, until the public mind was ripened for the bill for establishing religious freedom, which I had prepared for the revised code also. This was at length established permanently, and by the efforts chiefly of Mr. Madison, being myself in Europe at the time that work was brought forward.

To these particular services, I think I might add the establishment of our University, as principally my work, acknowledging at the same time, as I do, the great assistance received from my able colleagues of the Visitation. But my residence in the vicinity threw, of course, on me the chief burthen of the enterprise, as well of the buildings as of the general organization and care of the whole. The effect of this institution on the future fame, fortune and prosperity of our country, can as yet be seen but at a distance. But an hundred well-educated youths, which it will turn out annually, and ere long, will fill all its offices with men of superior qualifications, and raise it from its humble state to an eminence among its associates which it has never yet known; no, not in its brightest days. That institution is now qualified to raise its youth to an order of science unequalled in any other State; and this superiority will be the greater from the free range of mind encouraged there, and the restraint imposed at other seminaries by the shackles of a domineering hierarchy, and a bigoted adhesion to ancient habits. Those now on the theatre of affairs will enjoy the ineffable happiness of seeing themselves succeeded by sons of a grade of science beyond their own ken. Our sister States will also be repairing to the same fountains of instruction, will bring hither their genius to be kindled at our fire, and will carry back the fraternal affections which, nourished by the same *alma mater*, will knit us to them by the indissoluble bonds of early personal friendships. The good Old Dominion, the blessed mother of us all, will then raise her head with pride among the nations, will present to them that splendor of genius which she has ever possessed, but has too long suffered to rest uncultivated and unknown, and will become a centre of ralliance to the States whose youth she has instructed, and, as it were, adopted.

I claim some share in the merits of this great work of regeneration. My whole labors, now for many years, have been devoted to it, and I stand pledged to follow it up through the remnant of life remaining to me. And what remuneration do I ask? Money from the treasury? Not a cent. I ask nothing from the earnings or labors of my fellow citizens. I wish no man's comforts to be abridged for the enlargement of mine. For the services rendered on all occasions, I have been always paid to my full satisfaction. I never wished a dollar more than what the law had fixed on. My request is, only to be permitted to sell my own property freely to pay my own debts. To *sell* it, I say, and not to *sacrifice* it, not to have it gobbled up by speculators to make fortunes for themselves, leaving unpaid those who have trusted to my good faith, and myself without resource in the last and most helpless stage of life. If permitted to sell it in a way which will bring me a fair price, all will be honestly and honorably paid, and a competence left for myself, and for those who look to me for subsistence. To sell it in a way which will offend no moral principle, and expose none to risk but the willing, and those wishing to be permitted to take the chance of gain. To give me, in short, that permission which you often allow to others for purposes not more moral.

Will it be objected, that although not evil in itself, it may, as a precedent, lead to evil? But let those who shall quote the precedent bring their case within the same measure. Have they, as in this case, devoted three-score years and one of their lives, uninterruptedly, to the service of their country? Have the times of those services been as trying as those which have embraced our Revolution, our transition from a colonial to a free structure of government? Have the stations of their trial been of equal importance? Has the share they have borne in holding their new government to its genuine principles, been equally marked? And has the cause of the distress, against which they seek a remedy, proceeded, not merely from themselves, but from errors of the public authorities, disordering the circulating medium, over which they had no control, and which have, in fact, doubled and trebled debts, by reducing, in that proportion, the value of the property which was to pay them? If all these circumstances, which characterize the present case, have taken place in theirs also, then follow the precedent. Be assured, the cases will be so rare as to produce no embarrassment, as never to settle into an injurious habit. The single feature of a sixty years' service, as no other instance of it has yet occurred in our country, so it probably never may again. And should it occur, even once and again, it will not impoverish your treasury, as it takes nothing from that, and asks but a simple permission, by an act of natural right, to do one of moral justice.

Notes

1. 1796–1805. The acts not being at hand, the sums allowed are not known.
2. I found such an act, but not noting it at the time, I have not been able to find it again. But there is such an one.

IV

DOES LEGAL
GAMBLING
HURT OR
HELP THE
ECONOMY?

INTRODUCTION TO PART IV

Theoretically, people freely exchanging goods or services, with full knowledge, will perceive themselves as better off than they were before the transaction. And if some third party intervenes and forcibly prevents the exchange, the parties who wanted the transaction will presumably feel frustrated. Yet even the most enthusiastic defenders of free enterprise will probably concede that whole classes of people, for example, young children, should not be allowed to have the same degree of free choice as that allowed to competent adults. For while freedom is usually a good thing and frustration is usually a bad thing, protecting people from self-harm or even self-destruction is a valuable end.

Supporters of legalized gambling often argue that adults should be given the freedom to spend their money on gambling and should not be presumed incompetent to make those choices. In contrast, opponents of legalized gambling often argue that, while many adults can gamble responsibly, the consequences of those who do not gamble responsibly are serious enough to justify limiting legal opportunities for gambling. They further argue that increasing legal opportunities for gambling can increase the number of compulsive gamblers, who can harm not only themselves but also others, including their friends, families, and employees.

John Warren Kindt, a professor of commerce and legal policy at the University of Illinois-Urbana, believes that legalized gambling is generally more harmful than beneficial to a region's economy. He submits that in the long run legalized gambling tends to discourage investment in a region because companies and their employees will usually want to avoid the atmosphere created by gaming establishments, including increases in crime as well as taxes (needed to compensate for the lower productivity and theft caused by problem and compulsive gamblers.)

In short, Kindt submits that creating more opportunities to gamble will not strengthen an economy but weaken it by requiring businesses and governments to bear additional regulatory, crime, and social-welfare costs.

While Kindt asserts that there are economic costs created by gambling, economist Reuven Brenner contends that there are economic costs to prohibiting gambling. Allowing lotteries provides hope to the poor, while prohibiting them not only creates costs for law enforcement but also deprives the government of potential revenue, argues Brenner.

11. Legalized Gambling Is Bad for Business

John Warren Kindt

John Kindt, a professor of commerce and legal policy at the University of Illinois-Urbana and a prolific gambling policy analyst, argues that legalized gambling usually does not generate long-term or even medium-term economic development or tax revenues. What's more, he argues that there is evidence that legal gambling causes many personal bankruptcies, as in South Dakota, where the number of bankruptcies caused by gambling rose, he contends, after the introduction of casinos and state-wide video lottery terminals.

Kindt maintains that when legalized gambling establishments are brought to a population center, they disproportionately attract local compulsive gamblers, who within three or five years spend and lose their assets/credit base. Unless huge numbers of new tourists are attracted by legalized gambling activities after the first few years, the pre-existing economy and tourist trade, according to Kindt, are eventually depleted, preventing legalized gambling from providing state-wide economic growth, jobs, or tax revenues.

In fact, a region can, asserts Kindt, incur large economic losses after introducing legal gambling because of regulatory costs, crime costs, and social-welfare costs. "Economically speaking, legalized gambling is a sucker bet. Like the fairy tale, the economic Emperor of legalized gambling is wearing no clothes. It is a sad reflection upon society, and particularly legislative officials, that so many have ignored the business-economic negatives for so long."

"The Negative Impacts of Legalized Gambling on Businesses," John Warren Kindt in *University of Miami Business Law Journal* 4, no. 2 (Spring 1994), pp. 93–124. Reproduced here by permission.

Kindt holds that legalizing gambling can make a region unattractive to most businesses considering locating there. The reason, according to Kindt, is that legalizing gambling increases the number of problem gamblers both inside and outside the workplace, tempting local and state governments to raise corporate, personal, and real estate taxes. What's more, problem gamblers within the workplace, he says, are more likely to be absent, to produce less, and to steal more than the general population of workers.

He concludes by asserting that in the long run states with little or no legal gambling will have fewer personal and business bankruptcies, stronger financial institutions, more vibrant business economies, and better tourist, business, and community environments than states with more legal gambling.

Under good economic conditions, but particularly during recessionary periods, there is usually intense competition between states to attract new businesses. New businesses improve local and state economies by providing an influx of investment dollars, jobs, and new tax revenues. As states and municipalities attempted to boost economic growth during the recessionary U.S. economy of 1991–1992, the legalized gambling organizations in Nevada and in Atlantic City, New Jersey, saw the perfect opportunity to expand their organizations into previously unexploited regions.[1]

Gambling Interests Often Oppose New Legalization Measures

Notwithstanding contrary positions argued by legalized gambling interests in their efforts to gain and exploit new population bases,[2] and with rare exceptions, legalized gambling activities do not generate long-term or even mid-term strategic economic development or tax revenues.[3] Any profit generated by legalized gambling almost invariably comes from some consumer's pre-existing funds, and the resources devoted to gambling are taken from other activities.[4] In fact, legalized gambling interests have both promoted and discouraged legalized gambling when necessary to further their objectives. In one instance, major legalized gambling organizations conducted public relations campaigns arguing that their casinos would create economic development, jobs, and tax revenues in Illinois.[5] However, in order to undercut their competition in California and preserve their own gambling operations in Nevada, some of these same organizations simultaneously conducted public relations campaigns in California arguing just the opposite.[6]

Throughout the 1980s the legalized gambling organizations in Atlantic City and Nevada, in particular, felt competitive pressure from the nation-wide proliferation of state lotteries.[7] For example, in 1986 the legalized gambling interests in Nevada, and even Nevada state officials, opposed the initiation of a state lottery in California.[8] If the Nevada legalized gambling interests were concerned with the proximate competition of a California state lottery, they were more concerned with the potential "devastating impact" of a 1992 proposal for a moderately-sized casino operation in Adelanto, San Bernardino County, California.[9] Not only would the Adelanto casino "initiative" further saturate the legalized gambling market, but more importantly, it would also intercept the local population traveling from Southern California to Las Vegas[10] and open the door to more direct competition from casinos on Indian reservations throughout California.

Gambling Operations Face Market Saturation

The legalized gambling interests in Nevada were also concerned in general with future market saturation within the state. From years of marketing experience, the legalized gambling organizations were well aware that legalized gambling draws dollars from nearby local and state economies.[11] Therefore, the legalized gambling interests needed to expand their marketing bases to continue to attract consumer dollars. If the expansion process was forestalled for very long, the guaranteed population of legalized gambling "consumers" (10 percent "problem economic gamblers,"[12] which included 1.5 to 5 percent "compulsive gamblers"[13]) would be exhausted[14] and profits from those economies in which the legalized gambling organizations were located would diminish or evaporate.[15]

While the proliferation of state lotteries during the 1980s[16] jeopardized the regular tourist base attracted by legalized gambling, the major threat to the legalized gambling organizations was the long-term saturation of the market itself. Yet even while the expansion of state lotteries threatened the Nevada and Atlantic City legalized gambling interests, it also unexpectedly provided those interests with their strategic solution. The public's acceptance of state lotteries[17] had softened the image of legalized gambling and was laying the groundwork for the national acceptance of the "harder" forms of legalized gambling—that is, those forms with more of a "thrill factor."[18] This trend was further intensified by millions of dollars in advertising by state lotteries[19] aimed at softening concerns about legalized gambling activities and promulgating the widespread acceptance of games of chance.

Illinois serves as an example of an early state to develop legalized gambling activities. In Illinois, the state lottery was initiated in 1974;[20] a variety of lottery "games" proliferated throughout the 1980s;[21] major expansions in the numbers of off-track betting parlors occurred in 1990 and 1991;[22] riverboat gambling was legalized in 1990 and initiated in 1991;[23] video-machine gambling was also proposed in 1991–1992;[24] and Chicago Mayor Richard Daley proposed a $2 billion land-based casino complex in 1992.[25] Furthermore, by 1992 over 50 bills regarding legalized gambling activities were pending in the Illinois state legislature.[26]

Legalized Gambling Causes Bankruptcies

South Dakota serves as an example of an even more rapidly-developing gambling state. Until the initiation of its state lottery in 1987, there was no legalized gambling per se in South Dakota.[27] However, beginning November 1, 1989, the city of Deadwood, South Dakota, initiated land-based casino gambling after a state-wide plebiscite; casino gambling on the Indian reservations was in full operation by 1990; and by 1991, video-machine gambling was available throughout the state.[28]

Within two years of initiating these casinos and state-wide video lottery terminals (VLTs), an interesting business phenomenon was observed in South Dakota: a number of personal and business bankruptcies were being caused by gambling debts.[29]

> "There'd be significantly fewer bankruptcies without the gambling aspects," said Peder Ecker, a federal bankruptcy judge in Sioux Falls. "There's definitely a pattern of increasing bankruptcy filings because of the gambling."
> . . . .
> Ecker said he attributed most of the bankruptcies related to gambling to the state's video lottery, saying he saw *no cases that involved gambling debts before the game started in October 1989.* Gambling has grown to rival uninsured medical costs as *a leading cause of bankruptcies,* he said.[30]

These bankruptcies and the concomitant losses in jobs were a direct result of legalized gambling, and would not have occurred had VLT gambling, casino gambling, and even the "softer" gambling of the state lottery *not* been legalized.[31]

Clinical observations appear to confirm this phenomenon. The law firm handling most of the bankruptcy cases in South Dakota confirmed that while the overall number of filings were down, gambling was an increasing cause of bankruptcies in South Dakota.[32] Similarly, a 1992 Minnesota report also raised the proposition that increased legalized gambling activities in the state might be linked to the increase in bankruptcies.[33]

In any event, South Dakota and Illinois illustrate that with enough public relations dollars promoting legalized gambling activities,[34] both public officials and voters could be directed toward accepting the arguments that legalized gambling activities are traditional "businesses,"[35] and would provide net jobs and positive tax revenues on a statewide basis.[36] If these arguments were palatable to the U.S. public during a healthy economic climate, then these arguments would be even more acceptable and gain impetus during recessionary times.[37] That 1992 in particular was a time to capitalize on the economic fears of the public was reinforced by Bill Clinton's victory over President George Bush—when mounting concern over the U.S. economy was identified as the primary voter issue.[38] The window of opportunity had opened for the legalized gambling organizations, and the time had come for them to initiate a strategy of *carpe diem* and expand beyond Nevada and Atlantic City.[39] However, even a New Jersey Commission generally favorable to legalized gambling activities cautioned that "New Jersey should never risk weakening its regulatory systems to enhance the State's fiscal condition or offset possible *economic consequences occasioned by downturns* . . ."[40] Furthermore, the Commission noted it was "clear that retail business and retail employment in Atlantic City have continued to decline despite the presence of gambling. . . ."[41] The economic caveat is that state governments should not be prodded by perceived economic vulnerability into hasty and risk-developmental policies—such as legalized gambling—which might eventually intensify business-economic problems.[42]

Notwithstanding the generally poor economic conditions of 1991–1992, the timing for the legalized gambling organizations was propitious, and their strategy was simple: instead of waiting for tourists to come to them, the organizations would go to the tourists by locating in as many dense population centers as possible.[43] Those establishments successfully implementing this strategy would not have to worry about profitability for years since the legalized gambling activities would naturally take a major portion of the sixty-five percent "market cream" of the local population's gambling dollars.[44] This phenomenon means that there is a premium for being the first, most aggressive, or "most thrilling" form of legalized gambling established in a population center. Hence, it was not surprising that there were proposals during 1992 for major land-based casinos in Chicago and New Orleans[45]—both prime population centers.

Legalized Gambling Is Lucrative for the First Five Years

Once proposed gambling activities become legalized, the legalized gambling interests are concerned primarily with the quickest and most effective way to tap the local economy.[46] The fastest drain seems to be approximately three to five years before the 1.5 to 5 percent of local compulsive gamblers will "bottom-out," spending and losing their total asset/credit base. Therefore, while tourist campaigns and advertisements may be undertaken, legalized gambling organizations would almost invariably profit even if they did not attract a single tourist for approximately five years.[47]

Given the inherent nature of the legalized gambling markets, the first five years of business generally constitute the major revenue years for most legalized gambling organizations—after which they must find new markets and/or new marketing gimmicks to attract gamblers.[48] During the first five years, the profit margins can be surprisingly large. For example, in 1990 the *Excalibur* in Las Vegas opened as the largest hotel in the United States and then stunned the business world by paying its entire mortgage out of "operating revenues" in less than two years— while the rest of the country was in a recession.[49] In another scenario, the gambling riverboat in Alton, Illinois, sold more than $100 million in stock during its first day of trading.[50]

In any event, legalized gambling organizations cannot be characterized as conventional businesses and do not conduct traditional business activities despite efforts to market themselves as such.[51] Unless massive numbers of *new tourists* are attracted by the advent of legalized gambling activities, the pre-existing economy and tourist trade are eventually depleted, and consequently the legalized gambling will not provide statewide economic growth, jobs, or tax revenues.[52] Legalized gambling interests instead provide only the illusion of relative economic development, for where one locale might gain, others surely lose.[53] Across the region as a whole, there is no gain, but there can be large losses when the increased regulatory costs, crime costs, and social-welfare costs are factored into the analysis.[54] Economically speaking, legalized gambling is a sucker bet. Like the fairy-tale, the economic Emperor of legalized gambling is wearing no clothes. It is a sad reflection upon society, and particularly legislative officials, that so many have ignored the business-economic negatives for so long.

Any large infusion of money into a local economy can initially stimulate short-term economic development, new jobs, and tax revenues.

However, short-term progress does not always indicate long-term growth. For this reason it is essential to analyze legalized gambling and its projected economic impact for the intermediate term and long term. Only then can the actual economic effects of legalized gambling be adequately evaluated.

Eventually, Legalized Gambling Hurts the Economy

The legalized gambling interests, however, often focus public attention on possible short-term economic benefits as a technique to misdirect the economic debate.[55] What they conveniently omit is that the eventual results of legalized gambling are seriously debilitating. According to the authoritative nationwide statistics,[56] legalized gambling activities eventually effectuate:

1. economic dysfunction,[57]
2. the exploitation of minorities[58] and low-income groups,[59]
3. social dysfunction,[60] and
4. an eventual increase in taxes to address new social problems necessarily generated by legalized gambling.[61]

All forms of legalized gambling have a disproportionate impact on Hispanics[62] and Afro-Americans,[63] as well as on low-income groups,[64] who spend an average of 2.2 percent of their weekly income on legalized gambling.[65] These trends result in dramatic increased costs to social programs, increased unemployment for minorities, and more proportional unemployment for minorities than for whites.[66]

Since legalized gambling leaves the local community and state with increased social-welfare costs, inordinate pressures are placed on government officials to raise real estate taxes, state income taxes, and business taxes.[67] The promises of sustained economic growth promulgated by the legalized gambling organizations constitute, at best, illusory promises. As a result, the public contract between the legalized gambling organizations and the state to assist the economy constitutes a *nudum pactum*, or void agreement.

Business Investors Seek a Stable Environment

Businesses seek to locate in those local and state economies which have or can provide a stimulating business/economic environment.[68] Economically depressed areas often look beyond traditional manufacturing jobs to bolster their economies, and legalized gambling activities may be considered.[69] However, an actual accounting of the societal cost-benefit analysis is necessary to determine whether the activity, such as legalized gambling, would produce the desired economic growth and should therefore be introduced into the region.[70] The results of some economic studies[71] should "give pause to policymakers who are considering the use of casinos as a machine for growth in depressed regions."[72]

"Stability of expectations,"[73] is an essential ingredient of an attractive business environment. Businesses need to know that if they perform in a certain manner, they can minimize risk and maximize their expectations. While risk is always a factor in a changing business environment, the inability to calculate that risk is almost more destabilizing than the magnitude of any calculated risk.

One basic example of stability of expectations involves what is termed "the maintenance of a favorable legal order." On a national level, businesses want to know the "rules" under which they must operate. Commercial entities understandably become concerned in a society or country where, for example, the tax code is constantly changing, is not inherently "uniform," and/or is not being uniformly applied (or is even manipulated by the government).[74] Further, and as an extreme example, companies generally refuse to locate in countries undergoing revolution, or even threatened revolution. Regardless of any overwhelmingly positive concessions a pre-existing government may make, without stability of expectations businesses fear that those concessions will never be realized. Accordingly, a lack of stability of expectations can hamper or destroy any given business/economic environment by making calculation of risk difficult or impossible.

Throughout the twentieth century, and particularly since World War II, the maintenance of a favorable legal order and inherent stability have been two major strengths of the United States which have induced foreign investment within the U.S. economy. Presumably, the United States enjoys a higher stability of expectations than any other country, and this stability is crucial to maintain this pillar of the U.S. business/ economic environment. One of the unfortunate results of the U.S. savings-and-loan debacle of the 1980s was to chip this economic pillar, particularly in the minds of many U.S. citizens.[75]

Nationwide, the individual states have obviously benefited from these overall U.S. economic strengths and have successfully solicited foreign and domestic businesses to locate within their borders. Some states, however, have hurt their initially competitive positions for attracting new businesses by creating certain unstable business/economic factors. During 1991, for example, the states of California[76] and Illinois[77] were unable to pay their state obligations (such as wages to state employees in Illinois) and engaged in delays and sleight-of-hand to pay their bills. In so doing, these state governments effectively undermined the stability of expectations in their states,[78] decreasing the likelihood that businesses would choose them as locations for new subsidiaries.[79] Conversely, the bulk of states which did not have to delay payments enjoyed a relative advantage for attracting new businesses.[80] However, any concessions, such as tax concessions, offered by California or Illinois could more than offset the problem of "instability" of payments and thereby attract new businesses. Yet despite the potential concessions California and Illinois may make to new industries, they still suffer a competitive disadvantage because of the incidence of past instability. In essence, California and Illinois must now "pay" for the previous unstable business/economic conditions caused by their legislative budgeting anomalies.

Investors Dislike a High Crime Rate

In determining where to invest their dollars by building new plants or establishing new subsidiaries, corporations with large asset bases generally turn to "business location models."[81] Even small companies can utilize the less complex models,[82] but the models utilized by the larger companies,[83] such as the Fortune 500,[84] tend to be quite sophisticated.[85] Obviously, the major businesses like to keep these models confidential,[86] because the models can be the subject of large investments of time and money, and because competitors would gain some economic advantage from them. A classic example of a company utilizing sophisticated business location models involves a major fast-food chain, which is the leader in its area. Its competitors would obviously be quite interested in being able to predict ahead of time where and when that chain was going to establish new outlets and potentially locate there first.

One nuance strategy for the smaller competitors in such a market situation is simply to let the industry leader claim the primary location sites and then to follow the leader to those sites when they become public. This location strategy bypasses many of the expenses in utilizing business location models, but the escalating real estate costs which must be internalized by being the second, third, or fourth competitor into a prime market area may often be greater than the costs of utilizing the business location models. However, from the individual state's perspective, familiarity with business location models will very likely expand that state's opportunity for attracting new businesses and even for retaining established businesses.[87]

When faced with the decision-making process of where to locate initially or where to expand its presence, a company should examine the traditional business location models.[88] Some business models are used more than others, but many of the factors utilized therein are quite consistent with the economic variations that depend on the nature of the business.[89] Over time, the models often become quite sophisticated[90] as they adapt to the specialized needs of the company which makes use of them. It should also be noted that given their complexities, these models can easily take on "minds of their own" and the number of variables these models address can yield unexpected conclusions.[91]

Most of the traditional business location models include a category which is generically termed the "business environment."[92] A classic "red-flag" component of this category is "high-crime rate."[93] For example, a business location computer model would, by definition, identify a generic type of red flag to alert a company which was considering locating in a particular county if that county had the highest violent crime rate or the highest illegal drug use in the state.[94] Similarly, "legalized gambling activities" become an important factor in a company's decision whether to locate in certain communities.[95] While the advantages of locating in a given area might still overwhelm the notable disadvantages associated with its red-flag drawbacks,[96] that decision would have to be made as a type of managerial override of the red-flag alerts.[97] The point is that counties and states with these red-flag components are at a definite competitive disadvantage for attracting new businesses to their economies.

The question of whether high crime rates per se are associated with legalized gambling activities is beyond the scope of this discussion.[98] In addition, any specific red-flag areas are or should be separate components in business location models. Even so, pre-existing legalized gambling activities in any county or state constitute a definite negative in efforts to attract new businesses (and in keeping pre-existing businesses).[99] It is largely irrelevant whether the gambling activity has been legalized or not. The basic negative socio-economic impacts of an activity do not change just because an activity has been "legalized"—although the parameters of the negatives may be regulated or monitored more closely.

In the public domain, the best analysis interfacing a community environment with readily accessible legalized gambling activities is contained in "The Impact of Casino Gambling in New Orleans"[100] by the Division of Business and Economic Research at the University of New Orleans. This report referenced a 1989 survey[101] in which business leaders were asked what factors were "absolutely essential" in locating their businesses:[102]

> With respect to office locations, the business leaders listed eight factors that were important. Of these eight, two were related to the business climate: 1) the climate created by state and local government for business, which was ranked fourth with 29 percent of the respondents saying it was essential and 2) the ability to attract executives and professional[s] from outside the area, which was ranked seventh with 22 percent of the respondents saying it was essential. This is consistent with other surveys that have been done.[103]

It should also be noted that when these business leaders were polled about "other" cities, "[o]nly three percent felt that Las Vegas was an attractive place to locate a business today [1989]"[104] and "only 2 percent responded that they felt Las Vegas would be attractive in the next five years."[105]

An actual case example demonstrated several of these points when in March of 1992, Mayor Richard Daley announced and gave his support to a proposed $2-billion casino complex for Chicago.[106] Mayor Daley's plan was criticized as "increasing crime and other social problems and discouraging other businesses from locating [in Chicago]."[107] In this context, Mayor Daley claimed that he had first tried to attract another Walt Disney World to the Chicago area,[108] but failing in that attempt he was hoping to establish a $2-billion casino complex. Despite the many variables associated with such decisions, the speed with which the Mayor appeared to dismiss the Disney-type possibility hurt the Mayor's credibility. It seemed unreasonable that an attractive offer could not have been negotiated to attract the Walt Disney Company or a similar company—given the resources of the City of Chicago and the Governor of Illinois (whom Mayor Richard Daley did not consult prior to announcing the Chicago casino complex).[109]

Some Businesses Might Refuse to Locate Where There Is Legalized Gambling

Even so, it seemed illogical that a theme park the size of Walt Disney World would ever locate in the Chicago area once a $2-billion casino complex was approved. In other words, in business as in politics, the rule is that business persons should "never say never." However, in this hypothetical instance, the business location models and/or decision-making process for a Disney-size theme park would probably have "red flags" all over the "business environment" category, as well as many other categories. Of course this discussion is limited to only the impacts of legalized gambling activities, while many other factors in the business location models (such as the climate in Chicago) could have been of crucial importance.

In other hypothetical discussions, a related, interesting scenario could also occur. After the Walt Disney Company publicly announced plans in 1993 to establish a theme park in the area of Manassas, Virginia, a proposal for a legalized gambling riverboat complex was aggressively promoted for Richmond, Virginia—only ninety-four miles away.[110] Since tourism is the second leading industry in Virginia, it is interesting to consider whether a "pre-existing" legalized gambling complex in Richmond or in Washington, D.C. (only thirty-seven miles distant from Manassas) would have negated the decision of the Walt Disney Company. Perhaps the projected drawdown on the visitors to the Disney theme park would have been minimal given the distances involved. Perhaps other considerations of locale would have been more important to Disney than the socio-economic negatives associated with concentrated legalized gambling activities. Perhaps pre-existing legalized gambling complexes in Virginia would have caused Disney to reconsider Chicago. Regardless of these considerations and many other variables which may have been vital, the fact remains that Disney chose to locate first in a state with little or no legalized gambling activities.[111]

In this context, it is interesting to note that the 85-member Greater Washington (D.C.) Board of Trade quickly and unanimously rejected a 1993 proposal to bring casino gambling to the area.[112] There was apparently very little debate among businesses and the tourist trade in Washington, D.C.—compared with the debate in Chicago which began in 1992 and continued into 1994. The press report on the decision of the business leaders in the Washington, D.C. area was revealing.

> The Washington area's most influential business group . . . denounced Mayor Sharon Pratt Kelly's efforts to bring casino gambling to the District, attacking the idea as a poor use of city resources.
>
> In a rare public stand on a controversial political issue, the Greater Washington Board of Trade's *85-member board voted unanimously against the initiative*.
>
> The group, which includes many of the Washington area's most powerful business leaders, could have provided strong backing for Kelly's plans to use gambling to spur economic development. The mayor has courted the group on various financial issues.

"The addition of casino gambling would not enhance the city's image," the Board of Trade said in a statement. . . . "Directors believe that the city should concentrate on key economic development initiatives such as the convention center redevelopment, neighborhood revitalization and an aggressive business retention program," adding that gaming is "diverting the Kelly administration's attention away from well-outlined priorities."[113]

This decision by the Board of Trade was a significant reflection of business acumen and it unanimously rejected the standard claims of economic development promulgated by the legalized gambling interests.[114]

In any event, it should be emphasized that there are also fundamental differences in substantial portions of the tourist and nontourist clienteles attracted by complexes dedicated to gambling, as distinguished from other types of tourist attractions. These differences are important, despite the efforts of many legalized gambling facilities to disguise themselves as "family entertainment centers." "But a casino is *not* an adult Disneyland,"[115] according to law professor I. Nelson Rose, who summarized some of the issues differentiating a casino from a bona fide family entertainment center.

Disneyland would not exploit minors, or drunks, or compulsives [i.e., compulsive gamblers], even if it could get away with it. But some casinos do it every day and then lie about it, even to themselves.[116]

Considerable weight should be given to the argument that in many respects a Disney-style theme park and a legalized gambling complex are not just different, but fundamentally incompatible. These problems lead to the proposition that each state, particularly tourist-oriented states, must decide on their "tourist environment" as well as their statewide "business and community environments." Given some of Euro Disney's marketing problems during the early 1990s,[117] it would be difficult to believe that a Manassas theme park would not have some serious concerns about proximate legalized gambling facilities—particularly riverboats and casinos.

The main point is that counties, cities, and states must choose their respective business environments. Chicago needs to determine whether it wants to be known as "the City that Works" or "the City that Gambles."[118] Likewise, Illinois needs to determine if it wants to be known as "the State that Works" or "the State that Gambles." Virginia, Florida, and other tourist-oriented states will also need to decide on their "tourist environment."[119] As the Greater Washington Board of Trade emphasized, "[t]he addition of casino gambling would not enhance the city's image,"[120] or as Michigan Attorney General Frank Kelley concluded, "[c]ities trying to create a better image should stay away from gambling."[121] Before the twenty-first century, all U.S. counties, cities, and states will be faced with similar issues involving their community and business environments.

Businesses Should Not Locate in Legalized Gambling States

Sound economic reasons dictate that businesses should avoid locating in counties and states with legalized gambling activities if they can locate elsewhere.[122] Obviously, if the same degrees of legalized gambling pre-exist in all potential locations, the gambling activities component and related considerations may be largely irrelevant. However, those areas without legalized gambling activities have a competitive business-economic advantage over those states which have legalized gambling.

The best policy for most states is to establish themselves as "gambling-free" states. Gambling-free states escape the vast majority of socio-economic problems which encumber the local economies and governments of states with legalized gambling. States recently succumbing to pressures to enact state lotteries (such as Georgia in November of 1992) would be well-advised to disassociate their economies from legalized gambling activities and return to their previous status as gambling-free states. The longer the legalized gambling philosophy is allowed to influence an economy, the harder it becomes to revert to a gambling-free economy. However, economic history also demonstrates that gambling activities are generally recriminalized after an eventual erosion, and implosion, of the economy originally embracing them.[123]

A major reason that businesses do not want to be located in gambling states is [that] legalized gambling elevates social-welfare pressures on local and state governments to raise corporate, personal, and real estate taxes. Companies are naturally averse to paying higher corporate and real estate taxes to address these increasing problems. Business employees dislike higher personal and real estate taxes for the same reasons. Nor do businesses want to tack a salary bonus on their employees' paychecks to cover the increased taxes concomitant to living in a "high-tax state." The term "high-tax state" is a term which in the future will become more synonymous with "gambling state."[124] For example, in 1992 *Money* magazine found Sioux Falls, South Dakota, a prime community in which to live.[125] Interestingly, there were no personal income taxes in South Dakota. Naturally, potential employees want to live and work in such environments. Since 1988, however, with the initiation and subsequent rapid proliferation of legalized gambling activities in South Dakota, an eventual state income tax is likely, and such activities may cause Sioux Falls to lose its favorable community business environment.[126] By comparison, in 1988 *Money* magazine designated Atlantic City, New Jersey, as the least livable U.S. community.[127]

Of course, it is possible for a smaller gambling economy to live parasitically off of a larger non-gambling economy—Nevada and California, respectively—so long as the non-gambling economy cooperates.[128] It is well-documented that there is "a direct transfer of income and wealth from California to Nevada every year."[129] Gambling by Californians pumps nearly $3.8 billion per year into Nevada,[130] which translates into over one percent of California's Gross State Product.[131] In such an instance, it is therefore possible for a gambling state, such as Nevada, to be a low-tax state with no business or personal income tax.[132] Yet the previous points involving the economic advantages inherent in non-gambling states retain their validity, because until recently, the Nevada/California scenario was generally an exception. Furthermore, these principles can obviously be reflected across state lines in a more regional phenomenon; that is, companies will be less likely to locate in general "regions" of the country where the harder forms of gambling are legalized.

The Business Environment in Gambling States Is Inherently Destructive

The business environment is poor for business operations in gambling areas—except for legalized gambling organizations and their cluster services. For years, Nevada has had several communities with sufficient infrastructure to support numerous light industries, and yet those industries have chosen to locate elsewhere. There is no Silicon Valley or its equivalent in Nevada, and one major reason is that a substantial majority of pre-existing and potential employees do not want to work or raise families in a Nevada-like gambling environment.

Although the major Nevada communities competed vigorously throughout the 1980s to attract new businesses unrelated to legalized gambling and its cluster services, these negative factors have created an image which is not conducive to attracting new industries. Despite low taxes and a cheap pool of labor, most major companies have decided against locating in Nevada. One major company which was persuaded to locate in the Las Vegas area even changed its mailing address away from Las Vegas, allegedly to protect its company's image.

In any event, the "community environment" and its concomitant "business environment" appear to be the most important considerations reviewed by the Fortune 500 companies and other large businesses when considering where to locate. As Nevada illustrates, these considerations also appear to outweigh significantly the considerations pertaining to the availability of infrastructure, the demographics of the labor pool, and even tax rates.

Businesses Incur Higher Personnel Costs in Gambling States

Businesses can also expect major personnel problems if they choose to locate in a state with legalized gambling. Similarly, businesses will experience a premium in personnel costs if they allow the state in which they are presently located to legalize gambling. In this context, it is helpful to delineate strategic socio-economic factors which contribute to these increased personnel costs for businesses.

In a state with no legalized gambling, the population will contain approximately .77 percent compulsive gamblers and 2.33 percent "potential" compulsive gamblers.[133] The associated socio-economic costs are usually not readily apparent because they have already been subsumed into the pre-existing economy measured over decades. Once gambling activities are legalized and become socially "acceptable," however, the number of compulsive gamblers quickly increases to between 1.5 and 5 percent of the workforce.[134] To illustrate this point, if a business has 1,000 employees, the number of compulsive gamblers would increase from approximately eight to between fifteen and fifty employees. Furthermore, the "problem" economic gamblers (which includes the compulsive gamblers above) would total ten percent of the workforce, or 100 employees.[135] It is interesting to note that this ten percent parallels, and indeed corroborates, the reported clinical case load of problem gamblers in South Dakota, a state which only recently introduced casino gambling and VLTs at the end of 1989.[136]

As a direct result, then, businesses can anticipate increases of 100 to 550 percent in problems resulting from compulsive gamblers. Nationwide, an entirely new addicted workforce is being created as a result of legalizing gambling. In addition to the family and financial problems associated with compulsive gamblers which drain the resources of the local community, the state, and society at large, problems also directly and indirectly manifest themselves in the workforce. The internal problems which businesses can anticipate include increasing absenteeism and declining productivity. The average lost productivity for each compulsive gambler (at 1.5 to 5 percent of the workforce) has been calculated to be at least $15,000 per year,[137] but may be as high as $23,000 to $27,000.[138] To this total should be added the lost productivity of problem economic gamblers which, although not yet calculated within a range of specific dollar amounts, involves an added 5 to 8.5 percent of the workforce. Furthermore, the vast majority of those identified as compulsive gamblers often resort to theft from the workplace to finance their gambling.[139] Given this information, one observer has commented that "from a purely financial point of view, compulsive gambling is potentially worse [for an employer] than alcoholism and drug abuse combined."[140] In sum, personnel problems involving the dismissal of employees will presumably increase, and new legal grounds for dismissal may complicate the existing laws involving management-personnel relations.[141]

Furthermore, businesses are already facing increasing personnel problems, specifically rehabilitation costs, from employees engaging in illegal drug use and alcohol abuse, both "addictions" according to the American Psychiatric Association (APA). Several major companies have internalized the costs of treating their addicted employees for substance abuse, specifically alcohol and drugs. Added to these costs will be the costs of treating another APA-recognized addiction, gambling addiction.[142] Sociologists readily recognize the parallels between these three addictions. If conservative estimates of treating each gambling addict are utilized and absorbed by companies, the rehabilitative costs per employee can easily range from $15,000[143] to $42,000.[144]

Therefore, in a hypothetical company with 1,000 employees, the number of gambling addicts will be .77 percent, or seven to eight employees, *before* gambling is legalized.[145] This nominal sum often goes unnoticed and/or unaddressed by employers. Once gambling becomes legalized, however, a new addicted population will rise to include 1.5 to 5 percent of the workforce, and fifteen to fifty addicted employees can be anticipated. This 100 to 550 percent increase will transform a largely hidden problem into a significant and costly personnel quandary. Responsible firms that provide addiction treatment will face a conservative rehabilitative cost of $20,000 per gambling-addicted employee.[146] Increased personnel costs to a company with 1,000 employees would then amount to between $140,000 and $840,000. Add to this a lost productivity cost of $15,000 to $27,000 per employee,[147] and business could incur $35,000 in costs per gambling employee, for a total cost of $245,000 to $1.5 million.

It is unrealistic to think that state governments will directly shoulder these costs. State governments, traditionally pressured by taxpayers, place at least part of these rehabilitative and quality-of-life costs onto the businesses themselves. Businesses, then, will bear a substantial internal cost burden generated by the problems associated with compulsive gambling. Furthermore, a definite ten percent of our hypothetical workforce of 1,000 employees, or 100 people, will become problem economic gamblers, i.e., employees who are on their way to becoming compulsive gamblers, as well as those *already* compulsive gamblers.

Counties, cities, and states with legalized gambling activities are and will continue to become more competitively disadvantaged when trying to attract new businesses. In 1990, for example, Champaign County, Illinois, tried and failed to attract a $1-billion United Airlines facility. In 1992, the same county tried to attract a Spiegel distribution center promising 2,000 jobs, but failed. Interestingly, Champaign City was in the midst of a well-publicized legalized gambling controversy over off-track betting during this time. Both companies ultimately located in states with much less legalized gambling.[148]

These companies were probably utilizing business location models. Given the inherent nature of such models, the Champaign community, by embracing the gambling philosophy, was at a competitive disadvantage to non-gambling communities. Throughout 1990–1991, there were well over 150 media reports on the gambling controversy in the newspapers, radio reports, and television reports.[149] It would be difficult to suggest that this major community issue was not factored into the decision-making process by both companies as they investigated the Champaign County region.

Regardless of these determinations, legalized gambling communities and gambling states are in the process of developing poor community and business environments. The extent of negative consequences these communities face, however, is not always apparent, since companies rarely report their choices for location in a particular community based on its current or predicted deteriorating community environment. This is necessarily problematic for legalized gambling states which generate such deteriorating community environments. The economic trend is obvious; legalized gambling states will continue to hurt their economies as they embrace the gambling interests and the gambling philosophy. Savvy businesses should not, and probably will not, locate in legalized gambling states. Moreover, businesses should not expand their employee base in a gambling state, but should attempt to relocate as many jobs as possible to non-gambling states.

Businesses Will Be Attracted to Non-Gambling States

Those states which do not have any form of legalized gambling, including a state lottery, should not legalize gambling activities for purely fiscal reasons alone. From a business/economic perspective, the best strategy for a state is to declare itself a "gambling-free state" and then widely advertise itself as such. States which have already legalized gambling should re-criminalize gambling activities to boost their local economies. One major reason is that since most states are becoming infatuated with the gambling philosophy, those states without legalized gambling or with minimal legalized gambling will have several relative socio-economic advantages contributing to a positive business/economic environment. Even minimal legalized gambling in a state should be eliminated: once the Pandora's box of legalized gambling is opened, the socio-economic problems rapidly become ingrained in the economic fabric of the state.

Within the near future, businesses will start looking for gambling-free states or economies to which they can escape. Sooner or later, businesses will become disenchanted with the socio-economic problems and relatively high taxes of gambling states. Gambling-free states or states with less gambling will have advantages in attracting new businesses and in retaining pre-existing businesses. Strategically speaking, non-gambling states (or minimal-gambling states) will have more vibrant local economies, proportionately more consumer dollars, better sociological environments, more productive jobs, and lower taxes. As of 1992, Utah and Hawaii were the only remaining states without any legalized gambling activities whatsoever—although many states still had very limited legalized gambling activities. Given Hawaii's reliance on a tourist economy, the citizenry of Hawaii probably realized that any legalized gambling activities would severely injure the pre-existing tourist economy. Furthermore, Utah was recognizing and promoting its gambling-free status as an economic plus, and Utah Governor Mike Leavitt emphasized this advantage:

> We're the number one job creation state in the country. We're number two in personal income growth. . . . And there are a lot of people, frankly, that would like to move to a state where there is no gaming, where in fact you can have a safe place, a clean place to live . . . [150]

As other states expand legalized gambling activities, the gambling-free states and those states which minimize gambling activities will increase their competitive advantage in attracting and retaining non-gambling-related businesses.

Similarly, many businesspersons instinctively recognize many of these economic principles. When a land-based casino was projected in New Orleans, local entrepreneurs, including the New Orleans Business Council, actively opposed the casino and the guaranteed effect of legalized gambling facilities on pre-existing consumer dollars and tourist dollars. They feared that a casino would take customers from the native merchants and restaurateurs. Moreover, they failed to see how the Crescent City could benefit by dividing the substantial, existing tourist trade amongst itself. Not surprisingly, many New Orleanians were outraged that a proposed referendum on the casino issue was disallowed.[151]

In future years, businesses will invariably be attracted to non-gambling states, or to those states with less gambling, and their healthier economies with more consumer dollars, better business environments, and lower socio-economic problems. On a relative basis, the consumer dollars in non-gambling states will be less likely to be syphoned into the legalized gambling organizations, which are highly competitive in capturing local "consumer dollars" and transforming them into "gambling dollars."[152] Excepting the instances where a small gambling state lives parasitically off of the economy of a non-gambling state,[153] the corporate, personal, and real estate taxes should be proportionately lower for gambling-free states and states with minimal gambling. In sum, the less there is of legalized gambling, the more vibrant the economy will be.

In the long term, gambling-free states will also have proportionately more economic strength than gambling states. For example, Georgia should immediately revoke its state lottery, because as one of the last non-gambling states, its economy would prosper in comparison with its sister states. The local economies of gambling-free states will always have advantages in warding off recessionary economic trends. By comparison, these economic advantages will be unavailable to the gambling states, and since gambling economies have inherent recessionary trends, future recessions could be proportionately more severe in gambling states.

The legalized gambling interests frequently urge states to enact state lotteries or other forms of legalized gambling, claiming that gambling dollars are being lost to other states or communities. However, this argument that "everybody is doing it" is patently deceptive and inherently invalid as an argument for *anything*. Similarly invalid is the argument by legalized gambling proponents that gambling should be legalized because "it's fun."[154] An associated argument of legalized gambling proponents is that while there may be some more crime and some socio-economic negatives, gambling is going to be legalized so people simply ought to accept it and enjoy it. In other words, the state is going to get assaulted economically, so the state might as well accept it. Obviously, there are regional draws that cross state lines, but what the legalized gambling proponents ultimately fail to mention is that while gambling dollars may be "lost" to other states, so are many of the socio-economic negatives.[155]

When policymakers can avoid myopic fixation on the initial economic flash which the influx of dollars would create in any localized scenario, it readily becomes apparent that legalized gambling activities almost invariably raise taxes, cost jobs, and create large socio-economic problems. Across the spectrum of pre-existing non-gambling businesses, there must necessarily be a growing awareness of the difficulties of competing for those consumer dollars being transformed into gambling dollars[156] when legalized gambling activities enter a state and its communities. In the long term, gambling-free states should experience proportionately fewer personal and business bankruptcies, stronger financial institutions, more vibrant business economies, and better tourist, business, and community environments. All of these fundamentals translate into solid advantages for gambling-free states to attract and retain businesses unassociated with legalized gambling activities. In all, one thing remains certain: before the end of this century, all states and many countries will be faced with establishing and maintaining the parameters of their strategic business and economic environments.

Notes

1. See Better Government Association, Staff White Paper, "Casino Gambling in Chicago," apps. P, Q, and R (1992) [hereinafter Better Gov't Ass'n Report]. Of course, the present analysis deals exclusively with "legalized" or "legal" gambling activities and concomitant propositions, and all references to "gambling" should be interpreted as discussing legal gambling and not illegal gambling activities.
2. Ibid.
3. See generally Robert Goodman, *Legalized Gambling as a Strategy for Economic Development* (Ctr. for Economic Development, U. Mass-Amherst, 1994), pp. 16–19, 51–56.
4. Ibid., pp. 51–56.
5. Better Gov't Ass'n Report, apps. P and Q.
6. Ibid., app. R.
7. See generally Charles T. Clotfelter and Philip J. Cook, *Selling Hope* (1989), pp. 41–48.
8. Ibid., p. 130.
9. Better Gov't Ass'n Report, app. R.
10. See ibid.
11. See, e.g., California Governor's Office of Planning and Research, "California and Nevada: Subsidy, Monopoly, and Competitive Effects of Legalized Gambling" (December 1992), ES-1. ("Gambling by Californians pumps nearly $3.8 billion per year into Nevada, and probably adds about $8.8 billion—and 196,000 jobs—to the Nevada economy, counting the secondary employment it generates. . . . This is a direct transfer of income and wealth from California to Nevada each year.")
12. See Clotfelter and Cook, *Selling Hope,* 92–94 (approximately ten percent of the public gambles sixty-five percent or more of the gambling dollar). From a business-economic perspective, "problem economic gamblers" consist of gamblers who are in the process of becoming problem or probable compulsive gamblers, or who are already compulsive gamblers.

13. Ibid., pp. 124–25. See also Valerie C. Lorenz, *An Overview of Pathological Gambling* (booklet of the National Center for Pathological Gambling, 1990), pp. 2–4.

14. See generally Maryland Department of Health and Mental Hygiene, Alcohol and Drug Abuse Administration, Task Force on Gambling Addiction in Maryland (Valerie C. Lorenz and Robert M. Politzer, co-chairs, 1990) [hereinafter Maryland Report].

15. Indeed, Nevada and Atlantic City thrived thanks to the massive numbers of tourists attracted to these gambling meccas which exercised a practical monopoly on the more thrilling, or "harder," forms of legalized gambling in the United States.

16. See Clotfelter and Cook, *Selling Hope*, pp. 144–51.

17. See, e.g., ibid., pp. 151–58. Of course, the lottery issue was often the subject of rigorous public debate in many states. Ibid.

18. For a discussion of this "thrill factor" or "sensation seeking in gamblers" and a review of the relevant literature, see Kenny Coventry and R. Iain Brown, "Sensation Seeking in Gamblers and Non-gamblers and its Relation to Preference for Gambling Activities, Chasing Arousal and Loss of Control in Regular Gamblers," in *Gambling Behavior and Problem Gambling* (1993), p. 25.

19. Approximately 3.2 to 3.6 cents of each dollar spent on state lotteries is utilized for prizes, advertising and promotional activities [sic]. Clotfelter and Cook, *Selling Hope*, pp. 26–27, 199–202. More advertising expenses are spent in the lottery industry (2 to 2.2 percent) than in any other industry except amusement and recreation (3 percent). Ibid. at p. 200. Lottery states spend approximately $300 million per year on advertising. Goodman, *Legalized Gambling*, p. 14.

20. Clotfelter and Cook, *Selling Hope*, p. 5.

21. Ibid., p. 6.

22. See Illinois Economic and Fiscal Commission, *Wagering in Illinois* (1992), pp. 26–28.

23. Ibid., pp. 51–53 (Act approved February 7, 1990; operations began September 8, 1991, in Alton, Illinois).

24. Illinois State Representative E.J. Giorgi repeatedly supported video-slots/video-machine gambling during 1991–1992. See, e.g., Chuck Sweeny, "Giorgi, Bishop Clash Over Gambling," *Register Star* (Rockford, Illinois), December 12, 1991, p. 1.

25. Edward Walsh, "Chicago May Gamble on Casino Proposal," *Washington Post*, May 24, 1992, p. A-3.

26. For an example of how the process of legalizing gambling gains a momentum of its own, see Jack R. Van Der Slik, "Legalized Gambling: Predatory Policy," *Illinois Issues* (March 1990), p. 30.

27. Clotfelter and Cook, *Selling Hope*, p. 146. The state lottery was approved in 1986 and began operating in 1987.

28. Legalized video-machine gambling had begun on October 1, 1989. A vote to repeal the video-machine gambling was defeated by 62.8 percent to 37.2 percent on November 3, 1992. I. Nelson Rose, "Gambling and the Law: 1992 Elections, Endless Field of Dreams" (1992), p. 1 (unpublished article, on file with author).

A massive public relations campaign by the legalized gambling interests misdirected the voters into believing that repealing video-machine gambling would reduce the number of tax dollars going to education. For examples of how the public has been misled by arguments that legalized gambling will assist education, see Better Gov't Ass'n Report, app. Q; Clotfelter and Cook, *Selling Hope*, pp. 151–53. See also "Daley Seeks Teachers' Support for Casino," *News-Gazette* (Champaign, Illinois), March 29, 1992, p. B-8 (Mayor Daley of Chicago seeking the support of the Illinois Federation of Teachers for a casino complex in Chicago).

29. See, e.g., Todd Nelson, "S.D. Bankruptcies Down 5 Percent, Judge: Gambling Caused Most Cases," *Argus Leader* (Sioux Falls, S.D.), January 15, 1993, p. 1. Not surprisingly, this phenomenon had been predicted. See, e.g., JoDean Joy, Address before the South Dakota Citizens Forum on Video-Lottery Terminals, Sioux Falls, S.D. (October 18, 1992) (a nationally-recognized critic of legalized gambling activities).

30. "S.D. Bankruptcies," p. 1 (emphasis added).

31. It should be noted that the legalization of gambling activities increases the number of compulsive gamblers from .77 percent of the population to 1.5 to 5 percent. See above notes 12–14, and accompanying text.

32. "S.D. Bankruptcies," 1. According to one bankruptcy attorney, this phenomenon was puzzling:

> "I can't put my finger on why there were fewer filings," Blake said.
>
> "I consulted with a lot of people about bankruptcy that apparently didn't follow through. . . . It always mystified me when somebody comes in with $40,000 of debt and you don't see them again.
>
> Blake agreed that gambling is an increasing cause of bankruptcy.
>
> "I see people every month who tell me that it was because of video lottery," he said. "I see cases where people essentially gamble away $40,000 or $50,000 over a couple of years. Sometimes it's $5,000 to $10,000." (Ibid.)

It has been estimated that most compulsive gamblers tend to admit only approximately one-third of their actual debt due to gambling. Letter from Ms. Elizabeth George, Executive Director, Minnesota Council on Compulsive Gambling (December 21, 1992) (on file with author). In addition, the national statistics indicate the average debt of the "bottomed-out" compulsive gambler is conservatively estimated between $75,000 and $80,000. Maryland Report, pp. 60–61.

33. Minnesota Planning Office, *High Stakes: Gambling in Minnesota* (1992), p. 29.

34. Sponsors spent $5 million to promote a $2 billion proposal for a casino complex in Chicago. Patrick T. Reardon and Rick Pearson, "Casino Firms Say Patience Tapped Out," *Chicago Tribune*, December 4, 1992, pp. 2-7.

35. See, e.g., Illinois Gaming Board, *Annual Report and Wagering Study 1991* (1992), pp. 10–11. This governmental study basically accepts in toto the arguments of the riverboat interests and ignores the overall welfare of the Illinois public. Ibid., pp. 9–11. See Better Gov't Ass'n Report, app. Q, pp. 23–25 (internal public relations report "leaked" to the public, delimiting "'The Mob' as Businessmen").

36. See generally, Better Gov't Ass'n Report, app. Q; Goodman, *Legalized Gambling*.
37. Experts say the current recession causes people to gamble more, not less. As the economy sours, studies show, people look for quick solutions to their woes—especially the poor, who are hardest hit in bad times.

> "When economic times turn down, there will always be a segment of society that tends to try to hit a big score because the legitimate means for upward mobility have been reduced," says H. Roy Kaplan, sociologist and author of the 1978 book *Lottery Winners*. (Susan M. Barbieri, "'The Addiction of the '90s': Compulsive Gambling Comes into its Own in Recessionary Times," *Washington Post*, November 30, 1992, p. D-5.)

38. See, e.g., Howard Fineman, "The Torch Passes," *Newsweek* (November/December 1992), pp. 4, 6.
39. For specialized discussions of the evolution of legalized gambling activities in Atlantic City, New Jersey, see George Sternlieb and James W. Hughes, *The Atlantic City Gambler* (1983); Hawkins, "The Atlantic City Experience: Casino Gambling as an Economic Recovery Program," *Seton Hall Legis. J.* 6 (1982), p. 85; Kimberly J. Warker, *Casino Gambling as Urban Redevelopment: A Case Study of the Political Economy of Atlantic City, New Jersey* (1988).
40. New Jersey Governor's Advisory Commission on Gambling, *Report and Recommendations* (1988), p. 5 (emphasis added).
41. Ibid., p. 16.
42. Goodman, *Legalized Gambling*, p. 16.
43. See, e.g., Better Gov't Ass'n Report, apps. P, Q, and R (internal "leaked" planning documents of the legalized gambling industry).
44. See notes 12–14 above, and accompanying text. As one business source reported:

> "It will be impossible not to make a lot of money," one executive in New Orleans bragged before his casino had even opened. "It's like spitting and missing the floor." (James Popkin and Katia Hetter, "America's Gambling Craze," *U.S. News and World Report*, March 14, 1994, pp. 42, 43.)

45. See ibid. The efforts in New Orleans were substantially successful. In the form of a "compromise," Louisiana Governor Edwin Edwards signed a bill on June 18, 1992, authorizing but a single casino, although the legislation left open the possibility of future additional casinos. Rita Koselka, "Fantasyland," *Forbes*, March 1, 1993, p. 62.

The estimated increased costs of this casino to the New Orleans criminal justice system were estimated at $10.4 million per year for police and corrections costs, $2.3 million per year for attorney's fees, and $1.5 million for court costs. Illinois State Police, Division of Criminal Investigation, Intelligence Bureau, *How Casino Gambling Affects Law Enforcement* (April 16, 1992) [hereinafter Illinois State Police]; Terrance W. Gainor, Director of the Illinois State Police, Address before Annual IAODAPCA Luncheon, May 8, 1992, pp. 9–10 (transcript on file with author).
46. In Louisiana's case, this concern may have been reflected in the initial approval of but a single casino for New Orleans, because the population base could have

sustained more than one.

47. The pre-existing consumer base provides substantial dollars to legalized gambling activities upon their initiation—regardless of any inputs by tourists. See, e.g., Goodman, *Legalized Gambling*, pp. 51–56.

48. This factor also explains why gambling organizations are adamant about seeking and getting five-year tax waivers for the first five years of operation. See, e.g., Melissa Merlie, "Betting Parlor Operator Ties Danville Location to Tax Rebate," *News-Gazette* (Champaign, Illinois), August 2, 1990, pp. A-1, A-10.

49. James Coates, "Vegas' Tip to Chicago: Casino is Family Fun," *Chicago Tribune*, April 10, 1992, pp. 1, 10.

50. Ray Long, "$100 Million in Riverboat Stock Sold," *Chicago Sun-Times*, February 19, 1993, p. 13. Critics wondered about megaprofits for investors, considering that much of the riverboat stock was allegedly purchased for approximately one cent per share by the initial investors and that within two years the stock was being sold at between $19.25 and $21.50 per share. No illegality, however, was alleged. Floyd Norris, "Insiders Didn't Take Much of a Gamble with Argosy Gaming," *New York Times*, February 25, 1993, p. D-10.

51. Alf Siewers, "2 Reports Reveal Casino Strategy," *Chicago Sun-Times*, August 7, 1992, p. 14. See also Better Gov't Ass'n Report, apps. P, Q, and R (internal public relations documents "leaked" from the office of legalized gambling interests).

52. For a specific example of the importance of the tourist factor, see Better Gov't Ass'n Report, pp. 46–48.

53. See Goodman, *Legalized Gambling*, pp. 51–56.

54. See Illinois State Police, *How Casino Gambling Affects Law Enforcement*, p. 9.

55. For a review of fourteen studies analyzing the costs and benefits of various legalized gambling proposals, see Goodman, *Legalized Gambling*. Only one of these studies was considered "balanced," and most were criticized for "hiding the costs." Ibid., p. 16.

56. See Clotfelter and Cook, *Selling Hope*, pp. 96–104.

57. Ibid., p. 99.

58. Ibid., pp. 96, 98–100.

59. Ibid., pp. 96–98. See also *Congressional Record* 138, daily ed. January 22, 1992, p. S187 (statement of Sen. Simon) ("If you go into the *poorest section* of Chicago or East St. Louis, you will see people lined up to buy lottery tickets. . . . [W]e have to find way[s] of raising revenue that do not impose on the weakest and poorest in our society." (emphasis added)).

60. See Clotfelter and Cook, *Selling Hope*, pp. 104–06.

61. Ibid., pp. 99, 132–35.

62. Ibid., p. 96.

63. Ibid., p. 98.

64. Ibid., pp. 98–100. "[T]he prospect of households earning less than $10,000 per year averaging $550 per year on gambling, for example, as studies have shown for lotteries, is sickening to contemplate." Earl L. Grinols, "Analysis of the Major Impacts

of Off-Track Gambling in Champaign, Illinois" (September 23, 1991) (unpublished report, on file with the author), citing Clotfelter and Cook, *Selling Hope*, p. 99.

65. See Clotfelter and Cook, *Selling Hope*, pp. 99–100.

66. See, e.g., Better Gov't Ass'n Report, pp. 64–68. See also ibid., pp. 56–69, app. M.

67. See generally Andrew J. Buck et al., "Casinos, Crime, and Real Estate Values: Do They Relate?" *Journal of Research in Crime and Delinquency* 28 (1991), pp. 301–02; Simon Hakim and Andrew J. Buck, "Do Casinos Enhance Crime?" *Journal of Criminal Justice* 17 (1989), 409, 414–15.

68. See Buck et al., "Casinos, Crime, and Real Estate Values," pp. 301–02; Hakim and Buck, "Do Casinos Enhance Crime?" pp. 414–15.

69. Buck et al., "Casinos, Crime, and Real Estate Values," p. 289.

70. Ibid.

71. See, e.g., Goodman, *Legalizing Gambling*, and below.

72. Buck et al., "Casinos, Crime, and Real Estate Values," p. 302.

73. For explanations of this concept in the context of the McDougal/Lasswell decision-making model as applied to corporate development of national and international resources, see John W. Kindt, *Marine Pollution and the Law of the Sea* 1 (1992), pp. 11–17; John W. Kindt, "Prolegomenon to Marine Pollution and the Law of the Sea," *Environmental Law* 11 (1980), pp. 67, 70–72.

74. See, e.g., John W. Kindt, "The New Assault on Freedom of Thought: Section 263A of the Internal Revenue Code," *St. Louis U. L.J.* 33 (1988), p. 137.

75. See, e.g., Tom Schlesinger, "A Taxpayers' Program for Cleaning Up the S&L Mess," *USA Today* (September 1991), p. 22.

76. Steven V. Roberts et al., "California Crumbling," *U.S. News and World Report* (September 14, 1992), p. 69. See also Michael Meyer, "In a State of Collapse," *Newsweek* (August 17, 1992), p. 37.

77. See Mary A. Laschober, "The Link Between Current Tax Receipts and the Illinois Budget Crisis," *Illinois Business Review* (Fall 1991), pp. 8, 9.

78. See, e.g., H. Campbell Stuckeman, "Community Evaluation in Site Selection," in *Industrial Facilities Planning*, ed. H.M. Conway and Linda L. Liston (1976), pp. 97, 99.

79. See notes 100–105, below, and accompanying text.

80. Stuckeman, "Community Evaluation in Site Selection," p. 99 (the "state business climate"). "Are the state legislative, executive and judiciary branches performing as well as other state governments?" Ibid. This category constitutes one of the criteria in the site selection process for businesses.

81. For historical background and an introduction to business-related decision making in general, see Friedrich Rosenkranz, *An Introduction to Corporate Modeling* (1979). See generally, Jon E. Browning, *How to Select a Business Site* (1980); *Industrial Facilities Planning*, ed. H.M. Conway and Linda L. Liston (1976); William N. Kinnard and Stephen D. Messner, *Effective Business Relocation* (1970); Roger W. Schmenner, *Making Business Location Decisions* (1982); David M. Smith, *Industrial Location* (2d ed. 1981); John S. Thompson, *Site Selection* (1982); Alfred Weber, *Theory of the Location*

of Industries, trans. Carl J. Friedrich (1937).

82. See, e.g., Thompson, *Site Selection*, p. 167 (store location research for single stores), p. 197 (simplified guide to store location research).

83. For examples of the starting points for the business location models including the variable-cost model and operational models, see generally Smith, *Industrial Location*, pp. 149–313.

84. For general examples of business location analyses involving the Fortune 500, see Schmenner, *Making Business Location Decisions*, p. 60 and following.

85. For a summary of various theories of business location within the framework of spatial economic analysis, see Smith, *Industrial Location*, pp. 68–107. See also Weber, *Theory of the Location of Industries*.

86. Businesses express a need for confidentiality in various aspects of the decision-making process involving businesses location issues. For example, a company may "send several teams at different times to anonymously inspect each community." Stuckeman, "Community Evaluation in Site Selection," p. 97.

87. For examples of business location information of interest to state policymakers, see Kinnard and Messner, *Effective Business Relocation*, pp. 32–34 (public awareness and involvement); Smith, *Industrial Location*, p. 63 (public policy, planning, and the state) and pp. 359–92 (industrial location, development planning, and social well-being). See generally Browning, *How to Select a Business Site*, pp. 31–48.

88. For examples of starting points for formulating business location models, see note 81, above, and accompanying text.

89. See generally ibid.

90. See, e.g., Smith, *Industrial Location*, p. 149 and following.

91. For an introduction to the historical business decision-making models in general and their complexities, see Rosenkranz, *An Introduction to Corporate Modeling*. For a historical perspective on planning systems in the context of business decision-making, see James B. Boulden, *Computer-Assisted Planning Systems* (1975).

92. Perhaps "the most important qualification of all" is "community attitude" as part of the business environment. Stuckeman, "Community Evaluation in Site Selection," p. 99. "Community" and "Government Aspects" constitute "Major Factors that Shape Plant Location Searches." Schmenner, *Making Business Location Decisions*, p. 33. For examples of checklists involving the community business climate, see Browning, *How to Select a Business Site*, pp. 108–11, 125–28. The origins of this consideration are apparently found in "social and cultural" location dynamics. See, e.g., Weber, *Theory of the Location of Industries*, pp. 21–22. In current analyses, businesses are often encouraged to "hand-pick" their business community environments. See, e.g., Browning, *How to Select a Business Site*, pp. 87–114. In a juxtaposition of issues in this area, some traditional business ventures, such as retail liquor stores, carry the image of imposing various sorts of "negative environmental impacts" on the community and these businesses must accommodate community concerns before entering a chosen community. See, e.g., Kinnard and Messner, *Effective Business Relocation*, pp. 60–62.

93. See, e.g., Browning, *How to Select a Business Site*, p. 164 (checklist of "Police Aspects"); Conway and Liston, *Industrial Facilities Planning*, pp. 303–04 (civil disorders), p. 308 (crime); Stuckeman, "Community Evaluation in Site Selection," p. 99. For examples of analyses demonstrating the interface between crime and some business-economic issues in the area of legalized gambling, see Buck et al., "Casinos, Crime, and Real Estate Values," p. 288; Hakim and Buck, "Do Casinos Enhance Crime?" p. 409. Various impacts are incorporated under the general rubric of "crime."

94. For an example of a practical application of crime (specifically, robbery) as factored into "quality of life" considerations in business location decisions, see John M. Griffin and Norbert Dee, "Measuring the Intangible: How to Quantify Quality of Life," in Conway and Liston, *Industrial Facilities Planning*, pp. 219, 220–21.

95. For examples of various "pitfalls" to be considered in business location models, see Browning, *How to Select a Business Site*, pp. 205–211.

96. Ibid. Historical trends provide support for these propositions.

> During the first six years of the 1970s, seventy-three (almost 15 percent) of the Fortune-500 companies moved their headquarters. The most frequent reason was the decline of the cities. High crime rates, dirty streets, and the fact that increasing numbers of young executives offered a job at headquarters refused it have also contributed. (Ibid., p. 10.)

> Business location models delimit a *"[p]rimary concern for the quality of life in an area."* Schmenner, *Making Business Location Decisions*, p. 38 (emphasis in original).

97. The final question for the business location decision maker is often: "If the company transferred me to this location, would I want to move my family here?" Browning, *How to Select a Business Site*, p. 210.

98. See, e.g., Buck et al., "Casinos, Crime, and Real Estate Values," p. 409.

> For a summary of the socio-economic concerns associated with legalized gambling activities as they interface with the criminal justice system, see Frank Kelley, Michigan Attorney General, Address before the International Conference on Gambling, Nashville, Tenn. (February 11, 1994) ("I have been Michigan's Attorney General for more than thirty years, and there has never been an issue that has disturbed me any more than the proliferation of gambling in our state.") [hereinafter Michigan Att'y Gen.].

99. As a general observation in a related issue area involving business location decisions, "[m]any business activities are regarded as 'unsuitable neighbors] both for residences and for other types of more 'desirable' business activity." Kinnard and Messner, *Effective Business Relocation*, p. 61.

100. Timothy P. Ryan et al., "The Impact of Casino Gambling in New Orleans" (Division of Business and Economic Research, University of New Orleans, 1990).

101. This survey was undertaken by the economic development firm of Cushman and Wakefield, utilizing the polling firm of Louis Harris and Associates, Inc.

102. Ryan, "The Impact of Casino Gambling," p. 30.

103. Ibid., pp. 30–31.

104. Ibid., p. 32.

105. Ibid.

106. Walsh, "Chicago May Gamble," p. 3.

107. Ibid.

108. See generally, Chris Reidy, "Gambling Has Become the Nice Vice," *Boston Globe*, January 17, 1993, pp. 69, 71 ("The word gambling makes . . . [employees of legalized gambling organizations] uncomfortable. . . . In an era when casinos are designed with water slides and Disney-style theme parks, . . . [they prefer] such terms as 'gaming' and 'family entertainment.'").

109. John Kass and Rick Pearson, "Daley Folds Casino Hand," *Chicago Tribune*, January 8, 1993, pp. 1-1, 1-18. "[Mayor] Daley had sought the legislature's approval of the casino project last year without first discussing the idea with [Governor] Edgar, who is opposed to casino gambling in the city." Ibid., p. 1.

110. For an outline of the proposal to bring legalized riverboat gambling to Virginia, see Robert W. Cook, "Economic and Fiscal Impact of Riverboat Gaming in Virginia" (November 1993) (prepared for the Virginia Riverboat Council, calculating that seven riverboats would create $123 million in tax revenues, 7,000 direct jobs, and 17,000 indirect jobs). For a critique of this report, see Wayne K. Talley, "An Analysis of Economic and Fiscal Impact of Riverboat Gaming in Virginia" (February 1994) (prepared for the Assembly Group, concluding that seven riverboats would create only $10 million in tax revenues and 2,766 net jobs) (available from Prof. Wayne K. Talley, Old Dominion University, Norfolk, Va.). The large differences in these numbers indicate the typical parameters of the economic debate. Professor Talley's analysis was significantly more realistic and highlighted the problem of double counting which apparently occurred in the earlier analysis.

111. In any event, Virginia had considerably fewer legalized gambling activities than Illinois, which already had nine or ten riverboats, as well as off-track betting parlors in 1993. Virginia did, however, have the lottery, which was initiated in 1988. Clotfelter and Cook, *Selling Hope*, pp. 156–58 (referendum passed November 4, 1987). Presumably, the initial business location investigation would have begun years before Disney's public announcement in 1993.

112. Liz Spayd and Yolanda Woodlee, "Trade Board Rejects D.C. Casino Plan," *Washington Post*, September 25, 1993, p. A-1.

113. Ibid., p. 1 (emphasis added).

114. Ibid., pp. 1, 8.

115. I. Nelson Rose, "The Rise and Fall of the Third Wave: Gambling Will Be Outlawed in Forty Years," in *Gambling and Public Policy: International Perspectives*, ed. William R. Eadington and Judy A. Cornelius (1991), pp. 65, 72 (emphasis in original).

116. Ibid., p. 72.

117. See, e.g., "Euro Disney's Wish Comes True," *The Economist* (March 19, 1994), p. 83; "Meltdown at the Cultural Chernobyl," *The Economist* (February 5, 1994), p. 65.

118. Walsh, "Chicago May Gamble on Casino Proposal," p. 3 ("The dispute also has an emotional edge dealing with self-image. . . . 'If we become the gambling center of the Midwest,' [Chicago Alderman Lawrence] Bloom said, 'that's what we're going to be known as, and that's not what Chicago is.'").

119. See Spayd and Woodlee, "Trade Board Rejects D.C. Casino Plan," p. 1.

120. Ibid.

121. Michigan Att'y Gen., p. 4.

122. See, e.g., Buck et al., "Casinos, Crime, and Real Estate Values," pp. 301–02; Hakim and Buck, "Do Casinos Enhance Crime?" pp. 414–15.

123. See Rose, "The Rise and Fall of the Third Wave," p. 74.

124. An exception, however, is a small state, such as Nevada, living parasitically off of a larger state, such as California. California Governor's Office of Planning and Research, "California and Nevada," ES-1; California Governor's Office of Planning and Research, "Office of Planning and Research Releases Study of the Economic Relationship Between California and Nevada as it Relates to Legalized Gambling," December 17, 1992, pp. 1–2.

125. Marguerite T. Smith and Debra Wishik Englander, "The Best Places to Live in America," *Money* (September 1992), p. 110.

126. See also John W. Kindt, Address before the South Dakota Citizens Forum on Video-Lottery Terminals, Sioux Falls, S.D. (October 18, 1992).

127. Richard Eisenberg and Debra Wishik Englander, "The Best Places to Live in America," *Money* (August 1988), p. 83.

128. California Governor's Office of Planning and Research, "California and Nevada," ES-1, ES-4.

129. Ibid., ES-1; California Governor's Office of Planning and Research, "Office of Planning and Research Releases Study," p. 1.

130. California Governor's Office of Planning and Research, "California and Nevada," ES-1; California Governor's Office of Planning and Research, "Office of Planning and Research Releases Study," p. 1.

131. California Governor's Office of Planning and Research, "California and Nevada," ES-1.

132. Ibid.; California Governor's Office of Planning and Research, "Office of Planning and Research Releases Study," p. 1.

133. See generally U.S. Commission on the Review of the National Policy Toward Gambling, *Gambling in America* (1976), p. 73 [hereinafter U.S. Commission on Gambling].

134. See Rachel A. Volberg, "Estimating the Prevalence of Pathological Gambling in the United States," in *Gambling Behavior and Problem Gambling*, ed. W.R. Eadington (1992); Rachel A. Volberg and Henry J. Steadman, "Prevalence Estimates of Pathological Gambling in New Jersey and Maryland," *American Journal of Psychiatry* 146 (1989), p. 1618; Rachel A. Volberg and Henry J. Steadman, "Refining Prevalence Estimates of Pathological Gambling," *American Journal of Psychiatry* 145 (1988), p. 502;

Alberta Lotteries and Gaming, *Gambling and Problem Gambling in Alberta* (January 1994), p. 18 (summarizing twenty studies showing prevalence rates of problem and pathological gambling among the adult population of several states.

135. See Clotfelter and Cook, *Selling Hope*, pp. 92–94.

136. Nelson, "South Dakota Bankruptcies," 1 ("Ten percent of the clients who . . . went to the Consumer Credit Counseling Services of Lutheran Social Services of Sioux Falls openly admit[ted] that gambling underlies their financial problems . . .").

137. Maryland Report, p. 59; see ibid., pp. 59–61.

138. Robert M. Politzer et al., *Report on the Societal Cost of Pathological Gambling and the Cost-Benefit Effectiveness of Treatment* (1981), p. 9; Better Gov't Ass'n Report, p. 14.

139. Gerry T. Fulcher, "The Dark Side of a Trip to the Track," *Industry Week* (August 5, 1991), p. 13 ("85% of the thousands of identified compulsive gamblers admit to stealing from their employers, given the opportunity").

140. Ibid.

141. Perhaps the most interesting connection is that Type-A personalities—the very best blue-collar workers, the most productive white-collar workers, and the aggressive entrepreneurial managers—all fall within psychological profiles most susceptible to becoming problem gamblers. See Maryland Report, pp. 20–34.

142. American Psychiatric Association, *Diagnostic and Statistical Manual of Mental Disorders* (rev. 3d ed., 1987), § 312.31.

143. Some estimates are as low as $5,000 to $10,000 for out-patients, but $20,000 is a more reasonable number. Better Gov't Ass'n Report, p. 12.

144. In-patient care for compulsive gamblers ranges from $17,000 to $20,000 per month at the Compulsive Gambling Center, Inc., in Baltimore, Maryland, to between $15,000 and $42,000 per month at other facilities, such as the Philadelphia Psychiatric Hospital. Interview with Dr. Valerie C. Lorenz, Executive Director, Compulsive Gambling Center, Inc., Baltimore, Md. (November 10, 1992).

145. U.S. Commission on Gambling, *Gambling in America*, p. 73.

146. See notes 143 and 144 above, and accompanying text.

147. See Politzer et al., *Report on the Societal Cost of Pathological Gambling*, p. 9.

148. United Airlines settled in Indiana, and Spiegel located in Ohio. These companies undoubtedly utilized many factors in determining where to locate, and the Champaign gambling controversies may have been minor. For public relations reasons, however, no company would give precise reasons for choosing one community over another, and upper management might not have even realized the full extent of the direct and indirect gambling "red flags" which are inherent in most business location models and which may have been reflected in their specialized models. Concessions promised by the other sites might also have been the determining factors.

149. Public concerns involving alleged misinformation by the legalized gambling interests, as sometimes abetted by the media, was exemplified by the following letter, which is reprinted *in toto*:

To the editor:

On June 30, [1990] the Ministers Alliance, representing eight black congregations, came out against off-track betting facilities [OTBs] in the Champaign area.

The people of Champaign should ask themselves why most of the news organizations chose not to report or to downplay this obviously newsworthy story.

While WICD television reported this event on June 30 (and while WCIA did not), The News-Gazette has never mentioned this fact although The News-Gazette published stories on off-track betting on July 2, 4, 5, 6 (two articles) and July 7 (an article plus the "Week in Quotes").

Obviously, several opportunities to report or mention this development in the black community were ignored. Perhaps this should not be a surprise, since The News-Gazette's lack of objectivity and blatant favoritism encouraging a betting parlor for Champaign was apparent in most of these articles—but particularly in a full front-page article, with a color photograph, in the June 24 edition of the paper.

The public would prefer objective news, instead of editorial opinion and Mayor Dannel McCollum's propaganda disguised as news. (Letter to the Editor from Diane E. Pierce, *News-Gazette* (Champaign, Illinois), July 27, 1990, p. A-4.)

The public opposition to the OTBs was apparently extensive and vigorous. See, e.g., Letter to the Editor for J.E. Miller, *News-Gazette* (Champaign, Illinois), July 13, 1990, p. A-4 (indicating opposition to the OTBs from "at least 15 organizations"); Letter to the Editor from Connie Morenz, *News-Gazette* (Champaign, Illinois), July 23, 1990, p. A-4 (indicating opposition to the OTBs "from over two dozen civic and religious organizations" plus "eight ministers in the Ministers Alliance, representing the black community"); Letter to the Editor from Rev. Don Ehlers, *News-Gazette* (Champaign, Illinois), July 24, 1990, p. A-4 (indicating "[a] sizeable number of individuals from the community, especially from west Champaign, did oppose the location of an OTB in the city").

The OTB company's application first received general press exposure on May 30, 1990, but the application to the Illinois Racing Board was scheduled for action on June 12, 1990. Potential opponents had only eight working days to voice their opposition and had to travel over 130 miles to the hearing. See J. Philip Bloomer, "Nursery School Location Could Keep Betting Parlor Out," *News-Gazette* (Champaign, Illinois), June 9, 1990, pp. A-1, A-12; Letter to the Editor from Philip Miller, *News-Gazette* (Champaign, Illinois), June 16, 1990, p. A-4 (complaining about the "fast-track" procedures). Under the Illinois Open Meetings Act, all meetings of public bodies are required to "be held at specific times and places which are convenient to the public." *Illinois Rev. Stat.*, ch. 102, ¶ 42.01. As per this statute, or perhaps because of the public outcry, the Board's meeting was postponed. See Bloomer, "Nursery School Location," p. 1. See generally Kathleen Cardella, "Paperwork, Short Notice Help Stifle OTB Opposition," *News-Gazette* (Champaign, Illinois), October 10, 1991, p. B-2. These "political actions have stifled public access to pertinent information regarding the license applications decisions that the public is entitled to know." Cardella, "Paperwork," p. B-3.

> Along with these alarming changes, the Champaign and Danville off-track betting scenarios have highlighted the swift speed with which the Illinois Racing Board can approve an off-track betting license application. It requires no action on the part of local government and possibly can be approved without public support. . . . . Both the Champaign and Danville application processes underscore the short time frame that the public has to learn about this complex political issue and voice its concerns. It also demonstrates that public input is not always considered when approving off-track betting parlors.
>
> Unless there are changes in state law, other communities will be forced to act quickly to prevent the establishment of off-track betting parlors in their community. (Cardella, "Paperwork," p. B-3.)

150. *This Week with David Brinkley* (ABC television broadcast, March 20, 1994) (statement of Utah Governor Mike Leavitt).

151. Koselka, "Fantasyland," p. 63.

152. See generally Goodman, *Legalized Gambling*. See also William R. Eadington, "Economic Perceptions of Gambling Behavior," *Journal of Gambling Behavior* 3 (1987), p. 264.

153. See notes 128–132 above, and accompanying text.

154. See, e.g., *Illinois Journal* (WCIA-Channel 3 [Champaign-Springfield, Illinois] television broadcast, June 6 and 7, 1992) (interview with John Giovenco, President of the Gaming Division for Hilton Hotels Corp.). This argument is seductive because it suggests that public opinion is one the side of legalized gambling, when in fact it is rarely so when valid arguments are presented in a timely manner.

155. The rare exception to this scenario is exemplified by Las Vegas whose large tourist base means that the socio-economic problems associated with compulsive gambling are largely "exported" when the tourists return to their home states. The general rule is that states which legalize gambling and make it convenient to gamble are creating and retaining socio-economic negatives. These factors are widely recognized as the "acceptability factor" and the "accessibility factor."

156. See note 152 above, and accompanying text.

12. Prohibition of Gambling Is Costly and Does Not Achieve Its Intended Benefits

Reuven Brenner

Reuven Brenner, an economist at McGill University in Canada, maintains that gambling does not cause poverty or lower productivity. Rather, poor people and people whose economic situations are deteriorating, according to Brenner, tend to be attracted to lotteries and other forms of gambling. In fact, he maintains that lotteries and other games of chance are among the few items whose sale may increase during recessions.

Brenner rejects the proposition that lotteries should be outlawed because poor people disproportionately participate in them. He responds that it is mostly the poor and those in deteriorating financial conditions who tend to win lotteries, so that the money put into lotteries is principally distributed among the relatively poor.

He also rejects the argument that public lotteries should be avoided or banned because of the high cost of administering them. For he holds that public lotteries do more than generate public revenue: they also, according to him, provide an additional service to buyers by sustaining people's hope for a better future during harsh times. What's more, Brenner contends that prohibiting all lotteries would impose a large cost on government, as when government must pay the costs of enforcing anti-gambling laws. Still further, he argues that

---

This appeared as "Governments, Taxation, and the Impact of Prohibitions," in Reuven Brenner, with Gabrielle A. Brenner, *Gambling and Speculation: A Theory, a History, and a Future of Some Human Decisions* (Cambridge: Cambridge University Press, 1990), pp. 113–132, 143–49. Used by permission.

gambling prohibitions don't encourage gamblers to spend their money on other goods and services but rather simply criminalize gambling that will continue regardless of the prohibitions.

Nor would prohibiting gambling reduce crime, asserts Brenner: "Even if one does not label gamblers criminals, which would automatically increase the crime rate, the acts of illegal organizations that take over the gambling sector and enforce illegal gambling contracts increase the crime rate." Should the government spend more on enforcement while losing revenues from gambling, it would, he concludes, have either to raise taxes or to reduce its expenditures.

Brenner claims that decriminalizing private sector lotteries will not only reduce the power of organized crime but also help sustain hope for poor people. To help compulsive gamblers, he advocates allotting a small fraction of tax revenues obtained from legal gambling to treat compulsive gamblers.

Widespread legalization of lotteries and other games of chance in recent times is not just a sign that some government officials and other people recognize the fact that previous prohibitions were wrong-headed, that gambling is not a cause of either poverty or diminished productivity, and that the poor have a right both to choose their recreations and spend their money the way they want. It also reflects a need to finance sudden increases in government expenditures.

Government officials correctly perceived that there was an unexploited opportunity to raise money by legalizing gambling. There was clearly latent demand for games of chance; people gambled illegally, and the revenues from such illegal expenditures were untaxed; and enforcing prohibition involved expenditure. As a result, some governments decided to venture into the business while maintaining monopoly power, realizing that they could obtain the highest revenues by banning the sale of substitutes.

But it would be a mistake to conclude that unexpected increases in government expenditures or deficits in state budgets have *necessarily* led to the legalization of lotteries and other games of chance. Although the potential for raising revenues by this method was recognized, decisions were frequently made to maintain the ban. In England, in spite of the Treasury's interest since the 1920s in imposing a gambling tax and in suggestions concerning the state control of gambling and sale of lotteries, all proposals were rejected until the 1960s. And, as we have seen, similar decisions were made during the depression of the 1930s in the United States.[1] What had changed when some games of chance were legalized was not only that governments' expenditures suddenly increased and that the alternatives of raising taxes or of lowering expenditures seemed unfeasible, but also that views of what causes poverty and what the remedies are had significantly changed, that religious convictions had weakened, and that attributing a significant role to gambling in determining the productivity of workers had all but disappeared. At the same time the desire to gamble did not diminish. Movements up and down the social ladder continued and not only fueled the desire to advance, but were also behind the weakening of customs, of traditional ways of thinking, and of the conviction that luck, and not only ingenuity and hard work, determines whether or not one will strike it rich.

Although some of the old influential views about the detrimental effects of gambling have thus been discarded, new ones condemning gambling on other grounds have been invented. These newer views concentrate on the relationship among governments, taxation, crime, and games of chance. Whether they are erroneous or not will be examined in this chapter.

Revenues from Lotteries
Are Countercyclical

But first let us take a glance at the magnitude of the sums we are talking about and whether or not there is regularity in revenues from lotteries when they are legally permitted and no changes in the law occur. In England between the years 1802 and 1826, net revenues from lotteries represented between 0.3 and 1 percent of the government's net revenues (the gross share being between 1 and 2 percent).[2] In France between 1815 and 1828, net revenues hovered around 1 percent of the government's total receipts. More recently, in the United States between the years 1978 and 1983, net revenues from lotteries, as a percent of the respective state's general revenues, were between 3.7 and 5 percent in Maryland, 2 percent in Connecticut, and 1.5 percent in Massachusetts.[3]

As for a pattern in revenues from their sales, the evidence . . . leads one to expect that revenues from lotteries should be countercyclical; that is, increase during recession and turbulent periods and diminish during stable and good times. For during recessions people become suddenly unemployed, and frustrated expectations become the rule rather than the exception. In such circumstances, as we have seen, people are more likely to gamble; implicitly, both the statistical evidence presented in Chapter 2 [of the Brenners' book] and the more qualitative evidence presented later seem to confirm this statement.[4] It may be useful to emphasize the implications of this correlation for pragmatic reasons.

It is during recessions that governments experience relatively high expenditures because of commitments made when better times were expected, combined with suddenly diminished revenues, and face difficult choices. Imposing additional taxes, increasing debt, and revising previous commitments—none of these are very attractive. Lotteries and other games of chance are among the few items whose sales may rise during recessions, thus providing revenues for governments. Increased willingness to spend on games of chance also provides opportunities for entrepreneurs and for employment. Banning this sector not only makes the potential buyers, those already falling behind and the poor, even unhappier, but it also gives incentives to illegal entrepreneurship, thus cutting governments off from additional revenues. Moreover, the governments' expenditures must even rise, since law enforcement costs money. But, as can be inferred from the arguments presented earlier, there is more hiding behind the apparently simple recommendation "let your people gamble" (honestly, of course) than just the consideration of creating employment.[5] The question should be viewed in a much broader context: a policy that favors change and facilitates adjustment to it.

Condemnation of Lotteries as Regressive Taxation Is Wrong

Many social scientists condemn the government's monopoly of the sale of lotteries today on grounds of some vague and totally wrong new arguments. Lotteries are condemned because revenues from their sale are viewed as a form of regressive taxation; that is, on the ground that the poorer are spending a greater percentage of their wealth on lotteries than the relatively rich.

Why is condemnation on these grounds wrong? By examining facets of this question and discussing the evidence, we shall gain a still better understanding of the confusion that continues to surround the issue of games of chance in general and that of lotteries in particular.

The foundations of the traditional theory that perceives regressivity as bad, as diminishing happiness in a society, are so weak that they are hardly worth criticizing.[6] One of the assumptions behind it is that if the government redistributes wealth and achieves greater equality, this intervention could make society happier, since the unhappiness of the richer, from whom wealth is taken away, is more than compensated for by the additional happiness of the poor, who get the money.[7] How comparisons of people's happiness can be made, and who is making them in society and why, is not made clear within this framework. However, in order to reach the preceding conclusion, an additional assumption is made: that everybody in society is the same; that is, that from equal amounts of wealth people derive equal satisfaction. Wealth, and nothing else, matters.[8]

Condemning lotteries on the basis of this theory is wrong for additional reasons. It is true, as we have seen, that mainly the poor, the frustrated, and those falling or fearing to fall behind buy lottery tickets. But then, it is this group too who get the prizes, which represent 40 to 77 percent of the total receipts (the most frequent number is 60 percent).[9] Thus wealth in this case is mainly redistributed *among the relatively poor*, some of whom thus achieve, thanks to the prizes, a standard of living that welfare payments, no matter how generous, can never provide. The usual arguments about regressivity, even if they were right (as they are not), do not apply at all to the sale of lotteries.[10]

Other critics of the states' monopoly of the sale of lotteries have argued that raising income taxes by a small percentage can generate the same revenues as the sale of lotteries, and they point to the relatively high collection costs of taxation through lotteries. But this argument for condemning lotteries is wrong too, and for a number of reasons. First, comparing collection costs is valid only if one assumes that the only role of lotteries is that of providing revenues. Once the lottery is looked upon as providing an additional *service* to the buyers (since the private sector is not allowed to offer it)—and we have seen that it does, sustaining people's hopes for a better future during harsh times—the rationale for comparing the operating costs of lotteries with the cost of generating revenues by other forms of taxation disappears.[11] Second, the implicit assumption of the critics, which is that raising some taxes when lotteries are banned would leave other things unchanged, is erroneous. Prohibition imposes a large cost on governments and society with some long-term consequences that in turn are costly to correct; some of them will be examined later in this chapter.

Opposition to State Lotteries Implies Free Competition or Prohibition

If brought to its logical conclusion, the view that the state's sale of lotteries is bad leads to two courses of action: allowing competition or prohibiting their sale.

If it is the first option—permitting competition—that critics of the state's monopoly of the sale of lotteries have in mind, some questions must be raised. Is the fact that the poor are spending a relatively greater percentage of their wealth on lotteries under criticism? Or is the criticism that expenditures on lotteries are taxed because of the government's monopoly?

If it is prohibition that critics of lotteries today have in mind, then an accurate analysis justifying such a view requires raising the following questions. What will the previous buyers do if lotteries are prohibited? And what will governments do? Will they reduce their expenditures, and if so, on what items exactly? Or will they maintain expenditures and tax something else, and if so, what exactly? Without answering these questions, one cannot conclude that the present situation is better or worse than the alternatives.

Since the answers to questions concerning the option of competition are both easy and pave the way for examining the consequences of prohibition, let us look into them first.

One may argue that since governments had and still have today a monopoly of the sale of lotteries (since competition from both private companies and from other provinces' or states' lotteries is outlawed, and since there simply are no other financial investments that give the chance of getting rich by regularly spending a dollar),[12] the buyers may be paying a higher price for the tickets than they would if competition prevailed. It is only this difference, rather than the net revenues from lotteries, that may represent a tax—a sum redistributed from the buyers toward those who receive the money from the government. The reason for the previous statement being tentative is that there were circumstances when drawings were fraudulent in spite of competition. If the public in such cases believed that drawings could be kept honest only by restricting the sale of lotteries to governments, all of the aforementioned difference may not be perceived as a tax.[13]

Competing Lotteries Would Not Be Less Regressive than a Monopoly Lottery

Suppose, then, that because of innovations and better law enforcement, competition in the sale of lotteries is allowed, but the sale of tickets is taxed. What will happen? The public who buy the tickets would more or less stay the same as before (the poorer may even buy more tickets, since their price may be lowered), and the government would still collect regressive taxes, only in a different form. Thus the attacks on regressivity, when looked at from this angle—if the alternative to the state's monopoly is a taxed competitive sector—are hollow.[14]

There have been studies that attacked the government's sale of lotteries on the ground of regressivity from another angle, arguing that not only do the poor spend relatively more on the tickets, but the government's net revenues from lotteries are redistributed toward the relatively rich. On what premises were such conclusions reached?

Governments frequently point out the projects on which the net revenues from lotteries are spent, but make some peculiar statements. An official communication in Japan says that "gambling or lottery has never been considered as a taxable item in Japan," but then it is mentioned that 38 percent of the lottery's profits were "used for the development of educational equipment, road construction or repairs, construction of dwelling houses, expenses for public prosperity and welfare." (Is there any item in the government's budget that could not fit into one of these categories?) The famous Irish Sweepstakes, which is conducted by the Hospitals Trust, is required by acts of Parliament to pay out the net proceeds to 410 institutions that provide free medical and surgical services. The trust's communication also declares that the proceeds do not appear in the government's budget.[15] Such statements about the worthy projects on which net revenues from the sale of lotteries are spent are common in the United States and Canada too. Although in about half the states (Connecticut, Delaware, the District of Columbia, Illinois, Maine, Missouri, Ohio, Rhode Island, etc.) and one province (Quebec), the legislators had the good sense to provide that the net revenues from lotteries go to the general fund, there are other states and provinces that declare that the revenues will be used only for specific items: public education (California, Michigan, New York [at one time, but not any more], New Jersey, Ontario, etc.); conservation, parks, and recreation (Colorado, Alberta). It is on the basis of such declarations, pointing out specific uses for the net revenues from lotteries, that studies examining the regressivity of revenues from governments' sale of lotteries have been based too, and have argued that those who benefit most from these revenues are the richer.[16]

But such conclusions are also inaccurate. Can one seriously believe that, in the absence of revenues from lotteries, governments would not have decided to finance such expenditures by higher taxes, increased debt, or a reallocation of expenditures? The declarations should not be taken literally. All they imply is that less is allocated in the general fund in the directions that revenues are being used for.[17] Steven Gold, director of fiscal studies for the National Conference of State Legislatures in Denver, confirmed this view when stating that, because of the gains from lotteries, education programs sometimes lose equal amounts from general appropriations. In New York, which has the most efficient state lottery in the United States, according to the journal *Gaming and Wagering Business*, state officials said that over the twenty years the lottery had been running, the proceeds had substituted for other funds: "The primary debate in New York has been whether lottery funding becomes a supplementary source," said Paul C. Reuss, director of budget studies for the state Senate Finance Committee. "The truth is that it is just one of the funding sources, but if we didn't have the lottery, taxes would have to be increased by $650 million."[18]

Indeed, when New York instituted its lottery in 1967, the profits were set aside for education. But when the state faced a budget crisis in 1968, the legislature shifted the net revenues from lotteries into the general fund. A similar event took place in Connecticut. Until December 1975 lottery revenues were earmarked for education. But then a special session of the legislature voted to allocate the revenues first to education, with "the balance to become part of the general fund" (whatever this "balance" means).[19]

When lotteries were prohibited, government officials in various countries during the nineteenth and first half of this century were not slow to realize that the latent demand for them enabled cheaper servicing of debt if, instead of paying interest, they promised to give a few large prizes on some bonds, with the majority of holders just getting back their initial investment. Variations on such premium bonds, as they were called, were widespread in England, Sweden, and Ireland. But it is hard to believe that the fact that governments did not call such assets lotteries could have fooled anybody. The invention of these financial assets as well as the artificial allocation of receipts from lotteries just shows that it is naive to assume that if lotteries as such were not offered, governments would change their expenditures. The change was that of vocabulary, not content.[20]

Thus, those who have examined regressivity by just looking at either the buying patterns of the poor and the rich or the government's declarations are on the wrong track. They must look at the general patterns in the government's expenditures and regulations and not at one item in isolation. One may, however, ask: If this conclusion is accurate, why do governments bother to make the aforementioned misleading declarations? There may be two possible answers. One is that it may somewhat calm those who are opposed to the sale of lotteries on religious grounds. Since for this group lotteries are bad, state monopoly of their sale must be perceived as a second best: At least the product is taxed, thus diminishing participation; and the taxes seem to be spent on items these groups approve of. Still, this answer assumes that members of this groups take the government's declarations literally. A more plausible answer is that government officials and part of the public sometimes extrapolate without much thought from past evidence. As we have seen, revenues from lotteries were successfully used for building great American universities, charitable institutions, hospitals, and so forth. If such a method of financing was good for Harvard, Princeton, and Yale in the past, why shouldn't it be good for governments subsidizing education today? Students of regressivity have neglected the answer that the circumstances surrounding such financing in the past were different from today's, and that lotteries then fulfilled different roles (being either a substitute for financial institutions or an occasion for social gatherings), suggesting that their role in the past cannot be used to justify their role today. But then people do not always question the origins of customs, but often accept them unthinkingly: Since lotteries were tried out in the past and found to be good for financing education, why not try them again?

The unavoidable conclusion therefore seems to be simple. Those who criticize the states' sale of lotteries on the grounds of regressivity could logically have only one option in mind: banning their sale altogether. But justifying the viewpoint that lotteries should be banned requires much more complex consideration than just looking at people's expenditures on them. Some of these considerations are examined next.

Prohibition Stimulates Illegal Gambling

All lotteries were abolished by the revolutionary government in France in 1793, but the government revised its decision a few years later. The reason was that, being deprived of national lotteries, people played the foreign ones illegally. As a result the French government was losing both revenues and foreign currency.[21]

Before the French Revolution, baccarat used to be played in illegal gaming halls with a great deal of cheating. It is due to the common sense of de Sartine, chief of the French Sûreté, that the government of the day was persuaded to legalize baccarat; no further mention is made of cheating.[22]

Even when lotteries were sold by governments but were prohibited for sale by private firms, the impact of prohibitions was not significantly different. Between 1760 and 1826, when the price of a state lottery ticket in England was £13 (which meant that only the rich could buy it and that such gambling was therefore prohibited to the poor), "insurance" was invented, and hundreds of illegal offices selling it to the *poor* operated in London. When this practice was stopped in 1793, the move succeeded in creating not only a black market but also protection rackets. Once lotteries were prohibited at the beginning of the nineteenth century, illegal private lotteries on a small scale multiplied, and their clients continued to be the poor.[23]

When gambling was outlawed in Sweden (until 1930), the Swedes gambled on English soccer games, thereby smuggling out substantial amounts of Swedish currency. Once gambling was legalized, the criminal elements that were involved with smuggling and gambling disappeared. China inaugurated a state lottery (not accidentally) on July 31, 1933, but lotteries were not unfamiliar to the Chinese. Hwo-Wei, a form of illegal lottery, had been very popular among the lower classes in Shanghai.[24]

In the United States until the re-emergence of lotteries in the 1960s and 1970s, the dominant illegal games were numbers and "insurance" (also called policy). The latter got its start in connection with the drawings of authorized lotteries, which took a long time and were expensive. The reason for the time lapse between the issuing of tickets and the drawing was that each new lottery had to get a license from the government, and there was always the possibility of not obtaining it.[25]

"Insurance" disappeared with the abolition of lotteries at the beginning of the nineteenth century, but the numbers game continued to be played in the poorer districts of large cities, and charity raffles were regularly held in the richer districts.[26] None of these seemed to attract much attention. Both in the United States and England, attention was focused on gambling linked with horse racing.

Throughout the nineteenth century, the bookmaking industry in the United States was illegal yet very popular.[27] In spite of the illegality, Western Union provided communication services to disseminate race results and odds. When in 1904 Western Union was put under increasing pressure to stop providing its services for this industry, the result was that six months later John Payne of Cincinnati had acquired an illegal monopoly to provide the desired information.[28]

During the early 1920s pari-mutuel wagering was legal only in Kentucky, Maryland, and Louisiana. Yet horse racing and gambling on the races continued to prosper in other states, since the laws prohibiting racing and bookmaking continued to be unenforced. They could not be. Whereas the entrepreneurs involved with gambling quickly used new technologies, it took years for government agencies to catch up with the innovations. Bookmakers in New York used telephones fifty years before the state authorized wiretaps.[29] Moreover, the law itself was ambiguous. Since bookmaking was illegal, track managers invented a system of oral betting, which in *People ex rel. Lichtenstein v. Langan* (1909) was held to be exempt from the bookmaking law under the unconvincing argument that successful bookmaking required "the writing out of the list of the odds laid on some paper or material so that they can be seen by those who are solicited to invest." Thus, went the decision, oral betting did not constitute bookmaking.[30] Lack of enforcement also resulted from the fact that in some southern states hostility toward gambling could be found more in judicial opinions than in legislative enactments. Blakey speculates that this phenomenon may be due to the fact that whereas many judges received their legal training in the East, where features of the frontier life were frowned upon, legislators reflected the will of the voters, who were not concerned about gambling.[31] An additional reason for lack of enforcement may be that gambling had close links with urban politics. Gamblers, police, and politicians were frequently of Irish Catholic background in many American cities, and "it was not simply that gambling syndicates influenced political organizations, but that gambling syndicates *were* the local political organization. Local bookmakers or policy writers served as precinct captains, while the leaders of syndicates became ward leaders and often won elections as aldermen or state representatives."[32]

Americans, like the Swedish and the French, also gambled on out-of-state lotteries when forbidden to play within their states. As noted earlier, this was the reason for the Louisiana lottery's spectacular success during the nineteenth century; Louisiana was the only state with surviving lotteries. Australians too gambled on out-of-state lotteries when forbidden to play within their own state, thus diminishing local tax revenues. This was the reason why New South Wales, Victoria, Queensland, and Western Australia passed laws prohibiting the Post Office from carrying lottery tickets, thus preventing Tasmania from exporting its lotteries.[33]

The fact that prohibitions in other states or nations could be used to raise revenues (thus imposing a tax on "foreigners") was and is still perceived by politicians as one of the attractions of lotteries. With only 600,000 inhabitants, New Hampshire's lottery officials knew that to succeed they must appeal to out-of-state people. They did succeed; in 1964, 80 percent of the tickets were sold to residents of Massachusetts, New York, and Connecticut, even though out-of-state residents had to travel to New Hampshire's border towns to purchase the tickets (use of the mail to move them is prohibited by federal law in the United States too). After 1964 the residents of these three states had to travel less, since New York and Massachusetts introduced very successful lotteries.[34]

Residents of other states are still traveling some distance in hopes of getting really rich. Some Delaware residents drive more than twenty miles twice a week in order to participate in the Maryland lottery. Delaware has its own game, but the prizes are small. Hoping both to prevent the outflow of funds and to keep their gamblers happy, Delaware is now making plans to offer a four-state lottery in collaboration with Maine, New Hampshire, and Vermont, with first prizes varying between $1 million and $10 million, thus competing with the glittering prizes of New York's lottery.[35]

Premium bonds, discussed in the preceding section, were not the only invention made during the nineteenth century in response to prohibitions on gambling. New sweepstakes, prize competitions, and football pools became popular in both the United States and England during this period. Although at first prize competitions and sweepstakes were prosecuted as lotteries in both countries, eventually they were dubiously distinguished—legally, but not in the public's mind—on the ground that they required the exercise of skill.[36]

Enforcement of Prohibition Is Often Lax

But the prohibition had more serious consequences than the fact that people gambled illegally, that substitutes were invented, or that people had to travel to other states to buy tickets. The reason why the poor continued to bet in England, even after passage of the 1906 "class law," was that enforcement of the law was not always taken seriously.[37] In Scotland the law seemed to be used merely to raise revenues through penalties rather than to suppress illegal bookmaking.[38]

Lack of enforcement was due to a number of factors. Not long after the passage of the law, members of the police force criticized the law on the grounds that it was "antiquated, obscure, illogical, ineffective and falls unevenly upon different classes of the community."[39] Since the poor did not equate legality with legitimacy, the police, in attempting to enforce the law, were faced with an impossible task. The bookmakers had developed a tight organization, and the buyers sympathized with the bookmakers rather than with the police.[40] Members of the police were also bribed by the bookmakers, a corruption that led journalists to declare in the 1920s that confidence in the police was at its lowest ebb in half a century.[41]

Reactions were similar in the United States. In 1851 the New York

Association for the Suppression of Gambling was established, and the Green Law of 1851 was the harshest anti-gambling law passed up to that time. It imposed fines on anyone found guilty of keeping a gambling establishment, exhibiting gambling devices, or assisting in any game.[42] The legislation turned out to be ineffective, and according to some estimates 30,000 people in the New York of the 1850s made their living from gambling.[43] There were several reasons for this law's lack of impact. Whereas the legislation was passed by members of the Protestant establishment, in the years between 1825 and 1855 New York State's population doubled, primarily because of the immigration of penniless non-Protestants who wanted to gamble. Too, some politicians turned out to have an interest in the gambling industry. Eventually the police commissioner, who claimed to be ignorant of the law, declined to enforce it.[44]

Surprising as it may sound today, a comprehensive law prohibiting all forms of gambling was passed in Nevada in 1909 and gambling remained a criminal offense for two decades. The result was that government revenues from licensing were lost, a large number of games were played, and corruption and "protection" became widespread, bribes coming to seem like little more than a form of license. Commentators reached the same conclusions as those reached in England:

> The fact that the Nevada gambling prohibition had to be enforced along with the national liquor prohibition did not do much good in Nevada for either law enforcement program. The speakeasies had gambling tables and slot machines. The people who wanted only to gamble or only to drink felt a brotherhood. Both groups, of course, were outnumbered by that mass who wanted to both drink and gamble. One of the byproducts of all this was the creation of a lawlessness in attitude for a whole generation of Americans, and a class of dishonest law enforcement officers and public officeholders such as the nation had never known before.[45]

It was in 1930 that Nevada relegalized gambling. The change of mind can be attributed not only to the great crash of 1929 and impending crisis, but also to the recognition that people gambled anyway and that the moral reformers who were against gambling could not find any evidence of the desperation and ruin that were popularly associated with gambling.[46] The impact of the relegalization was that eventually, myths notwithstanding, the gambling industry in Nevada, which features a massive corporate structure, was characterized by honesty toward its customers.[47]

In spite of all evidence, and in contrast to the more liberal attitude adopted toward gambling in England during the 1960s, New York's legislature in 1960 passed a series of tough new *anti-*gambling laws whose purpose was to facilitate convictions and, by increased penalties, to have a detrimental effect on gambling. The law was passed in spite of the fact that public opinion in New York City did not seem to condemn gambling. This is what one may infer from the fact that a public opinion survey in 1963 revealed that few New Yorkers worried about the morality of betting on races, favoring it three to one.[48]

The law does not seem to have achieved its intended impact. Gambling and the organized crime associated with it persisted, but few convictions were obtained. If it had a significant effect, it was on the police, for whom, the Knapp Commission found, gamblers' protection money was the main source of bribes. A typical policeman on the gambling squad was able to get $300 to $1,500 per month, and his or her superiors got additional sums.[49]

These revelations led, as in England, to the decision by New York City's police commissioner, Murphy, to stop enforcing certain aspects of the gambling laws. He also argued that dismantling the gambling squads would not bring about any great increase in gambling. But it would, he argued, have the beneficial effect of diminishing corruption, enabling the police to concentrate on controlling violent crime and improving the morale of police and public.[50]

A similar sequence of events took place in Australia.[51] Legislation in Queensland in 1936 and in New South Wales in 1938, prohibiting off-course betting in newspapers or through broadcasting, led to the organization of illegal means of communication. People were employed to signal from the courses and used the telephone to handle transactions. The organizations also bribed policemen and employees of the telephone company. Because transactions were arranged by phone, a credit system was necessary; its enforcement depended on threats and the use of violence.

Prohibition Does Not Achieve
Its Intended Goals

A number of lessons can be drawn from this evidence and that presented in preceding chapters [of the Brenners' book]. Those who condemn gambling in general and recommend its prohibition must take into account the fact that the policy they have in mind does not lead to no gambling, to more progressive taxation, to less crime, or to people spending their time and money on church literature or socialist treatises. People continue to gamble, even if it is illegal, and the poor do so in particular; hence their expenditure patterns may not change. Neither is the result more progressive taxation: If the government imposes a tax on beer (as was done in England when lotteries were prohibited),[52] the situation of the poor may not improve, since they spend even more on beer than on lotteries, and more than the richer. The result of prohibition is not less crime either. Even if one does not label gamblers criminals, which would automatically increase the crime rate, the acts of the illegal organizations that take over the gambling sector and enforce illegal gambling contracts increase the crime rate. If, as a result, the government entangles itself more in this maze and spends more on enforcement (while losing the revenues of the gambling sector), it must either raise taxes or reduce its expenditures.

And all these effects are due in part to the fact that there was and still is a vocal opposition who may sincerely, but erroneously, believe in the detrimental effects of gambling. The sincerity cannot always be doubted; some people believe in ideas that have been repeated so many times that familiarity with them passes for evidence. However, one cannot discard the possibility . . . that the opposition's words disguise selfish interests.

Opposition to Legalized Gambling
Comes from Interest Groups

Religious groups have been aware of the fact that if people no longer hold traditional beliefs, they will spend less time praying and more playing games of chance.[53] And recall that the English statute of 1591 that forbade the use of houses for games of chance was passed on petition of the military lobby: those involved with the production of bows, arrows, and bowstrings.[54] Later, as we have seen, the argument was that both drinking and gambling diminished the workers' productivity. Yet only gambling was prohibited, and not drinking. Although the argument was offered that gambling is more harmful than drinking, it was never documented and was probably wrong.[55] The reason for the different legislative treatment was that brewers had a strong political lobby, being linked with agricultural and industrial interests as well as with finance and retailing outlets. The alcohol industry was also a major employer of labor; sellers of drink were as numerous, for example, as sellers of food.[56] In contrast, the gambling establishment, as we saw, came from a working-class background and had no political ties. The fact that all forms of gambling were forbidden except some linked with horse racing may also be explained by the fact that racing was a traditional major pastime for the wealthy and for social elites, whereas other forms of betting were less so.

In the United States, legislative efforts to curb gambling in connection with racing were widespread during the late eighteenth and early nineteenth centuries (statutes against it were passed in 1796 in Connecticut and in 1846 in New Jersey, and by 1860 most states in the Northeast had them), but the laws were frequently not enforced. Horse racing became a favorite pastime of the wealthy in the New World too.[57] How was racing exempted in the United States in spite of the fact that it was well known that it is not commercially viable without gambling? The lawyers found a legal solution. They declared that racing was a sport, not a game, and in *Van Valkenburgh v. Torrey* (1827), for example, the court gave a liberal reading to the word "racing" and declared that trotting was not affected by the law that prohibited races for bets or stakes. (Such plays on words are just another effect of prohibition, as noted in Chapter 3 [of the Brenners' book] in connection with the rise of contests.)[58]

Later, in the 1920s, the New Jersey Chamber of Commerce linked the following problems with the legalization of gambling when justifying its opposition:

> Department stores, clothing and shoe stores, manufacturers and wholesalers
> dealing in staple lines of merchandise were usually injured. Other established
> entertainment industries, such as motion picture theaters, suffer during the
> local racing season. Collections fall off, large numbers of individuals get
> behind on installment payments, and the incidence of defalcations and other
> petty crimes increase enormously during the racing season.[59]

There is no evidence to support the last statement, although . . . the rate
of petty crime is higher in places where there are more tourists. Transi-
tory crowds provide an easy prey, and the criminals themselves can more
easily disappear in the crowd. As for the first part of the statement, it is
probably true that some traditional leisure industries will fall behind when
a new one is emerging. But then the condemnation of gambling should not
be taken literally; it just reflects the fact that in practice those who may
fall behind will be against increased *competition*. In a society committed to
the idea of competition, representatives of threatened industries cannot be
expected to acknowledge that they want less of it. Instead, they can be expected to disguise their sentiments behind false accusations.

Today, in spite of the fact that there is a general trend toward
legalized gambling, opposition to it is still quite evident. But the vocal
opponents are no longer religious groups but, in Florida for example, business interests afraid of competition. Among the opponents are the amusement giant Disney World and, yes, pari-mutuel betting interests. In Texas,
where a vote on legalizing pari-mutuel betting was held in 1986 for the
fifth straight year, the opposition was still coming from religious groups
and neighboring states that already allowed such betting.[60]

The evidence seems quite clear; the correlation between opposition
to legalization and the opposition's private interests seems obvious. Yet
there is little doubt that at times opposition to gambling has been based
on ideas that some people believe in, erroneously but sincerely. The
implications of these findings concern more than just future policies
affecting games of chance.

Ideas as Well as Interests Explain Legislation

There is a line of thought popular today that says that laws are passed by small interest groups who expect to benefit from them, whereas the rest of society is mainly indifferent to paying a small price for them. This thought is not inaccurate, as clearly shown above, but frequently such ahistorical theorizing does not seem to lead one very far. For without a good understanding of human behavior and without attempting to enter into the minds of decision makers at a certain moment of time and understand their way of thinking and their beliefs, little can be said a priori about the type of legislation that one group or another might favor.

Could an interest-group theory predict why it was in the interest of the members of the Labor Party in England in 1906 to vote for the Betting Act, which went against the wishes, the revealed preference, of their constituents? Only if one discovers the idea that lurked behind the vote—the prospect that the opportunity to gamble, to become rich, works as an inducement for the poor to work harder in expectation of tasting the joys of capitalist society, and that the provision of such additional opportunities poses a threat to a socialist's ideology—can one understand the interest behind it. Was the vote in the *private* interest of members of the Labor Party? Or did the vote reflect a sincere belief that the whole *public* might benefit if socialism came sooner to England?

Even if one considers a narrower topic, it is not always easy to give a clear-cut answer to such questions. In 1906 senior officers of the London Metropolitan Police, whose opinions on the feasibility of enforcement of a prohibition law were sought, were not against the law. They declared that the police could enforce it.[61] One may be skeptical of such declarations and say that if the law was passed the police could reasonably expect to have more money allocated to them, an outcome that every bureaucrat favors. Thus the declaration benefited private interests. Yet one may argue that the reason for the police force's attitude in favor of prohibition reflected a genuine belief in the evils of gambling, a belief shared by many people at the time. Thus their stand might be in the public interest as some perceived it.

Twenty years later the police came out against the law, a stand taken once the press had begun to make frequent revelations of corruption. Was the new attitude in their private or in the public interest? After all, one can argue that policemen blamed the law in order to explain that their corruption was in fact legitimate, since the law was not. Also, being continually blamed for corruption is threatening, since with a diminishing reputation the resources allocated to the police (and thus the wealth of members of the force) diminish.[62] Was the change in mind due to this threat posed to the well-being of members of the police hierarchy, thus serving private interests? Or was it a sincere recognition by a majority of police that the 1906 law was illegitimate and that relegalizing gambling was in the public's interest (what some may call a social good)?

What is the public interest, anyway? And how much gambling is socially good? An answer to these questions, linked with a discussion of the elusive notion of happiness, is given in the next and final chapter [of the Brenners' book].

Regulation of Gambling Is Muddled

Belief in a large number of erroneous ideas, along with the political power of some interest groups, has brought many countries today to a situation where the betting laws are confused. The confusions and inconsistencies are striking as many people hold onto ideas inherited from the distant past without much questioning. When opinions are so strong, as among the vocal opponents of gambling, one could reasonably expect at least a moderate knowledge of facts. But we quickly discovered that this was too optimistic an expectation on our part. So what we have tried to do is not merely to gather as much evidence as we could so that future decisions can be made on a more reliable basis, but also to understand how societies got into the maze they are presently in, and so both provide a clear path out of it and prevent—perhaps—similar mistakes being made in the future. Of course we are not under the illusion that the problem will be simple. It is never easy for people to break with their customary thinking. Facts, even when set within a framework like the one we have tried to provide in this book, are not enough to fight long-held prejudices.[63]

Many changes in gambling laws during the twentieth century seem to be isolated attempts to deal with temporary problems, rather than the outcome of an in-depth examination of gambling and speculation.[64] Thus at times the liberalization of gambling laws was an attempt to suppress the involvement of organized crime (without noticing, however, that it was the anti-gambling law to start with that gave the incentive for organization of criminal acts). At other times the change was made just to raise revenues from an untapped source.[65]

However, because of old prejudices against gambling, liberalization did not lead toward permitting competition but toward providing the government with monopoly power over the sale of tickets. That meant that a government bureaucracy, at first lacking both experience and the threat of competition, was involved with the introduction of lotteries. Little wonder that some of the sales programs of the first states to offer lotteries were failures. Now the situation has changed, for one state's lottery competes with those of neighboring states.[66]

Gambling Should Be Open to
Private Competition

Since this is the situation today, it is unclear why the private sector should not be allowed to enter the game. There is always danger in a situation where a government bureaucracy is the only one allowed to offer a service and charge the pertinent taxes. The well-being of these bureaucrats depends on this form of revenue; to ensure the continuity of their own jobs and responsibilities, they may look for ways to expand their power, advertising their services and recommending excessive reliance on gambling activities as a source of revenue. After all, bureaucrats, like anybody else, are interested in preserving their jobs rather than in examining the role of gambling in society.[67] These are typical dangers with any bureaucracy. Bureaucrats may at first simply offer a service in a non-businesslike manner, failing to exploit the opportunities, and later offer too much service, having no interest in exploiting new opportunities but continuing in blissful bureaucratic inertia.

The recommendation reached here is therefore simple. The rationale for decriminalizing and demonopolizing gambling is not merely that such changes will eventually diminish the power of organized crime and keep bureaucrats on their toes. Rather, these steps lead toward a situation that both provides opportunities for employment and sustains optimism and hope among those who, in the game of life, have been among the hardest hit. Since, as Leo Rosten once wrote, optimism is often a narcotic to deaden anxiety, why not let people be optimistic?[68] Isn't that better than the alternative: dealing with anxiety?

Of course nothing comes free in this world, and society must deal with the small proportion of compulsive gamblers, probably by allocating a fraction of the tax revenues obtained from the gambling sector to treatment for such players and by making the sellers of games of chance liable if they know that the buyer is an addict. Yet even passing legislation that requires setting aside funds for treatment, and the treatment itself, may be easier when gambling is legal than when it is not. For if the sector is illegal, the gamblers, compulsive or not, will by definition be criminals. So voters might be less sympathetic when asked to pay for treatment, and compulsive gamblers may be less willing to come forward and admit their addiction, since they may find themselves imprisoned instead of cured.

Notes

1. See discussion and references in Chapter 3 [of the Brenners' book], section 6. A priori, one could think of another possible reason for banning lotteries: Since there is no doubt that compulsive playing is costly for society and the benefits of lotteries are diminished for the government when it has surpluses in its budget, one could imagine that the ban was associated with the appearance of such surpluses in the 1830s in Europe as well as on the American continent. But no such correlation can be found. In the United States, for example, there were periods of major expansion with federal government surpluses during 1825–26, 1844–46, and 1850–57, but deficits were run during the downswings of 1820–21, 1837–43, 1847–49, and 1858–60. Nor was there a trend toward diminishing government expenditures during the nineteenth century; expenditures continued to grow at least at the rate the economy was growing.

There is one change that could account for the diminished importance of lotteries at the state level in the United States (though nothing similar happened in Europe). Between 1790 and 1795 the states' wartime debts were taken over by the federal government, putting them on a sound financial basis. This could have diminished the states' incentive to offer lotteries (but not the federal government's). But there was another change during these years that, in principle, may have worked in the opposite direction to encourage the states' sale of lotteries. Under the new U.S. Constitution, the states lost their right to issue money (although the banks they created by acts of incorporation could do so, and did). Still, the loss of this right might have limited the local governments' options in generating revenues and redistributing wealth through inflation. In any case, in spite of the paper currency issues of "wildcat banks," there was no sustained inflation until the 1860s.

It should be noted, however, that frequently legalization of games of chance has followed one form or another of crisis: sudden decline in government revenues or sudden increase in expenditures. In Louisiana the introduction of lotteries followed the Civil War, and in Florida it was a response to the abrupt decline in tourism in the late 1920s and Florida's being hit by two of the worst hurricanes of modern times. Horse racing, on the other hand, was decriminalized with the Depression (Robert G. Blakey, *The Development of the Law of Gambling, 1776–1976* [Washington, D.C.: National Institute of Law Enforcement and Criminal Justice, 1977], pp. 282, 289, 290, 303, 398, 399). But Blakey remarks that in those states that traditionally took a firm position against gambling, people often chose to pay higher taxes rather than to legalize gambling (p. 399). Sometimes lotteries were introduced because they were preferred to alternative forms of taxation. For example, New Jersey had no income tax, and for years refused to introduce one. The lottery was established to provide required revenues (ibid., p. 109). In communist countries too, ideology notwithstanding, similar circumstances have led to the introduction of lotteries and casinos (recently in Hungary). See "The Jackpot: Gambling in the Soviet Block," in *Gambling*, ed. Robert D. Herman (New York: Harper and Row, 1967).

2.   For detailed information and sources, see tables in the appendix to this chapter [of the Brenners' book].

3.   For detailed information and sources, as well as information on other states and countries, see the appendix to this chapter [of the Brenners' book]. It should be noted that these revenues underestimate the impact of gambling. The advertisement of gambling generates revenues for newspapers and other channels of information. Horse racing generates revenues for agriculture, and both this and other types of gambling attract tourists. And one must take into account the fact that if gambling is banned, people will gamble illegally, the revenues from such gambling will be untaxed, and those now working in the underground gambling industry may even declare themselves to be unemployed and receive welfare. Thus it would be wrong to assume that if gambling were prohibited only the declared current revenues would be lost.

4.   A simple correlation between unemployment rates and revenues from lotteries

for the last ten years may not, however, be negative, for more and more games have been legalized during this period. Thus, whereas relatively few lotteries were available (or the number of locations where tickets were sold was small) in the early 1970s when unemployment rates were high, the number of lotteries and locations at which tickets are sold have both increased since the late 1970s, even though unemployment rates have been falling. We could not find sufficient evidence about locations to examine statistically the impact of lottery revenues on the relationship between locations and changing unemployment rates.

5.   George Bernard Shaw (*The Intelligent Woman's Guide to Socialism and Capitalism* [London: Constable, 1926], p. 52) once made the accurate observation that "creating employment" does not have an unambiguous positive meaning. Criminals create a lot of employment; they provide jobs not only to policemen but also to the producers of alarms and security locks, to doormen, and so forth. See Chapter 6 [of the Brenners' book] on the criterion of the "social good" implicit behind this statement.

6.   For a lengthy criticism, consult W.J. Blum and H. Kalven, Jr., *The Uneasy Case for Progressive Taxation* (Chicago: University of Chicago Press, 1966); for a non-traditional explanation, see Appendix 1 [of the Brenners' book].

7.   See Reuven Brenner, *Rivalry: In Business, Science, among Nations* (Cambridge: Cambridge University Press, 1978), ch. 5, for a discussion about the persistence of wrong ideas among "scientists." Alex Rubner (*The Economics of Gambling* [London: MacMillan, 1966], p. 3) notes that he examined 186 books on public finance and found that only 4 made reference to gambling. Recent books on public finance make no reference either, the reason being (as noted in Chapter 2 [of the Brenners' book]) that traditional economic theory has nothing useful to say about either gambling or risk taking.

8.   It should be noted that good arguments can be made to justify taxing the richer and redistributing the sums to those falling behind. One is that such redistribution prevents increased social instability. See Reuven Brenner, *Betting on Ideas: Wars, Invention, Inflation* (Chicago: University of Chicago Press, 1985), ch. 2. This argument, however, does not imply that selling lotteries is bad. Note also that E.J. Mishan ("A Survey of Welfare Economics, 1939–51," *Economic Journal* 70 [June 1960], p. 247) is among the few who mention that envy is absent from discussions of "welfare economics." But he does not have a clear view on the subject.

9.   See Rubner, *The Economics of Gambling*, ch. 11, pp. 118–19.

10.   Some may still argue that one must also examine what the government is doing with the money that is not redistributed through prizes. This issue is addressed later.

11.   See Christopher C. Hood, *The Limits of Administration* (London: Wiley, 1976), ch. 10 for this argument.

12.   Sweepstakes are substitutes, but they cannot always be found regularly, and the prizes are in general smaller than in lotteries.

13.   We saw in Chapter 4 [of the Brenners' book] that such seemed at times to be the perception in the United States.

14. Daniel B. Suits ("Economic Background for Gambling Policy," *Social Issues* 35, no. 3 [1979], p. 50) too points out that state-sanctioned gambling can raise revenues in two different ways: either by imposing a tax or by maintaining monopoly power. The burden—if there is one—is in both cases the same. When people say that lotteries provide a "voluntary tax," they confuse form and substance, for the tax on a ticket is no less a tax because the buyer is free not to buy it. Indeed, one reason for taxation is to diminish the quantity demanded.

15. See Rubner, *The Economics of Gambling*, ch. 3.

16. H. Roy Kaplan, "The Social and Economic Impact of State Lotteries," *Annals of the American Academy of Political and Social Science* 474 (July 1984), pp. 91–106; John R. Livernois, "The Redistribution Effects of Lotteries in Western Canada," Research Paper no. 85–23, University of Alberta, 1985; John L. Mikesell and C. Kurt Zorn, "Revenue Performance of State Lotteries," paper prepared for the 78th Annual Conference of the National Tax Association, Tax Institute of American, Denver, October 16, 1985. Mikesell and Zorn conclude, erroneously, that "lotteries are substantially less efficient vehicles of revenue generation than more traditional sources" (p. 12), whereas Livernois erroneously infers redistributive effects by looking at what net revenues from state lotteries are spent on. Kaplan ("The Social and Economic Impact," p. 99), however, concludes that the odds are that programs viewed as essential would have been funded if lotteries were not available. In general, he notes, politicians look on earmarked lottery revenues—for example, for education, the most commonly earmarked category—as an exchange item in their budgets. Monies realized by a lottery are allocated to education, but total education funds may not be increased, because a like amount may be withheld from other sources. Students and institutions do not receive a $50 million bonanza; they get what the legislature and governor thought they should have to start with.

17. See Blakey, *The Development of the Law of Gambling*, p. 399; Kaplan, "The Social and Economic Impact."

18. Kurt Eichenwald, "Are Lotteries Really the Ticket?" *New York Times* supplement, January 4, 1987.

19. Robert G. Blakey, "State Conducted Lotteries: History, Problems and Promise," *Journal of Social Issues* 35, no. 3 (1979), p. 76.

20. Rubner, *The Economics of Gambling*, pp. 14–17 for details about premium bonds. Such bonds are extremely popular now in China (Nancy Dunnan, "Yuan to Invest," *New York Times*, supp. "The Business World," November 29, 1987). Rubner also notes that when lotteries were suppressed in 1826, the abolition was attacked on the grounds of "depriving labourers of the privilege of drinking low-taxed beer. . . . Public opinion accepted as a foregone conclusion the raising of the beer tax to compensate the Chancellor for the revenue lost through the abolition of lotteries" (*The Economics of Gambling*, p. 20). On July 19, 1836, a London newspaper wrote that "a deficiency in the public revenue . . . will, however, be the consequence of the annihilation of Lot-

teries and it must remain for those who have . . . supported the putting a stop to Lotteries, to provide for the deficiency" (quoted in ibid., p. 21). Rubner also remarks that "while Gentiles spend more than twice the amount of money on alcohol than on gambling, the average British Jew's consumption pattern shows the opposite trend: gambling plays a much larger role than drinking. This presents a classical confirmation for the thesis put forward in this book that social evils are largely interchangeable. The compliment paid to the Jewish community for having to its credit a low rate of drunkenness ought to be seen in the perspective of the substitution effect, namely its proportionately larger participation in gambling" (ibid., p. 104). Also see pp. 32–37 on the sometimes wildly imaginative vocabulary used by government officials to justify one form or another of gambling. Blakey makes a similar observation when he notes that betting linked with horse racing was exempted from anti-gambling legislation in the United States when "in *Van Valkenburgh v. Torrey*, the court relied on a literal reading of the word 'racing' and declared that trotting was not affected by the law" (Blakey, *The Development of the Law of Gambling*, p. 175). Back to premium bonds: Their gradual disappearance during the second half of this century is, unsurprisingly, correlated with the legalization of lotteries and other games of chance.

21. See Reuven Brenner and Gabrielle A. Brenner, *Gambling and Speculation: A Theory, a History, and a Future of Some Human Decisions* (Cambridge: Cambridge University Press, 1990), ch. 1, n.46.

22. See Rubner, *The Economics of Gambling*, p. 12.

23. See discussion in Brenner and Brenner, *Gambling and Speculation*, ch. 1 and 3; David Miers and David Dixon, "National Bet: The Re-emergence of Public Lottery," *Public Law* (1979), pp. 376–79. Rubner (*The Economics of Gambling*, p. 19) remarks that the amount of money wagered on "insurance" was said to have equaled the sales volume of the actual lottery tickets, and that there were on average 200 insurance offices operating during this period. John Ashton (*A History of English Lotteries* [1893; Detroit: Singing Tree, 1969], p. 298) notes that at their peak there were 400 such offices. See also Blakey, *The Development of the Law of Gambling*, p. 897.

24. See Brenner and Brenner, *Gambling and Speculation*, ch. 2, n.68, for the sources on Sweden; Paul K. Whang ("The National State Lottery," *China Weekly Review*, August 19, 1933, p. 498) on China.

25. Charles Clotfelter and Philip J. Cook, "The Context of Lottery Growth," (manuscript, Duke University, 1987), p. 11, and discussion in Brenner and Brenner, *Gambling and Speculation*, ch. 4, section 5.

26. Blakey, *The Development of the Law of Gambling*, p. 913. Miers and Dixon ("National Bet," pp. 379–82) remark that with the enactment of the Lotteries Act in 1823, illegal private lotteries on a small scale multiplied, and apparently newspaper prize competitions became widespread.

27. See Blakey, *The Development of the Law of Gambling*, pp. 142–203; Edward C. Devereux, *Gambling and Social Structure* (Ph.D. thesis, Harvard University, 1949;

New York: Arno, 1980), pt. 3. But it should be noted that even racetracks were of questionable legality, since they derived their revenues from gambling.

28. Ibid., pp. 121–23; Peter Reuter, *Disorganized Crime* (Cambridge, Massachusetts: MIT Press, 1985), 15.

29. Blakey, *The Development of the Law of Gambling*, pp. 123–25.

30. Ibid., pp. 201–202. Judge Van, in his dissent, showed more common sense when he argued that "engaging in the business of public gambling by quoting and laying insidious odds to a multitude of people was the evil aimed at, not the making of record of the business which is comparatively innocent" (p. 202). Blakey also remarks that much legal discussion concerned the question whether horse racing was a game or a sport.

31. Blakey (ibid., p. 384) remarks that in Nebraska agrarian interests, reflecting their eastern origins, dictated an absolute ban on gambling as soon as they gained control of the legislature.

32. Blakey (ibid., p. 350), quoting an unpublished paper by Haller, "Bootleggers and American Gambling 1920–1945: An Overview," and also relying on Haller's "Urban Crime and Criminal Justice: The Chicago Case," *Journal of American History* (1970).

33. Blakey, *The Development of the Law of Gambling*, p. 674. Drawings from the Louisiana lotteries took place daily in Boston, Cincinnati, Denver, and San Francisco. And legislators were bribed. New York, in order to protect the success of its own lotteries, passed a law in 1759 that imposed a fine on anyone who sold foreign lotteries inside the state (ibid., p. 137). On Australia, see Rubner, *The Economics of Gambling*, p. 148.

34. Blakey, "State Conducted Lotteries," p. 73; *The Development of the Law of Gambling*, pp. 682, 701–702. Blakey, quoting Senator Eastland, also remarks that the impact of the mail prohibition was that the lottery statutes in their present form did not cover many forms of betting "transported daily across State lines, for they do not meet the traditional definition of a lottery. . . . Even out-and-out lottery tickets may be shipped across state lines with impunity if they are printed in blank, shipped, and then locally overprinted with the paying numbers" (*The Development of the Law of Gambling*, p. 583). But it was already during the Great Depression of the 1930s that the great success of the Irish Sweepstakes opened some government officials' eyes to the fact that government revenues could be obtained even during recessions without raising a public outcry, and that prohibitions made other governments richer. In fact, the Irish game was used in arguments during the 1960s to justify the legalization of lotteries.

35. See Lindsay Gruson ("Delaware Joins 3 States in Big Lottery," *New York Times*, April 19, 1987), from whose article one can infer that 50 percent of the buyers in Maryland's small communities near the border come from Delaware. She notes that Delaware's problem is faced by many of the twenty-two states that were operating lotteries: "It is getting more difficult to attract people to play lottery games that offer anything less than million-dollar jackpots." This is, of course, one of the results of

competition among the state-owned lotteries. Gruson also remarks that the attraction of big prizes "has led eight states, including New York, to consider banding together to offer regular multistate lottery drawings. Officials estimate that it could often produce jackpots of $80 million, nearly double the current record of $41 million, set two years ago in New York." But it should be noted that federal law still prevents the resurgence of nationwide private lotteries (Blakey, "State Conducted Lotteries," p. 71). In Prussia, a solution to competition among the states was found when the other German states gave up their lottery privileges and accepted a budget subvention in return for permitting the sale of Prussian tickets (Rubner, *The Economics of Gambling*, p. 148). In Nevada too, where by the 1960s gambling was the largest industry, similar aspects of the industry were not lost on the politicians, who realized that the state depended heavily on outsiders for its tax dollars (Blakey, *The Development of the Law of Gambling*, p. 467). According to William G. Blair ("16 States Consider Joint Lottery Game," *New York Times*, July 13, 1986), sixteen of the twenty-two states with lotteries and the District of Columbia were talking about banding together to offer a regular multistate lottery drawing that officials said would increase state revenues and produce jackpots of more than $50 million.

36. Blakey, *The Development of the Law of Gambling*, p. 381.

37. Hood, *The Limits of Administration*, p. 170.

38. Ibid., p. 170. Hood notes that this does not imply that the law was "ineffective." It prevented the development of large-scale bookmaking businesses, which could be visible, thus making betting more expensive for the poor and diminishing government revenues. The reason why the growth of large-scale businesses was hampered was that the system depended on bettors being personally known to the bookmakers' agents, both to ensure that casual bettors were not plainclothes policemen and because no written receipts were given.

39. David Dixon, "Illegal Gambling and Histories of Policing in Britain," paper presented at the Sixth National Conference on Gambling and Risk-Taking, Atlantic City, December 1984, p. 2 (Faculty of Law, University of Hull), quoting the assistant commissioner of the Metropolitan Police in 1923.

40. Ross McKibbin ("Working-Class Gambling in Britain 1880–1939," *Past and Present* 82 (February 1979), p. 159) notes that bookmakers would arrange for an arrest to be made if new officers were known to be on duty, so that the police who gave evidence in court could be identified and later avoided. See also Dixon, "Illegal Gambling," pp. 37, 63.

41. Dixon, "Illegal Gambling," p. 35. According to him, the evidence from England, based on autobiographies and memories of men who had contact with bookmakers after the passage of the 1906 law, is unanimous. Payoffs to the police were an inevitable part of the street bookmaker's expenses, taking the form of either a bribe or "betting with the bookmaker on the simple system of receiving on winners but not paying on losers" (p. 66), and he concludes that whereas "before the war, the police

had greeted the Street Betting Act as an addition to their power, they now began to perceive it as a threat to their authority" (p. 67).

42. Blakey, *The Development of the Law of Gambling*, p. 154.

43. Henri Chafetz, *Play the Devil: A History of Gambling in the United States from 1942 to 1955* (New York: Potter, 1960), p. 228; Blakey, *The Development of the Law of Gambling*, pp. 156–57.

44. Blakey, *The Development of the Law of Gambling*, pp. 154–58.

45. W. Turner, *Gambler's Money* (1965), quoted in Blakey, *The Development of the Law of Gambling*, p. 432.

46. Blakey, *The Development of the Law of Gambling*, p. 465.

47. Ibid., p. 466. Notice that this outcome is not unlike the situation in England, where the honesty of bookmakers is noteworthy.

48. David Weinstein and Lillian Deitch, *The Impact of Legalized Gambling: The Socio-economic Consequences of Lotteries and Off-Track Betting* (New York: Praeger, 1974); Blakey, *The Development of the Law of Gambling*, pp. 208–209.

49. Blakey, *The Development of the Law of Gambling*, pp. 195–98. He remarks that the 1971 Joint Legislative Committee on Crime discovered that an arrested gambler faced only a 2 percent chance of going to jail, and even then his sentence would be light. In one heavy gambling district, of 1,225 arrested bookies, only 10 were fined over $500, only 19 were imprisoned, and only 3 of these 19 received sentences in excess of ninety days. It was also estimated that each arrest cost the public forty times the fine recovered.

50. Ibid., pp. 197–98. In testimony before the legislature, it was revealed that the typical person involved in off-track betting earned $12,300 a year, was a high-school graduate 42 years of age on average, male, white, often of Italian or Irish extraction, very often Catholic, and a blue-collar worker who was not a compulsive gambler. Forty-three percent had prior experience with some form of illegal gambling. See ibid., pp. 211–12.

51. See John O'Hara, "Class and Attitudes to Gambling in Australia," paper presented at the Seventh International Conference on Gambling and Risk-Taking, Reno, 1987; and David Dixon, "Responses to Illegal Betting in Britain and Australia," paper presented at the Seventh International Conference on Gambling and Risk-Taking, Reno, 1987, and extensive evidence and sources quoted there.

52. See Rubner, *The Economics of Gambling*; Penry Williams, "Lotteries and Government Finance in England," *History Today* 6 (1956), p. 561; and discussion in Brenner and Brenner, *Gambling and Speculation*, ch. 3, section 3.

53. See discussion in Brenner and Brenner, *Gambling and Speculation*, ch. 3.

54. See discussion in ibid., ch. 3, section 2.

55. Brian Harrison, *Drink and the Victorians* (London: Faber and Faber, 1971), p. 65; James Walvin, *Leisure and Society 1830–1950* (London: Longman, 1978), p. 37; Donald Read, *England 1868–1914* (London: Longman, 1979), p. iii. Kathleen M. Joyce remarks that "the closest parallel to the treatment of gambling is the prohibition of al-

cohol, and many obvious comparisons are frequently drawn in the modern press. The . . . antilottery movement was part of a more general reform movement occurring in the latter part of the 19th century, which was antialcohol as well . . . although anti-lottery amendments were more common than antialcohol amendments" ("Public Opinion and the Politics of Gambling," *Journal of Social Issues* 35, no. 3 [1979], p. 149).

56. Blakey, *The Development of the Law of Gambling*, pp. 88–90, 174–78.

57. Ibid., p. 175. Pari-mutuel wagering, available in Europe from 1865, was not widely adopted in the United States until 1920, in part as a result of the political influence of the bookmaking lobby, notes Reuter (*Disorganized Crime*, p. 14).

58. For example, when usury was still prohibited, the word "interest" was invented, and paying it was legal.

59. Quoted in Blakey, *The Development of the Law of Gambling*, p. 104.

60. "Odds Improve for Legalized Gambling in Several States," *Wall Street Journal*, March 6, 1986, p. 1.

61. Dixon, "Illegal Gambling," section 1.

62. Dixon remarks that "police corruption must be taken into account as a likely social cost of the legislative creation of 'victimless' crimes: this is a widely accepted conclusion of extensive academic and official investigations in the United States" (ibid., p. 8), and he discusses facets of the corruption in England (pp. 8–22). He also writes that by the 1920s "attempts to enforce [the 1906 law] were stirring up open resentment against the police which was threatening the toe-hold of public consent upon which they depended" (p. 44) and that "consent to policing in liberal democracies relies heavily on the presentations and perception of the police as the enforcers of apolitically neutral law" (p. 45). Dixon also quotes E.P. Thompson's opinion in *The Making of the English Working Class* (1963) that a law that is partial and perceived to be unjust will prevent the law from performing its vital ideological work: It "will mask nothing, legitimize nothing, contribute nothing to any class's hegemony" (p. 45). Dixon concludes that "herein lies the significance of anti-gambling legislation of this type: it threatened not merely the 'moral standing' of the police which attempted to enforce it, but by necessary implication the legal system as a whole and the law itself as a legitimizing ideology" (p. 69).

63. See Brenner, *Rivalry*, ch. 5, on resistance to innovations in business and science.

64. Blakey, *The Development of the Law of Gambling*, pp. 364–65, 683–713.

65. Ibid., pp. 700–734, 873–75.

66. Ibid., pp. 683–713, "The Economic Case Against State-run Lotteries," and *Business Week*, August 4, 1975, where the critics failed to understand the reasons for the failure of the first lotteries. On bureaucracy in general, see Reuven Brenner, "Bureaucracy—A Useless Abstraction," Research Report no. 1787, Centre de Recherche et Développement en Economique, Université de Montréal, 1987.

67. See Brenner, "Bureaucracy."

68. See Leo Rosten, *Hollywood: The Movie Colony—the Movie Makers* (New York: Harcourt Brace, 1941), p. 39.

V

GAMBLING: SOCIAL MENACE OR SOCIAL BENEFIT?

INTRODUCTION TO PART V

There is no question that legal gambling has spread enormously in the United States since the 1970s. There is also no question that state governments have come increasingly to depend on lotteries for revenue. Yet there are serious questions about what role, if any, the federal government should play in directing and controlling gambling policy. It is already involved in permitting Native American gaming because of federal laws treating tribes as relatively sovereign political entities. There are different positions on whether Native American gaming is a good thing, as can be seen in the final section of this book. But there are also questions about whether the federal government should create a national gambling policy that would control policies in individual states.

Historically, the federal government has not tried to develop a comprehensive national gambling policy. Most federal senators and representatives have not been outspoken about gambling policy, which has been handled by states and localities. Republican senator Richard Lugar and former Democratic senator Paul Simon are unusual because they have been vocal in calling for federal hearings to examine the effects of gambling and to determine what further role the federal government should play in developing policy. Both men believe that the consequences of gambling are important enough to warrant hearings on the subject.

Although Lugar and Simon emphasize the importance of exploratory hearings, some policy analysts would like to see the federal government take an active role in developing a national gambling policy, to which state policies would be subordinate. To determine what such a national policy might look like, see Robert Goodman's contribution in Part VI..

Libertarian writer David Ramsay Steele offers an alternative to the proposition accepted by Simon and Lugar, that gambling tends to be a negative social force, unproductive at best and socially destructive at worst.

Against the claim that gambling is unproductive because it subtracts consumer dollars from other industries, Steele contends that such an argument would condemn running churches and manufacturing refrigerators, and it is usually manufacturing that many critics of gambling regard as the paradigm for productivity. He believes that, if manufacturing is productive, it is productive because it satisfies wants, and that gambling can satisfy wants as well as sports, religious services, or psychotherapy.

What's more, gambling, in Steele's view, can be as rational as any other activity. Just as people derive satisfaction from being insured against highly improbable but extremely unpleasant events, so people, according to Steele, can reasonably derive satisfaction from purchasing an opportunity to win a highly improbable but extremely pleasant prize, as in a lottery. What's more, he submits that most gamblers exercise moderation and seem to be aware of the odds.

Unlike many defenders of gambling, Steele does not try to defend it by asserting that it will enlarge public revenue. Rather, his defense of gambling rests principally on the conviction that it is fundamentally good for people to be entitled to do whatever they please with their own lives so long as they do not coerce or defraud others.

13. Gambling Has High Social Costs and Should Be Restricted by the Government

Senator Paul Simon

Paul Simon, a former senator from Illinois, reviews the history of gambling in the United States and then attempts to answer the following questions: How rapidly is gambling growing in the United States? What are its advantages and disadvantages? What role, if any, should the federal government play in regulating gambling?

After remarking that legal gambling has increased enormously in the United States since the 1970s, he suggests that there are costs and liabilities to generating public revenue through gambling. Simon asserts, for example, that gambling can weaken the work ethic and that government advertisements for the lottery mislead people into thinking that success requires only luck. He asserts further that gambling does not create nearly the number of jobs as manufacturing and does not produce value-added products or reinvestment in the market economy. What's more, the number of problem gamblers, he says, increases when gambling enterprises are established near a population center.

"The Explosive Growth of Gambling in the United States," speech by Paul Simon (U.S. Senate, July 31, 1995, from the Congressional Record for the 104th Congress). The text of this speech was downloaded from Thomas: Legislative Information on the Internet, which is run by the Library of Congress. The Web address for Thomas is http:/thomas.loc.gov/; the address for the speech is http://www.iquest.net/cpage/ncalg/the_expl.htm.

He contends, still further, that real property taxes for both residential and commercial properties have risen every year in some places where gambling has been legalized.

Because of the rapid growth of legalized gambling and the complex social and economic costs associated with it, Simon, along with Senator Lugar, introduced legislation to authorize a commission to examine the consequences of legal gambling and to suggest how best to design gambling policy. The nine-member commission was formed in 1997 and is headed by Kay Coles James, dean of Regent University's Robertson School of Government in Virginia Beach. Its findings are due no later than June 20, 1999. Although Simon wants the commission to arrive at its own conclusions, he believes that law can and should regulate gambling, as by requiring new gambling enterprises after a specific date to pay a tax of five percent on their gross revenue to avoid saturating the market. Because he fears that legal gambling may spread too quickly to control its social and economic costs, he suggests that states, Indian tribes, and local governments without legal gambling might be made eligible for per capita revenue-sharing assistance from the government so that they will not feel the need to resort to generating revenue from gambling. Simon concludes by asserting that the social and economic consequences of gambling are too far-reaching for Congress and the American people to ignore the need for a well-informed gambling policy.

Mr. President, in November of last year, when I announced I would retire from the Senate after 1996, President Clinton suggested that with the freedom from political restraint I now have, and with slightly more credibility because political opportunism would not be the immediate outcry of critics, I should, from time to time, make observations about our nation, where we are going, and where we should go.

One of the marks of our civilization, virtually unnoticed as we discuss the nation's problems, is our fastest-growing industry: gambling.

Local governments, Indian tribes, and states—all desperate for revenue—increasingly are turning to what appears to be a quick and easy solution: legalized gambling. And, temporarily, it often works. Poverty-stricken Indian tribes suddenly have revenue. Cities like East St. Louis, Illinois, with every possible urban malady, find themselves with enough revenue at least to take care of minimal services.

There are four basic questions:

1. How rapidly is this phenomenon growing?
2. What are its advantages?
3. What are its disadvantages?
4. Is there a role for the federal government to play, and should it play a role?

Gambling Has Flourished, Even When Illegal

Gambling is not a new phenomenon. The Bible and early historical records tell of its existence. Gambling surfaced early in U.S. history, then largely disappeared as a legal form of revenue for state and local governments. It remained very much alive, however, even though illegal, in the back rooms of taverns and in not-so-hidden halls, often with payoffs to public officials to "look the other way" while it continued. I particularly remember traveling overseas and back while in the U.S. Army. The troop ship became one huge gambling operation with dice or cards, activity slowed only by the occasional walking tour of a conscientious officer whose coming would be foretold by someone taking the voluntary watch for his fellow enlisted men—and they were then all men—who gambled. After the watchman's signal, suddenly that portion of the ship's deck or hold could meet the highest puritanical standards. Within seconds of the disappearance of the dreaded officer, the games would begin again. Participation had no appeal to me, not primarily for moral reasons, but I have always been too conservative with my money to enjoy risking it that way. What I remember about those shipboard activities was the enormousness of the stakes that could be built up—enormous for enlisted men on meager salaries in 1951–1953—and the ability of some of my friends to continue their activity with almost no sleep.

Gambling's appeal, particularly for the idle—and a troop ship is loaded with them—is clear.

Early in our nation's history, almost all states had some form of lottery, my state of Illinois being no exception. When Abraham Lincoln served in our state legislature from 1834 to 1842, lotteries were authorized, and there apparently was no moral question raised about having them. In 1839, for example, the Illinois House of Representatives voted unanimously to authorize a lottery to raise funds "for the purpose of draining the ponds of the American bottom" in the vicinity of what is now East St. Louis, an area that to this day has a severe drainage problem, and a city that today has a significant gambling presence.

In Illinois and other states the loose money quickly led to corruption, and the states banned all forms of gambling. Illinois leaders felt so strongly about it, they put the ban into the state constitution. For many years, Louisiana had the only lottery, and then in 1893—after a major scandal there—the federal government prohibited all lottery sales. Even the results of tolerated but illegal lotteries could not be sent through the mail.

But the lottery crept back in, first in New Hampshire in 1963, and then in 36 other states. [In 1994] states sold $34 billion in lottery tickets. Forty-two states now have some form of legalized gambling. Even states that technically outlaw gambling frequently manage to have some form of it. In one of the more peculiar decisions by Illinois Supreme Court justices—dependent for re-election at that time on campaign contributions—they ruled that betting money on horses was not gambling, because the ability of the horse and the skill of the rider were involved. Gambling is when everything is left to chance, they argued.

Legalized Gambling Has Grown Explosively

What we know as casino gambling was legal only in Nevada, then in New Jersey and now in 23 states. From a small enterprise in a few states, gambling has matured. In 1974, $17 billion was legally wagered in the nation. By 1992, it reached $329 billion, and it is now over $500 billion. Three-fourths of the nation's citizens now live within 300 miles of a casino. One article reports, "Airlines are exploring the installation of back-of-seat slot machines on some flights."[1] Other nations—particularly poorer ones—are expanding gambling operations. Within our country, the magazine *Gaming and Wagering Business* reports, "Old attitudes have been shattered. Barriers are crumbling, and doors have been flung open."[2]

At this point, let me digress to express my gratitude to scholars who have studied legalized gambling in the United States, with little attention and little gratitude from the community at large. Particularly helpful, as I prepared these remarks, was a book manuscript I had the opportunity to read by Robert Goodman, a professor at Hampshire College in Massachusetts. In October, the Free Press will publish his thoughtful and well-crafted manuscript under the title, *The Luck Business*. The subtitle is "The Devastating Consequences and False Promises of America's Gambling Explosion." John Warren Kindt, a professor at the University of Illinois at Urbana, wrote an excellent article for the *Drake Law Review* last year, "The Economic Impacts of Legalized Gambling Activities," and Henry Lesieur, who heads the criminal justice division at Illinois State University, edits a magazine in this field, *Journal of Gambling Studies*. I am grateful to them and to others who have pioneered research.

Legalized Gambling Can Yield New Revenue

What are the advantages of legalized gambling?

It brings in new revenue, at least temporarily and, in some cases, over a longer period of time.

One of the great weaknesses of American politics today—and one of the reasons for public cynicism toward those of us in politics—is our eagerness to tell people only what they want to hear. Polling is a huge business, and if a poll suggests some stand is unpopular, too many find a convenient way of changing course, even if the public good is served by the unpopular action.

An area of high sensitivity is taxation. That problem is compounded by the fact that at the national level no other industrial nation—with the exception of Israel—spends as much of its taxation on defense and interest as does the United States. These bring no direct benefit to people. Citizens of Germany, France, Great Britain and other nations pay much higher taxes, but they see health care and other benefits that we do not have. In addition, their parliamentary systems make it easier to make tough decisions than our system does.

So when someone comes along and says, "I have a simple way to get more revenue for you, and you do not have to raise anyone's taxes," that has great appeal to policymakers who must seek reelection. Those same people say to the policymakers, "Not only will I provide revenue for you without taxation, I will be very generous to you when campaign time comes." And they are.

Some Cities Have Been Helped
by Legalized Gambling

While the promises of what legalized gambling will do for a community or state almost always are greatly exaggerated, it is also true that many communities who are desperate for revenue and feel they have no alternative are helped. I have already mentioned East St. Louis, Illinois. Bridgeport, Connecticut, is another example. Small communities like Metropolis, Illinois, population 6,734, find that a riverboat casino brings in significant additional municipal revenue. And while other businesses in these communities often do not benefit—and some, like restaurants, are hurt—a poll by the Better Government Association, a highly respected Illinois civic group, shows that in some communities, the initial reaction to the riverboat casinos is more positive than negative: Rock Island/ Moline, 83 percent positive, though this has changed; Metropolis, 76 percent positive; East St. Louis, 47 percent positive; and Peoria, 64 percent positive.

Some officials in Chicago, desperate for revenue, wish to bring in a large casino operation with a $2 billion price tag. They say it will bring 10,000 construction jobs. That alone is significant. The initial press release said 37,000 construction jobs. And officials in Chicago, aware there are long-term dangers to the city from such an operation, also know that unless they solve short-term problems—and that takes revenue—the long-term picture for the city is not good. The state government has shown itself largely insensitive to the needs of the city, dominated as it is by suburban and rural leaders. Faced with a choice of lectures from the state about long-term problems and what appears to be easy, significant, immediate revenue, it is not difficult to understand Chicago's choice. On top of that, they face editorial prodding. Under a heading, "Casino a Great Bet for City," the Chicago *Sun-Times* called a casino "a cash cow" and noted: "The sooner state law changes to allow land-based casino gambling, the better. And the sooner Chicago finally gets in on the action, the better."[3] Almost unnoticed has been the report of the Chicago Crime Commission in response to a request by the Mayor: "Organized crime will infiltrate casino operations and unions, and will be involved in related loan-sharking, prostitution, drug activities . . . and public corruption."[4]

States Have Found Legalized Gambling Attractive

State governments are no more loaded with courageous leaders than is the federal government. They need revenue to solve their problems. In Illinois, for example, state support for public higher education has dropped from 70 percent of the costs in 1980, to 37 percent today, almost a 50-percent cut. (Here, I digress to observe that states have been partially bailed out by federal aid to students. We hear a great deal from states about unfounded mandates. We hear much less from states about sizable grants from the federal government.) Faced with needs in education at all levels, with growing health care costs that afflict both federal and state governments, and with decaying cities and decaying infrastructure, the states have two options: Tell people the truth and ask for the taxes to pay for these needs, or combine the growing practice of issuing bonds, states don't call them deficits and find some "easy" source of revenue, like legalized gambling. The courageous path is too infrequently taken.

Revenue from lotteries, race horse gambling, and riverboat casinos brings Illinois government approximately $820 million a year. That is state government revenue alone. I have made no attempt to calculate what revenue is lost because of money not being spent in other enterprises in the state. Most of those who wager in Illinois are from Illinois. When they spend on gambling, that is money that would otherwise go to clothing stores, groceries, and other businesses. That means less revenue to the state from those businesses. Also not calculated in the $820 million state revenue is the loss caused by the increased problem of gambling addiction.

Early promises to use Illinois lottery money for education have been technically complied with, but state support for education has declined substantially as a percentage of income for local schools since the lottery became a reality.

Wisconsin, not a big gambling state, has 17 Native American casinos. A study completed in April concluded: "Overall, the state gains $326 million in net revenue from the presence of the casinos." They added this caution: "However, this figure is reduced substantially—to $166.25 million—when even the lowest estimated costs of compulsive gambling are included in the calculations. With mid-range estimated social costs, the overall impact becomes negligible, while with higher social-cost estimates, the impact becomes clearly negative."[5]

Reservations Have Reaped Gains from Gambling

Indian reservations have misery as their constant companion. Unemployment rates, alcoholism rates, suicide rates, and poverty indexes all combine to paint a grim picture that should be a matter of shame for our nation. Not only has the federal government been weak in its response to these needs, but state governments, sometimes dominated by prejudice against Native Americans, often have been even worse. Listen to this Department of Health and Human Services report, given to a Senate committee this year (1995): "In 15 of the 24 states with the largest Native American populations, eligible tribes received nothing in 1993 from the more than $3 billion in federal funds (Title XX and Title IV-E child welfare services and protection programs) the states received. In the other nine states, Indians received less than three percent."[6]

It should not surprise anyone that tribal leaders who want to produce for their people seize what some view as a legal loophole that our courts and laws have created to get revenue for their citizens; 115 tribes now have some form of casino gambling. The gross revenue for the 17 tribes in Wisconsin is $655 million. And about one-fifth of that revenue comes from people who live outside of Wisconsin, higher than in most states, much lower than Nevada or Atlantic City. Connecticut is the prime example of a small tribe gaining big money. A casino operated by the Mashantucket Pequot Tribe in Ledyard, Connecticut, brings in approximately $800 million in gross revenue annually. Native American leaders who see long-term harm to their tribes from the gambling enterprises are hard-pressed by those who see immediate benefits, and not too much hope for sizable revenue outside of gambling.

Gambling Can Be Addictive

What are the disadvantages of legalized gambling?

The distinguished Nobel Prize-winning economist, Paul Samuelson, has warned us: "There is a substantial economic case to be made against gambling. It involves simply sterile transfers of money or goods between individuals, creating no new money or goods. Although it creates no output, gambling does nevertheless absorb time and resources. When pursued beyond the limits of recreation . . . gambling subtracts from the national income."[7]

A high official in Nevada told me, "If we could get rid of gambling in our state, it would be the best thing that could happen to us. I cannot say that publicly for political reasons. But major corporations that might locate their principal offices here or build plants here don't do it. They know that gambling brings with it serious personnel problems."

Personnel problems are but one disadvantage, but they are real. People can become addicted to gambling, as they can to drugs or alcohol or smoking.

My mother belongs to a church in Collinsville, Illinois, that had a fine substitute teacher at its Lutheran school. Unknown to the teacher's family, she had been visiting a gambling boat. Money the family thought had gone to pay the rent and family bills had, instead, gone into wagers. One day, she left a message for her family, drove her car to a shopping center and killed herself.

In a relatively affluent Chicago suburb, a 41-year-old man committed suicide after using more than $11,000 in credit card advances for gambling. He shot himself after leaving a gambling boat. Police found $13 in his pocket.

More typical is the experience of a friend, a professional man, who attended a statewide meeting of an association with which he is affiliated. While he went to the meetings, his wife went to a riverboat casino and "got hooked." She spent all the money she had and used all the available money from her credit cards, close to $20,000. Her husband knew nothing about it until he checked out of the hotel and found his credit cards could not be used because they had already reached their maximum. In this family, the situation has worked out, but that is not true for many.

A retired Air Force colonel has written me about the problem of casino gambling near Keesler Air Force Base that offers part-time work to personnel stationed there, but also 24-hour-a-day gambling availability and has brought serious problems of addiction and the social and criminal problems that go with it for the men and women stationed there.

Compulsive Gambling Leads to Crime and Suicide

Gambling addiction is a serious problem. We know that men are more likely to become addicted than women, that the appeal of gambling is greater for low-income people than those of above-average income, that there are approximately 9 million adults and 1.3 million teenagers with some form of gambling behavior problem and that the availability of gambling enterprises—their closeness to where a person lives—causes a significant increase in the addiction problem. Nationally, less than 1 percent, 0.77 percent, of the population are compulsive gamblers, but when enterprises are located near a population, that number increases two to seven times.

The greatest growth is among teenagers. University of Maryland football fans were stunned recently to read that their all-American quarterback had been suspended by the NCAA for four games because of betting on college games. The spread of gambling among teenagers has spilled over onto college campuses, and Maryland's football problem is evidencing itself on many campuses, a highly publicized tip of a much more serious iceberg.

Costs to society of the problem gambler vary from the most conservative estimate of $13,200 to $30,000 per year. I have no idea which figure may be correct, but we know there are costs. Arnold Wexler and his wife, Sheila Wexler, did a study for Rutgers University and noted:

> Compulsive gamblers will bet until nothing is left: savings, family assets, personal belongings—anything of value that may be pawned, sold or borrowed against. They will borrow from co-workers, credit union, family and friends, but will rarely admit it is for gambling. They may take personal loans, write bad checks and ultimately reach and pass the point of bankruptcy. . . . In desperation, compulsive gamblers may panic and often will turn to illegal activities to support their addiction.[8]

Prosecuting attorney Jeffrey Bloomberg of Lawrence County, South Dakota, testified before a U.S. House committee on his experiences dealing with Deadwood, South Dakota, a small community that became the first place outside of Atlantic City and Nevada to legalize casino gambling. He said they were promised "economic development, new jobs and lower taxes." Instead, casinos flourished, but other businesses did not. Businesses that provide

> the necessities of life such as clothing are no longer available . . . and customers of the town's only remaining grocery store walk a gauntlet of slot-machines as they exit with their purchases. For the most part, the jobs which were created earn minimum wage or slightly better and are without benefits. As for the claim that gambling brings tax relief, this simply has not proven

true. Real property taxes for both residential and commercial properties have risen each and every year since gambling was legalized. Crimes of theft, embezzlement, bad checks and other forms of larceny have increased. Our office has also seen an increase in the number of child abuse and neglect cases as a result of gambling. These run the spectrum from the children left in their cars all night while their parents gamble, to the children left at home alone while their parents gamble, to the children left at home alone while single mothers work the casino late shift, to the household without utilities or groceries because one or both parents have blown their paycheck gambling. Government is hooked on the money generated by gambling and in the long term the ramifications of this governmental addiction will be just as dire as for the individual who becomes addicted to gambling.[9]

One study conducted for insurance companies suggests that 40 percent of white-collar crime can be traced to gambling. Usually those involved have no prior criminal record.

The suicide rates for problem gamblers is significantly higher than it is for the general population. One out of five attempts suicide, a higher rate than for alcoholism or drug addiction.

State Lotteries Target the Poor

Pathological gamblers are much more likely to be violent with their spouses and abuse their children. Children of these gamblers generally do worse in school and have a suicide rate twice that of their classmates.

A survey of compulsive gamblers found 22 percent divorced because of gambling, 40 percent had lost or quit a job due to gambling, 49 percent stole from work to pay gambling debts, 23 percent [were] alcoholic, 26 percent [were] compulsive overeaters, 63 percent had contemplated suicide and 79 percent said they wanted to die.[10]

Treatment for gambling compulsion is rarely covered by health insurance policies, though physicians often will simply list depression as the cause for needed therapy, and that may be covered. A national conference will be held in Puerto Rico in September [1995] to discuss the growing problem of gambling addiction.

State lotteries disproportionately receive money from—and target—

the poor. While it is true that the purchases are voluntary and provide some entertainment, as a society we should be providing more substantial exits from poverty than the rare lottery victory. A bill before the Illinois legislature sponsored by Representative Jack Kubik to prohibit cashing welfare checks at race tracks, off-track betting parlors, and riverboat casinos died a quiet death.

Compounding all of this, state and local governments who receive revenue from legalized gambling often are its promoters, both to bring gambling in and to sustain it. Governments get hooked. While states receive revenue from alcohol and tobacco sales, no governmental unit— to my knowledge—promotes alcohol and tobacco. Generally governments appeal to our strengths, not our weaknesses. But gambling is different. Billboards are erected in poor areas to promote the Illinois Lottery. "This could be your ticket out," one proclaimed. If the state of Illinois had billboards promoting whiskey, beer or cigarettes, there would be a public outcry. The Pennsylvania lottery unashamedly advertises: "Don't forget to play every day." And of course the poor are the ones who succumb to that lure.

The Gambling Industry Makes False Promises

Industries that want to bring in casinos are generous with their promises. The poverty of Atlantic City would be virtually eliminated, the scenario read, but it did not happen. Poverty has not diminished, and problems with gambling addiction are up. Since the advent of the casinos, 40 percent of the restaurants not associated with the gambling enterprises have closed, and one-third of the city's retail business has closed. Unemployment in Atlantic City is now the state's highest. Crime is up significantly—almost tripled—and the population has dropped by one-fourth. Industrial consultant Nelson Rose told *U.S. News and World Report*: "Atlantic City used to be a slum by the sea. Now it's a slum by the sea with casinos."[11]

But not only Atlantic City has been affected. A study of crime patterns along non-toll roads between Atlantic City and New York City and

Atlantic City and Philadelphia found a significant increase in crime rates.[12]

The Better Government Association of Illinois survey of 324 businesses in towns with riverboat casinos found that 51 percent of the firms said riverboats had either no effect or a negative effect on their business. Of the 44 percent who gave a positive response, half said the lift their business got was minimal. Three percent said their business has been "helped a lot."[13] A Chicago *Tribune* survey found a similar result. An Aurora, Illinois riverboat casino gets all but 1 to 2 percent of its business from within the state, and the *Tribune* reported:

> "The casino is killing the small businesses in this area, and they claimed it would help us," said Mario Marrero, former owner of the Porto Coeli Cafe and Bakery, a block from the casino.
>
> As soon as the casino opened a year ago, Marrero saw his business drop by half, from about $4,000 a month to $2,000 a month, he said.
>
> In May, he was forced to close after nearly five years in business.[14]

Gambling's effect on government is more than income from gamblers and expenditures for dealing with problem gamblers and increased crime. Gambling operators are major contributors to campaigns—in the millions—and employ expensive lobbyists at both the state and federal level. A few gambling enterprises have formed the American Gaming Association and employed a former chairman of the Republican National Committee as its chief executive. Gaming is an influence to be reckoned with in dozens of state capitals, and its influence will grow markedly in Washington. In Illinois, the lobbyists for gambling include a former governor, a former attorney general, two former U.S. attorneys, a former director of the state police, a prominent former judge, a former mayor of Chicago and at least seven former state legislators. All of this is legal.

But gambling in Illinois has also been associated with the illegal. Back in 1964, as a state legislator, I co-authored an article for *Harper's* magazine titled, "The Illinois Legislature: A Study in Corruption." It did not enhance my popularity in that body, but it did some good, and I am pleased to report that today the Illinois legislature—in ethics, and in quality—is a much improved body over that period. But whenever there is easy money floating around, the temptation for corruption is present. We have had two governors in our state's history go to prison, one because of payoffs from legalized gambling. I recall particularly the deal worked out in which—on the same day—the sales tax in our state was increased from 2 cents to 3 cents, which then included food and medicine, and the tax on two politically well-connected racetracks was reduced by one-third. Every state legislator knew what was going on.

Gambling Attracts Organized Crime

Organized crime has frequently been a problem with gambling, whether legal or illegal. Big money attracts them. And it is big money.

Last year, one riverboat casino in Illinois netted—not grossed—$203 million. The Chicago *Tribune*[15] reported that two politically well-connected Illinois men were offered $20 million if they landed a casino in our state for a Nevada firm. When contacted by the *Tribune*, they said they had other offers that were higher.

The gambling elite are not only generous employers of lobbyists, they are multimillion dollar donors to political campaigns, and the combination makes them politically potent. The unsavory and unhealthy influence of lobbyists and legislators as a protector of this rapidly growing industry means sensible restraint will not be easily achieved.

But there is another side to that story. Public opinion is not with the gambling gentry. Even after well-financed campaigns, when there are referenda on whether legalized gambling should be expanded in a state or community, rarely do those initiatives win. Every referendum on a gambling casino held last year [1994] lost, and in the big one, Florida, it lost decisively. Donald Trump may have helped when he told the Miami *Herald* a few weeks before the referendum: "As someone who lives in Palm Beach, I'd prefer not to see casinos in Florida. But as someone in the gambling business, I'm going to be the first one to open if Floridians vote for them." Florida Commerce Secretary Charles Dusseau did an economic analysis of gambling possibilities in Florida and came to the conclusion it would hurt the state.

Opposition to legalized gambling also brings together an unlikely coalition. For example, Ralph Reed, [former] executive of the Christian Coalition, and the liberal state Senator Tom Hayden of California, agree on this issue.

To those who wish to go back to an earlier era in our nation's history when legalized gambling was abolished, my political assessment is that is not possible. But restraint is possible.

The Federal Gambling Commission Should Look at New Ideas

I have introduced legislation, cosponsored by Senator Lugar, to have a commission, of limited duration and a small budget, look at this problem. Congressmen Frank Wolf and John LaFalce have introduced somewhat similar legislation in the House. My reason for suggesting the limited time—18 months—and the small budget, $250,000, is that commissions like that often are the most productive. One of the finest commissions the nation has had, the Commission on Foreign Languages and International Studies, produced its report in a little more than one year on a small budget and had significant influence.

Let a commission look at where we are and where we should go. My instinct is that sensible limits can be established.

For example, what if any new gambling enterprise established after a specific date had to pay a tax of 5 percent on its gross revenue. Those who are already in the field who are not too greedy should support it because it prevents the saturation of the market. Financial wizard Bernard Baruch said of those who invest in the stock market, "The bears win and the bulls win, but the hogs lose." Gambling enterprises that are willing to limit their expansion are more likely to be long-term winners. And those who know the problems that gambling causes should support this idea because of the limitations.

Or suppose we were to move to some form of supplement to local and state revenue again. States, Indian tribes, and local governments that do not have any form of legalized gambling would be eligible for per capita revenue-sharing assistance. It would require creating a source of revenue for such funding, but would bring some relief to non-federal governments that do not want gambling but are desperate for additional revenue. There is no way—let me underscore this—of reducing the gambling problem without facing the local revenue problem.

Congressman Jim McCrery, a Republican from Louisiana, has proposed that lotteries—now exempt from Federal Trade Commission truth-in-advertising standards—should be covered. Why should the New York lottery be able to advertise: "We won't stop until everyone's a millionaire"?

These are just three possible ideas. The commission could explore others. The commission can look at how we deal with gambling opportunities that will surface later this year on an experimental basis on cable television and the Internet. How significant could this become? None of us knows.

We do know that two-thirds of problem gamblers come from a home where at least one parent had a problem with alcoholism. Should we be dealing more seriously with alcoholism, in part to deal with the gambling phenomenon?

These and other questions could be studied by a commission.

What should not be ignored by Congress and the American people is that we have a problem on our hands. We need to find sensible and sensitive answers.

Notes

1. Rob Day, "A Full House," *Hemisphere* (October 1994).
2. *Gaming and Wagering Business*, December 15, 1991–January 15, 1992.
3. *Chicago Sun-Times*, April 17, 1995.
4. Chicago Crime Commission, 1990.
5. William Thompson, Ricardo Gazel, and Dan Rickman, "The Economic Impact of Native American Gaming in Wisconsin," published by the Wisconsin Policy Research Institute.

6. George Grob, Deputy Inspector General, HHS, April 5, 1995, Senate Committee on Indian Affairs.

7. Paul Samuelson, *Economics* (McGraw-Hill, 1970).

8. Arnold Wexler and Sheila Wexler, 1992.

9. Jeffrey Bloomberg, testimony September 21, 1994, House Committee on Small Business.

10. Henry Lesieur and Christopher Anderson.

11. *U.S. News and World Report*, March 14, 1994.

12. Simon Hakim and Joseph Friedman.

13. Better Government Association of Illinois, 1994 survey.

14. *Chicago Tribune*, June 28, 1994.

15. *Chicago Tribune*, March 28, 1995.

14. Gambling Weakens the Work Ethic and the Family

Senator Richard Lugar

In his address to the National Coalition Against Legalized Gambling, Indiana senator Richard Lugar recommends the formation of a national commission on the effects of legalized gambling, which was formed in 1997 and is headed by Kay Coles James, dean of Regent University's Robertson School of Government in Virginia Beach. He asserts that civic leaders responsible for their communities' fiscal well-being need to have access to unbiased information concerning gambling and its social and economic impact. Furthermore, Senator Lugar contends that there are negative moral consequences associated with the implementation of gambling-based revenue programs, but that these negative consequences are often overlooked because of the false promises of immediate financial gain.

I am Senator Dick Lugar. I am pleased to have the opportunity to speak with you today about an issue you and I care deeply about: the spread of legalized gambling in America. You have gathered this weekend in Orlando to meet with colleagues and to hear from national experts and

Richard Lugar, U.S. Senator from Indiana, October 28, 1995, message presented on videotape to the National Coalition Against Legalized Gambling.

elected officials about the impact of gambling on our cities and communities. You have also come to find out what you can do individually, at the grassroots level, to make a difference.

As legalized gambling proliferates at breathtaking speed, it is touching the lives of millions of Americans. Hundreds of communities across the country are considering casinos, riverboat gambling, pari-mutuel racing, off-track betting, and other forms of wagering.

In the face of this explosive growth, I want to establish a temporary national commission to conduct an 18-month study on the effects of gambling. I testified last month before the judiciary committee of the House of Representatives in support of legislation to create this study commission. I was joined in this effort by the bill's sponsor, Senator Paul Simon of Illinois, and Congressman Frank Wolf of Virginia. Senator Simon and I have asked that public hearings also be held in the Senate.

We need to know the answers to questions like: What is the extent of gambling by teenagers? What is the impact of gambling establishments on other businesses? How does gambling affect crime rates? How does gambling affect low-income populations? And what links exist between gambling and organized crime?

Gambling Is a National Issue

One gambling industry lobbyist recently criticized the proposal saying, and I quote, "It's a state's rights issue." This argument is flawed for a number of reasons.

First, the federal government continues its regulation of gambling on tribal lands.

Second, the recent growth of electronic gambling via the Internet could have serious interstate and international implications when people use personal computers to gamble across state lines and around the world. We need to learn more about gambling via the Internet.

As a former two-term mayor of a vibrant midwestern city, Indianapolis, it is clear to me that the civic-minded folks facing the toughest decisions on whether to permit gambling are leaders at the local level.

They must do so in a vacuum of reliable, unbiased information, information desperately needed to make sound choices of what will affect both the social and economic futures of their communities. Many local leaders want to learn from the experience of other communities. Unfortunately, experts have found that many available studies were location-specific, unbalanced or funded by gambling interests. The *Washington Post* in a September 22 endorsement of the gambling study commission proposal stated, and I quote, "Those pushing casinos into communities made large claims about their economic benefits but the jobs and investment casinos create are rarely stacked up against the jobs lost and the investment and spending foregone in other parts of a local economy. The commission study could be of great use to communities pondering whether to wager their futures on roulette, slot machines and blackjack."

A steady stream of news accounts in the *New York Times*, the *Wall Street Journal*, and other national publications have chronicled the recent growth and expansion of gambling activities in America. Many of the studies describe the enormous profits generated almost overnight by gambling enterprises. The articles also relate the personal experiences of local residents who visit a casino instead of a restaurant or a ballpark, who spend their grocery money on a nearby instant-play video lottery game. Or who totally exhaust their personal or family savings at the casino tables.

Gambling Is Unproductive and Hurts Other Businesses

A major reason for the astronomical growth of gambling is the fact that state and local governments facing budget shortfalls are desperate for revenue. Another important and disheartening factor is our failure as concerned Americans to raise important questions about the spread of gambling. Hearing of gambling and instant promises of instant revenue, state and local government officials all too often accept gambling as the silver bullet solution to balancing their budgets without raising taxes. Even if a state or community is reluctant to host a gambling establishment, it can be drawn over the edge by the threat that gambling operations may locate in a nearby town or neighboring state. Studies have shown that casino operations have significant impact on neighboring economies. For many local officials, the legalization of gambling becomes an economic survival issue rather than a question of developing sound public policy. As gambling gains a foothold in the community, it enervates the notion of the work ethic. Gambling weakens our ability to teach our children the basics, if you will, the Cal Ripken values of hard work, patience, human achievement and personal responsibility. What is the message being sent to our children by clever television and radio commercials for lotteries that bombard us with the message that wealth is only a play away? It says that if you play enough you can hit the jackpot and be freed of the discipline of self-support through a job or a long commitment to ongoing education. This same erosion of personal responsibility is at the heart of family dysfunctions, drug abuse, criminal behavior and abortion. We cannot tolerate the get-rich symbolism of gambling, of pleading with our children to avoid other tosses of the dice that lead to unhealthy living and destructive behavior. The gambling industry does not choose to confront these moral questions. It would like for the gambling issue to be seen as an economic or entertainment choice. But even in the economic realm, the arguments for expanding gambling are weak at best.

Gambling-related employment pales when compared to other forms of employment such as manufacturing. Gambling does not produce value-added products or reinvestment in the market economy. Other businesses in the region often lose as consumer spending for all sorts of goods and services shifts to spending at casinos or casino-related activities. Long-term growth and prosperity for our communities is most often earned the old-fashioned way: through hard work, dedication, commitment to common purpose.

If we put our best minds to work on ways to finance the needs of our cities and communities, we can continue to ensure a higher standard of living and better quality of life for all Americans. As you continue your valuable work with the National Coalition on this important issue, I want to express my appreciation to you for your commitment to grassroots organization efforts to raise education and awareness about legalized gambling among our neighborhoods and communities. Thank you for the opportunity to speak with you today.

15. Gambling Is Productive and Rational

David Ramsay Steele

David Ramsay Steele defends the individual's freedom to gamble by trying to show that gambling is neither intrinsically wasteful nor necessarily irrational. Steele claims that it is misleading to accuse gambling of "cannibalizing" other activities, because that tendency is no more true of gambling than it is of any industry that competes with others for consumer dollars. He goes on to discuss what is meant by "productive," and contends that economic production means the satisfaction of wants, not necessarily the making of physical objects. Gambling is therefore truly productive if it yields "utility" (gratification of their wants) to gamblers.

Gambling is of two types, maintains Steele: recreational gambling and lottery playing. Steele holds that recreational gambling is a form of amusement or entertainment much like music, theater, chess, or sports. Recreational gambling often involves some skill, and in any case provides enjoyment to the participants. The possibility of monetary gain or loss adds spice to the game, but is usually not the main goal of the players.

Steele asserts that a lottery has a predominantly different motivation: it is played primarily for the chance of winning a big prize. Steele vigorously disputes the belief that there must be something irrational in playing the lottery. He maintains that there is no evidence that typical lottery players overestimate their chances or are in any way victims of a delusion or miscalculation. According to Steele, lottery players simply value an unlikely chance of

---

This is a condensation of part of the article, "Yes, Gambling Is Productive and Rational," which appeared in *Liberty* (September 1997). Used by permission.

becoming rich highly enough to pay a very small sum for that chance. In Steele's view, people who believe that playing the lottery has to be irrational often think this way because a lottery is technically an "unfair bet" or because the price of a lottery ticket is below what statisticians call its "expected value." Steele argues that it is not necessarily a mistake to take an "unfair" bet or to pay more for an opportunity than its "expected value."

Before we look at the claim that gambling involves nothing but sterile transfers of money or goods, let's first consider a related charge leveled by anti-gambling propagandists. One of their leaders, Robert Goodman, contends that gambling, when it is permitted after a period of prohibition, displaces or, as he picturesquely terms it, "cannibalizes" other activities.[1]

Goodman continually reiterates this charge, and doesn't seem to notice that it applies equally to any activity that consumes scarce resources—any activity whatsoever. If pizza restaurants were first prohibited and then legalized, the newly legal restaurants would attract some dollars away from other businesses. Buildings, kitchen equipment, tables, delivery vehicles, and employees would be bid away from other kinds of restaurants, and perhaps some resources would be bid away from non-restaurant activities, to cater to the consumers' newly-liberated demand for pizzas. One might then observe that pizza provision grows only by hurting other occupations—that pizzerias "cannibalize" other trades.

If, after being prohibited, a casino is permitted to open, this may well cause people to spend in the casino some money they would formerly have spent in a restaurant. Perhaps that restaurant has to close because of reduced business. Precisely the same would apply in reverse; if casinos were legal, but restaurants prohibited, and then restaurants were legalized, the newly legal restaurants would attract consumers' dollars away from casinos, and some casinos might have to close. Anti-restaurant fanatics could then proclaim that restaurateurs were nothing more than dastardly cannibals, gobbling up legitimate businesses such as casinos.

When a heretofore prohibited but widely desired activity is legalized, the expansion of this activity will necessarily curtail other activities, unless

total output increases. This does not mean that the change is unimpor-
tant. The fact that people pursue the newly legal activity demonstrates
that there was hitherto an unsatisfied appetite for that activity. The
people who formerly desired to take part in the prohibited activity, and
are now free to do so, experience an improvement in their situation, in
their own judgment. Their real incomes automatically rise, even though
this increase is not captured in national income statistics.

There are two important qualifications to what I have just stated.
First, the legalization of a formerly prohibited industry reduces the
demand for other industries below what it would otherwise have been,
not necessarily below what it has actually been. If total output rises—if
there is economic growth—casinos may attract business from restaurants,
and yet restaurants may keep the same business as before, or even
expand. Second, prohibition of gambling does not succeed in stopping
gambling. While prohibition reduces the total amount of gambling, some
gambling goes on illicitly. A major part of the expansion of legal gambling
following legalization takes away business from formerly illegal gambling
rather than from nongambling activities.

Production Means Satisfaction of Wants

What does it mean to say that some activity is unproductive? This
question was picked over quite thoroughly by economists in the
eighteenth and nineteenth centuries. One early view was that only agriculture was productive. Manufacturing (then a small part of total employment) was looked upon as unproductive, since it was obviously supported
by agriculture—the manufacturers had to eat. Another idea was that only
products that could be turned into gold and silver were truly productive.
Later these two theories lost any serious following,[2] but two others
remained popular for a while: that anything that did not result in a new
physical object was unproductive, and that what we would now call
"service" jobs were unproductive. (These two views are not the same, and
do not necessarily mesh together well, for a provider of services, such as

an architect, may assist in the creation of a new physical object, such as a house.)

After the end of the nineteenth century, leading economists no longer paid much attention to the classification of activities as productive or unproductive. The new theory of value based on marginal utility shone a flood of light on the question, and clearly exposed many of the old arguments as fallacious.

The conclusion of the new approach was that "production" means "satisfaction of wants." It is productive to make a physical object only insofar as that object enables someone to satisfy a desire. In satisfying desires, the physical object (such as a shirt) yields services. All production is ultimately production of *services* desired by consumers. The musician giving a live performance is being directly productive in the only way in which it is intelligible to be productive: he is satisfying the wants of consumers, in this case of listeners. The producer of a shirt is being productive more indirectly, by making an object that will yield a stream of future want-satisfactions to its wearer. If for some reason the shirt cannot yield these want-satisfactions, whether because everyone undergoes a conversion to an anti-shirt religion or because the shirt falls apart before it can be worn, then the labor of producing it has turned out to be unproductive, despite the fact that a physical object has been made.

One way of describing want-satisfaction is to talk about "utility." An activity is productive if it yields utility. According to the modern view, which is no longer controversial among economic theorists, domestic servants, entertainers, priests, and physicians are indeed productive, because they produce services their customers want; they enable those customers to get additional utility.

The same applies to activities in which people may engage either individually or collaboratively. It is productive for a musician to give a recital, assuming that the audience likes it, but it is also productive for a group of friends to get together and perform music for their own enjoyment, or for an individual to perform alone for his own satisfaction.

Does gambling satisfy the wants of its participants? Do gamblers enjoy gambling? If they do, then gambling is productive, in much the same way that sports, religious services, and psychotherapy are productive.

There Are Two Kinds of Gambling

The outstanding theorist of gambling, Reuven Brenner, points out that it comes in two types.[3] There is gambling—call it "recreational"—that takes up a lot of the gambler's time, and gambling that does not. Many people derive considerable enjoyment from recreational gambling. Recreational gamblers do not gamble primarily to gain financially, but to enjoy themselves by playing a game. The possibility of monetary gain or loss adds spice to the game.

Many forms of recreational gambling involve some skill, and these games are therefore not sharply different from games like golf or chess, where there is *some* luck and people pay to play competitively, the winners receiving substantial prizes. In poker, the amount of luck per hand may be high, but this evens out with many games, so that the element of skill will tend to predominate in the course of a few hours' play.[4] Recreational gambling is no less productive than tenpin bowling, ballroom dancing, or barbershop singing—all group pastimes that people pursue because they enjoy them.

Many people will readily agree that if a concert, a baseball match, or an evening's conversation are considered productive, a poker school might also be judged productive. But there is another kind of gambling: playing the lottery. Surely this can't be primarily an enjoyable way to pass the time. It seems to be done in hope of financial gain, but what if that hope is a product of delusion?

Anti-gambling dogmatists usually hold a distinctive interpretation of the motivation for gambling. They maintain that gambling occurs because individuals seek monetary gain, that this desire for monetary gain must be disappointed in most cases, and that therefore the persistence of gambling is irrational—either stupid or involuntary. It is often contended (or more commonly, just assumed) that a rational person would never gamble. Gambling, on this interpretation, occurs only because gamblers fail to understand elementary probability theory, or, understanding it, cannot bring themselves to act upon it. The cliché that lotteries are a "voluntary tax on the stupid" echoes Sir William Petty (1623–1687), who argued for state management of lotteries on the grounds that the state already had the care of lunatics and idiots.

Gambling prohibitionists are always falling over themselves to "explain" that "gamblers must lose in the long run," that "the odds are stacked against the gambler," that "gamblers as a whole can only lose," and so forth. They pronounce these marvelous insights as though they were gems of wisdom that gamblers must have overlooked. And perhaps a tiny minority of gamblers have indeed missed these earth-shaking commonplaces—after all, people have been known to make silly mistakes in all departments of life, from music to marriage, so there's no reason why gambling should be immune. But I cannot see any evidence that the general run of gamblers behave irrationally, or that they would stop gambling if they took a course in probability theory.

The claim that the gambler overestimates his chances is usually asserted as a blind dogma, with no supporting argument offered. However, some anti-gambling propagandists mention, as though it were significant, that the whole class of lottery players must lose on balance. In technical terms, playing the lottery is not a "fair" bet; the "expected value" of a lottery ticket is below the price of the ticket.[5]

It Can Be Rational to Place an "Unfair" Bet

The expenses of organizing a lottery have to be covered out of sales of tickets. Therefore, the amount returned in prizes is lower than the amount paid for tickets.[6] A technically "fair" lottery would be one in which the total prize money were equal to the total money paid for tickets. In such a lottery, what is called the "expected value" of a ticket would be the same as the ticket price. It is an error to suppose that this offers a criterion of rationality: that it must be irrational to play the lottery when the expected value is below the ticket price. That this supposition is faulty can be seen upon a moment's reflection.[7]

The proportion of total ticket revenues returned in prizes from lotteries is commonly around 60 percent, though it is sometimes more than 70 percent, and with some of the new state lotteries is little more than 50 percent.[8] If lotteries were purely private and open to competition, this figure would immediately rise to well over 90 percent (except where particular lotteries were openly allied with charitable donation),[9] but it could never reach 100 percent without the lottery's making a loss. Just suppose, however, that a lottery were subsidized, so that 105 percent of the prize money were returned in prizes. Would it then become rational to always buy lottery tickets, and irrational to fail to do so? If so, how many tickets? How much of one's income would it be obligatory, if one were rational, to allocate to lottery tickets? Suppose now that the lottery were hugely subsidized, so that, say, five times the ticket revenues were returned in prizes (but most entrants would still win nothing), what then? At what point, as we increased the subsidy to the lottery, would it become incumbent upon any rational person to buy a ticket?

There is no such point—though there would empirically be a point where the majority of people, or the majority of people with math degrees, would judge that one would have to be a lunatic not to buy at least one ticket. This kind of thing is a matter of personal preference, a matter of one's personality and world view. It is "subjective" in the sense that there is no single demonstrably correct answer for any rational agent. Such judgments can be influenced by miscalculations or other mistakes, but if all mistakes were eliminated, there would remain a diversity of preferences. Given these preferences, one's behavior is also affected by objective circumstances like one's income.

A lottery player will usually prefer a lottery that returns 90 percent of the ticket revenues to one that returns only 80 percent. Therefore, some will be induced to play at 90 percent who would not play at 80 percent. But someone who plays the lottery buys a chance of being in for a big win, and there is no justification for the assumption that the individual's valuation of this chance, the amount of utility he derives from being aware of it, has to coincide with the "expected value" of a lottery ticket (the prize money multiplied by the chance of winning). There are many cases where it clearly ought not to do so (for example, if the price of a ticket is one's entire income for the next few weeks, so that one will die of starvation unless one wins the prize, it would not be sensible to enter with a one-in-a-million chance of winning, even if the prize were so heavily subsidized that the expected value of a ticket were a thousand times the ticket price).

A rational person doesn't have to value a one-in-a-million chance of getting a million dollars at precisely one dollar. You may value such a chance at one cent or at five dollars—either way (though this may tell us something about your personality) there's nothing wrong with you.[10] However, assume for a moment that the "expected value" theory of rational gambling were correct. Suppose that you paid a dollar for a ticket giving you one chance in a million of winning $700,000, with $300,000 of ticket sales going to run the lottery and pay off the state. The expected value of your one-dollar ticket would be 70 cents. Only 30 cents would have to be explained by non-pecuniary elements (a sense of participation, giving something to a good cause, and so forth, or, if we want to indulge in flights of fancy, by "irrational compulsion" or "enhanced daydreaming"). It would follow that at least 70 cents out of each and every dollar spent on lottery tickets would indisputably be rationally allocated. Is this better or worse than the dollars spent on furniture or books? Casual discussion of the rationality of buying a ticket often tacitly assumes that "expected value" is the rule, but then proceeds as though the entire sum spent on tickets would be shown to be irrationally spent, when in fact (on the erroneous assumption that expected value should fix the buyer's valuation of a ticket) only something less than half of the ticket price would then, arguably, be spent irrationally.

The fact that a lottery is not technically "fair" follows automatically from the fact that the costs of running the lottery have to be covered out of ticket sales, and is otherwise a complete red herring from which no conclusions about the rationality of the players may legitimately be drawn. It's a feature of any system for re-allocating existing endowments, such as a subscription to the March of Dimes: organizing a subscription costs something, so the total paid to beneficiaries must be less than the total contributed. This is ineluctable, and in no way sinister. A lottery is simply a way in which many people each put in a small sum, and then a few of those people picked at random get large sums. Nothing in the world could possibly be more harmless or more innocent than this.

Notes

1.   Robert Goodman, *The Luck Business: The Devastating Consequences and Broken Promises of America's Gambling Explosion* (New York: The Free Press, 1995).
2.   The first is now almost precisely reversed in the minds of many followers of Ross Perot and Patrick Buchanan: only the building of gadgets, preferably of metal, is considered truly productive. "Hamburger flipping"—providing meals for people—has become the very paradigm of unproductiveness.
3.   Reuven Brenner, with Gabrielle A. Brenner, *Gambling and Speculation: A Theory, a History, and a Future of Some Human Decisions* (Cambridge: Cambridge University Press, 1990), pp. 20–21. This is the best book ever written on gambling. Although I agree with nearly all Brenner's criticisms of orthodox opinion on gambling, I reject the lynchpin of his own theory: that non-recreational gambling occurs only because people crave an increase specifically in their *relative* income, independent of their desire for an absolute increase in income.
4.   Where there is recreational gambling with some skill involved, a resourceful player may win in the long run. There is no reason why the "house" or the "bookie" would necessarily object to some players making consistent gains. The majority of recreational gamblers, whose interest in winning is less predominant, or whose skill is unremarkable, ultimately pay for the winnings of the monetary winners and the gains of the "house." This majority may still be "ahead" in non-pecuniary terms, in the enjoyment they derive from playing. In utility terms, which is all that matters, everybody may be a net winner. An interesting case is that of blackjack, where there is a sure-fire method of winning consistently. Although the existence of this method is very widely known, most blackjack players don't bother to learn it (which takes a few weeks of study), so casinos go on offering a game that they are bound to lose in the long run to any customers who apply the method. See the discussion of this in Willem Albert Wagenaar, *Paradoxes of Gambling Behavior* (Hove, England: Erlbaum, 1988), an interesting book that, like so many, never for a moment questions the reigning dogma that gamblers' motivations must involve irrationality.
5.   "Fair bet" and "expected value" are technical terms. They have nothing to do with the vernacular sense of these words. An "unfair" bet may be entirely fair, or vice versa, while an "expected value" is not what anybody expects.
6.   Under free competition, the return to investors in all industries, including gambling, will be roughly the same, on average, as the rate of interest.

7.   Consider whether you would rather have a dollar or a one-in-50,000 chance of $50,000. The one thing you will not say is that you can see no important difference between these options, that you are indifferent between them. But once a difference in the valuation of these two outcomes is acknowledged, it automatically follows that it may be rational to give up one in exchange for the other.

8.   Anti-gambling preachers frequently include in the "costs" of gambling all the money spent by gamblers, without subtracting the distributed winnings, which at a stroke multiplies the supposed costs several-fold. This is not willful deceit, just the normal intellectual laziness of these anti-gambling tub-thumpers.

9.   About 95 percent of the money wagered in Las Vegas casinos is returned as winnings. An appreciable chunk of the remaining 5 percent goes in taxes.

10. If someone you loved desperately could be saved from a painful and potentially fatal disease only by getting a million dollars, and the only possible way to get a million dollars were to play the lottery, wouldn't you play? Of course you would: it would be contemptible not to do so. The principle is not altered if the person you love so much is yourself, and the disease is not being rich.

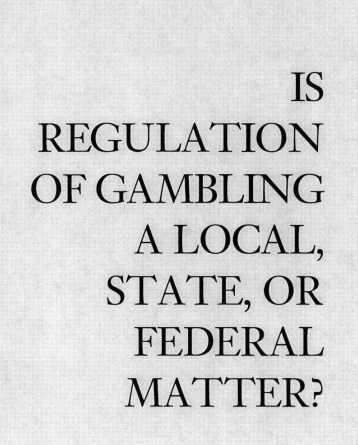

VI

IS
REGULATION
OF GAMBLING
A LOCAL,
STATE, OR
FEDERAL
MATTER?

INTRODUCTION TO PART VI

If gambling should be subject to governmental regulation, the question arises: from what level of government should most regulation come? Some policy analysts, for example, Robert Goodman (Chapter 18), argue that the federal government should largely direct gambling policy to ensure uniform laws that protect consumers. He believes that federal direction is necessary so that states can uniformly protect consumers instead of competing for their money. Apparently Goodman thinks that gambling policy should be informed not principally by a concern for states' rights but by a concern for consumers, especially impoverished ones.

Other analysts believe that gambling, in most circumstances, is a matter internal to states and appropriate to state governments. Still others argue that much gambling, such as that conducted in riverboats and casinos, directly affects local communities and so should be subject to local regulation. Today state gambling commissions have a great deal of power over gaming in different localities.

One critic of state-centralized gaming regulation is attorney Paul Delva (Chapter 16), formerly a law student at Temple University School of Law. According to him, gambling chiefly affects local communities and therefore gambling regulatory regimes, be they state or local, should accommodate the needs and preferences of people living in those communities.

Leah Lorber, a former law student at Indiana University School of Law, also sides with local interests in the matter of lands taken in trust for Native Americans (Chapter 17). Citing legal and historical precedents, she criticizes the Interior Department's recent policy of granting state governors absolute veto power over gaming facilities on newly acquired Indian trust lands.

16. Power to Regulate Gambling Should Stay with Cities and Counties

Paul Delva

Paul Delva, a Philadelphia attorney, argues that local governments and local citizens should play a leading role in forming and executing gambling policy. Developing his case by examining gambling policy in different states, where local communities have varying degrees of control over legal gambling, he looks at the case of riverboat gambling. While he notes that most legislation authorizing riverboat gambling gives local communities at the city and county levels authority to prevent gambling within their communities, the power to regulate legal gambling activities, once they are established, is normally vested in state gambling commissions, typically not answerable to local wishes and interests.

To illustrate how gambling might be regulated more locally, Delva examines some features of the Indian Gaming Regulatory Act (IGRA), a federal law allowing Indian tribes a good deal of latitude in regulating gambling within tribal territory. The act, for example, permits tribal governments not only to regulate gambling activities but also requires states to negotiate with Indian tribes to develop compacts governing gaming on Indian lands.

This first appeared as "The Promises and Perils of Legalized Gambling for Local Governments: Who Decides How to Stack the Deck?" in *Temple Law Review* 68 (1995), pp. 847–73. Used by permission.

Legal gambling is one of the fastest growing industries in the United States.[1] More and more states are in the process of liberalizing their gambling laws, transforming an activity once restricted by law into a hoped-for source of economic revitalization.[2] By authorizing new gambling-based enterprises, states hope to create jobs, revive local and regional economies, cultivate tourist industries, and tap into a newfound source of tax revenue.[3] As a result, state initiatives to legalize various forms of gambling have mushroomed in recent years. Gambling was the most popular ballot issue in the 1994 general election, with voters in eleven states facing a question on some aspect of the issue.[4] Although voters rejected many of these attempts—including, most notably, an attempt to legalize casino gambling in Florida[5]—new forms of legal wagering will continue to develop. The need for increased public revenues and continued public opposition to new income and consumer taxes mean increased state-sponsored gambling will very likely continue.[6]

Both the promises and the perils of legalized gambling carry distinctly local implications. Proponents of liberalized gambling laws promise jobs for local residents, tax revenues that will be used to improve local neighborhoods, and indirect benefits for local hospitality and tourist industries.[7] On the other hand, opponents of legalized gambling argue the claims of gambling proponents are exaggerated.[8] They warn of increased crime and traffic congestion in communities affected by gambling development, as well as damage to existing tourist and restaurant industries as dollars previously spent in them migrate to the new casino attractions.[9]

These "local" or "parochial" concerns[10] stand apart from broader social policy issues implicated by decisions to legalize gambling. Such social policy issues include the arguably regressive nature of legalized gambling as a source of taxation, and whether it is proper for states to organize and promote gambling.[11] These issues are not addressed directly here. That is, this article does not evaluate the competing claims of those for and against greater legalization of gambling, or attempt to draw conclusions about whether legal gambling is an appropriate source for public revenue or an effective means to promote economic development. Rather, this article examines the role of local governments in the regulation of gambling in the context of today's shifting gambling policies.

In the past, during an era characterized by gambling prohibition, local governments enjoyed considerable authority to regulate unlawful gambling.[12] This article argues that local governments should maintain this traditional exercise of local authority in today's increasingly permissive gambling policy environment. As gambling policy is reconceptualized and gambling legislation revised, local governments and local citizens should have a leading role in both the formation and execution of regulatory policies.

To address these issues, this article is organized into five main parts. Part 1 establishes the theoretical premises underlying subsequent analysis and discussion. Part 2 provides a historical overview of gambling regulation, tracing its development from past periods of prohibition to today's period of increasing acceptance. Part 3 examines how state and local governments have, to a large extent, shared gambling regulatory authority in the past "proscriptive" era. The doctrine of preemption is reviewed in order to analyze conflicts between state and local regulations. Part 4 reviews current state legislative approaches to one new form of legal gambling—riverboat gambling. These statutes are reviewed from the perspective of "local government autonomy." This term refers to the ability of "local actors"—city and county governments as well as local residents—to influence policies and regulation.[13] Part 5 analyzes the effect of riverboat gambling legislation on local autonomy.

The article concludes that new legislation authorizing gambling activities tends to decrease local autonomy, reducing the degree to which local people and governments can control events in their communities. The regulatory scheme governing gambling on Native American tribal lands is presented as a contrasting regime that provides a greater degree of local control over gambling activity in a given community. This conclusion suggests that legislation that purports to offer local or community choice over gambling should provide for greater local regulatory control over gambling activities after they are initially authorized by communities.

1. Local Autonomy Is Important

The conceptual distinction between centralized control and local autonomy underlies the analysis and discussion in this article. The concept of local autonomy refers to the ability of a locality—a city, town, borough, or similar "local" government unit—to act in a "purposeful, goal-oriented" fashion and "to act without fear of the oversight authority of higher tiers of the state."[14] In other words, local autonomy is the power of local governments to legislate for themselves.

In the United States, local governments do not formally have such power. Generally, local governments are revocable agencies of state governments. They are agencies of limited jurisdiction, and the scope of their powers depends upon the acts of state legislatures.[15] As a practical matter, however, because state governments are unable to deal with the intricacies of local affairs, much of their authority must be delegated to local governments.[16] Thus, the powers delegated to cities and towns are subordinate to the will of the state legislatures.[17]

Notwithstanding local government's subordinate relationship to state government authority, local self-determination and self-government constitute important and strongly advocated traditions.[18] They reflect the consensus that "self-determination by locally definable populations in regard to local problems is a desirable practice."[19] In drafting legislation, especially legislation devoted to local and regional economic development, state governments face important decisions about how much authority should be delegated to local government units.

This article begins, therefore, with the premise that local governments play an important role in the political process, despite their formally subordinate position to state governments, and with the normative assumption that local government is best able to reflect the needs, concerns, and aspirations of local communities. This assumption has supported local government authority to regulate gambling in the past "proscriptive era," and it should remain a valid basis of authority as states authorize new gambling activity as well.

2. Gambling's History Is Marked by Cycles of Prohibition and Promotion

Gambling[20] is a pervasive human activity.[21] And, like other income-producing endeavors, gambling has been used extensively by governments to generate revenue.[22] Lotteries have historically been viewed as a relatively popular means of raising public revenues. For example, during the American colonial period, the public preferred legalized gambling over additional taxes as the source of funding for the French and Indian Wars.[23] Many of the earliest forms of legal gambling in the United States were local lotteries organized to fund special projects.[24] Before the development of taxation, commercial banking, and public financing systems, governments used lotteries to pay for roads, bridges, canals, and other public works projects.[25] From 1790 to the Civil War period, states issued lottery licenses to colleges, schools, individuals, and private organizations for their own revenue-raising efforts.[26]

As lotteries grew in popularity and scope, however, corruption followed. Organized opposition to legalized gambling began to appear across the United States in the early 1800s.[27] By the end of the nineteenth century, 36 state constitutions had banned lotteries.[28] Gambling was generally prohibited from the late 1800s to the early 1960s because lotteries were perceived to be socially destructive.[29] At the same time, more sophisticated and efficient financing methods, which developed alongside industrial and commercial expansion, allowed governments to be less dependent on legalized gambling as a source of public funding.[30]

The history of legal gambling in the United States has thus been marked by cycles of government prohibition and promotion.[31] The latter has sometimes occurred in apparent response to fiscal crises. For example, an increased demand for public revenue caused a brief revival of lotteries—despite widespread public opposition—during and after the Civil War.[32] Since 1964, when New Hampshire introduced the first state-sponsored lottery in what may be referred to as the "modern legal gambling era,"[33] America has witnessed another surge in legalized gambling. Today, every state except Hawaii and Utah conducts a state-sponsored lottery.[34] Nevada and New Jersey permit high-stakes casino gambling. Oregon has expanded its state lottery to include on-line keno and video-poker machines throughout the state.[35] And, as discussed below, since the late 1980s several states have authorized limited gambling aboard riverboat casinos.[36]

Although more and more forms of gambling are permitted by state law, the practice remains largely prohibited in the United States by civil or criminal laws. Indeed, the increasing promotion of state-sponsored gambling contradicts state constitutional prohibitions and extensive criminalization of gambling in state law.[37]

While states generally prohibit gambling, they allow, by exception, state-run lotteries,[38] charitable "bingo," and similar games of chance (e.g., common raffles to support "worthy causes"),[39] pari-mutuel wagering on horse racing,[40] limited private or social gambling, and, increasingly, riverboat gambling and other forms of casino gambling.[41] Gambling that does not fall within such exceptions is, by definition, "unlawful gambling." Therefore, whether a form of gambling is unlawful or legal under state law is simply a matter of definition.

Persons convicted of unlawful gambling face sanctions that vary among the states. In California, unlawful gambling is a misdemeanor punishable by up to a $1,000 fine and up to six months' imprisonment.[42] Similar prohibitions can be found in Illinois,[43] New York,[44] Texas,[45] and other states' laws. In Pennsylvania, a person commits a first-degree misdemeanor if he or she "intentionally or knowingly makes, assembles, sets up, maintains, sells, lends, leases, gives away, or offers for sale, loan, lease or gift, any . . . device to be used for gambling purposes, except playing cards."[46]

3. Cities Have Some Authority to Regulate Gambling

Although state legislatures control gambling extensively through their criminal laws, local governments have historically played an important supplementary role in regulating gambling activity.[47] Local regulation of gambling has traditionally fallen within the local "police power"—the general authority of a town or city to legislate for "the public health, order, safety, morals and welfare."[48] The scope of this local authority depends on the legal traditions and customs of the particular state and locality under examination. Some states expressly grant their municipalities the power to suppress unlawful gambling.[49] For example, Illinois law gives cities and towns the same power to prohibit unlawful gambling, through the passage of supplementary local ordinances, as it does authority to suppress obscene publications and brothels.[50] In general, however, the local police power to suppress illegal gambling is perceived to be elastic in its response to local needs and demands.[51]

As a general rule, cities and towns may supplement state laws with local ordinances regulating gambling activity, but local regulations may not supplant or conflict with state laws.[52] Moreover, a local government's regulatory jurisdiction can be displaced, or "pre-empted," where a state's constitution or particular statute expressly provides that regulatory authority in a particular field is limited exclusively to the state legislature.[53] Where a state statute fully regulates a field, courts may be more reluctant to uphold local regulations impinging on that field.

For example, the Montana Supreme Court held that, where the state allowed the licensing of certain gambling games, it exercised exclusive authority to authorize those games.[54] The court reasoned that only where a state statute expressly grants local authority to regulate, as an exercise of local police power, would such authority be permitted.[55] On this reasoning, the court affirmed a trial court's order restraining a city from launching a local ballot initiative to restrict local gambling.[56] In that case, therefore, state regulation pre-empted a municipality's ability to regulate local gambling.

A court may also find an area of law pre-empted on constitutional rather than statutory grounds. For example, the Louisiana Constitution states that "[g]ambling shall be defined by and suppressed by the legislature."[57] The Louisiana Supreme Court has held that this constitutional language creates in the legislature the exclusive right to define and suppress illegal gambling activities. In *State ex rel. Corbello v. Bond*,[58] the Louisiana Supreme Court found that a local ordinance was unconstitutional because it defined unlawful gambling more broadly than did the state's gambling law.[59] The local ordinance prohibited gambling games in which some of the wagers were retained by the game's organizer (i.e., where the organizer "skimmed" or "raked off" a portion of the wagers).[60] The statutory definition of unlawful gambling was more limited. It proscribed gambling conducted as a business, so that "rake-offs" in non-business contexts were not forbidden by the state law.[61] The court held that, where the legislature exercised exclusive authority "to define that conduct which must be suppressed as gambling," the local ordinance violated the state constitution.[62]

Whether a statute fully regulates a field, however, is a question of judicial interpretation. In contrast to the Louisiana Supreme Court's approach, other state courts have affirmed the authority of local governments to supplement general state gambling laws with local ordinances.[63] In *State v. Khater*,[64] the Superior Court of New Jersey recently upheld a city ordinance that, in effect, prohibited amusement game machines that encouraged gambling, even though the machines themselves were not gambling devices.[65] The state statute at issue prohibited "slot machines" and other "gambling devices."[66] An ordinance of the city of Paterson, New Jersey, required that all amusement games be licensed, and forbade granting licenses to those games "used for the purpose of gambling."[67] Thus, the scope of the local ordinance was broader than that of the state statute, encompassing more types of devices than the state law. In holding that the city ordinance was valid, the Superior Court of New Jersey recognized that the city's police powers were limited by the state law.[68] However, the court found that the state's regulatory scheme was not comprehensive enough to preclude local regulation in the area of gambling devices.[69]

Similarly, in *Rice Street VFW, Post No. 3877 v. City of St. Paul*,[70] the Minnesota Court of Appeals upheld a St. Paul city ordinance regulating charitable games of chance, although the local ordinance was found to be more stringent than a state gambling law regulating the same subject.[71] The state law required profits of the games to be used only for charitable purposes.[72] The city ordinance at issue was more specific in defining how proceeds were to be spent, requiring ten percent of the games' profits to be donated to a special fund operated by the city.[73] The court reasoned that the St. Paul ordinance was merely a more rigorous regulation, consistent with the state law.[74] Therefore, the court held the ordinance to be within the municipality's right to adopt more stringent regulations with respect to charitable gambling.[75]

A municipality might gain the authority to regulate gambling activities not covered by a state law by expressly providing in a local ordinance that the ordinance be limited in scope to those games *not* regulated by the state statute. This practice was upheld by the California Court of Appeals in *In re Benson*.[76] The plaintiff in that case challenged a municipal ordinance of the City of Fullerton which prohibited a gambling game similar to bingo, arguing that California's state law regulating gambling pre-empted the field.[77] In upholding the city ordinance, the court found that the state statute did not preempt the field, and that the ordinance's language—prohibiting any gambling not included in the state law—avoided "preemption problems."[78] Thus, the court upheld a clear expansion of the state law.[79]

The cases analyzed above suggest that it is difficult to make generalizations about how conflicts between state and local gambling regulations are resolved. The resolution of a given conflict will more likely be guided by the specific constitutional and statutory language involved, as well as by the jurisprudence of the state at issue, than by any overarching legal doctrines.[80] The wide-ranging cases discussed here illustrate states' divergent approaches to similar issues, and highlight the importance of closely examining the specific statutory language involved in a particular case.

It is also notable that the cases discussed above, with the exception of *Rice Street VFW*,[81] involved state and local regulations *restricting* unlawful gambling rather than regulation *authorizing* or *taxing* legal forms of gambling.[82] The cases illustrate that local governments often have authority to restrict or suppress gambling under their general police powers. How local government's role as gambling regulator will evolve in a new era characterized by state promotion rather than restriction remains to be seen.

Where a state law provides for extensive regulation, courts may refuse to recognize local regulatory authority. For example, in *Plaza Joint Venture v. City of Atlantic City,*[83] the Superior Court of New Jersey held that Atlantic City did not have the power to regulate the conversion of rental property to condominium property.[84] Due to a shortage in rental housing caused by casino development, the city had passed an ordinance placing a one-year moratorium on rental-to-condominium conversions.[85] The court struck down the moratorium, finding that state gambling and anti-eviction laws, considered as a whole, had pre-empted the field and proscribed municipal regulation of the housing market.[86] Although *Plaza Joint Venture* provides an example of how local autonomy is affected by state laws authorizing and regulating gambling, its outcome should not be generalized to situations involving different statutory and factual contexts. The best indication of the roles envisioned for local governments and residents may lie in the new enabling laws authorizing new forms of gambling.

4. States Vary in the Degree of Local Control They Permit

Against this historical, legislative, and judicial background, this article now turns to an examination of riverboat gambling legislation introduced in recent years. States have adopted a variety of approaches in authorizing riverboat gambling. This variation demonstrates how historical, political, and other differences among the states are expressed in divergent approaches to legislation. Moreover, the differences among the various statutes illustrate how state and local governments can enact laws that offer specific solutions to specific local needs.

The statutes below are presented with an emphasis on "local control." Therefore, in this section, "local control" refers to the extent to which state laws grant local governments, and in some cases local residents, the power to influence riverboat gambling policies.[87] A given statute may place more or less power in the hands of local governments and local residents over decisions on whether to permit riverboat gambling in their communities. One state, for example, may require the majority of a county's voters to approve riverboat gambling through a county-wide special election.[88] Another state, alternatively, may require merely a resolution approved by the majority of the city or county council.[89]

Differences may also exist with respect to the burden placed upon local residents to act on their own behalf to prevent the authorization of riverboat gambling in their community. For example, one state may stipulate that voters must expressly approve riverboat gambling through a referendum, while another may presumptively allow the activity unless citizens organize opposition through petitions or other grass-roots methods.[90] Finally, once riverboat gambling has been authorized in a city or county, state legislation may confer more or less authority to local actors to subsequently revoke the authorization and once again prohibit the activity.

Existing state legislation provides useful examples of the range of options available to state legislators in crafting riverboat legislation. Furthermore, current legislation can be seen as a menu of possibilities for those contemplating similar laws. The degree of autonomy conferred upon local actors—those closest to the gaming activities being authorized—depends on the choices legislators make.

This section first discusses legislation that grants a greater degree of authority to local actors. It then discusses legislation that offers progressively less local control. Although not exhaustive of existing legislation on the subject, the statutes surveyed here provide an analytical basis for a critical review of riverboat gambling legislation in general.

A. The Dominant Model: Local Veto Power in Iowa

Riverboat gambling has been legal in Iowa since April 1, 1991.[91] Iowa authorizes riverboat gambling during an "excursion season" running from April through October.[92] It does so, however, in legislation distinct from laws regulating year-round lotteries and horse- and dog-racing. Like virtually all legislation authorizing gaming, the Iowa law created a state-wide commission, namely the "Iowa Gaming Commission."[93] The commission's primary responsibilities include: 1) licensing riverboat gambling operators, 2) regulating wagering activities, 3) enforcing gaming rules and regulations contained in the law, and 4) investigating rules violations.[94]

Riverboat gambling boats in Iowa may dedicate no more than 30 percent of their deck areas to gaming.[95] Moreover, the Iowa Gaming Commission requires as a condition for granting an operator's license that applicants' vessels "as nearly as practicable, recreate boats that resemble Iowa's riverboat history."[96] Boats also are required to include a section where Iowa-made arts, crafts, and gifts can be sold.[97] Guided by legislative intent, these provisions de-emphasize gambling activity, emphasizing instead the excursionary, historical, and tourism aspects of riverboat gambling.

Iowa's legislation is comparatively deferential to the wishes of local residents. Before riverboat gambling can be authorized in an Iowa county, the Iowa Code calls for a proposition to be approved by the majority of the county's voters in a special or general election.[98] In the event that a majority of voters reject riverboat gambling, the results of the election are binding; gambling cannot be authorized, and another referendum on the question cannot be held for two years.[99]

Iowa's legislation also triggers increased local powers should the small-scale nature of gambling currently authorized in the state change. At present, the state riverboat gambling law strictly regulates wagering in Iowa; a player cannot bet more than five dollars per play nor lose, in the aggregate, more than two hundred dollars per excursion.[100] If these relatively low maxima are ever raised, local residents would acquire the authority to revoke authorization for riverboat gambling in their communities. A 1994 amendment to the state's riverboat gambling law requires a referendum on riverboat gambling if betting limits are raised.[101] Moreover, if riverboat gambling were once again approved in this referendum, the question must be resubmitted to the electorate in the general election of 2002 *and* in the general elections at each subsequent eight-year interval.[102]

In addition to conferring powers over the existence of riverboat gambling, Iowa's legislation also allows a city or county to levy admission taxes of up to 50 cents per riverboat passenger per excursion,[103] but permits no other local taxes or fees to be charged.[104] The principal revenue-raising device in the law is a wagering tax of between five and twenty percent of a riverboat operator's adjusted gross receipts,[105] depending on the amount of receipts the operator takes in during a tax year.[106]

Although local voters play a significant role in approving riverboat gambling in Iowa communities, affected localities receive little of the revenue generated by the wagering tax. County and city authorities split one percent of the operator's adjusted gross revenue, while three times that amount is directed to a "gambler's assistance fund."[107] The remainder goes to the state's general fund.[108] The effect of these provisions, taken together, is that the revenue allocation scheme does not, on its face, compensate localities for relative increases in the gambling activities of an operator, even while it taxes the operator at a higher rate. In other words, although the tax rate on the operator increases with increased revenue, the city, county, and the gambler's assistance funds receive the same amount. Arguably, however, both the impact on local resources and the demands placed on the assistance fund would increase in direct correlation to the operator's receipts.

Iowa's riverboat gambling legislation is comparable to that enacted in Missouri[109] and Indiana.[110] Both states have local referenda provisions virtually identical to those in Iowa.[111] However, the taxation aspects differ. Missouri imposes a 20 percent tax on adjusted gross receipts.[112] Indiana imposes no taxes on wagering other than those sales and excise taxes that would apply under other provisions of Indiana law.[113] For the purposes of this analysis, however, these states' riverboat gambling laws are similar enough to be considered within the same rubric.

B. *Anticipating Citizen Initiatives: Mississippi*

Riverboat gambling legislation took effect in Mississippi on August 28, 1990. The state legislature enacted the Mississippi Gaming Control Act[114] notwithstanding the state's historically antagonistic view toward gambling. To this day, lotteries remain constitutionally prohibited in Mississippi.[115] In authorizing riverboat gambling, the Mississippi legislature defined riverboat gambling as a distinct form of activity not covered by the constitutional ban on lotteries. In an introductory provision, the law establishes that "[t]he Legislature derives its power to legislate upon gaming or gambling devices from its inherent authority over the morals and policy of the people and such power shall not be considered to conflict with the constitutional prohibition of lotteries."[116] As a result of this arguably inconsistent reasoning, players aboard Mississippi riverboats can play craps, blackjack, and slot machines, but no lottery tickets can be sold.[117]

Mississippi's approach to granting local authority differs significantly from the dominant model's approach. The state's legislation requires licensing of private riverboat operators.[118] Before a prospective riverboat operator is licensed, he or she must file a form known as a "notice of intent to apply for a gaming license." The legislation requires a notice to be published within ten days of the filing, plus once a week for the following two weeks, in a newspaper of general circulation in the county from which the proposed riverboat would operate.[119]

If there is opposition to riverboat gambling in a given Mississippi county, the county residents bear the burden of organizing opposition. In contrast to Iowa and Illinois, no affirmative act of approval is required by residents or their elected representatives. While a special election is required in Iowa,[120] and a county or city council resolution is required in Illinois,[121] gambling is approved in Mississippi by default unless a petition is produced in opposition.[122] To be effective, the petition must be signed by 20 percent or 1,500 of a county's registered voters, whichever is less. Furthermore, the petition must be produced within thirty days of the last publication of the notice.[123]

If no petition is produced, riverboat gambling will be permitted without formal approval by either the citizens or their local government representatives.[124] If a petition is produced, however, a special election is triggered.[125] If the outcome of the special election vote is against riverboat gambling, then the applicant cannot be licensed and another special election in the county cannot be held for one year.[126] However, if riverboat gambling is approved, by either default or referendum, then the question may never again be proposed in that county.[127]

If gambling is authorized in a city or county, then the three-member Mississippi Gaming Commission retains the power to revoke operators' licenses.[128] Residents and city and county councils, however, do not have such authority.

Mississippi's legislation allows the municipality or county where a riverboat casino is docked to impose wagering taxes.[129] The state government collects revenues through licensing fees imposed on the games operated aboard riverboat gambling vessels.[130]

C. Local Government Power in Illinois

Since 1990, riverboat gambling has been authorized on any navigable Illinois waterway other than Lake Michigan.[131] The principal focus of Illinois's legislation has not been on the economic development of large urban areas. Indeed, the legislation prohibits from docking in counties with populations over three million, effectively banning riverboat gambling from the metropolitan Chicago region.[132] The legislation targets one urban area for development, however. Of the ten licenses authorized state-wide by the legislation, one grants an operator the right to operate from East St. Louis, a city in social and financial crisis situated across the Mississippi River from St. Louis, Missouri.[133] Thus, Illinois's legislation at least in part perceives a role for riverboat gambling in urban development efforts. Policy makers hope that the jobs and revenues created by riverboat gambling enterprises will restore economic vitality to this struggling city.

Unlike Iowa, which requires voter approval of riverboat gambling,

Illinois vests authority in local government bodies, namely city and county councils.[134] The Illinois Gaming Board[135] may issue a license authorizing a riverboat to dock in a municipality upon the approval of the majority of the municipality's governing body.[136] In contrast to Iowa, control over riverboat gambling in Illinois is one step removed from direct control by the people. The practical difficulties of getting a council resolution passed, as opposed to getting a majority of voters to approve the activity, may present fewer hurdles for riverboat gambling proponents.

Although the local Iowa resident may arguably exercise greater control over riverboat gambling, the Illinois resident receives a greater share of revenues at the local level. Under Illinois legislation, a straight 20 percent tax is levied on a riverboat's adjusted gross wagering receipts.[137] One quarter of this tax goes directly to the local government of the municipality where the boat is docked.[138] The Illinois General Assembly can make appropriations from the remaining tax revenue to fund the administration of the Riverboat Gambling Act.[139] Any remainder is used to fund a state-wide "Education Assistance Fund."[140] In addition to the wagering tax, the Illinois legislation requires a two-dollar-per-person riverboat admission tax.[141] Half of the admission tax goes to the county or municipality where the boat is docked, and half goes to the state's general revenues.[142]

An additional Illinois provision proscribes gambling at the dock and limits the length of each riverboat gambling excursion to a maximum of four hours.[143] As opposed to Iowa, the Illinois law does not direct any of the revenues raised toward a gambling addiction fund or similar reservoir dedicated to addressing the social problems of gambling.

The municipality or county where the vessel docks receives all of the local revenues generated by the riverboat. However, the dock-site local government may contract with other local government authorities in the region to share revenues raised.[144] A municipality on a riverboat's cruise route could, for example, negotiate with the docking municipality to share some of the tax revenues in exchange for docking privileges. The idea, apparently, would be to develop more attractive routes, increase the number of passengers, and raise public exposure to riverboat gambling by increasing the number of stops en route. Although such regional cooperation is attractive, practical considerations make it unlikely. Under current law, no gambling is permitted when vessels are docked.[145] The riverboat's principal activity, and its operator's principal source of revenue, must cease at the dock. Docking stops en route could therefore be counterproductive under the four-hour excursion time limit. It seems unlikely that either the passenger-gamblers or the riverboat operator would wish to dock the vessel under such circumstances. Under the Illinois legislation, it is arguably more likely that excursions will be four-hour, non-stop loops characterized by continuous gambling rather than "hop-along" tourist excursions with brief stops at points along the way.

D. Centralized Control in New Jersey

While the states considered thus far provide some degree of local voter participation in the approval or disapproval of legalized gambling, New Jersey is notable for its highly centralized approach to gaming regulation and the relative absence of local input on centralized decision making. Legalized gambling in New Jersey is of a breadth far greater than any contemplated by the states that have passed or are contemplating riverboat gambling legislation. To some extent, therefore, New Jersey's laws are not relevant to a discussion of less far-reaching gambling laws. Nevertheless, New Jersey presents a useful reference point along the continuum from most to least local control over legalized gambling. Furthermore, in the context of possible legislation to allow some form of casino gambling in Pennsylvania, discussed below, examination of New Jersey's legislation is appropriate.

Through the New Jersey Casino Control Act,[146] the state exercises centralized control over all aspects of gambling in Atlantic City, the only municipality where gaming is permitted in the state. The five-member

New Jersey Casino Control Commission[147] has extensive powers. In addition to wagering, the commission regulates hours of operation,[148] casino leases,[149] and alcoholic beverage consumption.[150]

Residents in Iowa, Illinois, and Mississippi cities and counties participate in the gambling licensing processes through special elections, local government resolutions, and petition efforts, respectively. In contrast, Atlantic City residents retain no authority over decisions on gambling operations. Under New Jersey's gambling legislation, decisions are made by the commission.[151] Moreover, the authority of the commission extends to activities not tied to gambling which, in most municipalities, are considered within the local police power.

As an example of the degree to which New Jersey's centralized gaming authority exercises control over local concerns, consider the issues of traffic congestion and parking. Traffic problems are often generally among the drawbacks identified with legalized gambling. They are also among those concerns, often labeled "parochial" or "local," that are considered within local jurisdiction (i.e., traffic metering, parking regulations, and ordinances regulating turns and traffic direction). It is noteworthy that New Jersey's Casino Control Act regulates car parking at casinos in Atlantic City. Section 173.1 of the Act declared that the high cost of building and maintaining roads in Atlantic City was the product of high traffic volume caused by free parking, a shortage of hotel rooms, and inadequate public transportation. In response, the legislature adopted sections 173.1 to 173.3, which mandate that casinos charge parking fees of at least two dollars per vehicle per day. Of this, $1.50 consists of a tax paid to the state by the casino, the proceeds of which are used to promote better public transportation in Atlantic City. The legislation is apparently also designed to serve as a disincentive to motorists. If a casino elects to offer "free" parking by not charging the two dollar parking fee, or if a casino reimburses the patron for any part of a parking fee, then the casino must pay to the state the entire parking fee it collected, or at least two dollars.[152]

5. The Dominant Model of Gambling Regulation Is Centralized

A. *Local Autonomy Limited to Local Veto Power*

The legislation considered above clearly contemplates some degree of local control over riverboat gambling. However, this authority is largely one-dimensional, consisting, in effect, of a veto power over gambling in a given city or county. While the legislative models give local governments and citizens the power to prevent gambling, they vest in those local actors little power to regulate gambling once it has been authorized. Legislation, while vesting a large amount of ongoing regulatory authority in state-wide gambling commissions, is largely silent on the powers of local government. This is regrettable; greater ongoing regulatory authority at the local level would allow communities to meet local needs with local regulations.

The local authority most evident in the legislation considered above is a local veto power—the power of local government or local citizens to prevent the authorization of legal gambling in their communities. The primary distinctions among the various legislative models arise in the ways this veto power is exercised. Under the dominant model, evident in Iowa, Missouri, and Indiana, authorization through referenda by a majority of local voters is an express requirement and cannot be bypassed in the legalization process. In other words, for riverboat gambling to be authorized under this model, a majority of voters in a city or county referendum must approve it.

The veto powers contemplated by the other models place less power in the hands of voters, and more in the hands of local governments. In Mississippi, riverboat gambling in a city or county is authorized by default unless citizens take the initiative and petition for a referendum. Under this scheme, a local veto power exists, but it is not automatic. Finally, under legislation such as Illinois's, the veto power is exercised by city and county government elected officials rather than by individual citizens. Under this

model, only a resolution by the local governing council in favor of riverboat gambling is required. In this last model, therefore, riverboat gambling
becomes another municipal political issue, with elected officials choosing
positions based on traditional political factors.

Regardless of the type of local authority contemplated, however, all
share one characteristic. Each model offers local actors a before-the-fact
opportunity to reject riverboat gambling. Once riverboat gambling is
authorized, however, legislation is generally silent on the abilities of local
actors to regulate or terminate riverboat gambling in their communities.
Moreover, the authority vested in voters and local governments by these
enactments is not the equivalent of a licensing power. It is a power to
reject riverboat gambling, not necessarily to authorize it. In each of the
models considered here, the state's gambling commission retains discretion, even upon voter approval, to deny a license or to revoke a license
once it has been granted.

Recently considered riverboat gambling legislation in Pennsylvania[153]
has been consistent with the dominant model in these respects. Pennsylvania's Excursion Boat Gambling Act for Waterfront Economic Development, considered by the previous state general assembly[154] and reintroduced in substantially the same form in the current assembly,[155] requires
a majority of voters in a county-wide referendum to approve riverboat
gambling before a license can be issued.[156] Under the proposed legislation,
the governing body of a county could initiate a county-wide referendum
on the issue by passing a resolution.[157] If voters approve, riverboat gambling licenses could be issued by a state gambling commission created
under the act.[158] If voters disapprove, another referendum could not be
held for at least two years.[159]

Of some significance in the proposed Pennsylvania legislation, however, is the opportunity for local voters to disapprove riverboat gambling
after approval in a prior referendum. Under the proposed legislation,
additional referenda could be triggered either by a resolution of the
county's governing body[160] or by presenting the county board of elections
with a "valid petition."[161] If a majority of voters disapprove of riverboat

gambling in the subsequent referendum, no further licenses could be issued for that municipality.[162]

Such "recall" provisions add significantly to the veto power vested in local governments and citizens. However, they arguably also increase the risks faced by gambling boat operators. Under such legislation, operators face the prospect of having their licenses revoked as a result of a grass-roots backlash.[163] This added vulnerability may deter prospective operators from making long-term financial investments in the land-based elements of their gambling enterprises (such as dock-side reception facilities). On the other hand, the threat of revocation should arguably encourage operators to maintain local support for riverboat gambling by responding effectively to local concerns about safety, traffic, and development. In this way, the threat of revocation by local referendum functions as a local accountability mechanism.

Although provisions for additional referenda to repeal riverboat gambling offer local actors greater power, the nature of their control remains one-dimensional. Local control remains merely a veto; in reality a municipality may only reject legalized gambling. Where local actors "approve" the activity for their community, the logistics of the gambling activities themselves are governed by the state's enabling legislation.

Historically, local governments have been granted wide latitude to supplement restrictive state gambling laws with local ordinances.[164] Courts have often upheld the validity of these local ordinances, provided they do not conflict with state statutes or intrude upon a field pre-empted by state legislation.[165] It remains to be seen whether courts would uphold supplementary local ordinances in the field of riverboat gambling, where the state legislation is permissive rather than prohibitive. Given the extensive power vested in state-wide gambling commissions to regulate all aspects of riverboat gambling, it is likely that courts would find the field preempted by the state legislation.[166] However, if and when cities and counties begin to pass ordinances relating to riverboat gambling activities, challenges to commissions' authority to regulate these activities may arise.

Under the dominant model of gambling regulation, local actors trade whatever economic benefits riverboat gambling produces for less local regulatory authority. If local actors fail to exercise veto power, regulatory authority passes to the state gambling commission. State gambling commissions created under legislation considered above generally have extensive powers granted by the enabling statutes. Moreover, commissions are often managed by a handful of commissioners appointed by the governor and serve at his or her pleasure. Such a regulatory system is arguably the antithesis of local control. Indeed, it is the archetype of a centralized, bureaucratic control mechanism. Those who advocate decentralized control as most responsive to local needs should consider the implications of such a regulatory structure.[167] "Community choice" in the form of a one-dimensional veto power may leave municipalities with little regulatory control over legal gambling in their territories once riverboat gambling licenses are granted and the games begin.

B. Contrast: Indian Gaming as an Example of Increased Local Autonomy over Gambling Regulation

Current federal regulation of legal gambling on Native American tribal lands provides an interesting example of an alternative regulatory scheme. In contrast to the small amount of regulatory authority granted by state governments to local governments and local citizens under the gambling legislation considered above, Native American tribes exercise considerable local control over legalized gambling.[168]

In recent years Indian tribes have derived significant economic benefits from casinos operated for the general public on tribal lands.[169] Under a federal law—the Indian Gaming Regulatory Act (IGRA or "the Act")[170]— casino gambling on reservations is permissible if: 1) the state in which the reservation is located allows gambling for any purpose by any person,[171] 2) the tribe authorizes the activity,[172] and 3) the games are played in compliance with a compact negotiated between the tribe and the state.[173]

Under the state riverboat gambling laws considered in Part 4 above, regulatory power over riverboat gambling is vested in statewide gambling commissions once approval is obtained from local citizens, local government, or both, depending on the requirements of the state law at issue. Thereafter, the state commission regulates all aspects of the activity. In contrast to such a centralized regulatory structure, IGRA provides Indian tribes with some power to regulate gambling activities within their territories.[174] Self-regulation is allowed under the Act if the tribe can demonstrate that gambling activities have been conducted honestly and safely, and that the tribe has in place an effective system for accounting for revenues and investigating and prosecuting violations.[175] A self-regulated tribe is not subject to several requirements of the Act,[176] such as monitoring of operations, background investigations of employees, and on-demand inspections of books and records.[177] Thus, if a tribe wishes, it may self-regulate gambling activities on its reservation if it meets the requirements for self-regulation under IGRA.[178] Moreover, under IGRA tribes can sue state governments in federal court to negotiate compacts that govern gambling activities on tribal lands.[179] In other words, tribal governments may initiate gambling on their territories even where the state government at issue resists the effort. This power stands in contrast to the one-dimensional veto-power vested in local governments under the state gambling legislation considered in Part 4 above.

Obviously, the historical antecedents of Indian gambling and IGRA are significantly different from those of municipal regulation of gambling under state law. Nevertheless, IGRA illustrates how an alternative regulatory scheme might provide a significant degree of local self-sufficiency[180] and local authority, while still subjecting gambling activity to centralized (i.e., state) legislative control. Like riverboat gambling, Indian gambling has been regulated to develop local areas where the gambling is situated. Yet IGRA envisions a greater role for local actors than do the riverboat gambling laws reviewed above.

As society adopts a more permissive attitude toward gambling activity, and state laws recognize gambling as merely another form of regulated economic activity, state legislative schemes should allow local actors to play a greater role in the policy development process. Local participation in shaping gambling regulatory policies should move beyond the one-dimensional veto power provided in the referendum-oriented legislation that currently exists. States should aim for regulatory schemes that envision a greater, ongoing role for local governments and residents in determining how gambling happens in their communities, rather than the statewide commission model which provides for little dialogue with local government.

6. Legalization Has Diluted Local Authority

The growth of legal gambling in the United States presents important questions about the participation of local governments and citizens in policy decisions affecting their communities. The status of gambling in legal history has been marked by incongruity. On the one hand, governments have tolerated and at times promoted legal gambling as a means to raise charitable and public revenues. On the other hand, gambling has traditionally been restricted because of its socially destructive effects.

In this contradictory legislative context, local governments historically enjoyed wide latitude in supplementing state laws with local ordinances. When these ordinances were challenged, courts tended to uphold local gambling restrictions, as long as they did not contradict state law or intrude upon a field of law found to have been preempted by state legislation. To this extent, local governments have had a moderate degree of authority to regulate gambling. Shifting state gambling policies may alter this authority. Most legislation authorizing riverboat gambling, for example, gives local communities at the city and county levels absolute power to prevent gambling in their communities. States have delegated this local veto power in different ways. Most require voter approval through referenda before riverboat gambling can be authorized. Some require a less extreme expression of local approval such as a resolution of the city or county's governing body. The power of local actors to influence events in these respects is clear and significant. However, if riverboat gambling is approved, virtually all regulatory authority is normally vested in state gambling commissions, which centrally control most aspects of day-to-day gambling activities. As a result of this process, the status of the local police power to regulate gambling is uncertain.

As the state's posture toward gambling shifts from one of prohibition to one of promotion, local authority to regulate gambling in light of local concerns is unclear. The state's traditionally proscriptive position is reflected in existing enabling legislation that concentrates regulatory power in the hands of state gambling commissions. A better approach would provide for greater local regulatory authority. In any event, legislators and local residents should carefully consider the extent to which local authority over gambling is diluted by new legislation legalizing new forms of this historically pervasive activity.

Notes

1.   Robert Goodman, *Legalized Gambling as a Strategy for Economic Development* (1994), p. 6; see also I. Nelson Rose, "Gambling and the Law—Update 1993," *Hastings Comm. and Ent. L.J.* 15 (1992), p. 93 (more than $294 billion spent on legal gambling in United States in 1992).
2.   See, e.g., Dana Priest, "Lure of Gambling Has More States Rolling the Dice on Election Day," *Washington Post*, October 25, 1994, p. A4 (discussing campaign to legalize casinos in Florida and forecasting effects on state's economy).
3.   See, e.g., proposed legislation to legalize riverboat gambling in Pennsylvania, discussed herein at notes 153–63. In a statement of purposes and policy introducing the Excursion Boat Gambling Act for Waterfront Economic Development, the Pennsylvania General Assembly declared that "[t]he development of a historic riverboat industry is important to the economy of this Commonwealth in that it will assist in the continuing growth of the tourism industry and thus will benefit the general welfare of our citizens and create new jobs." Pa. H.B. 939 § 2(1), Pa. General Assembly, 1995 Sess. The proposed legislation provides for a 15 percent wagering tax (ibid., § 21(a)), in addition to initial license fees of as much as $30 million per riverboat gambling license. Ibid., § 8(b)(1).
4.   Priest, "Lure of Gambling," p. A4.
5.   An initiative to authorize 47 casinos throughout Florida was rejected by the state's voters at the November 8, 1994 general election, despite a $16.4 million advertising and lobbying campaign by gambling proponents. Michael Browing et al., "Casino Supporters' Expensive Campaign Takes a Big Beating," *Miami Herald*, November 9, 1994, p. 1A. More than 60 percent of voters voted against the proposition. Ibid. The initiative aimed to amend Article X, § 7 of the Florida constitution, which provides that "[l]otteries, other than the types of pari-mutuel pools authorized by law as of the effective date of this constitution, are hereby prohibited in this state." Florida Constitution, art. X, § 7.

6.   Ronald J. Rychlak, "Lotteries, Revenues and Social Costs: A Historical Examination of State-Sponsored Gambling," *B.C. L. Rev.* 34 (1992), pp. 11, 12.

7.   For example, in Philadelphia, riverboat gambling has been reported to be the hoped-for source of funding for a $209 million "neighborhood stabilization fund," part of a larger, $2.2 billion "Economic Stimulus Program." Vernon Loeb, "N. Phila. Tract is Target for a D-Day Attack on Urban Blight," *Philadelphia Inquirer*, June 6, 1994, p. B1; see also Nathan Gorenstein, "Questions Remain on Jobs Plan," *Philadelphia Inquirer*, January 30, 1995, p. E1 (estimating funds from riverboat gambling in Philadelphia would finance $200 million neighborhood revitalization plan, subsidize construction of downtown hotel, and partially pay for cut in city wage tax).

8.   See, e.g., John W. Kindt, "The Economic Impacts of Legalized Gambling Activities," *Drake L. Rev.* 51, 52 (1994), p. 43 (arguing increased tax revenues promised by proponents are usually overestimated and often do not materialize); Goodman, *Legalized Gambling*, p. 68 (pro-gambling interests exaggerate public benefits to increase public support for legislation).

9.   Opponents of efforts to authorize riverboat gambling in the Philadelphia area, for example, warn that because casinos offer cheap meals and free drinks to patrons, local restaurants and bars will be adversely affected. See "No Dice: 18 Reasons to Oppose Legalization of Riverboat Gambling" (1994) (relating statistics that gambling takes consumer spending from other regional businesses) (pamphlet produced by No Dice, a citizens' group opposed to legalized gambling in Pennsylvania). With respect to possible casino development in Chicago, Illinois, Governor James Edgar warned that the dollars spent in casinos would have been spent elsewhere, and that development could bring an overall *loss* of jobs. Kindt, "The Economic Impacts," p. 52. See also Goodman, *Legalized Gambling*, p. 51 (explaining that legalized gambling extracts money from other consumer spending).

10.   These terms refer to traditional "community" issues such as those relating to home, family, and neighborhood that are characteristically the subjects of local government authority. See Michael Libonati, "Home Rule: An Essay on Pluralism," *Wash. L. Rev.* 64 (1989), p. 51 (discussing local self-government and importance of localism in political process).

11.   For examinations of these issues, see generally David Weinstein and Lillian Deitch, *The Impact of Legalized Gambling* (1974), p. 5 (foreseeing new era of widespread legalized gambling); Kindt, "The Economic Impacts" (describing tax benefits of legalized gambling as overestimated); Edward J. McCaffery, "Why People Play Lotteries and Why it Matters," *1994 Wis. L. Rev* 71, p. 119 (questioning feasibility of funding public expenditures with lottery money); Rychlak, "Lotteries, Revenues and Social Costs," pp. 11–44 (reviewing historical development and social impact of legalized gambling); Todd A. Wyett, Note, "State Lotteries: Regressive Taxes in Disguise," *Tax Law* 44 (1991), p. 867 (arguing that state lotteries function as regressive taxes).

12. See herein notes 47–53 and accompanying text.

13. Regulation can be defined as "the expression of government, in the nature of a rule of conduct, imposed upon rather than implicit in a situation, conventional in character, and generally operating with form requirements, precise quantities, or administrative arrangements." C. Dallas Sands et al., *Local Government Law*, vol. 3, § 14.01, 14-2 (1994) (quoting Freund, *Legislative Regulations* [1932], p. 3).

14. Libonati, "Home Rule," p. 54 (quoting Gordon Clark, "A Theory of Local Autonomy," *Annals Ass'n Am. Geographers* 74, no. 2 [1984], pp. 195–208. Clark characterized local autonomy as the "power of initiative" and the "power of immunity." Clark, "A Theory of Local Autonomy," p. 198.

15. Sands et al., *Local Government Law*, vol. 1, 2-7.

16. Ibid., § 2.06, 2-14 to 2-15. The treatise finds justification for this delegation "[b]y reason of the inability of the legislatures themselves to deal with the great mass of detail in legal arrangements required by the complexity of modern society." Ibid., 2-14. Although the law of agency suggests that central authorities cannot delegate their authority, the power to prescribe local regulations is seen differently. For delegation to be appropriate—and not amount to abdication of the central government's responsibility as the sole law-making authority—delegation must be accompanied by standards and guidelines which direct and confine the scope of the delegated authority. Ibid., 2-15.

17. Ibid., § 2.03, 2-6 to 2-7. The treatise notes that "local governments are agencies of limited jurisdiction and powers, according to which the creature is legally capable of doing only that which the parent body or creating power has affirmatively authorized it to do." Ibid.

18. Professor Libonati refers to this tradition as concerned with "the decentralization of decision-making to give a forum to those whose lives are focused on the parochial—home, family, and neighborhood—and thus to bring government down to where the goats can get at it." Libonati, "Home Rule," p. 51.

19. Sands et al., *Local Government Law*, vol. 1, § 2.06, 2-15 (citing *Stoutenburg v. Hennick*, 129 U.S. [1889], p. 141).

20. "Gambling" comes from the Middle English word "gamen"—to amuse oneself. Ronald J. Rychlak, "Video Gambling Devices," *UCLA L. Rev.* 37 (1990), pp. 555, 556. Legally, gambling involves the elements of consideration, chance, and reward. *Black's Law Dictionary* (6th ed., 1990), p. 679.

21. See Rychlak, "Lotteries, Revenues and Social Costs," p. 13 (noting enormous popularity of state-run lotteries since their legalization); see also Weinstein and Deitch, "The Impact of Legalized Gambling," 7, discussing historical popularity of gambling.

22. Rychlak, "Lotteries, Revenues and Social Costs," p. 13. According to Rychlak, while lotteries have been successful in raising revenues, the cost has been shouldered by the poor. Ibid.

23. Weinstein and Deitch, "The Impact of Legalized Gambling," p. 8.

24. Ibid. For example, "[w]hen a group of citizens felt that a certain facility was needed and the colonial government was unable or unwilling to provide it, the group usually sought legislative authorization to conduct a lottery." Ibid.

25. Ibid.

26. Ibid., p. 9.

27. Rychlak, "Lotteries, Revenues and Social Costs," p. 32.

28. Ibid., pp. 12–13. In 1893, the Librarian of Congress wrote of a "general public conviction that lotteries are to be regarded, in direct proportion to their extension, as among the most dangerous and prolific sources of human misery." Ibid.

29. Ibid., p. 13.

30. Ibid., p. 12. Rychlak explained that states abandoned lotteries as they developed improved taxing policies. Ibid.

31. Ibid., p. 14. Professor Nelson Rose describes three waves of legalized gambling in American history. Rose, "Gambling and the Law," pp. 95–98. The first wave lasted from the time of earliest settlement through the 1820s and 1830s. During this period, state-sponsored lotteries were promoted as a means of raising funds for "worthy causes." A period of prohibition followed, however, and by 1862 only Missouri and Kentucky allowed lotteries. The second wave began after the Civil War period as states of the Old South used lotteries as a voluntary tax to raise money and rebuild their economies. However, the Louisiana Lottery scandal of the 1890s led to the enactment of strong federal anti-lottery laws, e.g., 18 U.S.C. § 1301 (1988) (enacted 1909), and by 1910 the country was again virtually free of legal gambling. The third wave, which continues today, began with the Great Depression. Today, a majority of states have lotteries and betting on horse races, dog races, or jai alai. Rose, "Gambling and the Law," p. 98.

32. Rychlak, "Lotteries, Revenues and Social Costs," pp. 38–39.

33. Ibid., pp. 44–45. In 1948, there were no legal lotteries in the United States. Ibid., p. 11. New Hampshire launched a new era in legalized gambling with the introduction of the New Hampshire Sweepstakes, a monthly lottery, in 1964. Ibid.

34. Ibid.

35. Rose, "Gambling and the Law," p. 97. See *Ecumenical Ministries v. Oregon State Lottery Comm'n*, 871 P.2d (Or. 1994), p. 106 (holding that video gambling devices do not violate state constitutional ban on casino gambling).

36. One commentator has observed that riverboat gambling, first introduced by Iowa in 1991, launched the current expansion of legal gambling because of its wholesome image in the minds of politicians and voters. Rose, "Gambling and the Law," p. 99. Riverboat casinos are seen as "islands of gambling," while land-based casinos are characterized as "hubs of decadence and decay." "If Governor I Would . . .," *Philadelphia Inquirer*, April 18, 1994, p. A15.

37. Rychlak, "Lotteries, Revenues and Social Costs," p. 12.

38. See, e.g., *Ill. Rev. Stat.* ch. 720, para. 5/28-1(b)(6) (1994) (making lotteries conducted by state in accordance with Illinois lottery law exempt from general

prohibition against gambling). If not exempted, "[a] person commits gambling when he . . . [p]lays a game of chance or skill for money or other thing of value." Ibid., para. 5/28-1(a)(1). Such a crime is punishable as a misdemeanor on first conviction and as a felony on second conviction. Ibid., para. 5/28-1(c).

39. See, e.g., ibid., paras. 5/28-1(b)(5), 5/28-1(b)(9) (exempting bingo and charitable games from prohibition against gambling). A New York statute states that the only justification for allowing gambling is to "foster and support such worthy causes and undertakings" as charitable raffles and bingo. *N.Y. Gen. Mun. Law* § 185 (McKinney 1994). Similarly, the Pennsylvania Bingo Law, 10 *Pa. Cons. Stat. Ann.* § 301 (1994), is exempted from the effect of Pennsylvania's law describing gambling as a misdemeanor, 18 *Pa. Cons. Stat. Ann.* § 5513 (1994).

40. See, e.g., *N.Y. Rac. Pari-Mut. Wag. and Breed. Law* § 222 (McKinney 1994) (permitting pari-mutuel wagering on horse racing). Pari-mutuel betting is a form of wagering in which bets are pooled and later paid, after subtracting a management fee, to holders of winning tickets. *Black's Law Dictionary* (6th ed., 1990), p. 1115.

41. See herein notes 87–145 and accompanying text for a discussion of legislation in various states that permit riverboat gambling.

42. *Cal. Penal Code* § 330 (West 1994) ("Every person who deals, plays, or carries on, opens, or causes to be opened, [any game] played with cards, dice, or any device, for money, checks, credit, or other representative of value, and every person who plays or bets at or against any of these prohibited games, is guilty of a misdemeanor . . .").

43. *Ill. Ann. Stat.*, ch. 720, para. 5/28-1 (Smith-Hurd 1994). The Illinois provision makes it a misdemeanor to keep open any gambling place other than the type authorized by the state's Riverboat Gambling Acts. Ibid. See herein notes 131–45 and accompanying text for a discussion of riverboat gambling legislation in Illinois.

44. *N.Y. Penal Law* § 225.05 (McKinney 1994) (stating that a person who "knowingly advances or profits from unlawful gambling activity" commits a Class A misdemeanor).

45. *Tex. Penal Code Ann.* § 47.02 (West 1994) (making gambling offense a misdemeanor).

46. 18 *Pa. Cons. Stat. Ann.* § 5513(a)(1) (1994).

47. Sands et al., *Local Government Law*, vol. 3, § 14.14, 14-40. The treatise explains that "[l]ocal government units traditionally exercise an extensive regulatory authority over all aspects of gambling activity, including regulation or prohibition of the use of premises for gambling and the possession of gambling devices or paraphernalia." Ibid. (citations omitted).

48. Ibid., § 14.02, 14-5.

49. See, e.g., *Ala. Code* § 11-47-111 (1994) (granting cities and towns express power "to restrain and prohibit gaming and the keeping of gambling houses").

50. *Ill. Ann. Stat.*, ch. 65, para. 5/11-5-1 (Smith-Hurd 1994).

51. See Sands et al., *Local Government Law*, vol. 3, § 14.02, 14-5 (describing local government's elasticity in response to economic and social change).

52. Meaningful general rules are difficult to draw because controversies are resolved with reference to the specific constitutional and statutory language involved. Ibid., § 14.04, 14-15. See herein notes 54–86 and accompanying text for specific examples of conflicts between state and local regulatory authority to regulate gambling and its effects.

53. Sands et al., *Local Government Law*, § 14.04, 14-15.

54. *DeLong v. Downes*, 573 P.2d (Mont. 1977), pp. 160, 162. The court concluded that the state statute did not empower local units to prohibit gambling in their jurisdiction. Ibid.

55. Ibid., p. 163.

56. Ibid., p. 162.

57. *La. Const.*, art. XII, § 6.

58. 441 So. 2d (La. 1983), p. 742.

59. Ibid., p. 744.

60. Ibid. The local ordinance provided that:

> it shall be unlawful for any person in this parish to gamble with cards, or to participate in any card game by whatever name the game may be called or known, at which money, or anything representing money, or any article of value shall be pledged, bet, or hazarded. This section shall not apply to any private game played in a private home occupied by a family as such, or game in private clubs, conducted without rake-off for gain. (Ibid., p. 742 [citation omitted].)

61. Ibid., p. 743 n.2 (quoting *La. Rev. Stat. Ann.* § 14.90 [West 1983]). The statute provides that "[g]ambling is the intentional conducting, or directly assisting in the conducting, as a business, of any game, contest, lottery, or contrivance whereby a person risks the loss of anything of value in order to realize a profit." Ibid.

62. Ibid., p. 744 (citing *City of Shreveport v. Kaufman*, 353 So. 2d [La. 1977], pp. 995, 997 (holding local ordinance unconstitutional where its definition of forbidden gambling went beyond legislature's to include social as well as business gambling)). The court granted defendant's motion to dismiss the case against him. Ibid. The defendant had been seen by sheriff's deputies taking cuts from the pot during card games in his home. Ibid., p. 743 n.5.

63. Sands et al., *Local Government Law*, vol. 3, § 14.14, 14-40.

64. 645 A.2d (N.J. Super. Ct. Law Div. 1994), p. 175.

65. Ibid., pp. 181–82.

66. Ibid., p. 178 n.4.

67. Ibid., p. 177 n.2. Included among such games were mechanical and video games which simulated casino games such as roulette wheel or keno.

68. Ibid., p. 181.

69. Ibid., pp. 181–82. In addressing the issue of whether the state law pre-empted the field of gambling device regulation, the court stated that:

> when the state regulatory scheme provides wide coverage and is broadly

inclusive of the subject matter, local controls may be discordant and disruptive, with no appropriate place in the legislative plan. On the other hand, if state law is only narrowly focused upon particular matters encompassed within a much broader spectrum of activity, local regulation may be entirely proper. (Ibid., p. 181 [quoting *Mack Paramus Co. v. Mayor of Paramus*, 511 A.2d (N.J. 1986), p. 1179].)

See also *Mannie's Cigarette Serv., Inc. v. Town of West New York*, 613 A.2d (N.J. Super. Ct. App. Div. 1992), pp. 494, 497 (upholding local ordinance in absence of conflict between state law prohibiting possession of gambling devices and local licensing scheme for devices that could be used for gambling); *In re Hubbard*, 396 P.2d (Cal. 1964), pp. 809, 813 (concluding that local ordinance could supplement general state prohibition where state had not fully occupied field).

70. 452 N.W.2d (Minn. Ct. App. 1990), p. 503.

71. Ibid., p. 505.

72. Ibid., p. 507. The law required that charitable gambling profits go to "lawful purposes" or expenses authorized by the state's charitable gambling board. The state law further defined "lawful purpose" to include youth groups. Ibid.

73. Ibid., p. 505. The ordinance provided in pertinent part that "[p]rivate clubs . . . [s]hall pay to the city-wide organization designated by the city council [10%] of the net profits from selling pull-tabs or tipboards to be distributed to other youth athletic organizations to be expended for such lawful purposes as specified [by law]." Ibid. (citation omitted). The city had amended what had previously been a 20 percent fee pursuant to state legislation. Ibid., p. 505 n.1.

74. Ibid., p. 506.

75. Ibid.

76. 218 Cal. Rptr. (Cal. Ct. App. 1985), pp. 384, 386.

77. The Fullerton municipal code provided that "[e]very person, firm, corporation or association who, for profit, or for anything of value or for commercial purposes of any nature, keeps, operates, conducts or maintains . . . any game, gambling or gaming *not mentioned or included in [the state law provision]* . . . shall be guilty of a misdemeanor." Ibid., p. 386 (emphasis added) (citation omitted).

78. Ibid., p. 387.

79. In upholding the Fullerton ordinance, the *Benson* court relied on *In re Hubbard*, 396 P.2d (Cal. 1964), p. 809. In *Hubbard*, the leading California case on gambling preemption, an ordinance of the city of Long Beach prohibited "any game of chance." Ibid., p. 810 n.1 (citation omitted). The state law at issue was narrower in scope, prohibiting a number of specifically enumerated gambling games as well as "any banking or percentage" game. Ibid., p. 810 n.2 (citation omitted). The defendant was arrested under the local ordinance for playing a gambling game that was neither one of the games enumerated in the state law nor a banking or percentage game. Ibid., pp. 810, 812. The Supreme Court of California rejected the defendant's argument that the state law pre-empted the field of gambling regulation, and upheld the validity of the

Long Beach ordinance. The court reasoned that "it is clear that the regulation of gambling in any form is within the purview of local police power." Ibid., p. 812. Thus, since the local ordinance did not directly conflict with the state law, and since the state law did not preempt the field, the local ordinance was a valid exercise of municipal authority. Ibid., pp. 812–15.

80. See Sands et al., *Local Government Law*, vol. 3, § 14.04, 14-15.

81. See above notes 70–75 and accompanying text for a discussion of *Rice Street VFW*.

82. Research has yet to uncover disputes between local and state regulation with respect to recent gambling enabling legislation such as the riverboat gambling legislation, discussed herein at notes 87–145. But see herein notes 83–86 and accompanying text for a discussion of *Plaza Joint Venture v. City of Atlantic City*, 416 A.2d (N.J. Super. Ct. App. Div. 1980), p. 71.

83. 416 A.2d (N.J. Super. Ct. App. Div. 1980), p. 71.

84. Ibid., p. 77.

85. Ibid., p. 73. The ordinance provided as follows:

(a) There is hereby declared a moratorium on the conversion of any rental unit into a condominium for a period of one (1) year commencing upon the passage of this Ordinance.

(b) During the existence of this moratorium no sales, or contracts for sale can be entered into; no prospectus issued; and no notice of intent is to be sent to tenants; and no one can request a tenant to vacate a unit as a consequence of conversion of a unit to a condominium.

(c) If the vacancy rate at the time when the aforesaid moratorium would have otherwise expired is less than five percent (5%), then this moratorium shall automatically be extended for six (6) additional months, but shall not be extended further.

(d) The Notice of Eviction . . . shall not be given until the termination of the aforesaid moratorium. (Ibid., pp. 73–74 [citation omitted].)

86. Ibid., p. 76. The court stated that, since legalization of casino gambling in New Jersey in 1976, "[t]he Legislature has continued to maintain close contact and scrutiny over problems developing within the industry and in Atlantic City." Ibid. The court continued, "[i]t is clear from [the anti-eviction and casino control laws] that the Legislature has viewed the housing crisis in Atlantic City, including the conversion of rental units to condominium, and casino gambling as an integrated problem and provided a comprehensive solution . . ." Ibid. See herein notes 146–52 and accompanying text for further discussion of New Jersey's gambling law and its effect on Atlantic City's autonomy.

87. See above note 14 and accompanying text for a discussion of local control and local autonomy.

88. E.g., *Iowa Code Ann.* § 99F.7.10.a (West 1984 and Supp. 1994).

89. E.g., *Mo. Ann. Stat.* § 313.807 (Vernon 1994).

90. E.g., *Miss. Code Ann.* § 19-3-79 (1994).

91. *Iowa Code Ann.* § 99F.3 (West 1994).

92. Ibid., § 99F.1.8.

93. Ibid., § 99F.4.

94. Ibid., §§ 99F.4.1 to 99F.4.22.

95. Ibid., § 99F.7.5.a. Allowing gambling on such a relatively small portion of the boat allows Iowa to avoid the impact of the Federal Gambling Ships Act, 18 U.S.C.A. § 1081 (West 1994). Barbara Powell, "The New Era of Riverboat Gambling," *Fed. Bar News and J.* 36 (1989), pp. 395, 397.

96. *Iowa Code Ann.* § 99F.7.3.

97. Ibid., § 99F.7.5.d.

98. Ibid., § 99F.7.10.a.

99. Ibid.

100. Ibid., § 99F.4.4.

101. 1994 Iowa Leg. Serv. (West), 28. Section 99F.7.10.c, which pertains to county elections to authorize riverboat gambling in Iowa counties, was amended to read, in pertinent part, as follows:

> If, after January 1, 1994, § 99F.4.4 [the maximum wager and loss provision] . . . is amended or stricken . . . the board of supervisors of a county in which excursion boat gambling has been approved . . . shall submit to the county electorate a proposition to approve or disapprove the conduct of gambling games on excursion gambling boats . . . at a special election at the earliest practicable time. If excursion boat gambling is not approved by a majority of the county electorate voting on the proposition . . . the commission shall cancel the licenses issued for the county within sixty days of the unfavorable referendum. . . . If the proposition . . . is approved by a majority of the county electorate . . . the board of supervisors shall submit the same proposition to the county electorate at the general election held in 2002 and, unless the operation of gambling games is not terminated earlier, . . . at the general election held at each subsequent eight-year interval. (*Iowa Code Ann.* § 99F.7.10.c.)

The amendment took effect March 31, 1994. Ibid. The same section before the amendment included the provision for canceling licenses in the event of an unfavorable referendum, but did not include the provision for repeated, subsequent referenda in the event of a favorable referendum. *Iowa Code Ann.* § 99F.7.10.c (West 1994) (as existing prior to amendment).

102. Ibid.

103. Ibid., § 99F.10.3.

104. Ibid., § 99F.10.5.

105. Ibid., § 99F.11. The tax is 5 percent of the first $1 million of an operator's adjusted gross receipts, 10 percent on the next $2 million and 20 percent on amounts over $3 million. Ibid., § 99F.11.

106. Ibid., § 99F.1.1. Adjusted gross receipts are defined as the total amount wagered minus the amount paid out in winnings. Ibid.

107. *Iowa Code Ann.* § 99E.10.1.a (West 1984 and Supp. 1994). The gambler's assistance fund is defined in the code's section on lotteries.

108. Ibid., § 99F.11.4.

109. *Mo. Ann. Stat.* § 313.812(10) (Vernon 1994).

110. *Ind. Code Ann.* §§ 4-33-1-1 to 4-33-15-4 (West 1994).

111. *Mo. Ann. Stat.* § 313.812(10) (Vernon 1994); *Ind. Code Ann.* § 4-33-6-19(c) (West 1994).

112. *Mo. Ann. Stat.* § 313.822. Adjusted gross receipts are defined as gross receipts less winnings paid. Ibid., § 313.800(1).

113. *Ind. Code Ann.* § 4-33-6-14.

114. *Miss. Code Ann.* § 75-76-1 (1994).

115. See *Miss. Const.* art. IV, § 98. The Mississippi legislature approached the subject with apparent ambivalence and defensiveness. The declarations prefacing the authorizing legislation state that "[n]othing in this chapter [authorizing riverboat gambling] shall be construed as encouraging the legalization of gambling in this state." *Miss. Code Ann.* § 75-76-3(1) (1994).

116. Ibid., § 75-76-3(2).

117. The Mississippi Gaming Act does what the state's constitution does not: it defines lotteries. Ibid., § 75-76-3(6). A lottery exists when (1) a player pays something of value for chances represented by a token, slip of paper or ticket, (2) winning is determined by a drawing, (3) a prize is awarded, and (4) there is no requirement for the physical presence of the player. Ibid. By defining lotteries this way, the legislature was able to authorize gambling activities that were not lotteries and that therefore could be legal under the state constitution. See also Rose, "Gambling and the Law," p. 101 (pointing out irony that Mississippi has no lottery but has riverboat gambling).

118. Ibid., § 19-3-79.

119. Ibid., § 19-3-79(1).

120. See above notes 91–108 and accompanying text for a discussion of Iowa's special election provisions.

121. See herein notes 131–45 and accompanying text for a discussion of Illinois's resolution requirement.

122. *Miss. Code Ann.* § 19-3-79(2) (1994).

123. Ibid., § 19-3-79(3).

124. Ibid., § 19-3-79(2).

125. Ibid., § 19-3-79(4). The section provides that the ballot include two choices, next to one of which the voter places an "x" or check-mark: "For [the other choice begins with "Against"] legal gaming aboard cruise vessels in the county as prescribed by law." Ibid.

126. Ibid.

127. Ibid., § 19-3-79(5).

128. Ibid., § 75-76-77.

129. Ibid., § 76-76-195. The local government can impose a tax of 0.4% on the first $50,000 of gross revenues collected per month, 0.6% on amounts over $50,000, and 0.8% on amounts over $134,000. Ibid.

130. Ibid., § 75-76-191. License fees are between $50 and $5,000, depending on the number of games operated. Ibid.

131. *Ill. Ann. Stat.*, ch. 230, para. 10/3 (Smith-Hurd 1994).

132. Ibid. The prohibition against riverboat gambling on Lake Michigan accomplishes the same end.

133. Ibid., para. 10/6.

134. Ibid., para. 10/7.

135. The board is composed of five members appointed by the governor.

136. Ibid. The applicant for an operator's license is required to submit copies of the resolutions with the application. Ibid.

137. Ibid., para. 10/13. Gross receipts are defined in Illinois as they are in most jurisdictions: the amount wagered minus winnings paid. Ibid.

138. Ibid.

139. Ibid.

140. Ibid.

141. Ibid., para. 10/12.

142. Ibid.

143. Ibid.

144. Ibid., para. 10/13.

145. Ibid., para. 10/11.

146. *N.J. Rev. Stat.* §§ 5:12-1 to 5:12-210 (1994).

147. Ibid., § 5:12-50.

148. Ibid., § 5:12-97. Atlantic City casinos may operate anything except 6 a.m.-10 a.m. on Saturday, Sunday and federal holidays and 4 a.m.-10 a.m. on other days. However, the commission may in its own judgment permit twenty-four-hour operation on any Saturday, Sunday, or federal holiday. Ibid.

149. Ibid., § 5:12-104.

150. Ibid., § 5:12-103g(1).

151. Ibid., §§ 5:12-84, 5:12-85. However, the mayor of Atlantic City exercises minimal influence over gambling development as a member, *ex officio*, of the Casino Reinvestment Development Authority. Ibid., § 5:12-153. The mayor is one of thirteen members of this authority, which grants to the state the right to make decisions on the redevelopment of Atlantic City. Ibid., § 5:12-160.

152. Ibid., § 173.3. This indicates that the parking fee is designed as more than a mere revenue source. If revenue were its only objective, what would explain charging a higher parking tax to casino operators who do not charge their patrons to park? The state would be happy to collect $1.50 per vehicle per day, regardless of who paid the tax. The idea of the legislation seems to be to encourage casinos to charge for parking, although one wonders how a $2-per-day parking fee could ever accomplish the supposed goal of encouraging people not to drive to Atlantic City.

153. H.B. 1883, Pa. General Assembly, Session of 1993 (Printer's No. 2303); H.B. 939, Pa. General Assembly, Session of 1995 (Printer's No. 1070). The 1993 bill was pending before the state general assembly's Committee on Finance at the close of the previous Pennsylvania General Assembly in 1994. The bill was reintroduced in the current assembly, with some changes, as H.B. 939 on March 1, 1995. Some commentators have suggested that riverboat gambling appears to be a secondary priority for the current legislature. See Nathan Gorenstein, "Questions Remain on Jobs Plan," *Philadelphia Inquirer*, January 30, 1995, p. E1 (noting that riverboat gambling is no longer high priority in Pennsylvania and [very] likely will not be discussed until fall 1995). Prior riverboat gambling legislation was defeated in the state's general assembly in 1991 by a vote of 118 to 81. Robert Zausner, "Odds Favor Riverboat Gambling," *Philadelphia Inquirer*, April 10, 1994, at p. B1. Former Governor William B. Casey threatened to veto any such legislation that reached his desk, but passage of authorizing legislation was said to be likely once Governor Casey left office. Ibid. Current Pennsylvania Governor Tom Ridge, elected November 8, 1994, supported riverboat gambling legislation during the Pennsylvania gubernatorial campaign, but after the election conditioned his support on approval in a statewide referendum. Gorenstein, "Questions Remain on Jobs Plan." The governor's insistence on a statewide referendum rather than local referenda in affected communities may make it more difficult to authorize riverboat gambling in Pennsylvania. Robert Moran, "Ridge Tackles Floating Casinos," *Philadelphia Inquirer*, November 11, 1994, p. B1.

154. H.B. 1883, Pa. General Assembly, Session of 1993, § 1 [hereinafter the "1993 Bill"].

155. H.B. 939, Pa. General Assembly, Session of 1995, § 1 [hereinafter the "1995 Bill"].

156. 1995 Bill § 12. The proposed legislation requires a county's board of elections to submit to qualified voters a proposition to approve or disapprove the "conduct of gambling games on an excursion gambling boat in the county." Ibid.

157. Ibid.

158. The act would create a state Excursion Boat Gaming Commission consisting of seven members appointed by the governor. Ibid., § 5(a).

159. Ibid., § 12.

160. Ibid.

161. 1993 Bill § 10(k)(1); 1995 Bill § 12. Under the 1993 bill, a "valid petition" was defined as a petition signed by the number of voters equal to "at least twenty-five percent of the highest vote cast for any office in the municipality at the last preceding general election." 1993 Bill § 3. Under the 1995 bill, a "valid petition" must have at least the number of signatures equal to 25 percent of the highest number of votes cast in the *county* at the last preceding general election. 1995 Bill § 3.

162. Ibid., § 12. The 1995 bill provides only that, if a majority of the county voters voting on the proposition do not favor the conduct of games, a license to conduct games in that municipality shall not be issued. Ibid. Under the 1993 bill, licenses in effect would be canceled within 60 days after a disapproving referendum vote. 1993

Bill § 10(k)(2).

163. In any case, of course, they would face the prospect of revocation for a breach of the gambling act or of a rule created under the act. 1995 Bill § 9(c).

164. See above notes 47–86 and accompanying text for a discussion of the authority of local governments to supplement state gambling laws with restrictive local legislation.

165. See above notes 54–86 and accompanying text for a discussion of judicial review of local ordinances that conflict with state statutes.

166. See above note 53 and accompanying text.

167. See Libonati, "Home Rule," above, note 10, and accompanying text.

168. The history and regulation of Native American gaming is complex and far beyond the scope of this article. The subject is raised here as an example of a regulatory scheme involving the grant of authority between a central authority (the federal government) and a local authority (Indian tribal governments). For analyses of other aspects of Indian gaming and, specifically, discussion of the Indian Gaming Regulatory Act, 25 U.S.C. §§ 2701-2721 (1988 and Supp. IV 1994), see, e.g., Amber J. Ahola, Comment, "Call It the Revenge of the Pequots, or How American Indian Tribes Can Sue States Under the Indian Gaming Regulatory Act Without Violating the Eleventh Amendment," *U.S.F. L. Rev.* 27 (1993), p. 907 (exploring exceptions to Eleventh Amendment sovereign immunity and concluding that Indian tribes can constitutionally sue states under IGRA); Eric D. Jones, Note, "The Indian Gaming Regulatory Act: A Forum for Conflict Among the Plenary Power of Congress, Tribal Sovereignty, and the Eleventh Amendment," *Vt. L. Rev.* 18 (1993), p. 127 (examining federal courts' approaches to Indian tribal sovereignty issues and concluding federal judiciary has failed to resolve tribal and state claims equitably); Joseph J. Weissman, Note, "Upping the Ante: Allowing Indian Tribes to Sue States in Federal Court Under the Indian Gaming Regulatory Act," *Geo. Wash. L. Rev.* 62 (1993), p. 123 (tracing development of IGRA and stressing importance of Indian tribes' ability under IGRA to sue states in federal courts).

Author's note: Subsequent to the publication of the original article, the U.S. Supreme Court, in a 5–4 decision, held that the 11th Amendment *prevents* Congress from authorizing suits by Indian tribes against states to enforce federal legislation that requires states to negotiate in good faith with Indian tribes toward tribal-state compacts governing gaming on Indian lands. See *Seminole Tribe of Florida v. Florida*, 116 S. Ct. (1996), p. 1114. Thus, the power of the "local units" has been diminished somewhat, although the contrast between IGRA and state gambling legislation still stands.

169. Weissman, "Upping the Ante," p. 123.

170. 25 U.S.C. §§ 2701-2721.

171. Ibid., § 2710(d)(1)(B). Since only Utah and Hawaii prohibit all gambling without exception, only those states, under IGRA, could regulate gambling on tribal lands. Weissman, "Upping the Ante," p. 129 n.45.

172. 25 U.S.C. § 2710(d)(1)(A).

173. Ibid., § 2710(d)(1)(A). IGRA gives tribes the right to sue state governments for negotiations if states fail to negotiate in good faith. Weissman, "Upping the Ante," p. 124.
174. 25 U.S.C. § 2710(4) (1988 and Supp. IV 1994).
175. Ibid.
176. Ibid., § 2710(c)(5).
177. Ibid., §§ 2706(b)(1)-(4).
178. Ibid., § 2710(c)(4).
179. Ibid., § 2710(d)(7)(A)(i).
180. The designated purpose of IGRA is to "provide a statutory basis for the operation of gaming by Indian tribes as a means of prompting tribal economic development, *self-sufficiency*, and strong tribal government . . . and to ensure that the Indian tribe is the primary beneficiary of the gaming operation. . . ." Weissman, "Upping the Ante," p. 128 (quoting IGRA, 25 U.S.C. § 2702) (emphasis added).

17. States Should Stop Encroaching on Tribal Sovereignty

Leah Lorber

Leah Lorber, former law student at the Indiana University School of Law, discusses a legal conflict between American Indians who seek to acquire new land to open off-reservation gambling establishments and state governments and governors opposed to the spread of off-reservation gambling. The American Indians appeal to the Indian Reorganization Act of 1934, allowing the federal government to acquire off-reservation land and convert it into Indian land for the tribes' benefit. That process, according to Lorber, is objectionable to some states because it leaves state and local governments with little or no control over activities possibly harmful to their communities. What's more, lands taken into trust for tribes become exempt from local governments' taxes and zoning and other land-use regulations.

Although Lorber appreciates state governments' interests in off-reservation lands, she places a high value on tribal self-determination, which, she asserts, has been legally recognized since the principles implied in an 1832 case, Worcester v. Georgia. Since that case American Indian tribes have been officially recognized as domestic dependent nations, which have distinct interests

---

This article appeared as "State Rights, Tribal Sovereignty, and the 'White Man's Firewater': State Prohibition of Gambling on New Indian Lands," in *Indiana Law Journal* 69 (1993), pp. 255–74. Used by permission.

that are supposed to be protected by the federal government and over which states have limited jurisdiction.

According to Lorber, the U.S. Supreme Court has developed canons of construction that require courts broadly to construe federal action that establishes or reserves Indian rights and narrowly to construe action that limits Indian rights. It is in the light of that judicial history that she criticizes the Interior Department's recent policy of granting state governors absolute veto power over gaming facilities on newly acquired Indian trust lands. Lands taken into trust for Indians, argues Lorber, belong to them and should be controlled by them without explicit congressional intent to authorize state governors to control them.

She concludes that the Department of the Interior should reverse its policy giving states an absolute veto over gaming on new Indian lands. Since the Secretary of the Interior already considers state interests when determining whether to take land into trust for tribes, state interests, according to Lorber, are already properly valued even if state governors have no power to veto gaming on new Indian lands.

Indian-sponsored gambling, from bingo parlors to Las Vegas-style casinos, exploded onto tribal lands during the 1980s. Essentially free from state regulation,[1] Indian gaming halls bring millions of dollars a year to scores of once economically depressed Indian communities.[2] Now, with the success of on-reservation gaming, tribes are seeking to acquire new land to open off-reservation gambling establishments in cities as diverse as Detroit, Michigan, and Salem, Oregon. State officials, who in the mid-1980s unsuccessfully fought to extend state gambling laws over reservations, vigorously oppose the spread of off-reservation gaming. They question the ability of tribes, acting with the federal government, to remove land in the heart of cities from state jurisdiction, convert it into Indian land, and open Indian-regulated gaming on it—thereby preventing the states from exerting control over what they see as an unsavory activity with a detrimental impact on state residents.

State Governors Can Veto Gambling
on New Indian Lands

The Indian Gaming Regulatory Act of 1988 (IGRA),[3] comprehensive federal legislation that governs the operation of Indian gambling establishments, addresses this concern. Section 2719 of the IGRA prohibits gaming on lands acquired in trust for Indian tribes (and thus exempt from state gambling laws) after October 17, 1988—with several exceptions. The major exception allows the Secretary of the Interior to lift a prohibition on gaming on newly acquired trust lands if:

> [A]fter consultation with the Indian tribe and appropriate State and local officials, including officials of other nearby Indian tribes, [the Secretary] determines that a gaming establishment on newly acquired lands would be in the best interest of the Indian tribe and its members, and would not be detrimental to the surrounding community, *but only if the Governor of the State in which the gaming activity is to be conducted concurs in the Secretary's determination.* . . .[4]

The practical effects of this language, however, are by no means clear. Some interested parties, such as the Western Governors Association, have criticized this language as vague and sought clarifying amendments to the act.[5] Others, such as the State of Oregon and the Confederated Tribes of the Siletz, brought lawsuits to determine the meaning of the section.[6] The Department of the Interior, which decides whether to take land into trust for gaming, has vacillated on the legislation's requirements. Until recently, the Interior Department interpreted this section to allow the state governor to voice concerns about off-reservation Indian gaming, which the department would consider in determining whether to allow gambling on newly acquired trust lands.[7] In December 1992, however, the department reversed itself and announced a policy that essentially makes the governor's veto dispositive in these gaming decisions.[8]

This new policy highlights the ongoing battle for power between states and Indian tribes. Since 1831, when the Cherokee Nation challenged Georgia's attempts to abolish the Cherokee government and distribute

Indian land over five counties, Indians have fought steadily, but not always successfully, to prevent state governments from exercising jurisdiction over tribes.[9] In fact, states have regularly disregarded Indian interests when exercising or attempting to exercise jurisdiction.[10] The Interior Department's new policy of allowing a state governor to unilaterally veto tribal plans for gaming on newly acquired off-reservation lands presents an impermissible encroachment of state regulation onto the lands of a separate sovereign body, and an impermissible intrusion into tribal affairs.

As the issue is just beginning to draw attention, few cases or scholarly articles address § 2719, or otherwise discuss the state's ability, or lack thereof, to exercise control over tribal use of newly acquired lands. This Note discusses two possible attacks on the Interior Department policy granting a state governor absolute veto power over gaming facilities on newly acquired sovereign Indian trust lands.[11] Part 1 discusses the various interests of the states and tribes involved. Part 2 details congressional action on this issue. Part 3 analyzes § 2719 in accordance with the canons of statutory construction of American Indian law, determines that the Interior Department's interpretation of the statute is erroneous because it disregards the longstanding methods used to interpret federal actions concerning Indians, and presents an alternative interpretation. Part 4 argues that the Interior Department's interpretation poses a constitutional problem and thus should be invalidated under the commonly recognized principle of statutory interpretation that courts should prefer a meaning which satisfies constitutional scrutiny.

1. Gambling Is a Boon to Many Reservations

High-stakes Indian bingo parlors opened in Florida in the late 1970s and quickly spread to one-third of the 330 reservations in the United States.[12] Since then, Indian gaming—the "white man's firewater"[13]—has been a financial windfall to more than 150 tribes across the United States during the 1980s. Exempt from state gambling regulations, Indian bingo halls can offer higher pots and longer hours than state-approved bingo parlors.[14] More than $720 million was bet on Indian lands in 1991;[15]

gamblers from nearby states take advantage of package-fare deals and fly or ride chartered buses to the reservations.[16]

This windfall income is helping Indian tribes become self-sufficient through tribal economic development, a goal the Reagan administration announced in 1983.[17] Gambling profits, which reached $400 million in 1991,[18] have made up for cuts in federal spending during the last decade,[19] and paid for health, education, and community development programs. For example, tribes in Minnesota have withdrawn from federal assistance programs, using income from casino-related jobs to pave roads, build water and sewer projects, and community centers, and fund chemical dependency programs, college educations, and free medical care. Some tribes distribute gambling profits to their members in per capita installments. The Shakopee Mdewakanton Sioux Community guarantees tribal members a free college education and trust fund payments of up to $140,000, beginning at age eighteen.[20] Contrast this relative prosperity with the situation ten years ago, when 70 percent of the people were on welfare and living in trailers with two or three families to a home.[21]

Indian gaming on reservations is also a boon to nearby economically depressed cities. In Turtle Lake, Wisconsin, when the St. Croix tribes opened a casino on reservation lands in May 1992, jobs and real estate development boomed while deposits at the Bank of Turtle Lake jumped ten percent.[22] In Redwood Falls, Minnesota, a 4,900-person town and the site of an on-reservation casino, unemployment in 1992 was less than two percent, single-family homes sold within days in a once-depressed housing market, and new businesses moved in.[23]

Tribal representatives were thrilled with the benefits that gambling brought their communities. "It represents growth in any area you can imagine," said Leonard Prescott, chairman of the tribal company that runs a new $15 million casino in Mystic Lake, Minnesota.[24] "It represents a strong tribal government; it represents self-determination; it represents pride."[25]

State officials and their supporters often view the issue differently, raising concerns about immorality[26] and organized crime.[27] Since tribal governments are not required to report large cash transactions, law enforcement authorities worry that Indian halls will be used to launder drug money.[28] "Who [is] making sure the machines [are not] rigged, the payoffs [are] being made and the income [is] being used for community activities?" asked one state official.[29] Others noted the impact that Indian on-reservation gaming could have on revenues from state-sanctioned gambling—one Nevada senator put the figure at $15 billion in 1985.[30] Finally, some officials are reluctant to recognize tribal sovereignty and its accompanying limits on the state's ability to exercise jurisdiction over tribal lands. "I know the tribes don't want State regulation. I know that. They want sovereignty," said Arizona Attorney General Robert Corbin. "But they are part of the State of Arizona. And I think they should comply with our laws."[31]

Whether Indian on-reservation gaming has had a detrimental impact on nearby communities has yet to be proven. In 1992, the Justice Department reported that it found no widespread or successful effort by organized crime to infiltrate Indian gaming operations. In fact, the Department said the Federal Bureau of Investigation reported fewer than five open investigations of organized crime family activity related to Indian gaming.[32] On the other hand, calls for police service, traffic accidents, and congestion increased after a casino was built near Redwood Falls, Minnesota.[33] And in the Minneapolis-St. Paul area, where tribes operate several casinos, membership in the area Gamblers Anonymous increased nearly sixfold in the past ten years and calls to the group's hotline tripled during 1991.[34]

With the financial success of on-reservation gaming, tribes began to seek to acquire lands and open bingo halls and casinos in urban areas.[35] They did so by seeking to capitalize on provisions of the Indian Reorganization Act of 1934, which allow the federal government to acquire off-reservation land and convert it into Indian land for the tribes' benefit.[36] This process, though, generally leaves state and local governments with little or no control over activities that could be harmful to their communities.[37] The states' concerns (and the tribes' potential for income) increase when Indian gaming operations are established off the reservation. In addition to concerns discussed earlier,[38] lands taken into trust for tribes are removed from local governments' tax rolls[39] and from the reach of zoning and other land-use regulations.[40] Urban traffic and crime problems may be increased by the proximity of a casino, but are still the city's responsibility to solve. A city's decision to welcome tribal gaming may be less well-considered if the tribe is also negotiating with the city next door. Rolling Meadows Mayor Carl Couve said he was concerned that the neighboring suburb would accept the Chippewa casino if Rolling Meadows rejected it, forcing the suburb to live with the detriments of a casino without reaping any of its benefits.[41]

The issue peaked in late 1992, when the Confederated Tribes of the Siletz asked the federal government to take twenty acres in northeast Salem, Oregon, into trust so the tribe could open an $8 million casino. The recently recognized tribe, whose land holdings are scattered primarily among tracts of steep timberland on the Oregon coast, sought the land because of its proximity to the Portland-Salem-Eugene metropolitan area and to the Interstate 5 corridor. Interior Secretary Manuel Lujan first announced in November 1992 that he planned to take the land into trust despite the objections of Oregon Governor Barbara Roberts, following a longstanding Department policy that considered the governor's opinion advisory. He reversed his decision—and the Interior Department's interpretation of the Indian Gaming Regulatory Act of 1988—after the state filed a lawsuit to determine how much control § 2719 gives the governor in determining whether gaming should be allowed on new Indian lands.[42]

2. Congress Legislated on Indian Gaming in the 1980s

Early congressional action considered the idea of prohibiting gaming on new, off-reservation Indian lands. This idea drew little attention, however, as lawmakers focused more on creating a regulatory scheme that would protect tribal sovereignty and states' interests in fighting crime. The first bill on Indian gambling activities, House Bill 4566 in the 98th Congress, made no mention of gaming on trust lands and eventually died in committee.[43]

In 1985, the 99th Congress considered several bills to regulate Indian gaming. One bill, House Bill 3130, was specifically introduced by Nebraska Representative Douglas Bereuter to prohibit the granting of trust status to non-Indian lands for gambling activities unless the tribe obtained "the concurrence of the governor of the state and the legislative bodies of all local governmental units in which the land is located."[44] In introducing his bill, Representative Bereuter noted that extending trust status to land not contiguous to Indian reservations "would create ill feelings . . . in areas where relationships are already strained."[45] He also stated that although he supported tribal sovereignty and economic development, gambling was not an "appropriate activity" to justify adding new trust lands and that Nebraska charities were fearful of losing income from state-approved bingo games to competing Indian bingo halls.[46] Similarly, the Department of the Interior and the Justice Department presented a plan to restrict gaming to the reservations proper and on trust lands where the tribe resides as a community and exercises governmental authority.[47] Bereuter's bill drew little discussion at the committee level,[48] as House members were preoccupied with considering House Bill 1920, which provided for a comprehensive Indian gambling regulatory scheme.[49] These bills also died in Congress.

In the 100th Congress, senators considered two bills that apparently reflected the intent of Bereuter's earlier bill to grant a state governor the ability to veto gaming on newly acquired lands: Senate Bills 1303 and 555. The first, Senate Bill 1303, allowed the prohibition against gaming on new lands to be waived if the tribe "obtains the concurrence of the Governor of the State, and the governing bodies of the county or municipality in which such lands are located."[50] This section drew occasional criticism from Indian supporters, who saw the section as either an impermissible encroachment on tribal sovereignty[51] or an out-and-out attempt to limit competition for non-Indian gaming interests.[52] The potential constitutional violation in the section's language also concerned the Justice Department. The Justice Department suggested revising the section to comply with the demands of the Appointments Clause,[53] noting that this was essentially the approach taken in the other bill, Senate Bill 555.[54] Senate Bill 555 was adopted and became the Indian Gaming Regulatory Act of 1988.[55]

3. The Interior Department's Interpretation of the Governors' Veto Is Wrong

Tribal sovereignty, the power of tribes to govern themselves and determine their futures, is a concept cherished by Indians[56] and their supporters.[57] The concept encompasses tribal authority over Indian lands, for example, to enact and enforce tribal laws, tax, grant marriages and divorces, provide for the adoption of children, zone property, develop the tribal economy, and regulate the use of natural resources on tribal land.[58] "Indian people will never surrender their basic desire to control the relationships both among themselves and with non-Indian governments, organizations and persons," said Wade Miller, chairman of the tribal council of the Omaha Tribe of Nebraska.[59]

Although Congress's view of American Indian independence and self-determination has fluctuated during the past 150 years, the federal government recognizes the tribal sovereignty doctrine first set forth by Chief Justice Marshall in *Worcester v. Georgia*.[60] Although the *Worcester* doctrine has since been modified to accommodate changing circumstances, its basic principles remain:[61] state jurisdiction over Indians is limited, but tribes do not enjoy the full range of sovereignty of foreign nations. They are instead perceived as "domestic dependent nations" with a relationship to the United States that "resembles that of a ward to his guardian."[62] This trust relationship places upon Congress the responsibility to act to protect Indian interests.[63] Since Congress's intent in dealing with the Indians is presumed to be benevolent, the United States Supreme Court has developed canons of construction that dictate that federal action should be read, when possible, to protect Indian rights.[64] For example, courts should broadly construe federal action that establishes or reserves Indian rights, and should narrowly construe action that limits Indian rights.[65] This rule of construction, though, can only go so far: congressional intent,[66] as evinced by the language, legislative history, and surrounding circumstances of an act,[67] will ultimately control. Still, Congress must "clearly and specifically express" its intention to delegate jurisdiction over Indian country, since state jurisdiction over Indian country erodes tribal self-government and federal protection, two long-favored aspects of the trust relationship between Indian tribes and the United States.[68]

Reading § 2719 against the traditional "backdrop"[69] of Indian sovereignty that gives meaning to federal laws governing Indian affairs indicates that the Interior Department's new interpretation of the section is improper. The interpretation, which gives a state governor veto power over the Secretary's decision to allow gaming on new Indian lands, conflicts with these long-recognized canons of construction. Because lands taken into trust by the Secretary become Indian country,[70] the Interior Department's interpretation is proper only if it confirms a clear showing of congressional intent to allow the governor to exercise jurisdiction over these lands.[71] No such clear showing is present, as indicated by an examination of the language, legislative history, and surrounding circumstances of § 2719 and of the structure of the IGRA itself.

A. Ambiguous Language and an Alternative Interpretation

The language of § 2719 is ambiguous, obscuring the roles which the Interior Secretary and the state governor are to play in determining whether new tribal lands should be used for gaming. The act prohibits gaming on lands acquired after October 17, 1988, with several exceptions. The exception at issue allows the Interior Secretary to lift a prohibition on such gaming if:

> [T]he Secretary, after consultation with the Indian tribe and appropriate State and local officials, including officials of other nearby Indian tribes, determines that a gaming establishment on newly acquired lands would be in the best interest of the Indian tribe and its members, and would not be detrimental to the surrounding community, but only if the Governor of the State in which

the gaming activity is to be conducted concurs in the Secretary's determination.[72]

It is unclear whether the language of § 2719 delegates the ultimate decision-making authority to waive the ban on gaming to the Interior Secretary alone, to the state governor alone, or to both parties jointly. In fact, two federal agencies have given this language different interpretations. The Interior Department's new policy construes the language such that the state governor has the ultimate power to ban or approve off-reservation gambling.[73] The Justice Department has interpreted the language as ultimately assigning this decision to the Interior Secretary.[74]

The ambiguity of this section apparently reflects legislative attempts to avoid a potential constitutional violation. Earlier versions of the IGRA clearly provided a blanket grant of power to the state governor to approve or disapprove gaming on new Indian lands; the Interior Secretary was given no control over these decisions.[75] This grant of power drew criticism from the Justice Department, which noted a potential Appointments Clause[76] violation: the section would give individuals not appointed in accordance with constitutional provisions the power to waive a federal statute.[77] The Justice Department believed the constitutional requirements could be met if lawmakers reworded the section's language to ensure that the Interior Secretary, an executive officer, would ultimately be responsible for determining whether to lift the ban.[78] The Justice Department also noted that the language of Senate Bill 555, another regulatory proposal, took that approach and met constitutional requirements.[79] Aware of this need to make the Interior Secretary ultimately responsible for lifting the gaming ban, Congress adopted Senate Bill 555 as the Indian Gaming Regulatory Act of 1988.

In light of these events, it is most probable that Congress intended to grant the Interior Secretary ultimate authority to determine whether to lift the ban on off-reservation gaming. It is unlikely that lawmakers intended to grant this authority to the state governor, since they knew of the potential constitutional problems that it would pose. Even if the Secretary and the governor jointly exercised that authority, the constitutional problems would remain because the governor would be responsible for waiving a federal statute. Still, Congress most likely intended for the state governor's opinion to carry weight in the Secretary's decision on lifting the gaming ban. Throughout discussions on the IGRA, lawmakers emphasized tribal-state cooperation and the need to develop a gaming regulatory scheme that protected state as well as Indian rights.[80] The proper reading of § 2719 would make the Secretary of the Interior responsible for determining whether to allow gaming on newly acquired, off-reservation lands—but would require the Secretary to give great weight to the state governor's *advisory* opinion when making this determination.[81]

The existence of a second plausible interpretation of this ambiguous language indicates that the Interior Department erred when it interpreted § 2719 to grant the state governor absolute veto power over gaming on new Indian lands. Congress did not clearly, specifically, and unambiguously state an intention to give the governor this power. Congress, however, is fully aware of the need to use clear and specific language when granting states jurisdiction over Indian country, and it has done so in the past. For example, when Congress passed Public Law 280 to give five states criminal and civil jurisdiction over reservation Indians, it stated:

> Each of the States . . . shall have jurisdiction over offenses committed by or against Indians in the areas of Indian country listed opposite the name of the State . . . to the same extent that such State . . . has jurisdiction over offenses committed elsewhere within the State . . . and the criminal laws of such State . . . shall have the same force and effect within such Indian country as they have elsewhere within the State.[82]

Similarly, Congress also stated:

> Each of the States listed . . . shall have jurisdiction over civil causes of action between Indians or to which Indians are parties which arise in the areas of Indian country listed . . . to the same extent that such State has jurisdiction over other civil causes of action, and those civil laws of such State that are of general application to private persons or private property shall have the same force and effect within such Indian country as they have elsewhere within the State.[83]

Without a similarly clear and specific expression of intent to grant state governors unilateral control over gaming on newly acquired land, § 2719 cannot be interpreted as granting such jurisdiction.

B. A "Framework" of Sovereignty

In addition to the ambiguous language of § 2719, the structure of the IGRA itself precludes an interpretation that would allow a state to encroach upon tribal sovereignty by vetoing gambling on new Indian lands. As the sponsors of the IGRA addressed the need for enforcement of gaming laws and regulations, they were emphatic about preserving the sovereign rights of tribal governments to regulate activities and enforce laws on Indian lands. In fact, the Senate Select Committee on Indian Affairs intentionally developed a "framework"[84] for these Indian gaming regulations which: "provides that in the exercise of its sovereign rights, unless a tribe affirmatively elects to have State laws and State jurisdiction extend to tribal lands, the Congress will not unilaterally [sic] impose or allow State jurisdiction on Indian lands for the regulation of Indian gaming activities."[85]

In just one example of congressional concern for the integrity of tribal sovereignty, Congress repeatedly included safeguards for tribal sovereignty when it drafted § 2710(d) of the Act, which governs the ability of tribes to operate casino gaming, horse and dog racing, jai alai, and certain other gambling (all referred to as Class III gaming) on Indian lands. In drafting this section, Congress sought to balance the law enforcement interests of the states with the economic development and self-government interests of the tribes. This section of the Act states in part that: "(1) Class III gaming activities shall be lawful on Indian lands only if such activities are . . . (C) conducted in conformance with a Tribal-State compact entered into by the Indian tribe and the State."[86] Section 2710(d) was drafted to ensure that tribes wishing to offer Class III gambling could negotiate such regulatory compacts with the state as "equal sovereigns,"[87] and to prevent states from using these regulatory compacts as a subterfuge for imposing state jurisdiction on tribal lands. Congressional protections for tribal sovereignty permeate the section.

For example, states are required to act in good faith when negotiating tribal-state compacts. Tribes have the affirmative right to sue the state if a compact is not negotiated. In such a case, the state must prove it acted in good faith[88] and any demand by the state for direct taxation of the tribe or Indian lands is evidence that the state did not negotiate in good faith.[89] The courts can appoint a mediator to attempt to negotiate another compact.[90] Finally, if that attempt fails, the Secretary of the Interior has the power to prescribe procedures, in consultation with the tribe, under which Class III gaming may be conducted on the tribal lands.[91] Under this scheme, no state consent is ultimately needed for tribal jurisdiction over Class III gaming on Indian lands.

Given the Act's emphasis on the protection of tribal sovereignty, the Interior Secretary's ultimate authority, and limits on state jurisdiction elsewhere in the Act, a policy allowing a governor to prohibit gaming on newly acquired lands would be at odds with the purpose of the Act and Congress's interest in tribal sovereignty. These textual and structural arguments and their reliance on a backdrop of tribal sovereignty should prevail.

C. Legislative History and Surrounding Circumstances

The Interior Department's interpretation of § 2719 is undermined by further examining the IGRA's legislative history: analyzing § 2719 against a backdrop of tribal sovereignty. In light of this examination and the goals of the IGRA and the Indian Reorganization Act of 1934 (IRA),[92] § 2719 does not clearly and specifically show congressional intent to allow a governor to unilaterally veto tribal gaming on new lands.

Both the IGRA and the IRA share the goal of attaining tribal self-sufficiency through tribal economic development. Under the IGRA, Congress set up a gaming regulatory scheme to preserve tribal self-sufficiency while minimizing the risk of criminal involvement.[93] Under the

IRA,[94] the federal government was allowed to take lands into trust for Indian tribes in order to "rehabilitate the Indian's economic life and to give him a chance to develop the initiative destroyed by a century of oppression and paternalism."[95] At present, tribal use and development of trust property represents "one of the main vehicles for the economic self-development necessary to equal Indian participation in American life."[96] Gaming profits have helped tribes provide more government services than otherwise would have been possible, just as lotteries and other forms of gambling have contributed to state and local government coffers. Often these profits mean the difference between adequate tribal programs and skeletal programs totally dependent on federal funding.[97]

States, however, often resent Indian gaming's success, because of fears of lost lottery revenue, increasing crime, moral concerns, or pressure from non-Indian gambling interests.[98] States also have a lengthy history of ignoring or disparaging tribal interests in economic development and other areas when enacting legislation,[99] and therefore they are not the proper entities to wield unfettered control over American Indian economic development efforts. As one federal court pointedly explained:

> [S]ubjecting [Indian lands] to local jurisdiction would . . . subject [ ] Indian economic development to the veto power of potentially hostile local non-Indian majorities. Local communities may not share the usually poorer Indian's priorities, or may in fact be in economic competition with the Indians. . . . Indians and surrounding communities are often likely to have differing views of the relative priority of economic development, environmental amenity, public morals, and the like.[100]

In light of congressional attempts to foster tribal self-sufficiency and economic development in this and other legislation,[101] it is unlikely that Congress intended to create a policy under which a hostile state governor could unilaterally and arbitrarily prevent a tribe from acquiring land to start what has become a highly lucrative economic development activity for tribes.

4. The Interior Department's Interpretation
Poses a Constitutional Problem

Under a commonly recognized canon of statutory interpretation, if there is a potential problem with a statute's constitutionality, the statute is ordinarily to be interpreted in a manner that avoids constitutional doubt.[102] The Interior Department's current interpretation of § 2719(b) poses constitutional concerns because it conflicts with the Appointments Clause.[103] Therefore, courts should prefer an interpretation of § 2719(b) that vests ultimate authority in the Secretary of the Department of the Interior.[104]

The Interior Department's interpretation allows a person who is not an executive branch official to waive a federal statute. Under case law interpreting the Appointments Clause, any person who exercises significant authority under the laws of the United States is considered an "Officer of the United States" and must be appointed by the President with the "Advice and Consent of the Senate" in accordance with the procedures prescribed by the Clause.[105] A person exercises "significant authority" if, for example, she can make decisions that bind not only the parties involved, but also a cabinet member and the President.[106]

In the instant case, a state governor acting under the Interior Department's interpretation of § 2719(b) exercises significant authority under federal law. The statute prohibiting gaming on new Indian lands[107] can be waived only if the state governor permits it to be waived. This permission would only come if the governor agreed that gaming on the new lands would benefit the tribe and would not be detrimental to the surrounding community. If the governor does not agree, the prohibition cannot be lifted. The governor's decision whether to agree, therefore, determines the Secretary's actions and is binding on the Secretary. The responsibility of determining when to waive a federal law must fall under the responsibility to execute the laws, which is entrusted to the Executive Branch.[108] Here, though, this executive responsibility is given to the governor, a person not considered an Officer of the United States and *not* appointed by the President with the advice and consent of the Senate. An interpretation of § 2719(b) that grants a governor this veto power would render the section unconstitutional, as would an interpretation that granted power to waive the gaming prohibition *jointly* to the governor and the Interior Secretary.

Although such an argument is not unassailable,[109] it does present a serious constitutional concern with the Interior Department's current interpretation of § 2719(b). As discussed in Part 3, an alternative interpretation of § 2719(b) would make the governor's opinion advisory and would give the Interior Secretary the sole authority to determine whether to lift the ban. Two interpretations of the statute are possible, one constitutional, one unconstitutional. Following the Supreme Court's rule of statutory interpretation, the Interior Department should adopt the constitutional interpretation, which gives the Interior Secretary the ultimate decision on gaming on newly acquired lands. The purpose of the statute—to ensure that off-reservation gaming would benefit the tribe and not harm the surrounding community—would still be met, because the Interior Secretary would have to seriously consider this information and the governor's opinion when making this decision. The Department should reject its current interpretation, which poses constitutional problems.

5. Governors Should Not Have an Absolute Veto

The Department of the Interior should reverse its policy giving states an absolute veto over gaming on new Indian lands. The benefits to tribes from gaming have been well documented; the harm from gaming feared by the states has not been demonstrated. The Secretary of the Interior already considers state interests when determining whether to take land into trust for tribes,[110] so state interests would be accounted for even though state governors would not possess veto power. Given the emphasis of the IGRA and the recent federal policy of protecting tribal sovereignty, there is no reason to limit it by adopting a potentially unconstitutional interpretation of the ambiguous language of § 2719.

Notes

1. State bingo regulations and other civil or regulatory gambling laws do not, absent tribal consent, apply to Indian lands. See *California v. Cabazon Band of Mission Indians*, 480 U.S. (1987), p. 202; *Barona Group of Capitan Grande Band of Mission Indians v. Duffy*, 694 F.2d (9th Cir. 1982), p. 1185, *cert. denied*, 461 U.S. (1983), p. 929; *Seminole Tribe v. Butterworth*, 658 F.2d (5th Cir. Unit B Oct. 1981), p. 310, *cert. denied*, 455 U.S. (1982), p. 1020; *Mashantucket Pequot Tribe v. McGuigan*, 626 F. Supp. (D. Conn. 1986), p. 245; *Oneida Tribe of Indians v. Wisconsin*, 518 F. Supp. (W.D. Wis. 1981), p. 712. Additionally, under a provision of the Indian Gambling Regulatory Act of 1988, Congress explicitly provided that tribes who wish to offer activities such as pari-mutuel dog and horse racing, casino games, and jai alai must in good faith negotiate a tribal-state compact that will govern the operation of such gaming on Indian lands. 25 U.S.C. § 2710(d) (1988).
2. By 1991, Indian tribes operated about 150 gambling halls, generating $1.3 billion in revenue and $400 million in net profit in that year alone. "Indians Want to Block States' Role in Reservation Casinos," *Boston Globe*, July 21, 1992, Nation Section, p. 13 (quoting the National Indian Gaming Commission) [hereinafter "Reservation Casinos"]. A March 1992 study by the New York investment banking firm of Wertheim Shroder found that at least 27 Las Vegas-style casinos were run by tribes in nine states, with more than 50 applications pending before the federal government. Janan Hanna, "Suburb's Casino Plan Still Quite a Gamble," *Chicago Tribune* (Lake ed.), November 15, 1992, section 2, 3.

    In constant 1990 dollars, economic development spending by the Bureau of Indian Affairs (BIA) fell from $144 million in 1977 to $36 million in 1990, a drop of 75 percent. *Congressional Record* 138 (daily ed. March 12, 1992), S3426 (remarks by Arizona Sen. John McCain, quoting statistics from the National Indian Policy Center).

    > From 40 to 45 percent of reservation Indians and 22 percent of off-reservation Indians live below the poverty line. In 1985, the Bureau of Indian Affairs reported a 39 percent unemployment rate among its population. Fourteen percent of Indian reservation households, three times the rate for the United States as a whole, had an annual income under $2,500, and 25 percent of Indian reservation households are on food stamps. (Ibid., S3425.)

    Only 40 percent of the working age population on Indian reservations are employed more than 40 weeks of the year, and most of those who work earn less than $7,000 a year. Ibid. (quoting statistics from the National Indian Policy Center).
3. 25 U.S.C. §§ 2701-2721 (1988).
4. Ibid., § 2719(b)(1)(A) (emphasis added).
5. Pat Flannery, "Governors Raise Gambling Ante: New Deal Asked on Tribal Gaming," *Phoenix Gazette* (Final ed.), June 23, 1992, p. A1 (quoting Arizona Governor Fife Symington).

6. "Oregon Files Suit to Stop Siletz Tribes' Casino Plan," *Seattle Times*, November 26, 1992, Northwest Section, p. E1, WESTLAW, available in DIALOG, file no. 707 [hereinafter "Oregon Files Suit"]; Carmel Finley, "Siletz Tribes File Suit to Save Casino Plan," *Oregonian*, December 23, 1992, Metro/Northwest Section, p. E6.

7. Hanna, "Suburb's Casino Plan," p. 3.

8. "New Policy Gives Engler Veto Power Over Indian-Run Casinos," UPI Newswire, December 23, 1992, available in LEXIS, Nexis Library, Wires File.

9. *Cherokee Nation v. Georgia*, 30 U.S. (5 Pet.) (1831), p. 1. In this highly controversial case, an outgrowth of Georgia's attempts to assert jurisdiction over the Cherokee Nation (and incidentally its gold-rich lands), the Cherokee Nation filed suit to test the state's jurisdiction over crimes occurring on tribal lands. Chief Justice John Marshall avoided deciding the touchy question of the extent of the state's jurisdiction by first focusing on whether the Cherokee Nation had standing to sue in federal court. Looking to an aberrational and no longer valid case from the early 1800s, Marshall ruled that the Cherokee nation had no standing to bring the case. In so holding, however, Marshall created a special status for Indian tribes. See text accompanying notes 61–63 herein.

10. See note 99 herein.

11. Indian trust lands are off-reservation lands acquired by the federal government under 25 U.S.C. § 465 (1988) and held in trust for the benefit of Indian tribes. Trust lands are usually considered Indian country and are governed primarily by federal and tribal law. See note 70 herein.

12. Chuck Haga, "Indians Snare Chunk of Jackpot; Tribes See Casinos as Chance to Reverse Economic Stagnation," *Star Tribune* (Minneapolis), September 24, 1990, News Section, p. 1A, WESTLAW, available in DIALOG, File no. 724.

13. David Fritze, "Minnesota Tribes Roll Dice, Win with Gambling," *Arizona Republic*, May 24, 1992, p. A1, WESTLAW, available in DIALOG, File no. 492.

14. *California v. Cabazon Band of Mission Indians*, 480 U.S. (1987), p. 202; *Barona Group of Capitan Grande Band of Mission Indians v. Duffy*, 694 F.2d (9th Cir. 1982), p. 1185, *cert. denied*, 461 U.S. (1983), p. 929; *Seminole Tribe v. Butterworth*, 658 F.2d (5th Cir. Unit B Oct. 1981), p. 310, *cert. denied*, 455 U.S. (1982), p. 1020; *Mashantucket Pequot Tribe v. McGuigan*, 626 F. Supp. (D. Conn 1986), p. 245; *Oneida Tribe of Indians v. Wisconsin*, 518 F. Supp. (W.D. Wis. 1981), p. 712.

15. "Wisconsin Tribes Attend War Council on Gaming," *St. Paul Pioneer Press* (Wis. ed.), October 7, 1992, p. 3D.

16. Fritze, "Minnesota Tribes Roll Dice."

17. Indian Policy, Statement of the President, *Wkly. Comp. Pres. Doc.* 19 (January 24, 1983), pp. 98, 99.

18. "Reservation Casinos," p. 13.

19. Ibid.; Haga, "Indians Snare Chunk of Jackpot."

20. Fritze, "Minnesota Tribes Roll Dice."

21. Haga, "Indians Snare Chunk of Jackpot."

22. Steven Morris, "Gambling Drums are Beating in Illinois," *Chicago Tribune*, November 16, 1992, § 4, pp. 1, 3. Patrick Wick, the president of the Bank of Turtle Lake, said the bank received about $3.5 million in deposits from the casino and its employees. Ibid.

23. Richard Meryhew, "Casino Gives Nearby Town a Shot in the Arm, Pain in the Neck," *Star Tribune* (Minneapolis), July 18, 1992, News Section, pp. A1, A8.

24. Fritze, "Minnesota Tribes Roll Dice."

25. Ibid.

26. Oregon Governor Barbara Roberts vetoed plans for an Indian casino in Salem, the state capital, citing concerns that "a casino in Salem would erode the social and moral fabric of the community and that quality of life would decline." "Oregon Files Suit." Others have stated that the government should steer clear of supporting or conducting such a "destructive and improper activity" as legalized gambling, citing religious and social concerns and referring to gambling as an "economic parasite." "Gaming Activities on Indian Reservations and Lands: Hearing on S. 555 and S. 1303 Before the Senate Select Comm. on Indian Affairs," 100th Cong., 1st Sess. 436–38 (1987) [hereinafter "Senate Hearing on Gaming Activities I"]. Finally, some have voiced concerns about opening the reservations to unregulated "cockfighting, tattoo parlors, nude dancing, houses of prostitution, and other illegal but profitable enterprises." *California v. Cabazon Band of Mission Indians*, 480 U.S. (1987), pp. 202, 222 (Stevens, J., dissenting).

27. See *Cabazon Band of Mission Indians*, 480 U.S., p. 211; "Senate Hearing on Gaming Activities I," pp. 82–84, 92, 141–44; "Indian Gambling Control Act: Hearing on H.R. 4566 Before the House Comm. on Interior and Insular Affairs," 98th Cong., 2d Sess., pp. 15–39, 66–75 (1984).

28. Haga, "Indians Snare Chunk of Jackpot."

29. Ibid.

30. For example, Nevada Senator Chic Hecht's study estimated that the 32 states with Indian reservations could lose from $28 million to $123 million in lottery revenues and from $89 million to $199 million in state-approved bingo revenues in 1985. "Senate Hearing on Gaming Activities I," p. 187.

31. "Indian Gambling Control Act: Hearings on H.R. 1920 and H.R. 2404 Before the House Comm. on Interior and Insular Affairs, Part I," 99th Cong., 1st Sess., p. 56 (1985) [hereinafter "House Indian Gambling Hearings, Part I].

32. Michael Murphy, "Casinos Mostly Crime-Free, Official Says," *Phoenix Gazette*, June 23, 1992, p. A1.

33. Meryhew, "Casino Gives Nearby Town a Shot in the Arm," p. A8.

34. Fritze, "Minnesota Tribes Roll Dice."

35. For years, only two off-reservation gaming halls existed. But recently, tribes began seeking to open off-reservation casinos around the country. For example, in Detroit, two developers have offered to donate a parcel of land in the trendy "Greektown" area to the Sault Ste. Marie Chippewa tribe for use as a casino. Mayor Coleman Young favors the plan; a majority of city residents and Michigan Governor

John Engler do not. See Tina Lam and Joel Thurtell, "Casino Foes Fight Odds: Detroit Plan's Lawyer Confident," *Detroit Free Press*, November 20, 1992, p. 1A. In the northwestern Chicago suburb of Rolling Meadows, the town aldermen decided to lend their support to a casino proposed by the Wisconsin-based St. Croix Chippewa tribe; Illinois Governor Jim Edgar refused to approve the plan. Hanna, "Suburb's Casino Plan Still Quite a Gamble," p. 1. In Hudson, Wisconsin, voters endorsed the sale of a greyhound racing track to an Indian tribe that plans to add a casino there. Wisconsin Governor Tommy Thompson has said he does not want to expand gambling operations but would consider the wishes of local communities. Maureen M. Smith, "Hudson Voters Narrowly Endorse Sale of Dog Track," *Star Tribune* (Minneapolis), December 4, 1992, p. 1A.

36. 25 U.S.C. § 465. That section states: "The Secretary of the Interior is authorized, in his discretion, to acquire, through purchase, relinquishment, gift, exchange, or assignment, any interest in lands . . . for the purpose of providing land for Indians. . . . Such lands . . . shall be exempt from State and local taxation." Ibid.

37. *Florida Dep't of Business Reg. v. United States Dep't of the Interior*, 768 F.2d (11th Cir. 1985), p. 1248 (holding that an Interior Department decision to take land into trust for Indians is unreviewable as within the Secretary's discretion), *cert. denied*, 475 U.S. (1986), p. 1011. But c.f. *Scotts Valley Band of Pomo Indians of the Sugar Bowl Rancheria v. United States*, 921 F.2d (9th Cir. 1990), p. 924 (holding that the city's tax and regulatory concerns gave it protectable interest in an Indian action to have land restored to trust status); *City of Sault Ste. Marie, Mich. v. Andrus*, 458 F. Supp. (D.D.C. 1978), p. 465 (holding that statute waived the federal government's sovereign immunity status so the city could challenge the Interior Department trust decision).

38. See above notes 26–34 and accompanying text.

39. 25 U.S.C. § 465. Although not favored by the IGRA, tribes often negotiate agreements to pay local governments money to make up for the loss of tax dollars. The St. Croix Chippewa tribe promised to pay the cities of Rolling Meadows and East St. Louis $10 million a year in lieu of sales and other taxes lost when land was taken into trust for new casinos, and to provide each city with 2,000 new jobs. Morris, "Gambling Drums," p. 3. The potential loss of taxes inherent in land-trust actions, however, has led some local governments to fight federal trust decisions made for other reasons. See, e.g., *Scotts Valley Band*, 921 F.2d, p. 924; *City of Sault Ste. Marie*, 458 F. Supp. 465; *City of Tacoma, Wash. v. Andrus*, 457 F. Supp. (D.D.C. 1978), p. 342.

40. 58 Interior Dec. pp. 52, 54 (1942); 25 C.F.R. § 1.4 (1992).

41. Hanna, "Suburb's Casino Plan Still Quite a Gamble," p. 3.

42. Finley, "Siletz Tribes File Suit." After Secretary Lujan decided not to take the land into trust, the Siletz tribes filed a federal lawsuit attacking the Secretary's interpretation of § 2719 as unconstitutional. Ibid.

43. Gary Sokolow, "The Future of Gambling in Indian Country," *Am. Indian L. Rev.* 15 (1990), pp. 151, 155. Sokolow's article presents a detailed history of attempts to regulate Indian gambling prior to the passage of the IGRA.

44. H.R. 3130, 99th Cong. § 1(b), reprinted in "Indian Gambling Control Act: Hearings on H.R. 1920 and H.R. 2404 Before the Comm. on Interior and Insular Affairs, Part II," 99th Cong., 1st Sess., p. 18 (1985) [hereinafter "House Indian Gambling Hearings, Part II].

45. Ibid., p. 18.

46. Ibid., pp. 22–29.

47. Ibid., p. 52.

48. One lawmaker, Ohio Representative John F. Sieberling, a supporter of H.R. 3130, suggested including the requirement that an off-reservation gaming hall on new trust land should be established according to state requirements as well as federal requirements. "House Indian Gambling Hearings, Part II," pp. 28–29.

49. "House Indian Gambling Hearings, Part I," pp. 5–13 passim; "House Indian Gambling Hearings, Part II."

50. S. 1303, 100th Cong., 1st Sess. § 4(b) (1987), reprinted in "Gaming Activities on Indian Reservations and Lands: Hearing on S. 555 and S. 1303 Before the Select Comm. on Indian Affairs," 100th Cong., 1st Sess. pp. 46–47 (1987) [hereinafter "Senate Hearing on Gaming Activities II"].

51. See, e.g., ibid., p. 433 (statement of Charles W. Blackwell of American Indian Tribal Government and Policy Consultants, Inc.).

52. See, e.g., ibid., p. 505 (letter from John M. Peebles, Steier and Kreikemeier, P.C., to Sen. Daniel Inouye).

53. *U.S. Const.*, art. II, § 2, cl. 2. For further discussion of the Justice Department concerns regarding a potential Appointments Clause violation, see herein notes 76–81, 103–10 and accompanying text.

54. *S. Rep. No. 446*, 100th Cong., 2d Sess. p. 32 (1988).

55. 25 U.S.C. §§ 2701-2721.

56. See, e.g., "Establish Federal Standards and Regulations for the Conduct of Gaming Activities Within Indian Country, Hearing on S. 902 Before the Senate Select Comm. on Indian Affairs," 99th Cong., 2d Sess., pp. 471–72, 481 (1986) [hereinafter "Senate Hearing on Federal Standards"] (statement of Roger A. Jourdain, Chairman of the Red Lake Band of Chippewa Indians). The letter states:

> The threat to the sovereignty of American Indian tribes is one of the most critical issues that we face today. In addition to the ever increasing difficulty of dealing with economic survival, the maintenance of cultural traditions, languages, customs and spiritual existence that all Tribes have faced for centuries, the constant erosion of the sovereign rights of American Indian Tribes poses a threat to our very existence as a separate and distinct people. Indian tribes have survived since the creation because we have always understood and respected our own sovereignty and because we have fought to protect it in war, in court and in the Congress. . . . Sovereignty is a state of mind, supported by actions, and it is our responsibility to take those actions necessary to protect it.

57. Felix S. Cohen, a former solicitor for the Interior Department, an Indian law scholar, and a longtime Indian rights supporter, described the importance of tribal sovereignty this way:

> In the history of Western thought, theologians, missionaries, judges, and legislators for four hundred years and more have consistently recognized the right of Indians to manage their own affairs. . . . For four hundred years, men who have looked at the matter without the distortions of material prejudice or bureaucratic power have seen that the safety and freedom of all of us is inevitably tied up with the safety and freedom of the weakest and tiniest of our minorities. . . .
>
> [M]ay not the world profit, if in a few places in our Western Hemisphere there is still freedom of an aboriginal people to try out ideas of self-government, of economics, of social relations. After all, there are so many places all over the world where we Americans can try out the ideas of economics and government that we know to be right. Is there not a great scientific advantage in allowing alternative ideas to work themselves out to a point where they can demonstrate the evils that we believe are bound to flow from a municipal government that maintains no prisons, or from a government that gives land to all members of the group who need it? . . .
>
> [W]hen those of us who never were Indians and never expect to be Indians fight for the cause of Indian self-government, we are fighting for something that is not limited by the accidents of race and creed and birth; we are fighting for what Las Casas and Vitoria and Pope Paul III called the integrity or salvation of our own souls. We are fighting for what Jefferson called the basic rights of man. (Felix S. Cohen, *The Legal Conscience: Selected Papers of Felix S. Cohen*, ed. Lucy K. Cohen [1970], quoted in "Senate Hearing on Federal Standards," pp. 358–60 [statement of Wade Miller, Chairman of the Omaha Tribe of Nebraska].)

58. Kirk Kickingbird et al., *Indian Sovereignty* (Inst. for the Dev. of Indian Law, 1983), pp. 8–12, 39.

59. "Senate Hearings on Federal Standards," p. 361.

60. *Worcester*, 31 U.S. (6 Pet.) 515 (1832).

61. *Williams v. Lee*, 358 U.S. (1959), pp. 217, 219. Over the years, the tribal sovereignty doctrine evolved to accommodate changing circumstances, allowing (in the absence of a governing act of Congress) limited state jurisdiction "in cases where tribal relations were not involved and where the rights of Indians would not be jeopardized." Examples include allowing state court jurisdiction over crimes committed by a non-Indian against another on Indian land and over lawsuits by Indians against an outsider. Ibid., pp. 219–20.

62. *Cherokee Nation v. Georgia*, 30 U.S. (5 Pet.) (1831), pp. 1, 17.

63. For a history and critique of the trust doctrine, see Note, "Rethinking the Trust Doctrine in Federal Indian Law," *Harv. L. Rev.* 98 (1984), p. 422.

64. *Felix Cohen's Handbook of Federal Indian Law*, ed. Rennard Strickland et al. (1982), p. 221.

65. Ibid., p. 225. More specifically, the United States Supreme Court has ruled: 1) ambiguous expressions must be resolved in favor of the Indians, *McClanahan v. Arizona State Tax Comm'n*, 411 U.S. (1973), pp. 164, 174; *Carpenter v. Shaw*, 280 U.S. (1930), pp. 363, 367; 2) treaties must be construed to favor Indians, *Choctaw Nation v. United States*, 318 U.S. (1943), pp. 423, 431–32; *Choate v. Trapp*, 224 U.S. (1912), pp. 665, 675; and 3) treaties should be construed as the Indians would have understood them. *Choctaw Nation v. Oklahoma*, 397 U.S. (1970), pp. 620, 631; *United States v. Shoshone Tribe*, 304 U.S. (1938), pp. 111, 116. See also *Felix Cohen's Handbook*, p. 222 (discussing canons). These canons of construction apply to statutes, executive orders, and administrative regulations as well as to treaties, since their purpose is to carry out the special trust relationship between the United States and tribes. In addition, Congress has not distinguished between treaty tribes and non-treaty tribes when implementing the federal-tribal relationship. Ibid., p. 224.

66. *Rosebud Sioux Tribe v. Kneip*, 420 U.S. (1977), pp. 584, 586 (holding that congressional intent controls the court determination of whether reservation boundaries were diminished by subsequent congressional enactments); *DeCoteau v. District County Court*, 420 U.S. (1975), pp. 425, 444 (reasoning that congressional intent to terminate a reservation must be clear on the face of the act or in the surrounding circumstances and legislative history).

67. See, e.g., *DeCoteau*, 420 U.S., p. 444; *Mattz v. Arnett*, 412 U.S. (1973), pp. 481, 505 (concluding that language surrounding the circumstances and legislative history of the act did not indicate congressional intent to terminate the reservation); *Frost v. Wenie*, 157 U.S. (1895), pp. 46, 59 (holding that Indian treaty rights will only be abrogated if the express language of the act makes such a construction unavoidable); *United States v. White*, 508 F.2d 453 (8th Cir. 1974), pp. 456–59 (concluding that the language and legislative history of the Bald Eagle Protection Act do not clearly indicate congressional intent to modify reservation hunting rights).

Recently, the U.S. Supreme Court determined the surrounding circumstances of an Indian law issue by looking to other statutes as well as the statute before it. See *Cotton Petroleum Corp. v. New Mexico*, 490 U.S. (1989), p. 163 (ruling that explicit language in the prior statute granting states the ability to tax oil and gas production on Indian land provoked the conclusion that a 1938 mineral leasing statute allowed such taxation even though the statute was silent on the issue). For a discussion of whether courts should look for an express statement of congressional intent in statutory language before abrogating Indian rights, rather than implying legislative intent by looking to extrinsic evidence, see Charles F. Wilkinson and John M. Volkman, "Judicial Review of Indian Treaty Abrogation: 'As Long as Water Flows or Grass

Grows Upon the Earth'—How Long a Time is That?" *Cal. L. Rev.* 63 (1975), p. 601.
68. *Felix Cohen's Handbook*, p. 361; see, e.g., *Montana v. Blackfeet Indian Tribe*, 471 U.S. (1985), p. 759 (disallowing the state to tax royalty payments for mineral leases under a statute that lacked a clear expression of congressional intent to allow taxation); *County of Oneida v. Oneida Indian Nation*, 470 U.S. (1985), p. 226 (holding that subsequent congressional action lacked plain and unambiguous language and thus did not ratify unlawful land treaties); *Bryan v. Itasca County*, 426 U.S. (1976), pp. 373, 381 (concluding that congressional enactments gave no express grant of authority to county to tax personal property on the reservation); *Fisher v. District Court*, 424 U.S. (1976), pp. 382, 387–89 (finding jurisdiction over adoptions in the tribal court, and not the Montana state court, where all parties were tribal members living on the reservation).
69. *McClanahan*, 411 U.S., p. 172.
70. Off-reservation lands acquired for tribes become Indian country once they are taken into trust. Indian country is governed primarily by federal and tribal law rather than state law. It has three definitions under federal law:

> (a) all land within the limits of any Indian reservation under the jurisdiction of the United States government, notwithstanding the issuance of any patent, and, including rights-of-way running through the reservation, (b) all dependent Indian communities within the borders of the United States whether within the original or subsequently acquired territory thereof, and whether within or without the limits of a state, and (c) all Indian allotments, the Indian titles to which have not been extinguished, including rights-of-way running through the same. (18 U.S.C. [1988], § 1151.)

There is little case law discussing the status of land held in trust for Indians; however, the Supreme Court has stated that lands held in trust are set aside for the benefit of the Indians and are thus considered Indian country. *United States v. John*, 437 U.S. (1978), p. 634; *United States v. Celestine*, 215 U.S. [1989], p. 278.
71. See *Felix Cohen's Handbook*, p. 361.
72. 25 U.S.C., § 2719(b)(1)(A).
73. See above note 8 and accompanying text; cf. Hanna, "Suburb's Casino Plan," p. 3 (explaining the Department of Interior's prior interpretation of the policy that the governor's opinion was advisory only).
74. See herein notes 78–80 and accompanying text.
75. The first piece of proposed legislation to address gaming on newly acquired lands, H.R. 3130, would have prohibited the Interior Secretary from taking land into trust if the land was to be used for gaming purposes. H.R. 3130(1)(a), reprinted in "House Indian Gambling Hearings, Part II," p. 17. This prohibition would not apply if: "the Indian tribe requesting the acquisition of land in trust status obtains the concurrence of the governor of the state and the legislative bodies of all local governmental units in which the land is located." H.R. 3130(1)(b), reprinted in "House Indian Gambling Hearings, Part II," p. 18.

Subsequent attempts to create a more comprehensive regulatory system for Indian gambling imposed similar requirements of state approval. For instance, H.R. 1920 provided that the ban on off-reservation gambling on new trust lands: "shall not apply if the Indian tribe requesting the acquisition of such lands in trust obtains the concurrence of the Governor of the State, the State legislature, and the governing bodies of the county and municipality in which such lands are located." H.R. 1920(3)(b), reprinted in "Senate Hearing on Federal Standards," p. 17. Additionally, S. 1303 provided that the gaming ban "shall not apply if the Indian tribe requesting the acquisition of such lands in trust obtains the concurrence of the Governor of the State, and the governing bodies of the county or municipality in which such lands are located." S. 1303(4)(b), reprinted in "Senate Hearing on Gaming Activities II," p. 47.

76. *U.S. Const.*, art. II, § 2, cl. 2.

77. This criticism was made by Assistant Attorney General John Bolton in a lengthy letter to Senator Daniel K. Inouye, Chairman, Select Committee on Indian Affairs. The pertinent section states:

> Section four of S. 1303 generally prohibits tribes from running a gaming operation anywhere but within the boundaries of their present reservations. It provides that gaming regulated by the Act shall be unlawful on lands acquired in trust for the tribe after the effective date of the Act. However, the section does not apply "if the Indian tribe requesting the acquisition of such lands in trust obtains the concurrence of the governor of the State and the governing bodies of the county or municipality in which such lands are located." This provision would give individuals not appointed in accordance with the Appointments Clause, Article II, section 2, clause 2, the authority to waive a federal statute. In order to avoid the constitutional problems inherent in such a situation, section 4(b) should be revised to begin "Subject to the approval of the Secretary," a change that would ensure that implementation of this part of the statute remains in the hands of a properly appointed executive branch officer. We note that this, in essence, is the approach adopted in the comparable provision in S. 555, section 20(b)(1). (Letter from Assistant Att'y Gen. John Bolton to Sen. Daniel K. Inouye [January 14, 1988], reprinted in *S. Rep. No. 446*, pp. 22, 32 [hereinafter Letter to Inouye].)

The existence of a potential Appointments Clause violation is examined herein notes 102–09 and accompanying text.

78. See Letter to Inouye.

79. The language of S. 555, § 20(b)(1) is identical to the IGRA's language prohibiting gaming on new off-reservation lands. 25 U.S.C. § 2719. The language states that the ban on off-reservation gambling can be lifted when:

> [T]he Secretary, after consultation with the Indian tribe and appropriate state and local officials, including officials of other nearby Indian tribes, determines that a gaming establishment on newly acquired lands would be in the best

interest of the Indian tribe and its members, and would not be detrimental to the surrounding community, but only if the Governor of the State in which the gaming activity is to be conducted concurs in the Secretary's determination. (Ibid., § 2719[b][1][A].)

The discussion of S. 555 and the IGRA shed little light on the convoluted wording of this section, making little mention of the extent to which a governor could wield power to prohibit gaming on new lands. See "Senate Hearing on Gaming Activities I"; *S. Rep. No. 446*. The Justice Department, however, believed that this language was sufficient to grant the Interior Secretary the ultimate power to lift the gaming prohibition, thereby fulfilling the requirements of the Appointments Clause. See Letter to Inouye.

80. See *S. Rep. No. 446*; "Senate Hearing on Gaming Activities I"; "House Indian Gambling Hearings, Part I"; "House Indian Gambling Hearings, Part II"; "Senate Hearing on Gaming Activities II"; and "Gambling on Indian Reservations and Lands, Hearing Before the Senate Collect Comm. on Indian Affairs," 99th cong., 1st Sess. (1985).

81. It is not unusual for federal officials and courts to give far more mandatory language than that of § 2719 a less than mandatory reading when such language deals with Indian tribes. See, e.g., 57 Interior Dec. (1940), pp. 162, 167–68 (explaining that, although a statute said the Secretary of the Interior "shall" permit state health and education inspection and enforcement on Indian lands, the word "shall" should be construed as "may" in this case, giving the Secretary discretion); *Menominee Tribe of Indians v. United States*, 391 U.S. (1968), pp. 404, 410 (holding that, although a reservation termination act provided that state laws should apply to the tribe and its members "in the same manner as they apply to other citizens . . . within their jurisdiction," this did not make the Indians subject to state game and fishing laws so as to abolish hunting and fishing rights).

82. 18 U.S.C. § 1162(a) (1988).

83. 28 U.S.C. § 1360(a) (1988).

84. *S. Rep. No. 446*, p. 5.

85. Ibid., pp. 5–6.

86. 25 U.S.C. § 2710(d)(1)(C). The compact could cover licensing issues such as days and hours of operations or wage and pot limits, the application of state and tribal criminal and civil laws necessary for licensing and regulating gaming, and the allocation of criminal and civil jurisdiction between the state and the tribe. Ibid., § 2710(d)(3)(C).

87. *S. Rep. No. 446*, p. 13.

88. 25 U.S.C. § 2710(d)(7)(B)(ii).

89. Ibid., § 2710(d)(7)(B)(iii)(II).

90. Ibid., § 2710(d)(7)(B)(iv)–(vi).

91. Ibid., § 2710(d)(7)(B)(vii).

92. 25 U.S.C. § 465 (providing the method by which Indian lands are taken into trust).

93. *S. Rep. No. 446*.

94. 25 U.S.C. § 465.

95. *H.R. Rep. No. 1804*, 73d Cong., 2d Sess. (1934), p. 6.
96. *Santa Rosa Band of Indians v. Kings County*, 532 F.2d (9th Cir. 1975), pp. 655, 664, *cert. denied*, 429 U.S. (1977), p. 1038.
97. *S. Rep. No. 446*, pp. 2–3.
98. See above notes 26–34, 38–40 and accompanying text.
99. See, e.g., *County of Yakima v. Confederated Tribes and Banks of the Yakima Indian Nation*, 112 S. Ct. (1992), p. 683 (addressing tribal contentions that state attempts to extend tax laws to reservation activities crippled Indian economic development); *Cotton Petroleum Corp. v. New Mexico*, 490 U.S. (1989), p. 163; *Washington v. Confederated Tribes of the Colville Indian Reservation*, 447 U.S. (1980), p. 134; *Worcester v. Georgia*, 31 U.S. (6 Pet.) (1832), p. 515 (addressing state attempts to eradicate tribal government and exercise jurisdiction over tribal lands). The U.S. Supreme Court also recognized state-Indian tensions when it upheld federal jurisdiction over certain on-reservation crimes, stating: "[t]hese Indian tribes . . . owe no allegiance to the States, and receive from them no protection. Because of the local ill feeling, the people of the States where they are found are often their deadliest enemies." *U.S. v. Kagama*, 118 U.S. (1886), pp. 375, 384.

   In discussions on the IGRA, Arizona Representative John McCain charged states with taking part in the creation of the IGRA with the "true interest [of] protecti[ng] . . . their own games from a new source of economic competition. [T]he State and gaming industry have always come to the table with the position that what is theirs is theirs and what the Tribe have [sic] is negotiable." *S. Rep. No. 446*, p. 33.
100. *Santa Rosa Band*, 532 F.2d, p. 664 (footnote omitted).
101. See, e.g., Indian Self-Determination and Education Assistance Act of 1975, 25 U.S.C. §§ 450(a)–(n) (1988) (authorizing tribes to plan and administer federally funded programs themselves); Indian Financing Act of 1974, 25 U.S.C. §§ 1451–1453 (1988) (enhancing tribal economies through tribal economic development efforts); Indian Mineral Development Act of 1982, 25 U.S.C. §§ 2101–2108 (1988) (authorizing a variety of mineral development arrangements to promote Indian self-determination and tribal economic development); Indian Tribal Governmental Tax Status Act of 1982, 26 U.S.C. § 7871 (1988) (extending to tribes tax advantages enjoyed by states to strengthen tribal governments, provide additional sources of income, and eliminate an unfair tax burden).
102. This rule falls under the justiciability doctrine, which also holds that the Supreme Court refuses to answer unnecessary constitutional questions, formulates constitutional rules only as broadly as necessary for the case before it, and prefers to render decisions on non-constitutional grounds. *Ashwander v. Tennessee Valley Auth.*, 297 U.S. (1936), pp. 288, 346–48 (Brandeis, J., concurring) ("[I]f a serious doubt of constitutionality is raised, . . . this court will first ascertain whether a construction of the statute is fairly possible by which the question may be avoided."); *Schneider v. Smith*, 390 U.S. (1968), p. 17 (Act delegating executive officials authority to safeguard

merchant ships from sabotage construed narrowly to prevent constitutional violation inherent in attempt to condition employment on ships on non-membership in the Communist Party); see also *Scales v. United States*, 367 U.S. (1961), pp. 203, 211 ("Although this Court will often strain to construe legislation so as to save it against constitutional attack, it must not and will not carry this to the point of perverting the purpose of a statute.").

103. The Appointments Clause states:

> [The President] shall nominate, and by and with the Advice and Consent of the Senate, shall appoint . . . all other Officers of the United States, whose Appointments are not herein otherwise provided for, and which shall be established by Law: but the Congress may by Law vest the Appointment of such inferior Officers, as they think proper, in the President alone, in the Courts of Law, or in the Heads of Departments. (*U.S. Const.*, art II, § 2, cl. 2.)

104. The Confederated Tribes of the Siletz, the Indian tribe whose plans for gaming on new lands in the city limits of Salem, Oregon, were recently scuttled by the Interior Department's new policy, filed suit in January 1993, on the grounds that this reading of the statute violated the Appointments Clause. Finley, "Siletz Tribes File Suit," p. E6. An earlier version of this section of the IGRA, S. 1303 § (4)(b), was criticized by the Justice Department as potentially posing the same constitutional problem. See above text accompanying note 53.

105. *Buckley v. Valeo*, 424 U.S. (1976), pp. 1, 126 (holding that the composition of the Federal Election Commission, as to all but its investigative and informative powers, violates the Appointments Clause).

106. *United States v. Mississippi Vocational Rehabilitation for the Blind*, 794 F. Supp. (S.D. Miss. 1992), pp. 1344, 1354 (no Appointments Clause violation existed in the makeup of an arbitration panel because the Secretary of Education appointed its members pursuant to statute).

107. 25 U.S.C. § 2719(a).

108. "[I]t is to the President, and not to the Congress, that the Constitution entrusts the responsibility to 'take Care that the Laws be faithfully executed." *Buckley*, 424 U.S., p. 138.

109. Such an argument may first be attacked on the grounds that a governor acting pursuant to § 2719 would not be considered an "Officer of the United States." A person whose "position is without tenure, duration, continuing emolument, or continuous duties, and [who] acts only occasionally and temporarily" is not an "officer" for purposes of the Appointments Clause. *Auffmordt v. Hedden*, 137 U.S. (1890), pp. 310, 327; see also *United States ex. rel. Newsham v. Lockheed*, 722 F. Supp. (N.D. Cal. 1989), pp. 607, 613 (finding that parties authorized to bring qui tam proceedings "do not have a tenure beyond the lifespan of the particular suit"). Arguably, a governor acting under § 2719(b) would only be called on occasionally, whenever a tribe sought to open off-reservation gaming on new trust lands, and would only make limited decisions.

Second, a similar Appointments Clause argument was struck down on the grounds that Congress has the power under the Necessary and Proper clause to appoint such persons. *United States v. Ferry County*, 511 F. Supp. (E.D. Wash 1981), p. 546 (upholding a requirement that the local government concur before land is taken into trust in such a way as to make it non-taxable). The court stated that the Appointments Clause "does not put Congress into such a 'rigid box' as to preclude conditioning [the] operation of [a federal law] on the consent of local officials." Ibid., p. 552. The court did not explain its reasoning.

110. 25 C.F.R. § 151.10(e)–(f) (1993) requires the Secretary to consider "the impact on the State and its political subdivisions resulting from the removal of the land from the tax rolls[, and] jurisdictional problems and potential conflicts of land use . . ." In addition, the further away from the Indian reservation, the more compelling need for the land the tribe must show.

18. We Need a Federal Plan to Control Gambling

Robert Goodman

A prominent critic of current gambling policy, Robert Goodman, a professor of environmental design and planning at Hampshire College, views the gambling industry as a "scavenger" economy, often exploited by state governments that "promote destructive behavior and false promises." He does not, however, support a total prohibition of gambling, since he thinks the popularity of gambling makes a total prohibition neither practical nor desirable. Rather, he advocates several specific reforms, designed to protect the poor, who disproportionately gamble. He thinks that the federal government should have more authority over gambling policy not because of constitutional reasons but because he believes consumers require uniform protection.

He advocates a national moratorium on expanding gambling ventures, especially electronic gambling machines and those involving at-home interactive TV or telephone betting. He calls for limiting the ways in which states and private businesses can promote, advertise, and encourage gambling so that all ads are required to meet the truth-in-advertising standards. He recommends that the federal government and state governments undertake studies reviewing the impacts of gambling on small businesses, compulsive gamblers, and the economy generally. He calls further for federal oversight and coordination of a national gambling policy to minimize the competition among states to expand gambling opportunities. He calls for changes in current state lotteries that

From *The Luck Business: The Devastating Consequences and Broken Promises of America's Gambling Explosion* (New York: Free Press, 1995), pp. 173–91. Used by permission.

would make the habitual purchase of lottery tickets a more reasonable investment. For example, he believes that states should cap prizes in the range of $10,000 and repay non-prize-winning ticket holders who have accumulated at least $100 worth of tickets in a one-year period their original ticket price, plus interest, after five years. "Interest would be calculated on an annual basis at 2 percent less than the rate of a five-year bank certificate of deposit at the time the ticket was purchased. The state could use this pot of money to make low-interest loans to local businesses." In short, Goodman thinks that government should play an active role in regulating gambling to minimize the social and economic costs, especially to the poor.

In the mid-1980s, Lee Iacocca was probably America's most admired corporate executive. Having taken charge of the Chrysler corporation when the automotive giant was accumulating millions in weekly debt, he negotiated an unprecedented $1.2 billion loan from the federal government. The company averted bankruptcy and thousands of jobs were saved in Detroit and other cities.

Several years later, in his best-selling autobiography, Iacocca trumpeted the need to restore the beleaguered ideals of American enterprise. "I learned there are no free lunches," he wrote. "And I learned the value of hard work. In the end, you've got to be productive. That's what made this country great—and that's what's going to make us great again."[1] As the hard-working son of Italian immigrants, Iacocca had become the embodiment of the American dream—at one point, he was even touted as a candidate for president of the United States.

But only ten years after his feat at Chrysler, Iacocca had switched gears. By 1994, he had left the company, moved to Los Angeles, and set up his own investment company. The new focus of his business was gambling, including efforts to open casinos in Michigan's economically depressed cities and futuristic concepts such as in-flight gambling for airline passengers.

Iacocca's professional transformation—from leader of one of America's flagship manufacturing industries to his emergence in the ranks of gambling entrepreneurs—is a dramatic vignette of the shifting paradigm of American economic development. His career path provides a disturbing picture of where we are headed, and why we need to change direction. It underscores the urgent need to fundamentally rethink the ways in which state and local governments are using gambling as public policy, and why the federal government must play a more active role in reforming this process.

Iacocca's Transformation Parallels America's Industrial Decline

In his autobiography, Iacocca warned of what we faced if American businesses did not counter the surge of competition from abroad. "I don't know when we're going to wake up, but I hope it's soon. Otherwise, within a few years our economic arsenal is going to consist of little more than drive-in banks, hamburger joints, and video game arcades."[2] Less than ten years later, his dismal prediction was turning out to be right on the money, with slot machines and casinos as the adult counterpart to video game arcades. And Iacocca himself was now scrambling to become a major player in creating that future.

By 1993, Detroit, in spite of the federal bailout of Chrysler, was mired in even more desperate straits. The American auto business had rebounded, but it had done so largely by shedding employees and shifting production to lower-wage areas in the South and abroad. Detroit and many smaller midwestern cities that once constituted the bedrock of automobile manufacturing found themselves with empty factories, growing welfare rolls, and shrinking tax bases. The quick-fix promise of casino gambling became a tantalizing option.

In the fall of 1993, a Detroit entrepreneur announced that he was taking applications for casino jobs. That no casino had in fact been legalized seemed to be of no concern to him. The applications were being sought, he explained, so that his company would have time to train workers in the event his proposed casino was approved. On a cold November morning, three hours before the doors opened for this bogus job fair, hundreds of people started lining up. As the day progressed, nearby streets had to be closed off to accommodate the overwhelming turnout. By the day's end, more than 10,000 people, most of them black, had filled out applications for nonexistent jobs as blackjack dealers, security guards, cocktail waitresses, and busboys. Casino opponents lambasted this spectacle, which never led to any real jobs, as a cruel tactic to raise people's hopes in a ploy to create political pressure for the legalization of gambling.

The following year, when Detroit and several other Michigan cities continued to mull over legalized gambling, Lee Iacocca marched prominently in the parade of suitors. That summer, he was in Flint, a left-for-dead city made famous in Michael Moore's academy-award winning documentary *Roger and Me*, where he reportedly scouted sites for a new casino. In the film, Moore pilloried General Motors for its indifference to the plight of its laid-off workers and mocked the city's pathetic efforts at economic revitalization. By the end of that year, Iacocca, who had already joined the board of directors of MGM Grand, owner of the Las Vegas mega-casino, merged his investment firm with Full House Resorts, another casino firm.[3]

Lee Iacocca's shifting roles mirror the plight of America's industrial cities and their decision to pursue gambling as economic development strategy. While his switch from productive to scavenger economic enterprises may seem contradictory, there is a consistent theme in his activities. Both of his efforts—at Chrysler and in developing gambling ventures—embrace the idea of an explicit partnership between business and government.

Some Business Interests Support Industrial Policy

Although only a few companies have needed the level of government aid provided to Chrysler, many American industries find themselves with a declining share of world markets, smaller workforces, and a more precarious global position. As a result, our cities are being forced to deal with swelling ranks of the unemployed, enormous public-budget shortfalls, and dwindling opportunities for work. Meanwhile, crime rates and drug problems have escalated. Political and business leaders have been looking for solutions to these problems through new partnership arrangements between the public and private sectors at all levels of government.

At the federal level, the question of whether government should support economic development has crystallized into a debate over what is called "industrial policy." Broadly speaking, federal industrial policy proposes to identify those technologies and industries that are most critical to the country's economic future, and to provide these industries with specially targeted government support, including outright grants for research and development, loan guarantees, tax breaks, tariff protection from foreign competitors, research at government labs, and guaranteed availability of government as a client and buyer of products.

The hope is that federal industrial policy will help make the country's global position in critical international trade markets more secure, by helping America gain preeminence in the research and development of new technologies.[4] Policymakers and economists who argue against this approach maintain that the free market, not government, should dictate which businesses succeed and which fail. Government involvement in "picking winners," they say, will only distort the market and lead to public subsidies to support inefficient operations. The free-market arguments, however, tend to be based on an idealized abstraction of a perfectly level playing field, while in most developed countries, particularly Germany and Japan, the foreign companies that American businesses must compete against are already heavily supported by the governments.

The U.S. government has always had a hand in "picking winners," especially in the postwar era. The clearest example is the government's close relationship with military and space exploration contractors.[5] There is also a long-standing precedent of government assistance for agricultural ventures through price support and agricultural research programs— subsidies that have long been considered sacrosanct by many liberal as well as conservative politicians in Congress. Earlier, private railroad companies were supported by free grants of land, while oil and gas energy firms were assisted with government energy depletion allowances. Today, many American businesses, faced with the need to compete more aggressively with foreign firms, are edging toward supporting ad hoc models of partnership with government.[6]

State Support for Gambling Contradicts
Federal Support for Productive Industry

While business and political leaders on the federal level have been slowly moving toward establishing partnerships in developing such products as semiconductors and clean-burning fuels for cars, the primary form of partnership between government and business at the state and local levels has ironically been based on gambling.[7] This reliance on gambling as a kind of ad hoc industrial policy actually contradicts federal efforts to promote productive and cutting-edge industries by putting public support behind a parasitic economic activity.

As Chapter 9 [of Goodman's book] explains, using gambling as industrial policy sets the stage for future government fiscal crises by feeding off the remains of America's productive economic base and by creating new costs for dealing with increased crime and problem gambling.

Unfortunately, the money that state and local governments allocate to promote gambling far outweighs what they spend to support and develop productive businesses. As indicated in Chapter 8, the states currently spend over $350 million a year nationally simply to advertise their lotteries, but they provide only $50 million nationally for all their industrial extension programs—programs that provide important technical advice to the country's 350,000 small and medium-sized firms. Some state industrial assistance programs are so starved for funds they simply cannot met the needs of their local firms. Georgia Tech, the engineering university in Atlanta, for example, operated one of the most successful government-sponsored industrial extension services in the country, but doesn't advertise its services for fear it wouldn't be able to handle the requests for help if it did.[8]

In 1991, Congress's Office of Technology Assessment criticized

America's meager governmental commitment to support business efforts to bring new technologies to market. It contrasted the situation in this country with the extensive aid that the national and local Japanese governments provide to their businesses. In Japan there is a nationwide system of 185 technology extension centers, funded at about $500 million, with money from both the national government and the prefectures. In addition, many Japanese cities and other local governments support industrial halls that offer similar services to their industries, including regular workshops on common manufacturing problems, demonstrations of new technologies, and other forms of research and development advice. While the Japanese and many of their European counterparts are offering assistance to a wide range of productive local industries to foster regional economic development, American state and local governments are helping to develop new products in the gambling industry.

Until very recently, the federal government simply ignored the issue of gambling proliferation, leaving it to the often conflicting decision making of individual state, local, and tribal governments. While national political leaders have expended enormous amounts of time, resources, and public debate on policies like NAFTA and GATT, they have done almost nothing to develop rational policies to address the destructive economic and social impacts being produced by states competing for each other's gambling dollars. The last federal review of the impacts of gambling was completed by the Commission on the Review of the National Policy Toward Gambling in 1976—a time when the only legalized casinos in America were in Nevada.[9] Now, with almost every state in the country already engaged in some form of legalized gambling and most contemplating the expansion of their gambling enterprises, the time for the creation of a new national policy is long past due.

Resignation in the Face of Gambling Expansion Is Short-sighted

In interviewing politicians, business people, and people in the media, I've repeatedly heard the argument that while the proliferation of gambling may be problematic, the genie is out of the bottle, and there's no putting it back. New forms of local convenience gambling, the argument goes, are simply here to stay, and states can either get into the game themselves or watch the revenues pile up in their neighboring states. Governments have become hooked on their gambling revenues, goes another strain of this analysis, and they cannot give them up without tremendous fiscal hardship.

While some of this may be true, it is an extremely short-sighted view of both what is possible and, perhaps even more important, what is actually happening. In considering future policies, it is crucial to understand that gambling expanded not because of a popular movement clamoring for more opportunities to gamble, but because of aggressive lobbying by the gambling industry and the promotional efforts of politicians who haven't been able to find more productive alternatives for economic development. While such efforts may have been successful in the past, they have reached the point of diminishing returns. As described in Chapter 4 [of Goodman's book], the gambling industry's own research demonstrates that the more gambling expands, the less acceptable it is becoming to the American public.[10]

Although the gambling industry and its political allies will continue to aggressively promote more expansion in the future, the growing popular discontent suggests that it is not only possible to contain this expansion, but in many cases, it can actually be reversed. As Chapter 4 explains, many states have already rejected expansion, even in the face of unprecedented multi-million-dollar lobbying efforts by the gambling industry. In the elections of 1994, for example, all of the many state-wide proposals for new casino gambling were defeated by voters.

There are several possible scenarios for the future. Public and business community reaction to the growing cannibalization of local business sales and jobs, as well as the growing visibility and costs of problem-gambling behavior, are likely to bring about increased pressure for reform. As more and more people experience gambling within their own communities, its costly problems will become more evident. This has happened before in our history. The current gambling boom has obvious parallels with the one which occurred in 19th-century America, when gambling ventures proliferated until corruption and abuses produced federal legislation outlawing all forms of gambling in the 1890s. There are already strong grass-roots movements in states like Louisiana and South Dakota to repeal laws that allow electronic gambling machines.

But in spite of growing opposition, there is likely to be continued pressure in the years ahead for still more expansion. Although some regional markets are already close to saturation, there are still plenty of economically distressed communities which the gambling industry will try to entice with its claims of an economic cure. With aggressive political lobbying and marketing, it is possible to draw many more consumer dollars out of other parts of the national economy. While there were already falling casino profits, bankruptcies, and large-scale worker layoffs in some markets by 1995, the larger gambling firms have the financial muscle to survive local shakeouts, and to promote their wares in other parts of the country. The strategy of the largest casino companies is to argue for limiting the number of licenses to firms with "experience" and "integrity."[11] This could effectively result in a few large companies with even more monopolistic control of the industry in the future.

Meanwhile, state governments themselves have shown little restraint in spending money in their attempts to recruit more people to gamble. Few of the businesses endangered by new gambling ventures, such as restaurants, other entertainment businesses, and clothing stores, have anywhere near the lobbying resources of the gambling industry with which to fight expansion. In the absence of more government oversight, planning, and regulation, especially at the national level, the overall situation could get much worse before it gets better.

Gambling's Expansion Needs to Be Curbed

Since there are many people who want to gamble, there will always be politicians who would like to use gambling to bolster tax revenues. Under these circumstances, total prohibition is not only impractical, but undesirable. Rather, the formation of a rational gambling policy should be based on a number of key points.

What is needed most immediately is a national moratorium on the expansion of gambling ventures, especially the most pernicious forms, including electronic gambling machines and those involving at-home inter-active television or telephone betting. This will provide an opportunity to assess the impact of the rapid gambling proliferation that has already taken place and allow a chance to reflect before becoming committed to new and untried forms of gambling.

There is also a crucial need to consider limits on the ways in which states and private businesses can promote, advertise, and encourage more gambling. At the very least, state governments should have to meet the same truth-in-advertising standards as private businesses—standards from which the federal government now exempts the states.

At the same time, the national government, as well as the individual states, should undertake reviews at the national and state levels of the impacts of gambling. These must include looking at the economic effects on the nation's small businesses, at the private and public costs of dealing with gambling addiction, at the consequences of government dependence on gambling revenues, and at the growing concentration of economic and political power within the gambling industry. There is also a crucial need for the creation, based on the findings of these reviews, of a national plan which would help determine the future direction of gambling in this country. Such a plan needs to address such questions as what types of gambling should be made available to the public, how many gambling ventures are appropriate, where they should be located, and how revenues from these ventures should be redistributed to local and state governments.

Even if it proves to be difficult to develop mechanisms to enforce such a plan in its entirety, the very process of creating it will help focus atten-tion on the national impact of gambling proliferation. Furthermore, this process will generate ideas for legislation and initiatives at all levels of government to both counteract the negative impacts of gambling legalization and to enhance those which are positive.

The federal government has a critical role to play in restructuring the ways in which state and local governments use gambling as industrial policy. Left to their own devices, states and cities have few options but to compete with adjacent governments in using gambling ventures to attract one another's residents. Many local politicians, even those who oppose expansion, find themselves favoring casino development simply as a defensive measure to keep state residents from betting in neighboring cities, states, or nearby Indian reservations. Federal oversight and coordination of gambling development can help prevent this kind of competitive scramble among neighboring jurisdictions.

State gambling legalization processes also need to be reformed. The gambling industry, with deep financial pockets, can not only vastly outspend grass-roots efforts opposed to gambling expansion, but it can return again and again with new proposals even after voters have rejected their original plans. This not only mocks voters' rejection of their proposals, but more fundamentally undermines the democratic process. As part of a reform effort, the federal government and the states should consider spending limits on lobbying and promotional campaigns for legalizing gambling.

The federal government should also require, or at least encourage, state and local governments to commission their own independent impact studies to measure both the benefits and costs of legalizing new gambling operations, rather than relying on gambling industry studies. At the very least, states should conduct independent evaluations of the gambling industry's own research efforts—much as they do for the environmental impacts of certain industrial and public works projects. In addition, those states which already have gambling should conduct an independent analysis of the social and economic impacts of gambling in their states on a regular basis—possibly every five years.

We Need a Federal Plan of Action

The outline of an effective plan of action to redirect national gambling policy should include:

1. A national commission to assess the local and national impact of

expanded gambling on the American economy. This review should be directed by an independent federal government commission with input from state and local governments, as well as representation from such federal agencies as the Federal Reserve Bank, the President's Council of Economic Advisors, the Small Business Administration, and the Labor Department. The commission would address such questions as: What are the real costs and benefits of using gambling as industrial policy? How are state and local gambling expansion efforts affecting the incidence of problem gambling and how are the costs of problem gambling affecting public- and private-sector economies? What are the impacts and implications of state and local gambling expansion policies on federal and private-sector efforts to expand the national economy? How, for example, are federal government efforts at improving America's global competitiveness affected by state and local government gambling expansion policies?

2. The creation of a national plan for coordinated and cooperative efforts among federal, state, local, and tribal governments in expanding the economy. This would include a coordinated effort at national gambling policy and an end to the situation in which states are forced to legalize and/or expand gambling in order to prevent local gambling dollars from crossing borders.

3. The development of innovative investment opportunities for the public, to provide alternatives to the present attractions of pure gambling opportunities. These alternatives, one of which I describe later, would combine investment strategies with people's willingness to gamble as a way to raise funds that could be used to encourage expansion of productive business enterprises. They could also be used to raise money for such public purposes as expanding state industrial extension programs.

The first steps toward a federal effort at examining the impacts of existing gambling policies, with the goal of developing more effective national policies, were actually taken in late 1994. At that time, New York State Congressman John J. LaFalce, then Chairman of the Committee on Small Business, held hearings on the "National Impact of Casino

Gambling Proliferation." The committee heard testimony from experts in economic development, law enforcement, public policy, and the treatment of compulsive gambling. Most of the speakers agreed that national attention to the issues raised by gambling proliferation was highly desirable. After the hearings in early 1995, LaFalce and Virginia Congressman Frank R. Wolf each introduced bills calling for a national review of the impacts of gambling.

A Lottery Could Be Combined with Investment

There actually could be more productive ways for government to be involved in financial risk taking or even gambling, without the dangers of the current approach. These should be based on some simple, common-sense observations. The first is that people want to use their money to make more money—through both investment and gambling. Second, governments need more money than they are currently able to raise through taxes and borrowing. While these traditional ways of raising public revenues have never been popular, growing public revenue needs and citizen resistance to paying increased taxes have made them even more politically unpopular. Third, business will always need to raise capital to expand its operations, and fourth, people will continue to be dependent on business expansion for their jobs.

The question is, how can government be involved in meeting these desires and needs in ways that do not prey on people's lack of better opportunities to make money? The determining factor in whether or not people have good opportunities to invest their money has a great deal to do with their economic status. Since attractive investment opportunities usually require substantial amounts of money, lower-income people are often locked out. Whatever money they're able to put aside is rarely enough to net anything more than the meager returns of a savings account. Under these circumstances, feeding slot machines or buying $20 worth of lottery tickets becomes extremely appealing. As discussed in

Chapter 3 [of Goodman's book], research indicates that the lower a person's income, the more that person tends to see gambling as an investment opportunity.

While the lotteries and slot machines prey on people's limited investment options by offering the illusion of a chance to get ahead, government could develop a fundamentally different approach. This might still involve offering people the chance to win significant amounts of money. But it's possible to do this in a way that at the same time encourages people to make real investments with their money.

To illustrate one way we could move toward this end, I suggest we go back about 300 years and consider reviving one of the original government ventures in gambling. In 17th-century England, the royal government financed some of its projects by selling lottery tickets. However, in contrast to our contemporary state lotteries, prizes were won by some few lucky players and the rest of the ticket holders were repaid, with interest, over a period of years.[12]

What I propose is adoption of a similar approach. States that now have lotteries would sell one-dollar investment lottery tickets with the chance to win prizes that are capped in the range of $10,000 (as opposed to the current, escalating mega-million-dollar, change-your-life jackpots). The state would also repay non-prize-winning ticket holders who have accumulated at least $100 worth of tickets in a one-year period their original ticket price, plus interest, after five years. Interest would be calculated on an annual basis at 2 percent less than the rate of a five-year bank certificate of deposit at the time the ticket was purchased. The state could use this pot of money to make low-interest loans to local businesses.

The criteria for receiving such a loan would be a business's economic viability and its willingness to use such a loan to expand its employment rolls. The money would be lent at two percentage points less than whatever the current bank rate is for commercial loans. The state's return on its lottery revenues could be used to pay for lottery prizes and administrative costs, and to accumulate a reserve fund against failed loans to business.

I don't mean to suggest that the introduction of this kind of investment lottery would cause an immediate or overwhelming shift of players away from existing lottery games. What is likely to happen, though, is that some percentage of players—perhaps 10 to 15 percent—would shift their playing habits. With the alternative of a win-win situation, instead of the currently mostly-lose situation, a considerable number of people could be persuaded to change their gambling habits, especially if lottery advertising were redirected from enticing people to spend a dollar on a dream and instead encouraged genuine saving and investment. Over time, if the investment lottery helped support local business and create jobs, state officials might find themselves persuaded by the results. Political pressure might cause a shift away from regressive gambling ventures and toward this kind of investment hybrid.

I propose this investment lottery approach not so much to endorse these particular details, but as a way of illustrating the broad possibilities for rethinking government involvement in gambling policy. The overriding goal would be to move from government's current approach of simply promoting more opportunities for people to lose their money and toward policies that could actually encourage savings, investment, and the creation of productive jobs. This is obviously only one aspect of what needs to be a much broader federal, state, and local effort to redirect America's problematic expansion of gambling opportunities.

We Are Creating a Scavenger Economy

As our economy continues to shed productive jobs in favor of ever more popular ways of taking chances with money—from trading vintage Barbie dolls to building sumptuous gambling palaces—we invest less in basic research, in the education of young people, and in support of innovative industries. We handsomely reward the designers of clever lottery scratch tickets and analysts who chart the future value of collectible trinkets, while we neglect the talents that built our basic industries. What we are creating is a scavenger economy that relies more on the milking of existing wealth than on the creation of new wealth. It is quite possible that at no other time in history have so many people been trying so hard to make money without having to work for it.

So long as we continue to tolerate the growth of this approach to economic development, more states will become convinced that they have no choice but to enter the destructive fray, and ever more options will be defensively added to their gambling menus in the frantic hope of not losing revenue to neighboring competitors.

But it is not just local economies that are at a risk in the proliferation of gambling—it is the very health and integrity of our political system. At a time when faith in government is arguably at an all-time low, political leaders around the country are asking people to believe that they will have a more secure future through access to more gambling. This is quite a distance from the past promise of governments to actually develop serious programs to create jobs and spur the economy. Where we once had government-backed rural electrification, farm irrigation projects, and industrial extension programs, we now get government-backed lotteries, off-track betting, and themed casinos.

Bernard Goldstein, owner and developer of some of the country's first riverboat casinos in Iowa, got it right when he said, "We are beating our plowshares into amusement centers."[13] Right next to where he moored his boats stand the factories that produced machinery that plowed and harvested the agricultural heartland that in turn fed America, along with a good part of the world. Now these buildings serve as the grim backdrop for an industry that, in the words of casino executive Stephen Perskie, "doesn't produce anything."[14]

Politicians and government officials, upon whom citizens rely to make judgments on ventures that could permanently alter the economic and social conditions of their states, are abdicating their responsibilities. During the many hours I have spent in legislative hearings on gambling and in examining testimony, nothing has distressed me more than to see politicians thoughtlessly repeating the trumped-up revenue figures and job projections supplied to them by the gambling industry. Only rarely have they bothered to commission their own objective research. Having done little serious analysis of their own, they turn to leaders of the gambling industry for answers. At a 1992 hearing before a legislative committee of the Connecticut state legislature, Steve Wynn, the CEO of the Mirage casino company, was asked how he planned to help Bridgeport with a new casino and how it would fit into their city.

"You can't put a jewel in a slum," he told them. "You've got to make a tremendous barrier around it so that the presentation is proper. Otherwise," said Wynn, "who is going to come?" At that same hearing, legislators asked him to analyze the impact of the casino on their state's economy: Would his casino draw dollars away from their race tracks? The state lottery? Would the state's highways and airport be big enough to handle his casino's future traffic? Wynn explained he would have his people provide the answers. Then, turning to the question of the airport, he told them that it had looked big enough to him when he arrived in his private jet earlier that day.[15]

Gambling Lobbyists Wield Political Clout

As it expands across the country, the gambling industry is becoming a major new political power. Indeed, in many states it has become the leading lobbying group; politicians have already grown dependent on its contributions for campaign financing. Never before in their histories have so many states been host to promotional campaigns on the scale of those which have been mounted by America's gambling industry.

We are told by an increasing number of political leaders to expect less from our government, and that for most of us, this will be a good thing. Less money from out of our pockets, less government on our backs. But the enthusiasm with which state and local governments have ushered in the gambling industry suggests an altogether different direction. Why, we should ask, are governments so willing to enter into profit-sharing partnerships with gambling companies, but so averse to making similar arrangements with other, potentially more productive industries? How is it that the total cumulative amount that state governments across the entire country spend on their industrial extension programs is less than what New Jersey alone spends to regulate its gambling industry? And, ultimately, we must ask, do we really want our government aggressively promoting enterprises that are potentially addictive, demonstrably increase crime, and drain money from firms struggling to survive?

The boosters' last line of defense is to invoke the principles of freedom and choice. No one, after all, is being forced to gamble away his or her money. It is simply an entertainment option, one among many, and why should local citizens be deprived of it? These arguments are rife with euphemisms and misleading information. Legalized gambling is a highly controlled, monopolistic business that preys on the most vulnerable people in our society. There is hardly much free choice when jobs are scarce or don't pay well, and when government and private casino companies spend hundreds of millions of dollars on behavior modification studies and advertising to tell people they can change their lives through gambling.

Citizens should be able to look to government to protect their basic rights, not to promote destructive behavior and false promises. There is a lot that government can do to support job growth and to ease the dislocation and unpredictability that has become part of our economic system. To move away from the culture of chance and toward policies that promote genuine economic development will mean going beyond the hype of magic bullet cures and focusing instead on incremental, long-term policies. We should seek to better understand and correct the economic circumstances that have forced state and local governments to consider gambling in the first place. This process will require patience, careful analysis, and honest discussion among leaders and their constituents. The reward will be not only the protection of our economy, but a shift from the pathologies of hope to the creation of real hope.

Notes

1. Lee Iacocca, *Iacocca: An Autobiography* (New York: Bantam Books, 1984).
2. Ibid., p. 323.
3. See stories by Janice Leary, "Iacocca Eyes Flint for Casino," and "Iacocca Gambling Deal Reported with Five Michigan Tribes," *Flint Journal*, August 5, 1994, p. A1 and August 20, 1994.

4.   Bennett Harrison, *Lean and Mean: The Changing Landscape of Corporate Power* (New York: Basic Books, 1994), p. 224. Harrison writes: "There are cases in which the firm (or region) that achieves a certain critical minimum market share or a monopoly over a new technology may, by attaining economies of scale, name recognition, or head start in learning by doing, sustain a competitive advantage over a long period of time."

5.   Laura D'Andrea Tyson, *Trade Conflict in High-Technology Industries* (Washington, D.C.: Institute for International Economics, November 1992), p. 289. According to Laura D'Andrea Tyson, Chairwoman of the president's Council of Economic Advisors, "America's military industrial policy has been the primary driver of technological development and diffusion in the United States since World War II."

6.   The Bush administration, which originally opposed industrial policy, moved toward limited forms of this idea out of concern about the growing dependence of the United States on foreign sources of military hardware and about foreign competition with American business. By the time Bush left office, his administration had endorsed a Critical Technologies Institute, with a mandate to identify emerging technologies for federal support. When Bill Clinton replaced him, ideological and financial support for industrial policy increased. Important policymakers in Clinton's administration, Laura D'Andrea Tyson, for example, argued that, with the end of the Cold War, military R&D budgets had been slashed, resulting in fewer spinoff benefits for America's civilian businesses. In high-tech areas like biotechnology, semiconductor manufacturing, robotics, artificial intelligence, and high-definition displays, innovations were increasingly being driven by civilian, rather than military, applications. See Tyson, *Trade Conflict*, pp. 290–91.

Under Clinton, the National Institute of Standards and Technology proposed raising its yearly advanced technology program to over $750 million by 1997—an increase of greater than tenfold. The White House also announced it would use up to $5 billion of the $25 billion spent by federal laboratories each year (much of which was then being used for nuclear weapons research) on joint federal government/private industry projects, with equal financing provided by the government and industry.

7.   See Edmund L. Andrews, "Clinton's Technology Plan Would Redirect Billions from Military Research," *New York Times*, February 24, 1993, and Keith Bradsher, "Reason to Smile Again: Clinton Industrial Policy," *New York Times*, March 8, 1993, 9.

8.   Congress of the United States, Office of Technology Assessment, *Competing Economies—America, Europe and the Pacific Rim: Summary* (Washington, D.C.: U.S. Government Printing Office, October 1991).

9.   Commission on the Review of the National Policy Toward Gambling, *Gambling in America, Appendix 1: Staff and Consultant Papers, Model Statutes, Bibliography, Correspondence* (Washington, D.C.: U.S. Government Printing Office, October 1976).

10. Harrah's Casinos, *The Harrah's Survey of United States Casino Entertainment: 1994* (Memphis, Tenn.: Harrah's Brand Communications, February 1994).

11. See, for example, talk by Promus CEO Michael Rose, "The Gambling Industry and Economic Growth," at American Legislative Exchange Council, National Leadership Summit on Economic Growth, San Antonio, Texas, April 14–17, 1994.

12. See *Gambling in America, Appendix 1*, pp. 9, 10.

13. Paul Glastris and Andrew Bates, "The Fool's Gold in Gambling," *U.S. News and World Report* (April 1, 1991), pp. 22, 23.

14. Stephen P. Perskie, Interview on the "Dale Arnold Show," WEEI Radio, Boston, Mass., June 14, 1994.

15. Casino Gambling Task Force Invitational Forum, Finance, Revenue, and Bonding Committee, State of Connecticut, Hartford, Conn., October 13, 1992.

VII

THE IMPACT OF GAMBLING ON THE TRIBAL RESERVATION

INTRODUCTION TO PART VII

A. Origins of Contemporary Indian Gaming

While Indian gaming operations exploded after 1988, when Congress passed the Indian Gaming Regulatory Act (IGRA), the popularity of tribal gaming began in the mid-1970s. Then tribes in Florida, Connecticut, Wisconsin, and California operated low-stakes bingo halls on their reservations. To reduce reliance on federal revenue and to move toward economic independence, tribes came to expand their gaming enterprises. When they began offering higher stakes, staying open longer, and using paid workers rather than volunteers, they came into conflict with state law. When state and local law-enforcement officials charged the Indians with violating the law, tribal leaders responded that they were exercising their sovereignty and the laws did not apply to reservations. Until 1987 states and tribes fought inconclusively in courts over who had the legal authority to regulate tribal gambling. Then, in 1987, a majority in the U.S. Supreme Court ruled in the precedent-setting decision *California v. Cabazon* that tribes could conduct and regulate any gaming activities legal elsewhere in the state. The Court held that since the California legislators permitted the state lottery, horse racing, church bingo, and private card rooms, they intended the law to regulate rather than to prohibit gaming.

B. The Indian Gaming Regulatory Act: Landmark Federal Law

The *Cabazon* decision led many tribes throughout the country either to begin or to expand gaming operations without the fear of state intervention. Unable either to control the rise of tribal gaming or to collect taxes from it, state officials turned to Congress, which in 1988 disappointed them by passing the Indian Gaming Regulatory Act (IGRA), requiring state officials to negotiate in good faith compacts with tribes and creating licensing regulations.

The IGRA was intended as a compromise between the tribal position that states have no right at all to affect activities on the reservation and the states' position that all state and local laws should apply. Although it was designed to force each side to treat the other as an equal, the IGRA to some degree disappointed both sides. The states resented the federal government's giving tribes a competitive business advantage: the nontaxable opportunity not only to compete with state lotteries and racetracks but also to operate commercial gaming enterprises in the state. From the perspective of many Indians, however, state officials were hypocritical for supporting state-run lotteries or off-track betting and then objecting to tribal bingo halls and casinos. Since the IGRA there has at times been cooperation between states and tribes, but perhaps more often there has been conflict.

At times state officials have refused to negotiate in good faith with tribes, and tribes have sued them in federal court. The states have argued as follows. Despite Congress's intention, through an explicit provision in the IGRA, to give tribes the right to sue states for not negotiating with them, forcing states to negotiate with tribes violates the Tenth and Eleventh Amendments to the U.S. Constitution, relating to the balance of power between state and federal governments.

While some federal courts have agreed with the states' contentions and suspended negotiations in certain states, other federal courts have rejected the states' arguments. The U.S. Supreme Court has not resolved the constitutional question whether Congress can lawfully force states to make agreements with tribes.

There are other legal issues than the right of tribes to sue states for not negotiating with them. One issue concerns the degree to which tribes may acquire land outside their reservation specifically for gaming. When Congress passed the IGRA, it thought it was creating policy principally for reservations. Since the passage of the law, however, a number of tribes on remote reservations have bought land in or near cities in the hopes of building casinos there. In fact, some cities have struck deals with tribes to bring gambling to their areas over the resistance of state legislators. What's more, even some casino companies would like to see tribes get land in cities so that the companies can manage those businesses.

Once the federal government approves of land for Indian use, the land has the legal status of a reservation and becomes exempt from state and local laws and taxation. While states argue that they have a legitimate interest in activities or property in or near their cities and agree with the IGRA requirement that a state's government should approve land transfers to Indians, tribes want the requirement removed. Leah Lorber's article in Part VI of this anthology deals specifically with the issue of new land acquisitions.

C. The Economics of Indian Gaming

To understand the amount of money involved in Indian gaming, consider the following data. In 1993, the Mashantucket Pequots' Foxwoods casino in Connecticut became the most profitable casino in America, earning net profits of about one million dollars a day. By the beginning of 1994, tribal gaming revenues were grossing an estimated $2.6 billion a year. By 1994, nearly one hundred tribes in nineteen states, or about one-third of all tribes outside Alaska, conducted gaming operations, often in casinos larger than those in Las Vegas and Atlantic City.

Although casinos are highly controversial for some tribes, many tribal leaders view them as providing a much-needed opportunity for economic independence to a people often forcibly moved to unproductive land and denied access to investment capital.

D. Controversies Within the Tribes

Among Native Americans there are both many who advocate gaming for economic development and many who strongly reject it. In fact, one conflict led to homicide, when several members of the Mohawk tribe in upstate New York were killed in fighting between pro- and anti-gambling factions. Some tribal members see agreements involving non-Indian bureaucrats, judges, and police as invitations to outside influences and a yielding of tribal sovereignty.

While advocates of Indian gaming point to its economic benefits, critics worry that it will threaten traditional values, and increase the incidence of problem gambling and its attendant evils. At times the critics have literally outvoted the advocates, as in 1994 when the Seneca tribe in New York State voted against casinos. While many Indians view gaming as the best opportunity for tribal development, others see it as selling out their culture.

Collectively, the chapters in this part show the complex questions at issue in suggesting or evaluating Indian gaming policy. The statement put out by the National Indian

Gaming Association, attempts to defend Indian gaming by answering the usual objections. The article by Jon Magnuson, expresses the ambivalence many Christians feel as they try to harmonize their general disapproval of gambling with their respect for Indian sovereignty. The piece by Paul Pasquaretta examines how reservation gambling has affected different elements within the Native American community and transformed contemporary Indian identities. David Segal's article paints a largely negative picture of current Indian gaming. Though not unconditionally condemning the idea of Indian gaming, Segal calls for tighter governmental controls to protect Indians against managerial corruption and mismanagement and infiltration from gangsters.

19. Tribal Gaming Benefits the Reservations

National Indian Gaming Association

One way to support tribal gaming is to defend it against the usual objections. This is exactly what the following piece, put out by the National Indian Gaming Association, attempts to do.

1. Myth: The Indian Gaming Regulatory Act (IGRA) created Indian gaming.

Fact: Gaming is a right of Indian nations.

Gaming is one of the oldest forms of recreation; not only did Europeans bring new games to the New World, but Indians have traditional games still played today. In fact, Indian gaming existed long before Europeans settled in America. Large-scale Indian gaming, mainly in the form of bingo, predated IGRA by about 10 years. The U.S. Supreme Court in 1987 recognized Indian people's right to run gaming when it ruled that states had no authority to regulate gaming on Indian land if such gaming is permitted outside the reservation for any other purpose (*California v. Cabazon*). Congress established the legal basis for this right when it passed IGRA in 1988.

"Tribal Gaming: Myths and Facts," National Indian Gaming Association (Internet web site: American Indian Gambling and Casino Information Center, http://www. dgsys.com/~niga/myths.html). Used by permission.

2. Myth: Indian gaming is commercial, for-profit gaming.

Fact: Gaming on Indian reservations is operated by tribes to fund governmental programs.

IGRA requires that all revenues from tribal gaming operations be used solely for governmental or charitable purposes. Much like state government and the use of funds from forty state lotteries, tribal governments determine how gaming proceeds are to be spent. In direct contrast to the opulent expenditures on yachts and jets by commercial casino operators such as Donald Trump, Indian tribes are using gaming revenues to build houses, schools, roads, and sewer and water systems; to fund the health care and education of their people; and to develop a strong, diverse economic base for the future.

3. Myth: Tribal gaming is an unregulated magnet for organized crime.

Fact: Indian gaming is more heavily regulated and more secure than commercial gaming.

The tribes, as governments, are the first to be vigilant in protecting the integrity of projects they rely upon to feed, clothe, educate, and employ their people. Even before IGRA created a federal framework for regulating certain forms of tribal gaming, tribes regulated reservation gaming activities by exercising their inherent police powers and, when necessary, taking violators to court. Many tribes have had existing law enforcement and court systems for years. In compacts negotiated between state governments and tribal governments, such issues as law enforcement and security measures are considered. States like Arizona, for example, have reached agreements with tribes to coordinate background checks and other security measures. While many of the opponents of Indian gaming challenge its security, they have no evidence to support their claims. In fact, at an October 1993 House hearing, Jim Moody, FBI section chief for organized crime, testified there is "no information to support claims" that organized crime has infiltrated Indian gaming.

"We've heard more rumor and innuendos than we've been able to prove," Moody told lawmakers. The third level of regulation is the federal government: the Department of Justice, FBI, and Bureau of Indian Affairs provide oversight on crimes committed on reservations. Finally, the law (IGRA) established the National Indian Gaming Commission, which became operable in February 1993, to regulate Indian gaming.

4. Myth: Indian people do not pay taxes.

Fact: Indian people pay all taxes required by state and federal law.

All Indian people pay federal income, FICA, and social security taxes. Most Indians also pay state income and property taxes. Only the small percentage of Indians who live and work on federally recognized reservations—not unlike soldiers and their families living on military installations—are exempt from paying state income and property taxes. However, they still pay taxes such as sales and federal income tax.

Indian tribes are governments with responsibilities to their citizens, but tribes almost uniformly lack a tax base to support their governmental needs. Some tribes have found in gaming a means to provide not only jobs and economic activity on their reservations, but also a source of badly needed government revenue. As sovereign governments, tribes do not have to pay taxes on their revenues to any other governments. Do states pay taxes on their resources derived from gaming or from any other source? NO!

5. Myth: IGRA has not worked and cannot work.

Fact: Indian gaming is providing substantial economic benefits in states where IGRA has been given a chance to work.

IGRA is working to the benefit of Indians and non-Indians in several states, including Minnesota, Wisconsin, Michigan, and Connecticut. Reservations are slowly recovering from decades of failed government programs and building new houses, community centers, roads, and much more. Indians and non-Indians are proudly leaving welfare rolls and getting on payrolls. They are taxpayers instead of tax users. Local and state governments are enjoying increased tax revenues. Only where states failed to negotiate compacts in "good faith" in violation of IGRA has the process not worked.

6. Myth: IGRA is an unconstitutional infringement upon states' rights.

Fact: States have reneged on the deal they proposed and accepted.

The states' ongoing assault on IGRA starts from the faulty premise that they have some inherent long-standing right to regulate or curtail tribal gaming. States are now trying to renege on a deal they proposed and accepted when Congress passed IGRA in 1988 by unjustly and wrongly asserting that IGRA violates the 10th and 11th Amendments to the U.S. Constitution. To the contrary, the Supreme Court's *Cabazon* decision was a clear recognition of the right of Indian tribes to regulate gaming on their lands free of state laws if the state permitted those activities outside the reservation.

7. Myth: Tribal gaming drains resources and tax dollars from surrounding non-Indian governments and communities.

Fact: Indian gaming creates additional resources and tax dollars for surrounding non-Indian governments and communities.

Indian gaming is now a 5-billion-dollar industry according to *Gaming and Wagering* magazine. Indian gaming creates jobs, increases economic activity, and generates tax revenue both on and off the reservation. Consider the following: in San Diego county alone, tribal gaming has been responsible for the creation of more than 5,000 well-paying new jobs, with a payroll of $22 million per year (and the associated payroll taxes and employee income taxes). In Minnesota, Indian gaming has become the state's seventh largest employer, having created more than 12,000 new jobs—three-fourths of which are held by non-Indians. And in Connecticut, a single Indian gaming facility will provide more revenues to the state than its largest taxpayer, which is one of the country's largest defense contractors—direct jobs created nationally, with the majority of employees being non-Indian.

Tribes have spent millions of dollars for construction. In addition, they spend many more millions per year for goods and services—almost all locally.

8. Myth: Better economic development alternatives to gaming are available to tribes.

Fact: Indian gaming is the first—and only—economic development tool that has ever worked on reservations.

Many reservations are in remote, inconvenient locations on land that nobody else wanted. Before tribal gaming, there had been little successful public- or private-sector economic development on reservations. The federal government/Bureau of Indian Affairs has not been successful in economic development on reservations. The states have not proposed any specific or credible alternatives to Indian gaming as a meaningful source of tribal revenues and jobs. However, tribal governments are using the gaming proceeds to diversify and conduct other economic enterprises.

9. Myth: Tribal gaming has little public support among non-Indians.

Fact: A majority of Americans support Indian gaming.

Public opinion surveys, both nationally and within various states, conclusively demonstrate that the public strongly supports expanded gaming on Indian reservations. A national Harris poll in October 1992, and polls in Arizona, California, Kansas, Minnesota, New Mexico, Nebraska, and Washington, all show that the general public favors casino-style gambling on Indian lands but opposes expanded non-Indian gaming opportunities.

The reasons given for supporting tribal gaming are consistent with the purposes behind IGRA: the revenues will help the tribes and surrounding communities become economically self-sufficient and the tribes should have the right to govern their own lands.

20. White Unease about Indian Gambling May Reflect Nostalgic Imperialism

Jon Magnuson

Jon Magnuson, a Lutheran campus pastor at the University of Washington and co-chair of the Church Council of Greater Seattle's Native American Task Force, tries to explain how complicated the issue of Indian gaming is.

After giving a personal account of his experiences of Indian gaming, he describes some of the legal history of Indian gaming within a larger historical context, when two court cases (one in California, the other in Florida) were instrumental during the 1980s in broadening Indian gaming. Magnuson explains that giving tribes a wide latitude in running gaming establishments rests on a standard expressed by Supreme Court Justice John Marshall, who wrote in the nineteenth century that tribes are "domestic dependent nations, recognized as sovereign within their territories, with power of self-government over activities on their reservations."

It is the concern for Indian sovereignty and a respect for Indian self-government that makes it difficult, according to Magnuson, for many religious persons who disapprove of gambling fully to condemn Indian gaming.

Understanding the concern over gambling expressed by both Native and non-Native Americans, he asserts that some disapproval of Indian gaming is either hypocritical or racist, as when people condemn Indian gaming while condoning state-sponsored lotteries. Magnuson argues that some of the moral

---

"Casino Wars: Ethics and Economics in Indian Country," in *Christian Century* (February 16, 1994), pp. 169–71). Used by permission.

indignation and masked anger at Indian gaming is probably rooted in what is termed "nostalgic imperialism," "an unconscious sentimentalizing and romanticizing of that which a dominant culture has destroyed."

Other critics of Indian gaming, he writes, are simply trying to advance their own interests, as when Donald Trump sued the federal government for "supposedly giving tribes regulatory breaks."

He argues finally that whatever people think of gambling in general, evaluations of Indian gaming must be sensitive to the unfortunate history and treatment of the American Indian.

The "Ghost Trail" weaves through 7,000 acres across one of Washington state's largest Indian reservations. My informant tells me it carries no visible markings. For outsiders the path remains a hidden part of that indigenous community's spiritual geography. I'm told that some Salish avoid crossing the trail casually. They regard it as one that their forest spirits travel. Only initiates into the *Seyouwin*, or winter dance society, continue to perceive the trail; those who practice the thousand-year-old secret rituals are pledged to protect and honor it.

I stand in a parking lot with a longtime employee of the tribe's Treaty Protection Task Force, who musingly points out that the ghost trail ends a few yards in back of me at the doorway to the tribal casino, which operates 24 hours a day. This is my second visit to the tribe's gaming enterprise. We casually wander over to the renovated warehouse that now houses bingo games, roulette wheels, and blackjack tables. The central image on a cedar totem pole near the entrance is a bear holding a deck of cards. Next to the door a world map invites visitors and customers to mark their points of origin. Hundreds of red and green tacks fill the display, representing dozens of countries in Europe and Asia, as well as North America. Approaching the casino's entrance, I lift my hand to trigger a motion activator hidden inside a Halloween skeleton. The "Addams Family" theme song echoes from a speaker mounted just out of sight.

It's busy this afternoon. As in big-time casinos, there are no windows, no clocks, and no places to sit down apart from gaming and bingo tables.

Employees are cordial, floors spotless. State regulations prohibit liquor from being served here, and although food is available, it's apparent that no one has come to linger, eat, or socialize. The atmosphere reminds me of Las Vegas and Reno. There is a feeling of peculiar seriousness in such establishments, perhaps because the rules seem so straightforward. This is about winning. And money.

As is true on most Indian reservations, this casino is leased to a national gaming organization, with a contract stipulating that it turn over full operation to tribal leaders in three or four years. Meanwhile, plenty of sophisticated marketing techniques have been put into place. Not long ago this nondescript warehouse was an empty building on the edge of a bay next to a lonely ferry dock. What was once an abandoned storage area is now an expansive, neatly ordered parking lot filled bumper to bumper with cars and vans. Each day hundreds of bingo and blackjack fans enter what was once a sleepy tourist and fishing town, oblivious to ghost trails, Indian treaty rights, or the ancient masked dances that still go on near here on rainy winter nights. I get myself some coffee, and my friend introduces me to a young tribal woman dressed in medieval jester's garb, working as one of the hostesses. She is friendly, and mentions with pride that 60 percent of the employees are tribal members. She's a single mother with three children. The pay is good, she says. My colleague, one of the tribe's cultural specialists, points, smiling, to a blackjack table. He says the dealer, a man with long dark hair, is one of the leaders of the *Seyouwin*.

Gambling Has Become Acceptable

This small but obviously lucrative casino is only one example of the sudden growth of legalized gambling on Indian reservations. It is also a sign of the sweeping shift in public morality that is underway in virtually every municipality, Indian and non-Indian, across the country. Gambling has become an acceptable form of mass-market entertainment. In 1992 Americans spent more on legal games of chance than on films, books, amusement attractions, and recorded music combined. That same year

Americans spent three times as much money at Indian gambling casinos as on movie tickets. According to Wall Street forecasts, spending on gambling will double within a decade. "If there weren't more demand than supply, we'd all be doing something else," says Bruce Turner, a casino analyst for Raymond, James, and Associates.

Twenty states now have Indian gambling, ranging from bingo parlors to casinos as big and glamorous as those in Nevada. Fifty-eight tribes are currently involved in gaming ventures. The Foxwoods casino in Connecticut is the single largest contributor to that state's tax coffers; it alone will provide the state with $113 million this year. Minnesota, with its Native American gambling halls, currently has more casinos than Atlantic City. Eager to jump aboard the economic boom, a promoter in northwest New Jersey has recently offered to donate land to the Delaware Indians if a few members of that tribe will come back from Oklahoma to sponsor a casino.

The use of reservation lands for large-scale commercial gaming designed to attract non-Indian players is a relatively new trend. Two court cases in the early 1980s set the standard for states: In both *Seminole Tribe v. Butterworth* (in Florida) and *State of California v. Cabazon* the courts used the "criminal-prohibitory and civil regulatory" test. This test holds that if state law criminally prohibits a form of gambling, then the tribes within that state may not engage in that form of gaming free of state control. To further regulate tribal gaming, Congress passed the federal Indian Gaming Regulatory Act in 1988. This act affirms Indian sovereignty over gaming based on provisions established by the country's first interactions with tribal entities. Supreme Court Justice John Marshall, who shaped the earliest federal policy toward Native Americans at the beginning of the 19th century, wrote that Indian tribes are "domestic dependent nations, recognized as sovereign within their territories, with power of self-government over activities on their reservations." The legal ramifications of this position have proved to be complex, and subject to modifications by the reservations' federally appointed trustee, the Bureau of Indian Affairs. The 1988 act, for example, places restrictions on tribes that are not imposed on state gaming operations. It ensures that tribal governments are the sole owners and primary beneficiaries of gaming. It further states that tribes may not conduct casino-type gambling without a valid tribal-state compact regulating such issues as what games are played and the percentage of payoffs.

Native Peoples Disagree about Tribal Gaming

For many native peoples, gaming has become the method for building the strong economic base that they claim they need for their independence. For others, the proliferation of gaming is a spiritual cancer eating away at what is left of the soul of Native American communities.

Driving south from Minneapolis, we take Highway 42 west off Interstate I-35. My companion, a former church worker for Indian ministry in northern California, says, "You gotta see this." He's right. Mystic Lake is Minnesota's most spectacular new gaming facility. Owned by the Shakopee Mdewakanton Dakota tribe, Mystic Lake is a $15 million gaming entertainment center, the largest gambling casino between Las Vegas and Atlantic City. Crowning the facility is a teepee formed by searchlights extending hundreds of feet into the sky. The 135,000-square-foot casino boasts more than 75 blackjack tables and 1,000 video slot machines. One of its promotion brochures proclaims, "The excitement of Vegas . . . Without the desert." The Twin Cities' *Southwest Metro Entertainment Guide* reads, "If it's big money you're looking for, Mystic Lake Bingo offers games with mega jackpots. Megabingo starts at $500,000 and grows each night until someone cashes in." This is the pinnacle of Indian bingo, a dazzling feast of lights and sound where a new car is given away every night, where the food and beverage service is elegant and sophisticated, and where free shuttles from Minneapolis and St. Paul hotels arrive around the clock.

Walking through the doors, I'm taken aback by the glitter and noise of hundreds of slot machines and video games. The structure's circular design, our host says, symbolizes "the great circle of life, the four seasons, and the three cycles of life. Within the concentric circles of the main casino, all seven tribes of the Sioux nation are represented." I wander into the 1,100-seat Bingo Palace located at the west end of the structure and pause, disoriented by the mixture of spiritual and cultural images that frame this setting. A clergy friend from northern Minnesota had told me that the radio advertisements for Mystic Lake use a drum and the voice of an "authentic" shaman to lure customers to its gaming tables. Mysticism of a kind abounds here, but I'm not sure it is exactly what Black Elk had in mind.

On one level, the Native American boom in commercial gaming looks like a sure bet. In Minnesota, gambling is well on its way to becoming one of the state's largest employers, having created over 10,000 jobs. Members of some Indian nations receive checks as a share of casino profits. Three Dakota communities in southern Minnesota give out payments that vary from $2,000 to $4,000 per month, depending on profits, to each enrolled member of the tribe. The figures are staggering. After a lengthy legal struggle to regain the tribe's original 2,000-acre reservation, the Pequot nation finally got a financial guarantee from the Bureau of Indian Affairs and a loan from the Arab-American Bank in New York. Its casino opened in 1992 and is expected this year to earn over $500 million for tribal members. The tribe has had to open a genealogy office to judge the claims of long-lost relatives to membership in the group, which is now up to 256 members, all of whom are at least one-eighth Pequot by blood.

Some of the tribes, like the Oneidas of Wisconsin, have gained respect and admiration from both Indian and non-Indian groups as they collectively have made decisions about how to use their windfalls of revenue. Thanks to their new gaming facility, the Oneidas' unemployment rate fell from 40 percent in 1976 to 17 percent in 1991. With proceeds from their bingo hall, they have built a $10.5 million hotel and convention center, as well as an environmental testing lab that has won state and federal contracts. They have also subsidized their own Head Start program and built an elementary school. Other tribal councils, like Washington State's Suquamish, are using proceeds to purchase back reservation lands that were long ago taken away by state and federal policies. An attractive, state-of-the-art pamphlet for Mystic Lake concludes with some direct advocacy: "Tribal governments realize that casino gaming is not an end in itself. It is a means to achieve what no other federal economic development program has been able to in more than 200 years—the return of self-respect and economic self-sufficiency to Indian people."

Christians Vary in Their Responses to Indian Gambling

The varied responses to Indian gaming emerging from Christian churches warrant special attention. As a non-Indian and a member of the clergy, I believe these responses reflect important deeper issues about ethics, spirituality, and the complex face of racism and cultural identity. An immediate and common response was related to me in the form of a question by a denominational executive not long ago. "What are we going to do about Indian gambling?" he asked. In light of his strong, sensitive record of supporting treaty rights for northwest tribes, he was finding himself in a moral quandary. He was pondering the dilemma of how the Christian community could affirm the proliferation of what has long been considered a vice by most Protestants. To best answer this question it is important to acknowledge that the issue poses several ethical and moral dilemmas. The first, and perhaps the most elemental, is the right of Native peoples to decide their own destinies, a right protected by treaty provisions. Only in states that already allow gambling are commercial Indian games of chance legal.

In the larger social context, it is unsettling that there has been so little opposition by church leaders to the proliferation of state lotteries. The exploitation of low-wage workers and the abdication of any corporate public commitment to building a solid, equitable tax system is dismally evident to economists, whatever their political loyalties. It might be good to clean one's own house before suggesting that Native Americans should clean theirs. For historical reasons, America's 200 Indian reservations face overwhelming internal and external conflicts in developing strategies for survival. As Rick Hill, Oneida tribal chairman, stated in his welcoming speech to the Native American Journalists Association in 1992, "We have been reduced to gaming, but I feel at this time it offers the only chance we have for economic self-sufficiency."

Some perceive the results of Indian gaming as a humorous kind of revenge. Thomas Donlan, writing recently for the financial weekly *Barron's*, reminds us that one of the fundamental principles of economics is that a fool and his money are soon parted. What can be said in favor of a gambling casino, he says, is that it concentrates fools, money, and those who would part the two, thus contributing to economic efficiency through moral decay. Donlan enjoys the irony. The people who were "defeated by imported alcohol and disease," then corrupted by paternalistic management, he writes, "now find themselves, through a legal loophole, able to erect institutions to corrupt their oppressors."

A second popular response to the rise of gaming in Indian country is often moral indignation and masked anger. This is voiced quietly by many political liberals and whispered privately by progressive church leaders. Such an emotional response is probably rooted in what anthropologists call "nostalgic imperialism," an unconscious sentimentalizing and romanticizing of that which a dominant culture has destroyed. It is a fascination with indigenous people and culture, *exclusively* from an historical and artistic point of view. Such an "emblematic" relationship with Native cultures, anthropologists suggest, is a form of racism that many of us, including many Native Americans, share. In other words, others in the culture can gamble, but not the "noble American Indian."

While creative, powerful traditional values are still embodied in the remnants of Native spiritual religions and customs, it is important to remember there is no more "pure," unblemished spiritual teaching in indigenous cultures than there is in the varieties of Christian expression. The question "How could Indians be involved in commercialized gambling?" betrays our own longings for an innocent culture in touch with the best of earth and heaven. A good corrective might be to recognize that among Native Americans there is no consensus on the commercial gambling boom. The Mohawks of New York State have broken out in armed conflict over casino operations. The struggle to protect big-time tribal operations from organized crime continues. Traditionalists around the country grapple with tribal governments over the direction in which their communities are moving.

A third response to the increase in commercial Indian gaming is the plea by some for an "even playing field." The accusation that Native Americans have been given special privileges reflects a superficial reading of American history, as well as an ignorance of treaty rights and the historical relationship of tribes to the U.S. government. One of the more entertaining legal struggles against the explosion of Indian gaming has been waged by Donald Trump, seeking better odds for his own gambling ventures. Trump has sued the federal government for supposedly giving tribes regulatory breaks. His testimony before the federal courts was embarrassing and amusing to many Native American journalists, as he showed little if any understanding of the peculiar but critical history of the tribes' right of sovereignty, which has been affirmed since the earliest days of the Constitution. The defense of aboriginal rights in courts has been won over and over again in the last half of the 20th century. That legacy will undoubtedly remain part of our country's ongoing jurisprudence.

I'm on my way to British Columbia for a two-day stay at a Benedictine monastery. I turn on my car radio and hear an advertisement for the Lummi Indian casino 50 miles to the west. Switching stations, I find a public radio broadcast of a speech in Vancouver by a recent recipient of the Visiting Scholar Award sponsored by Simon Fraser University's Institute for the Humanities. The announcer introduces the speaker as Ovide Mercredi, grand chief of Canada's 600,000 aboriginal people. Although schooled as an attorney, his thoughts are expressed in typical Native style, in a personal, informal, and somewhat circuitous way. Mercredi's closing remarks are about the future of his people, the recovery by his children and grandchildren of their culture, traditions, and religion. "We're growing stronger," he says. "When we reclaim what once was ours, you will see us differently. We will win it back, buy it back, the land that was taken from us. You will hear our voices. Our Indian culture is renewing itself. In the years ahead," he concludes almost matter-of-factly, "you're not going to like us very much."

21. Modern Gambling Is Unlike Traditional Indian Games of Chance

Paul Pasquaretta

Although discussions of Indian gaming commonly focus on legal and economic questions, Paul Pasquaretta, who has done doctoral research on North American Indians, focuses, in the article reprinted here, on how reservation gambling has affected Native Americans and their cultural identities. While acknowledging that Indian gaming has had a profound effect on tribal economies, he notes how it has provoked controversy within Indian communities, aggravating already existing conflicts.

Tribal leaders supporting gaming point to tribes that have used gaming profits for education, housing, and other valuable purposes, but critics worry that tribal leaders and crime bosses will develop powerful alliances. Reservation gambling can also threaten elected leaders and traditional governing councils, according to Pasquaretta, because it can create new leaders politically and economically independent of current political structures. He asks: "Are these 'bingo chiefs' appropriating a corporate tribal sovereignty for personal gain, or are they expressing their own fundamental rights as tribal people?"

Many critics, with whom he has some sympathy, see gambling as a vice forced on Indians to ruin their culture and to provide further opportunity for state and federal governments to impose more laws and restrictions on Indian territories. While Pasquaretta admits that games of chance have been part of

---

"On the 'Indianness' of Bingo: Gambling and the Native American Community," in *Critical Inquiry* 20 (Summer 1994), pp. 694–714. Used by permission.

Indian culture before European settlement, the games of chance important to Indian culture, he argues, have carried ceremonial meaning and have reinforced social bonds. Those games, he believes, do not foster or reward individual acquisitiveness in the way that Vegas-style gambling is thought to do so.

By focusing on describing conflicts occasioned or exacerbated by gaming within Native American communities, Pasquaretta tries to clarify how Indian gaming means different things to different Indians and how a source of hope to some can also be a source of conflict.

In recent years a great deal of attention has been paid to the development and apparent success of the American Indian gambling industry. Discussions in the national media have generally focused on the legality and economic impact of reservation gambling, especially because of its power to redistribute wealth and transform regional politics. Without ignoring the importance of those issues, I will examine how reservation gambling has affected the Native American community itself and contributed to the ongoing transformation of contemporary Indian entities.

The proliferation of reservation gambling began in the late 1970s. Offering high-stakes bingo to the public, the earliest reservation gambling facilities in Maine and Florida were enormously profitable. Soon tribal councils throughout the United States were developing plans for their own bingo facilities. Their progress, however, was hindered by growing opposition. Before the emergence of Indian bingo, state governments had complete authority to control and limit high-stakes gambling within their borders. By claiming sovereign rights of their own, the tribes challenged that authority. As the number of reservation gambling establishments grew, lawmakers sought ways to limit and abolish their operation.

The U.S. Government Supported
Reservation Gambling

The controversy might have ended at the state level if tribal operators had not found an unlikely ally in the federal government. In an apparent effort to stimulate reservation economies, the federal government supported the development of high-stakes reservation gambling. Throughout the 1980s it consistently ruled in favor of federally recognized American Indian tribes that sought to establish or maintain such an operation. In Connecticut, for example, the legislature's rejection of high-stakes gambling prompted the Mashantucket Pequot Tribe to bring two federal suits against the state. The first, in 1986, was initiated when the state threatened to prosecute the tribal council if it proceeded with its plans to establish a high-stakes bingo operation. The second, in 1989, was filed when the state refused to negotiate a gaming compact for a tribally owned and operated casino. In both cases federal rulings favored the Pequots, and Connecticut was compelled to recognize the legitimacy of Pequot gambling.[1]

In 1988 the federal government established the Indian Gaming Regulatory Act (IGRA). Under the provisions of the act, states are required to negotiate gambling compacts with recognized tribal governments, if the proposed form of gambling is legal in that state, because the latter are nonprofit organizations. Indian high-stakes bingo and Las Vegas-night gambling, therefore, should be treated just like any other nonprofit fundraising event. One of the most recent and severe tests of the IGRA came in 1992 when the State of Arizona was forced to renegotiate its Indian gaming policy. Federal agents seized hundreds of illegal video slots purchased by tribal governments. One group, however, the Fort McDowell Yavapai Indians, refused to hand over the games. A stand-off followed and the agents withdrew. Months later the tribes and the state negotiated a new compact that allows three different tribes to run electronic games.[2] This compromise allowed the states a measure of regulatory control without denying the Indians the right to own and operate a high-stakes gambling facility.

Endorsed by the federal government, the Indian gambling industry has grown rapidly. Table games, slot machines, and poker have been incorporated into existing tribal operations and full-scale, Las Vegas-style gambling casinos have cropped up across North America. Today, an estimated two hundred high-stakes Indian gambling operations can be found in the U.S., and more are likely to emerge in the coming years.

By testing the limits of the law as well as the limits of their own political sovereignty, tribal governments (with the support of non-Indian lawyers, legislators, and financiers) have dramatically altered the structure of tribal economies throughout the United States. In many places this has led to the virtual re-creation of economies plagued by chronic poverty and unemployment. Yet the "casinoization" of Indian territories has tended to exploit the limited sovereignty tribal entities are granted under the law, and this has provoked controversy within Indian communities.

As a radical enactment of tribal sovereignty, reservation gambling is partly the natural by-product of the tribal system. Imposed on indigenous peoples by the federal government, the tribal system has facilitated the erosion of traditional governing structures and thus the traditional base of Indian culture. As the existence of a tribal government is dependent on the existence of a centralized, federal government, so too is the existence of the tribe itself. In other words, a tribe is a legal construct that cannot exist independently of the colonial structure that calls it into being.[3] On the other hand, tribes are also the remnants of formerly sovereign nations subjugated by European and Euro-American expansion. As such, a tribe may be indistinguishable from an American Indian nation. Does reservation gambling, then, support the proliferation of a federally mediated tribal culture to the detriment of American Indian nationhood? Or can the tribally run American Indian gambling industry be appropriated in ways that support indigenous identities and traditions?

Gambling Has Worsened Disagreements among Native Americans

The answer depends to a large extent not on how conflicts with external forces are resolved but on how factions within Indian communities come to understand one another. For the presence of high-stakes gambling facilities has aggravated existing conflicts within the Native American community itself. Throughout the U.S., tribal leaders have argued that gambling revenues provide the most available means to stimulate reservation economies. This claim is supported by the great success of a number of tribal communities. Gambling on the Mashantucket Pequot Reservation has transformed an all-but-abandoned Indian territory into a thriving and dynamic community. In other places, however, gambling has had a more negative impact. In the most dramatic example, the establishment of high-stakes gambling operations at Akwesasne divided the Mohawk community into gambling and anti-gambling factions. At the height of the controversy two men were killed. The Mohawks continue to be plagued by this fundamental division.

The trouble at Akwesasne, as elsewhere, invokes the issue of sovereignty. While the proliferation of gambling facilities on American Indian lands is, in part, a product of the limited sovereignty such lands are granted under federal law, some have argued that establishing games of chance is not the appropriate means to test the limits of tribal sovereignty. Gambling is a notorious industry, and many Indians are concerned that tribal leaders and crime bosses will develop powerful alliances. In California, for example, mobsters attempted to gain control of the Rincon Tribal Council's high-stakes bingo operation. Their efforts were eventually thwarted by internal tribal politics and the work of federal agents. Nonetheless, the possibility remains that Indian gambling operations could be infiltrated and run by organized crime.[4]

Reservation gambling also creates new leaders who are politically and economically independent of both elected and traditional governing councils. Are these "bingo chiefs" appropriating a corporate tribal sovereignty for personal gain, or are they expressing their own fundamental rights as tribal people? That question is related to another regarding the long-term economic effects of reservation gambling: Will high-stakes gambling stimulate the growth of viable reservation economies, or will it contribute to a greater disparity in the distribution and use of Indian resources?

Other gambling opponents within the Native American community have argued that high-stakes gambling is merely another vice foisted on Indians to promote further cultural ruin and greater assimilation into mainstream American society, while providing yet another opportunity for state and federal governments to impose more laws and restrictions over sovereign Indian territories.[5] This understanding informed the decision of Akwesasne's Mohawk Nation Council to oppose the unlicensed and unrestricted development of gambling operations on the reserve. Distinguishing Mohawk nationhood from federal tribalism, the council sought to inhibit the growing entrepreneurialism of the reserve's gambling operators. The council's traditionalist stance, however, is problematized by the heterodox and heterogeneous nature of Mohawk society. At Akwesasne, as in American Indian communities throughout the U.S., interracial bloodlines, intercultural attitudes, and new, post-contact traditions have all but overwhelmed traditional lifestyles and beliefs. Consequently, it is often difficult to know which traditions and life ways might be threatened by the advent of a gambling economy. This development is further aggravated by the diminishing availability of traditional resources, that is, fisheries, hunting grounds, and arable lands. Over the centuries these have either been destroyed by Euro-American expansion or reduced to the point that they are no longer central to a reservation's economy or lifestyle. In a new tribal world of consumer economics, federal subsidies, and wage labor, what can be recognized as authentically Indian? If gambling operators lack Indianness, where does a true Indianness reside? I want to examine these issues by returning in greater detail to the experiences of the Akwesasne Mohawks and the Mashantucket Pequots. When viewed in contrast, the experiences of these two distinct indigenous communities illustrate many of the major problems and opportunities precipitated by the rise of high-stakes reservation gambling. The comparison may also shed light on the complicated and thoroughly problematic nature of contemporary Indian identity in North America.

Gambling Pre-dates European Immigration

As it does throughout most of the rest of the world, gambling has ancient roots in indigenous North American culture. An estimated 130 tribes from 30 different linguistic stocks played dice games of various kinds centuries before European settlement.[6] Unlike Euro-American games of chance, which function as secular rituals and foster acquisitiveness, individual competition, and greed, traditional Native American games of chance are sacred rituals that foster personal sacrifice, group competition, and generosity.

For instance, among Hodenausaunee Iroquois traditionals *Gus-ka'-eh*, the ancient peach stone game, is considered one of just four divine amusements made by the creator for the happiness of the people.[7] Taught to men when the world was young, the game is an important rite of the *Midewiwis*, or Midwinter Ceremony. According to Trudie Lamb Richmond,

> the Midewiwis . . . concludes the end of one cycle and marks the beginning of another. The Sacred Bowl Game is one of the Four Sacred Rituals of Midwinter and symbolizes the struggle of the Twin Boys to win control over the earth. The Midwinter is a time of praying and awaiting the rebirth, a renewal of life. It is a time of giving thanks to the spirit forces and to the Creator. . . . The Iroquois explain that the Sacred Bowl Game . . . when played during the four-day Midwinter, is not only meant to maintain a balance of nature but also to amuse life-giving forces; to please the plant and animal world; and to make the Creator laugh.[8]

Because *Gus-ka'-eh* occupies a central place in Iroquois cosmology winning is less important than the attitude a player brings to the game. Playing with right attitude means staking one's most valuable possessions on the outcome of the contest and playing for the good of the whole community, if not for the sake of creation itself. This understanding of the game is informed by its history. According to Hodenausaunee tradition, the peach stone game was first played by the divine twins, Skyholder and Troublemaker. Evenly matched with his brother, Skyholder won the contest by sacrificing a part of his creation.

Ordinarily bowl games are played with stones, fruit pits, nut shells, or some other two-sided object. These are placed in a small wooden bowl. The players take turns smacking the bowl on the ground or some other hard surface. This action throws the pieces into the air; beforehand, the players bet on how they will fall. Skyholder chose to play with the heads of several small birds he had created. By killing the birds and playing with their heads he gained the crucial advantage he needed to defeat his powerful twin. In this way he retained his right to govern the earth. To commemorate his victory and to ensure that the game is played in the proper manner something of great value should always be staked on its outcome.[9]

Native American Games of Chance Were Unlike European Ones

Unlike Euro-American games of chance, which emphasize individual competitiveness, traditional Native American forms of gambling are often practiced as team competitions. Mourning Dove's account of the traditional Salishan stick game emphasizes the social, competitive, and team nature of the game:

> In the evening, people made large bonfires in the open air and challenged other tribes to play stick games. Lively songs were sung by both sides, and each team tried to distract the other while it was trying to hide the two bones. The object of the game was for the other side to guess which hand had a particular bone. Each side had a long pole stretched across in front and pounded on it with short sticks, keeping time with the songs. Bets of robes, blankets, coins, and so forth were piled in the middle. Anyone could bet on a team, even women. Women also had their betting games, which could last for a few hours or several days. All bets had to be absolutely matched. Anyone who wanted to make a bet had to match it against one for the other side. After the game, a winner got back double on the bet. . . . All gambling required good sportsmanship. It was shameful for poor losers to grieve. They would get no sympathy.[10]

The Iroquois bowl game is also practiced as a team competition. In the nineteenth century Lewis Henry Morgan reported that the game was normally contested between neighboring communities or different clans within a particular community. The victory belonged to both the gambler and his clan or nation. Thus, gamblers were chosen by the whole group for their skill at betting or throwing dice.[11]

Indigenous gambling practices have had other important functions. In *Manitou and Providence* Neal Salisbury has argued that northeastern woodland dice games like *hubbub* reinforced native systems of resource management and helped to maintain harmonious group relations. Within a classless society gambling losses and gains contributed to the fair and equal distribution of the group's communal resources. According to Salisbury, even sachems played and lost all they had in playing. Thus, *hubbub*, like other "mechanisms of political organization," also "served to counter the centralization of authority."[12]

This kind of sacred and social gambling has little to do with Vegas-style gaming, high-stakes bingo, and video slots; the comparison casts into sharp relief the great difference between gambling organized as a profit-making venture and ceremonial gambling practiced in traditional American Indian contexts. As Gerald Vizenor has argued, "pull tabs are not moccasin games, and bingo is far from a traditional tribal giveaway to counter materialism."[13] Insofar as casino gambling fosters materialism, acquisitiveness, and self-interest divested of group interest, it might also represent the last phase in the complete assimilation of indigenous North American peoples.

Handsome Lake's Code Warns Indians Against Playing Cards

Vizenor's concern finds antecedents in many places, but the most pertinent to this discussion is found in the Iroquois *The Code of Handsome Lake*. Handsome Lake was a Seneca prophet who "rallied the Iroquois at a time when some of them were selling their entire winter harvest of furs for hard liquor."[14] His code, established in the early nineteenth century, is meant to provide the people with a way to resist the evils of colonial occupation.

According to *The Code of Handsome Lake*, the time of trouble began when the "Evil One" duped a young European preacher into importing to North America the means to effect the destruction of the people: playing cards, money, fiddles, rum, and witchery. This preacher, having confused the devil with the savior, believed these things would be used to good purpose. "'Take them to these people,' he is told, 'and make them as white man are'" (*CHL*, 17). To carry out these instructions the preacher enlisted the help of Christopher Columbus, who carried the evil objects to North America. Once here they brought about the wholesale destruction of Iroquois people and beliefs and, in general, threatened to obliterate the community's special character and traditions:

> Then did [the Evil One] laugh and then did he say, "These cards will make them gamble away their wealth and idle their time; this money will make them dishonest and covetous and they will forget their old laws; this fiddle will make them dance with their arms about their wives and bring about a time of tattling and idle gossip; this rum will turn their minds to foolishness and they will barter their country for baubles; then will this secret poison [the witchery] eat the life from their blood and crumble their bones."[15]

The threat posed by each object deserves a thorough analysis. The cards, however, explicitly raise the issue of gambling. By the sixteenth century playing cards were common in every European country, and they were undoubtedly among the first things that traders and trappers introduced to North America. Native peoples could easily adopt the practice of playing cards, which, in some ways, was similar to their own gambling rituals, like the dish game. Both may share a common origin. In much the same way as dice, cards may have evolved from the practice of gambling on how sticks and arrows would fall (early Chinese playing cards were developed from sticks that later were widened, shortened, and designed with images).[16]

In *The Code of Handsome Lake*, playing cards pose a devastating threat to the community. Alien to the life ways and traditions of the Iroquois, card playing constitutes a profane and destructive practice that causes the people to "gamble away their wealth and idle their time." But gambling itself, as we have seen, is not prohibited by Iroquois tradition. Even in the code, which is, in fact, a bicultural document, the peach stone game is described as a divine amusement. Governed by ritual and sanctioned by myth, it constitutes a sacred and creative manner of negotiating chance and uncertainty. In this context *wealth* seems to refer to cultural as well

as economic stock and should be distinguished from the mere acquisition
of money.

For Mohawk traditionalists who follow the teachings of Handsome
Lake and participate in the traditional longhouse government of the
Iroquois, high-stakes bingo and gambling operations are likewise viewed
with suspicion, particularly when they are owned and operated by non-
traditional factions of the Mohawk community. However, this traditionalist stance is problematized because the entire Iroquois community has
been forced to adopt certain features of European culture. Such cultural
adjustments are also advocated by Handsome Lake. In many places he
promotes the use of Euro-American practices, particularly ones involving
land use:

> Three things that our younger brethren (the white people) do are right to
> follow:
>
> Now, the first. The white man works on a tract of cultivated ground and
> harvests food for his family. So if he should die they still have the ground for
> help. If any of your people have cultivated ground let them not be proud on
> that account. If one is proud there is sin within him. . . .
>
> Now, the second thing. It is the way a white man builds a house. He
> builds one warm and fine appearing so if he dies the family has the house for
> help. Whoso among you does this does right, always providing there is no
> pride. . . .
>
> Now the third. The white man keeps horses and cattle. Now there is no
> evil in this for they are a help to his family. So if he dies his family has the
> stock for help. Now all this is right if there is no pride. No evil will follow
> this practice if the animals are well fed, treated kindly and not overworked.[17]

In this way the code makes important distinctions among a variety of alien
practices and technologies. Some are considered inherently dangerous and
avoided at all costs, and others are considered necessary for continued
Iroquois survival. For the modern Iroquois living in a postinvasion world,
success often depends on the selective use of Euro-American things. The
code itself is a complex hybrid of Native and Euro-American practices and
beliefs; it attempts to constrain a new mode of living within an existing
code of ethics. The new mode, based on farming and livestock production,
dominated Akwesasne life for over a hundred years. Two drastic changes

coming in the twentieth century, however, have threatened to make the code and the way of living it institutionalized obsolete: the industrialization of the surrounding non-Indian territory and the establishment of a gambling economy on the reserve.

Pro- and Anti-gambling Factions Contest in Akwesasne

The population of Akwesasne is approximately 6,500 persons. Its territory around the banks of the Saint Lawrence River encompasses roughly 27 square miles. Bisected by the U.S.-Canadian frontier, five different non-Indian governmental offices claim jurisdiction over various parts of the reserve: the New York State government, the federal government in Washington, D.C., the provincial governments of Ontario and Quebec, and the Canadian federal government in Ottawa. Partly because of this division of external authority, internal authority at Akwesasne is contested among five distinct groups: the Mohawk Nation Council, the Saint Regis Tribal Council (recognized by New York State and Washington, D.C.), the Akwesasne Tribal Council (recognized by Ottawa, Ontario, and Quebec), the Mohawk Sovereignty Security Force, and entrepreneurial Mohawks, that is, cigarette smugglers and casino owners and operators. When high-stakes gambling came to Akwesasne in 1983, the Saint Regis Tribal Council was controlled by a pro-gambling faction, who, with the support of non-Indian builders and financiers, established the Mohawk Bingo Palace, the reserve's first high-stakes gambling facility. By 1989 six other casino, bingo, and electronic slot machine facilities had been established by independent operators. These new facilities were built on tribal lands without a formal agreement with either the tribal council or the State of New York. Nonetheless, the emerging bingo chiefs, as some called them, had a great deal of support within the Mohawk community. They provided important new sources of income and channeled a great deal of cash into the reserve's struggling economy.[18]

Their success, however, threatened some of the existing powers at Akwesasne and divided the reserve into anti-gambling and pro-gambling factions, which continue to exist today. The anti-gambling factions are dominated by three main groups: the Akwesasne Tribal Council, the Mohawk Nation Council, and anti-gambling factions within the Saint Regis Council. Funded by Parliament, the authority of the Akwesasne Council is legitimated by the Canadian government. Traditionally, Canadian Indian policy has emphasized "ethnicity or race rather than residence and territory" and, in turn, has supported a strong alliance between the Akwesasne Council and the Mohawk Nation Council.[19] The legitimacy and power of both groups is derived from precontact features of Mohawk culture, particularly its language, religion, and political constitution. The gambling interests, they argue, threaten to further unravel the fabric of Mohawk community and tradition. According to Barbara Barnes, director of the North American Indian Travelling College at Akwesasne, "'we were in the midst of a glitter-gulch strip, [with] no community controls, no government approval, no tribal regulations, and no profits to the people.'"[20] Moreover, both groups have supported plans to establish a single government for the whole territory. By distancing themselves from Parliament, which outlaws high-stakes gambling, the New York Mohawks have further aggravated the legal divisions imposed on the community by Euro-American governments. Anti-gambling leaders within the Saint Regis Council objected to independent gambling operations for similar reasons. The independents also threatened the ability of the council to regulate gambling within its jurisdiction.

Gambling at Akwesasne is supported by factions of the Saint Regis Council, independent gambling operators, cigarette smugglers, and the Mohawk Sovereignty Security Force, or the Warriors. The pro-gambling chiefs in the tribal council support the negotiation of state compacts and a regulated gambling economy; however, they did nothing to limit the operation of unlicensed facilities. The operators themselves ignored pressure from an increasingly active anti-gambling faction to shut down and refused to limit operations until state compacts could be reached. They argued that the same sovereignty which allowed the tribal council to build and operate a gambling facility on Mohawk land extended to them as individuals. Positioning themselves as entrepreneurs possessed with the true spirit of laissez-faire, they also claimed to have created hundreds of well-paying jobs and a Mohawk economy no longer dependent on state and federal welfare programs or the unpredictable fluctuations of the building industry.[21] Years before this group emerged, cigarette smugglers, or "butt-leggers," had been exploiting Akwesasne's special legal and political resources. Profiting from their tax-exempt status as Mohawks and from high Canadian taxes on tobacco sales, the butt-leggers thrived on a commodity no one else could supply: cheap cigarettes for Canadian smokers. In the early eighties the traditionals had unsuccessfully attempted to regulate this emerging entrepreneurial class. By the end of the decade the butt-leggers had a great many interests in common with independent gambling operators, and, in many cases, were the same people.

The Warriors represent themselves as descendants of ancestral braves and protectors of Mohawk sovereignty.[22] In the early seventies they won two major confrontations with provincial and state police. The first was at Kahnawake, the Mohawk reserve near Montreal. The Canadian-backed tribal council at Kahnawake was supporting the efforts of non-Mohawks to settle on the territory. After a standoff with Canadian police, the Warriors forced the tribal council to alter its position. The second confrontation involved a tract of land near Moss Lake in New York where the state had purchased 612 acres for a wilderness reserve. In 1974 the Warriors occupied this land and claimed it as part of their own sovereign territory. Although the confrontation threatened to erupt into violence between Mohawks and state police, New York eventually opted for negotiation, and, after three years of talks, the Warriors won a ruling that allowed Mohawks to hunt, fish, and grow crops at Ganienkeh, five thousand acres of state-owned land west of Moss Lake.[23]

Having established their legitimacy at Ganienkeh and Kahnawake, the

Warriors began to extend their influence at Akwesasne. In 1989 when anti-gambling factions invited state police and F.B.I. agents to crack down on the unlicensed operators, the Warriors established roadblocks to prevent the arrest of casino operators or the confiscation of their property. Although they never officially supported unlicensed gambling at Akwesasne, the Warriors opposed intervention of any kind from federal agents and border police on Mohawk territory. Funded by the underground economy and the flourishing butt-legging trade, they also had economic interests of their own at stake. Their posture revealed a schism between themselves and other traditionalists at Akwesasne and points to another important division within the Mohawk community.

In the late 1970s state police with allies in the Saint Regis tribal office blockaded a group of Akwesasne traditionals on Racquette Point. The traditionals had provoked elected tribal officials by confiscating chain saws and stopping work on a project to remove timber from the area. Backed by widespread public support, the longhouse people won this contest.[24] Ten years later, however, many of these same traditionals backed intervention by state and federal officials against gambling operators. In so doing they lost a great deal of public support and strengthened the position of the Warriors. Their resolution cemented a developing distinction between the two groups. In 1980 Peter Matthiessen, in an article on the Racquette Point controversy, drew no distinction between the traditional longhouse people of Akwesasne and the Warriors who had occupied Moss Lake. In Rick Hornung's account of the Akwesasne gambling war, *One Nation Under the Gun* (1991), as well as in Bruce E. Johansen's more recent study, *Life and Death in Mohawk Country* (1993), Warriors and Akwesasne longhouse traditionals are represented as two distinct and unrelated groups. Although both groups claim to follow the Constitution of the Five Nations and support traditional values, a closer look distinguishes the emergence of a traditional Warrior faction with a militant and entrepreneurial philosophy from an Akwesasne traditional longhouse faction with a conservative economic philosophy rooted in the agricultural past.

Until their most recent generations, the Mohawk people had greatly depended on the quality of their arable lands, fisheries, and hunting grounds. In this century, however, the area surrounding the community was heavily industrialized. In 1903 the Aluminum Company of America (Alcoa) built its first smelter a kilometer from Akwesasne. Completion of the Saint Lawrence Seaway in the 1950s and the availability of inexpensive hydropower attracted more plants to the area. Three aluminum smelting plants and a General Motors casting factory are still operating within a kilometer of the reserve.[25] These have reportedly discharged PCBs into the Saint Lawrence River and fluorides into the atmosphere. The fisheries were gradually ruined, the cattle poisoned, and the ground contaminated. At the same time, large numbers of Mohawks were employed as steel workers to build the factories. They became expert at this craft and were later employed to build skyscrapers and bridges across North America. Construction-related jobs eventually filled the employment and resource void created by the environmental disasters.

As the quality of the land diminished the decline of precontact features of Mohawk culture continued at an accelerated pace. Today, less than 10 percent of Mohawk children under the age of ten speak an Iroquois dialect. The number of Mohawks who participate in the functions of the traditional longhouse government is less than a thousand.[26] During this same period the number of entrepreneurial and working-class Mohawks has dramatically increased. This development all but overwhelmed the social, political, and economic life of the Akwesasne traditionals and led the council to take the unprecedented step of supporting police intervention on the reserve. The casinos were shut down, many of their operators were arrested, and the leader of the Warriors was convicted of conspiring to interfere with the ongoing police investigation. Nonetheless, the influence of the Mohawk Nation Council continues to wane, and high-stakes, for-profit gambling remains an important institution at Akwesasne.[27] Thus many Mohawks are seeking a new home elsewhere. Efforts are being made to secure land in the Mohawk River Valley, the traditional home of the Mohawk people. It is hoped that this place, to be known as Kanatsiohare, "the clean pot," will provide a haven for Mohawk families that wish to relearn and share traditional beliefs.[28]

The Mashantucket Pequot Have
Made Great Gains from Bingo

In the quiet, semirural town of Ledyard, Connecticut, the Mashantucket Pequot Tribe has enjoyed a completely different kind of experience with the high-stakes gambling industry. In the late 1960s, little development of any kind could be found on the tribe's rocky, tree-covered reservation. Two dozen people resided there and the tribal council was all but bankrupt. A great many other Pequots were scattered throughout the region. All, regardless of their residence, existed on the margins of southern New England society. That, however, was soon to change. By the late 1980s the Pequots had become one of the most dynamic and powerful communities in the region. Bingo profits led the way.

In the context of the last three hundred and fifty years of their history, contemporary Pequot resurgence is nothing short of miraculous. In the 1630s the Pequot Nation was brutally disbanded and outlawed by the General Court at Hartford. Led by Captain John Mason, colonial forces killed as many as seven hundred women, children, and men on a single dawn raid. The few hundred who did survive the war of 1637 were compelled to sign a treaty that declared them extinct as a people and forbade the use of their name forever.[29] Able-bodied men and women were sold into West Indian slavery; the rest were distributed among their Mohegan and Narragansett Indian neighbors or indentured to their English conquerors.[30]

Despite ongoing violence and oppression two independent bands of Pequots survived the war. One of these, the eastern, or, as they are now known, Paucatuck Pequots, continued to occupy their traditional territory on the eastern border of Connecticut. In 1667 the western, or Mashantucket Pequots, were granted three thousand acres in Ledyard. At the time, however, this group was residing at Noank on the coast. They refused to occupy the wooded and rocky inland tract and did not claim it as their home until 1712, the year the town of Groton passed a law allotting their Noank holdings to English colonists. Despite Pequot complaints the Connecticut General Assembly confirmed this ruling two years later, and the Ledyard Reservation, for better or worse, became the official home of the group.[31]

Since those times Mashantucket Pequot survival has adopted many forms. To supplement traditional occupations like hunting and fishing, Pequot men in the eighteenth and nineteenth centuries found employment off the reservation, working as domestic servants, field hands, militiamen, and whalers. The women often remained on or near the Ledyard tract protecting the tribe's territorial rights while raising families, tending crops, and weaving baskets for sale.[32] As the area grew up around them, however, state overseers became increasingly indifferent to their needs, and the life of this independent indigenous community continued to decline. The lack of suitable housing and economic resources caused a slow exodus of Mashantucket Pequots into the surrounding communities. By the 1940s only one family remained on the reservation. Yet, having come so close to being abandoned entirely, a Pequot presence in Ledyard was maintained by the tribe's elders, Elizabeth George Plouffe and Martha Langevin Ellal. Together they held the line on territorial encroachments through the late 1960s. Trespassers were driven off the reservation at gunpoint, and every effort was made to resist the implementation of state laws on Indian land. Despite the absence of public assistance, they managed to preserve the group's identity, land base, and meager economic resources.[33]

The re-emergence of the Pequots began in the late 1960s. Inspired by American Indian activism throughout the U.S., Connecticut Indians lobbied for changes in the state's Indian policy. The creation of a new Indian-staffed board to deal with Indian affairs in the state meant that, for the first time, indigenous peoples had a say in Connecticut's Indian policy.[34] During this same period the Mashantucket Pequots revamped their organizational structure. In 1974 they established a constitution and adopted their current, tribal form of government. A chairman, a vice-chairman, and three members now serve on the tribal council. In 1975 tribal members elected Richard Hayward chairman. Under his leadership a number of economic redevelopment projects were quickly undertaken. In the decade before the opening of the bingo hall the tribe produced maple syrup for sale, sold reservation timber, raised livestock, and established a sand and gravel pit. In the early eighties a hydroponic greenhouse was constructed to grow lettuce and other vegetables.[35]

None of these enterprises, however, generated enough income to sustain their own operation, much less a long-term tribal redevelopment effort. In each case the Pequots found themselves in competition with well-established non-Indian producers of the same products. Indigenous commodities, like hand-woven baskets and brooms, had disappeared generations before. In 1983, the same year that the Mohawk Bingo Palace was opened, the Pequot council's efforts received a tremendous boost. The Pequots had won federal recognition, and with it, federal dollars. The subsequent influx of these monies helped the tribe to improve its infrastructure, provide basic services for its members, and develop its organizational capability.

Federal recognition also gave the Pequots the legal footing they needed to develop a new "Indian" commodity: high-stakes bingo. Undoubtedly, the council's plans to establish a gambling operation caught state legislators and town residents by surprise. The Ledyard tract was generally thought to be a poor resource. Over the centuries small portions of it had been used for grazing and agriculture. The rest, composed of rocky, wooded hills and swamp, was considered unsuitable for development. What could the tribe do with this land that hadn't already been done? In this instance, however, the quality of the land was less important than its status under the law. Unaware of the opportunities that lay before the tribe, state legislators supported the council's bid for federal recognition.

The process of negotiation that culminated in federal recognition for the Mashantucket Pequot Indians had begun six years earlier when the tribal council sued Ledyard residents for the return of 800 acres of reservation lands ceded by the state in 1855.[36] This action placed a cloud on property titles, and town residents were unable to sell, develop, or subdivide their properties. At the same time, the Pequots negotiated a land claims settlement with Congress. They sought three things: the right to repurchase land ceded in 1855, a trust fund to accomplish the repurchases, and a federal relationship. In return the tribal council promised not to sue for anyone's private residence or compel anyone to sell their land. This arrangement was equitable to both the residents and the state. The state also saw an additional benefit in removing the land from state tax lists, a necessary consequence of federal recognition and land transfer. According to Congressman Sam Gejdenson, the state derived very little tax benefit from the acreage the Pequots sought to reclaim. He argued that the state could actually save money by deferring to the federal government its responsibility to the tribe.[37]

In retrospect, Gejdenson's opinion was uninformed, but not incorrect. Since the establishment of reservation bingo the state has gained millions of dollars in revenue from licensing fees and state payroll taxes. Nonetheless, the news that the Pequots were planning to establish a high-stakes gambling facility was not met with enthusiasm. In fact, the tribe's plans were delayed for three years by Connecticut's chief state attorney, Austin J. McGuigan, who threatened to prosecute the tribe if it proceeded with its plan. Consequently, bankers were hesitant to meet the council's 3.8-million-dollar loan request. In response, the Pequots entered a civil action against the state in federal court and, in 1986, won a favorable ruling.

On July 5, 1986, the bingo hall opened. With management support from the Penobscot Indians, who had been running their own high-stakes bingo operation since 1976, Pequot bingo opened its doors to the public. Enormously successful, its profits first complemented and, later, far outstripped federal and state grants. In its first full year of operation Pequot bingo netted over 2.6 million dollars in profit.[38] In 1989, in an effort to further capitalize on the economic opportunities presented to them, the council demanded that the state negotiate a compact for a tribally owned and operated casino. The state refused to negotiate and a second federal suit was initiated. Again, the ruling favored the Pequots.

Victory in both cases has brought radical change to southeastern Connecticut. In little more than a generation the Pequots have become one of the wealthiest communities in the Northeast. The reservation's population has increased eight-fold, its land base ten-fold. Quality housing is now available to a majority of the tribe's membership, and all enjoy use of its walk-in health-care center, child-development center, recreational facilities, and college scholarship fund. The tribe's casino and bingo complex creates more revenue than all but a handful of the state's most profitable corporations. Employing over 3,200 workers, it also has one of Connecticut's largest payrolls. Most recently, the tribe has begun construction on a second casino and hotel/entertainment complex. Complete with a shopping mall and entertainment center, these new facilities are expected to open in late 1994 and will become the most visible monuments to this extraordinary transformation.

Pequot re-emergence has come at a timely moment. Throughout the latter part of the twentieth century New London County has been supported by large defense contracts to Electric Boat, the designer and builder of the U.S. Navy's nuclear submarine fleet. The so-called peace dividend has meant greatly reduced federal expenditures on large weapon systems of all kinds, and E.B. layoffs threaten to increase dramatically the number of the region's unemployed. During this same period the Mashantucket Pequots have become New London County's second largest employer; casino work is replacing defense jobs. In the coming years the economic fortunes of the region will largely depend on the success of the tribe's many endeavors. Thus, where a few families had struggled to maintain themselves, a large and thriving community now dwells; in a region whose economy had begun to shrink, an Indian tribe has provided jobs for thousands of people.

Pequot Gambling Is an Example of Crossblood Adaptability

Not surprisingly, the Mashantucket Pequots have had a great deal more success than the Akwesasne Mohawks in appropriating the Euro-American gambling industry. The Pequots are a small community with a total membership of only about three hundred persons. Anti-gambling factions within the community are either nonexistent or too weak to affect the debate on Pequot gambling. Chosen by and responsible to the entire adult population of the tribe, the elected council manages the economic and political life of the whole community. Externally, it must contend with only three distinct agencies: the Town of Ledyard, the State of Connecticut, and the U.S. federal government. The advantages inherent in this organizational structure, however, are the by-products of a nearly genocidal assault against Pequot people and culture. This fact points to an important distinction between their world and that of the Mohawks.

At Akwesasne, many aspects of precontact Mohawk culture have survived into the twentieth century. The Mashantucket Pequots, on the other hand, have been compelled to restructure nearly every aspect of their traditional social and economic institutions. Decimated in the early seventeenth century, they have spent 350 years adjusting and readjusting to the systems imposed on them. In contrast, the Mohawks were largely independent until at least the 1780s. Moreover, unlike many tribes that live in remote and unpopulated regions of North America, the Ledyard Indians are situated within 100 miles of approximately 10 percent of the total population of the continental United States. Consequently, the Pequots have had more contact with non-Indians over a longer period of time than most indigenous North American communities.

These factors have contributed to a radical reconfiguration of the group's genetic structure. The Pequots are a tribe of mixed-bloods and are descended from Pequots, other northeastern Indians, African Americans, French Canadians, Irish, Scottish, and English peoples.[39] The bulk of this new blood is African American. As the Pequots reconstituted themselves from the triple demons of war, disease, and impoverishment, intermarriage with free blacks became a vital necessity. As long as the Pequots remained invisible, unrecognized, and powerless, it mattered little that they were "black Indians." Pequot anonymity, however, is a thing of the past. Contemporary Mashantucket Pequots are extremely visible, and, insofar as they are perceived as black people, they are also perceived as non-Indians. Many outsiders feel this lack of indigenous blood delegitimizes other tribal claims, including their right to own and operate a casino. This attitude is compounded by the fact that the Pequots pay no state or federal taxes on their enormous profits. As Jack Campisi has so pointedly remarked, "the only thing more despicable than a poor Indian is a rich Indian."[40] Yet, as a community of black Indians, the contemporary Pequots provide an example of how indigenous North American communities have continually transformed themselves. This phenomenon is largely unrecognized and little understood.

Euro-Americans have generally labeled Indians according to tribal blood quotas; in Euro-American discourse Indians are often referred to as full-bloods or mixed-bloods. Full-bloods are generally viewed as noble but vanishing, and mixed-bloods as irredeemably degenerate. In 1833 a local historian described the Mashantucket Pequots as vicious and ugly. This is owing, he claimed, to them being more mixed with "negroes" and whites.[41] These distinctions are also enforced by Native American groups themselves, particularly ones that have a stake in maintaining traditional clan structures. Yet such a classifying system, regardless of who advances it, rests on the assumption that something like a pure Indian exists from which degrees of Indianness can be measured. Moreover, the biological classification emphasizes genetically inherited qualities. In this paradigm indigenous peoples are denied the right to change and adapt to new conditions. It also limits the criteria for establishing tribal rolls.

Vizenor's term *crossblood* can provide an alternative approach to conceptualizing contemporary indigenous experience. According to Vizenor, crossbloods are "survivors" of "racialism, colonial duplicities, sentimental monogenism, and generic cultures."[42] This description emphasizes both the historical context within which contemporary tribal communities have emerged and the transformative powers of those communities. Outside of facile binary structures like savage and civilized, Indian and white, traditional and modern, full- and mixed-blood, crossbloods are the products and producers of an open-ended and ongoing negotiation. Within this cultural paradigm Vizenor's writing has explored the development of high-stakes reservation gambling.

In his 1991 novel *Heirs of Columbus*, Vizenor envisions a crossblood community with cultural and genetic ties to the archcolonialist himself, Christopher Columbus. Like many other contemporary tribal people these "heirs" have a bicultural inheritance. They also own and operate a high-stakes gambling facility named, appropriately enough, the Santa Maria Casino. A floating barge anchored near the international border, it may be understood as the appropriation of an expropriated people. Nearby, a full-scale replica of the *Nina* serves as a floating restaurant, and the *Pinta*, a tax-free market. As a whole, this simulated fleet serves as a metaphor for the contemporary crossblood experience. Vizenor's tribal community, legitimate heirs of European colonists as well as indigenous North Americans, has transformed European inventions and histories into tribal ventures and traditions. In this context, reservation gambling is the symbolic fruit of the ongoing Columbian exchange. Although Vizenor's novel presents an extremely optimistic view of imposed systems and technologies, it serves the need to expand the limits of self-definition and, hence, the limits of action and response available to contemporary indigenous people.

Vizenor's concept may inform our understanding of the Mashantucket Pequot Indians. Their selection of tribal members regardless of race or ethnicity may be regarded as one manifestation of a successful crossblood response to contemporary needs. The casino is another. Despite generations of intermarriage with the people of distant continents as well as the radical restructuring of their social, economic, and political institutions, the Mashantucket Pequots have maintained a governing structure that fosters consensus and a strong communal ethos based on ties of kinship. Like their seventeenth-century ancestors, the contemporary tribe is harvesting a crop that the environment readily offers, and each enterprise they pursue is informed by their sense of themselves as a distinct and sovereign people. Although high-stakes, Las Vegas-style gambling has only recently become a feature of their culture and traditions, contemporary Pequots have shown that it can be employed in ways that support their corporate claims, needs, and aspirations.

Such adaptive reconfigurations are often viewed with suspicion, and many Native American leaders are concerned that tribalism is being engaged merely to advance the gambling industry. Traditionalists I spoke with at Akwesasne suggested that a group without its native language, traditional culture system, or pre-Columbian genetic heritage is Indian in name only. A pro-gambling stance is further evidence of a basic lack of Indianness. The longhouse people have good reasons for holding these opinions. Painfully aware of the forces that can make bingo and gambling operations socially divisive, they are also deeply concerned about the steady decline of traditional Mohawk culture. If allowed to go unchecked, they believe the process of cultural annihilation will eventually claim the distinct character and traditions that have made the Mohawk Nation a recognized and sovereign entity.[43] In this context, Vizenor's thoughts are once again pertinent:

> Tribal sovereignty is inherent, an essential right that is limited but not given by the government. Congress, however, negotiated treaties with the tribes and has the absolute power to terminate reservations. That tension between the idea of limited sovereignty and assimilation could be resolved by congressional resolutions in favor of state governments. Casinos could be the last representation of tribal sovereignty; the winners could become the losers.[44]

The "casinoization" of American Indian reservations has precipitated debate on many levels, the most basic of which may involve the nature of Indianness itself. Since the advent of European contact the indigenous peoples of North America have been compelled to negotiate their identities with hostile colonists, federal commissions, and state governments. This negotiation has taken a heavy toll on both individuals and groups; nevertheless, by engaging dominant categories and structures (that is, Indianness, tribalism, and capitalism) their descendants have cultivated opportunities to reclaim a measure of their Native inheritance. In all cases, that inheritance is limited, mediated, and, as the events of Akwesasne have demonstrated, disputed within indigenous communities themselves. Furthermore, over three hundred distinct communities, each with its own history and traditions, are formally recognized as American Indian Tribes. Scores of other groups consider themselves to be independent nations, which in theory, if not in practice, are sovereign entities. In such a context, the imagined, debilitating, and effective definitions of *Indianness* will continue to be negotiated. Because of its enormous profit potential, reservation gambling has heightened the importance of the issue. As the events at Akwesasne and Mashantucket have illustrated, gambling has dramatically affected the Native American community. The question remains, Will gambling provide a means to support the independent life of an indigenous community or contribute to the erasure of its boundaries and the complete assimilation of its people?

Notes

1. See James D. Wherry, afterword, in *The Pequots in Southern New England: The Fall and Rise of an American Indian Nation*, ed. Laurence M. Hauptman and James D. Wherry (Norman, Okla., 1990), p. 218; and "Mashantucket Pequots Win!" *The Eagle*, May-June 1991, pp. 1, 22.

The success and proliferation of such tribally run operations has also threatened non-Indian casino owners. A recent suit filed by Donald Trump in federal court contends that the Indian Gaming Regulatory Act violates the sovereign right of states to "tax, regulate and police gambling activities conducted within their borders" (quoted in "Donald Trump Targets Indian Gaming Rights," *The Eagle* [early summer 1993], p. 7). Designed to protect Trump's own substantial casino market, this suit could force a restructuring of Indian gambling regulations.

2. See "F.B.I. Agents Raid Casinos on Five Indian Reservations," *New York Times*, May 13, 1992, p. A16; and "Three Tribes Allowed to Run Gaming Machines," *New York Times*, February 18, 1993, p. A15.

3. For a discussion of the important distinction between *tribe* and *nation*, see Ward Churchill, *Indians Are Us? Culture and Genocide in Native North America* (Monroe, Maine, 1994), pp. 291–357.

4. See Paul Lieberman, "Mafia Tied to Indian Gambling Takeover Bid," *Los Angeles Times*, January 1992, p. 5; rpt. *Akwesasne Notes* (midwinter 1992), p. 5.

5. See Gerald Vizenor, "Gambling on Sovereignty," *American Indian Quarterly* 16 (Summer 1992), pp. 411–13.

6. See Jim Roaix, "Games and Toys of the American Indian: Dice Games," *The Eagle*, May-June 1991, p. 20.

7. See Arthur C. Parker, *The Code of Handsome Lake, the Seneca Prophet*, in *Parker on the Iroquois*, ed. William N. Fenton (Syracuse, N.Y., 1974), p. 41 [hereafter *CHL*].

8. Trudie Lamb, "Games of Chance and Their Religious Significance among Native Americans," *Artifacts* 8 (Spring 1980), pp. 10–11.

9. This aspect of the peach stone game was explained to me by Mike McDonald, a lecturer/historian with the North American Indian Travelling College, Cornwall Island, Ontario.

10. Mourning Dove, *Mourning Dove: A Salishan Autobiography*, ed. Jay Miller (Lincoln, Nebr., 1990), pp. 102–03.

11. See Lewis Henry Morgan, *The League of the Iroquois* (1962; Secacus, N.J., 1972), p. 292.

12. Neal Salisbury, *Manitou and Providence: Indians, Europeans and the Making of New England, 1500–1643* (New York, 1982), p. 46.

13. Gerald Vizenor, *Crossbloods: Bone Courts, Bingo, and Other Reports* (1976; Minneapolis, 1990), p. xii.

14. Bruce E. Johansen, *Life and Death in Mohawk Country* (Golden, Colo., 1993), p. 115.

15. *CHL*, p. 18.

16. See Carl Sifakis, *Encyclopedia of Gambling* (New York, 1991), p. 56.

17. *CHL*, p. 38.

18. See Rick Hornung, *One Nation Under the Gun* (New York, 1991), pp. 17–19.

19. Ibid., p. 22.

20. Quoted in Johansen, *Life and Death in Mohawk Country*, p. 26.

21. See Hornung, *One Nation Under the Gun*, pp. 21–22.

22. See ibid., p. 18.

23. See ibid., p. 23.

24. See Peter Matthiessen, "Akwesasne," *Indian Country* (New York, 1984), pp. 127–64.

25. See United Nations Transnational Corporations and Management Division to the Working Group on Indigenous Populations, "Transnational Investments and Operations on the Lands of Indigenous Peoples," 1992, excerpted in *The Eagle*, early winter 1992, p. 3.

26. McDonald, conversation with author, June 21, 1992.

27. According to Joe Gray, public relations director of the Saint Regis tribal office, two bingo establishments are currently in operation at Akwesasne: Billy's Bingo Hall, owned and operated by the Saint Regis Tribal Office, and the Mohawk Bingo Palace, independently owned and operated.

28. See "Kanatsiohare: The Clean Pot," *Akwesasne Notes*, Fall 1992, p. 28.

29. See Barry O'Connell, introduction, in *On Our Own Ground: The Complete Writings of William Apess, a Pequot*, ed. Barry O'Connell (Amherst, Mass., 1992), pp. xxv.

30. See Jack Campisi, "The Emergence of the Mashantucket Pequot Tribe, 1637–1975," in *The Pequots in Southern New England*, p. 118.

31. See John W. De Forest, *History of the Indians of Connecticut from the Earliest Known Period to 1850* (Hamden, Conn., 1964), pp. 423–25.

32. See Campisi, "The Emergence of the Mashantucket Pequot Tribe, 1637–1975," pp. 127–28.

33. See ibid., pp. 137–38.

34. See Robert L. Bee, "Connecticut's Indian Policy: From Testy Arrogance to Benign Bemusement," in *The Pequots in Southern New England*, p. 198.

35. See Wherry, afterword, in *The Pequots in Southern New England*, pp. 215–18.

36. See Richard A. Hayward, "Mashantucket Pequot Tribunal Council: Prepared Statement," in House Committee on Interior and Insular Affairs, Settlement of Indian

Land Claims in the States of Commercial and Louisiana: Hearing on H.R. 5358 and H.R. 6612, 97th Cong., 2d sess., 1982, pp. 61–64.

37. See William H. Coldiron, statement, in House Committee on Interior and Insular Affairs, Settlement of Indian Land Claims in the States of Connecticut and Louisiana: Hearing on H.R. 5358 and H.R. 6612, p. 35.

38. See Wherry, afterword, in *The Pequots in Southern New England*, p. 219.

39. Charlene Prince, tribal librarian, Mashantucket Pequot tribe, conversation with author.

40. Campisi, "Mashantucket Pequot" (paper presented at the second Mashantucket Pequot history conference, Mystic, Conn., October 22, 1993).

41. See William T. Williams, introduction, in Lion Gardener, "Lion Gardener: His Relation of the Pequot Warres," *Collections of the Massachusetts Historical Society*, vol. 3, 3d ser. (Cambridge, Mass., 1833), p. 134.

42. Vizenor, *Crossbloods*, p. vii.

43. McDonald, conversation with author.

44. Vizenor, "Gambling on Sovereignty," pp. 412–13.

22. Gambling Is a Threat to Native American Culture

David Segal

Washington journalist David Segal expresses deep concerns over the consequences of Indian gaming, especially for Native Americans. While noting that dozens of tribes have turned to gaming to generate revenue for education, housing, and other positive ends and some have achieved some success, he submits that many tribes have run into unintended consequences. "Wherever it's been tried, gambling has been accompanied by a dramatic increase in violent and property crimes, alcoholism, and drug abuse." Yet many Indians, according to Segal, are hesitant to criticize gaming because there appear to be few other economic opportunities, especially since the eighties, when there were budget cuts for Indian assistance.

The dangers and adverse unintended consequences of gaming are often overlooked, he submits, because many people, both Indians and non-Indians, want gaming to work. Yet Segal believes that infiltration from organized crime is a serious danger, given that banks are reluctant to give loans to Indians, whose land cannot legally be foreclosed. He asserts that as Indians are tempted to look elsewhere than banks for start-up capital, they can find themselves, at times unwittingly, receiving financial backing from organized crime.

Although Segal does not want Indian gaming banned, he does think that the federal government, as through the National Indian Gaming Commission, should take a more active role in providing technical assistance and useful information for Indians and in protecting them from dishonest predators.

"Dances with Sharks: Why the Indian Gaming Experiment's Gone Bust," in *The Washington Monthly* (March 1992), pp. 26–30. Used by permission.

Plastic garbage bags stand in as roofs; faucets along a dirt road serve as showers. A 12-year-old might call this a scout camp, but the Kickapoo tribe of Eagle Bend, Texas, calls it a nation—and it's clearly a nation in trouble. A quarter of the population is unemployed, more than half is illiterate, and much to the embarrassment of tribal leaders, the signal crop in the community vegetable garden is marijuana.

By the looks of it, the Kickapoo reservation needs several basic things, including electricity, plumbing, and a school. But it *wants* only one thing: bingo, and step on it. "We're desperate for the money," says Julio Frausto, a tribal leader. And the Kickapoos are not the only ones. In the four years since Congress passed the Indian Gaming Act, which guaranteed the tribes the right to run gambling enterprises on their reservations, more than a hundred tribes from North Dakota to Florida have gotten into the act, eager to translate blackjack and bingo into better education and opportunity.

But while the Kickapoo look to Las Vegas for inspiration, they might be wiser to first glance a few hundred miles north, to Miami, Oklahoma.

When the leaders of the Seneca-Cayugas there hired Wayne Newton Enterprises to run their high-stakes bingo parlor in October 1990, they thought their troubles were behind them. The parlor had been shut down for several months after the tribe terminated its contract with a British management company that failed to turn a profit after running the hall for a year. But now they had a real Las Vegas concern working for them, and Wayne himself—half American Indian—came to the grand opening to give away the evening's big prizes. Sure, the tribe was asked to throw in $224,000 to help restart the operation—over and above the $300,000 it had already spent to build the hall—but Wayne was going to ante up $125,000, he was sending his best people, and anyway, business during November was good. No worries.

By December, worries. On most nights the huge hall, with its mirrored ceilings and pastel interior, was packed with 1,400 players. But profits were nowhere to be found. Neither, for that matter, was Wayne's $125,000. In December 1991, Newton Enterprises' own ledger sheets reported a gross of $12.5 million for the year, improbably offset by enough expenses to leave a debt of $360,000, which the company asked the tribe to cover. For the whole year the Seneca-Cayugas received $13,000—barely a seventh of the salary of Newton Enterprises' on-site manager. The final outrage came in December, when two jackpot winners were unable to get their checks cashed at the bank. The tribe retaliated by surrounding the bingo hall with pick-up trucks while Newton's security forces barricaded themselves inside. After a tense five-day standoff, a federal judge ruled that the hall was to be returned to the tribe. The question of who will pay the hall's debt is now headed for arbitration.

Although tribes have always kept criminal and financial data to themselves, and while the government seems equally disinclined to discuss the subject of troubles in Indian gaming, there's a growing body of evidence that what happened to the Senecas is not unusual. Since high-stakes, Indian-owned bingo parlors made their first appearance in the late seventies, tribes with gaming operations have been beset by difficulties ranging from graft to fratricide. What Congress envisioned as a fast track out of poverty and unemployment for American Indians has evolved into a billion-dollar-a-year industry that has added precious little to social services on reservations throughout the country.

"If we get the money from bingo, we're going to set up a vocational training program," says Kickapoo administrator Frausto. "Even if the kids don't go to college, they'll have a trade." Perhaps. But they may also get more than they bargained for. In one extreme instance, the Mohawks of upstate New York split into pro- and anti-gambling factions and commenced a brief civil war because profits from their seven on-reservation halls were going exclusively to hall owners and their non-Indian management team. Two tribe members were left dead.

While it's easy—and partially correct—to blame American Indians for the unfolding gambling fiasco, the real culprit may be bureaucrats in Washington, D.C. After all, Indian gaming is an experiment that might convince even Milton Friedman that government regulation is in order: inexperienced, financially desperate Indians entering a slick and crime-infested business. But the Indians don't want help, and the commission the government created to regulate Indian gambling, the National Indian Gaming Commission (NIGC), is equally disinclined to provide it, preaching laissez-faire as tribe after tribe gets taken. The shame is that a few tribal success stories suggest that, if properly run and carefully regulated, Indian gambling can pay off as promised—in housing and modern plumbing, scholarships and jobs. Instead, as the Kickapoos break in the tables without expertise or government assistance, the deck has quietly been stacked against them.

Gambling Brings Crime, Alcoholism, and Drug Abuse

To anyone familiar with the effects gambling has had on other communities that have legalized it, the Indians' venture into gaming may sound less like a shortcut to prosperity than a quick way to finish off tribal life once and for all. Wherever it's been tried, gambling has been accompanied by a dramatic increase in violent and property crimes, alcoholism, and drug abuse. Yet there is surprisingly little breast-beating on the reservations about how gambling could destroy what is left of Indian culture. (Could names like "Stands With 17" be far behind?) One reason is that Indians are a little more modern than we think. Another is that, after a decade of penetrating budget cuts, they have few other options.

Indian gaming took hold in the eighties, as most everything else on the reservation was withering away. While funds for education decreased only slightly in the Reagan-Bush era, other aid programs plunged. In 1980, the National Health Service Corps sent 155 physicians to reservations; a decade later it was sending seven. Housing and Urban Development, which had authorized 6,000 new units of Indian housing during Carter's last year as president, was building only 1,500 new units by 1988. The Economic Development Administration, which had funded bricks-and-mortar projects, was slashed to near extinction, while the Community Services Administration, which granted money for development projects, was wiped out altogether.

"The Reagan cuts devastated tribes," says Frank Ducheneaux, who served as counsel on Indian Affairs for the House Committee on Interior and Insular Affairs during this period. "Since most have high rates of unemployment and poverty and rely heavily on the government for social services, Indians had to find alternative sources of funding." And as the need for alternative funding became evident, the legal grounds for gaming were being won.

The first test came in Florida back in 1979, after the Miami Seminoles defied a state law prohibiting bingo prizes of more than $100 and began offering $10,000 jackpots in a 1,200-seat hall. The state sued, but in 1982 a federal appeals court ruled that since the Seminoles were a sovereign nation, state civil regulations did not apply to them. Tribes nationwide took note, and within five years, 113 bingo operations around the country were grossing $225 million annually. Legal challenges from states abounded, but in 1987 the Supreme Court decided that Indians could operate any form of gambling already permitted by the state—and could do so with their own regulations. In the 14 states that allowed groups to run highly restricted "Las Vegas nights" for charity, the door was opened for Indians to start up full-blown casinos.

A year later, Congress bestowed its approval with the Indian Gaming Act, which advocated gambling as "a means of promoting tribal economic development, self-sufficiency, and strong tribal governments." Yet Congress wasn't altogether sanguine about gaming—nor should it have been, considering the then-vivid example of Atlantic City, where the felony crime rate skyrocketed in the first few years of legalized gambling. (Las Vegas was steadier, ranking either first, second, third, or fourth in per capita felonies in the country's metropolitan areas between 1960 and 1984.) Nevertheless, Congress agreed that the Indians had both the legal right to establish gaming parlors and little prospect of raising badly needed money from other sources. So to shield Indians "from organized crime and other corrupting influences" and ensure that "the Indian tribe is the primary beneficiary of the gaming operation," it devised a complicated system of regulation. Yet to date, no government or private agency has examined the successes or failures of Indian gaming—Congress didn't apparently have much of a plan for overseeing how its well-intentioned rules would work. According to the FBI, troubles began almost as soon as the gaming did—and those troubles have included organized crime.

Reservations Are Vulnerable to Mafia Infiltration

When Stewart Siegel, a dealer and manager at casinos from Las Vegas to the Caribbean, was hired to run the Barona reservation's bingo hall in San Diego, he brought a pro's touch to the reservation's games: Grand prizes like cars and $60,000 in cash were regularly won by planted shills, who then gave the money back to Siegel. After pleading guilty in 1986 to four counts of grand theft, including bilking the tribe of $600,000 a year, he joined the witness protection program and started talking. Testifying before the Senate Select Committee on Indian Affairs with a hood over his head, he claimed that he knew of at least 12 halls that were controlled by the Cosa Nostra but guessed that nearly half of all Indian casinos were tainted by it, either directly through management and investors or indirectly through suppliers.

The allegation is hardly far-fetched, given the economics of starting up a gaming hall. Indians are especially vulnerable to mafia infiltration because few banks make loans to tribes: their land, which is sovereign, cannot be foreclosed. So when tribes look elsewhere for start-up money, well- and not-so-well concealed mafiosi are often their most willing backers. According to the FBI, the trendsetting Seminoles unwittingly hired the mob when they opened their hall in 1979. (The FBI routed them out.) Two years later, the Cabazons, a tiny tribe in Riverside County, California, retained Rocco Zangari, a member of a Southern California organized crime family, to run their card room. When tribal vice-chairman Alvin Alvarez accused the management of skimming profits, he was forced out of office. Months later, he and two other critics were found shot to death. The case has yet to be solved.

Disorganized crime may be just as threatening. Under the most common contracts that tribes negotiate with management companies, the

Indians are promised 60 percent of "profits after expenses," a clause that often means the tribe gets nothing. Examples of management companies cooking the books are legion. On the Mohawk reservation where the intratribal gambling war broke out, non-Indian investor Emmet Munley was found by his Indian business partner to have deducted $186,000 in traveling expenses and $120,000 in accounting fees. At the Seneca-Cayuga hall, Wayne Newton Enterprises was clearing $20,000 to $30,000 a month, according to Don Deal, who used to work for the company and saw the accounting sheets, while the tribe earned next to nothing. The Winnebagos of Wisconsin got a Halloween party and a back-taxes bill from the IRS for $800,000 but have yet to get any profits from their management company, the Genna Corporation.

Even worse, gambling has cut off the little federal support the Winnebagos had before gaming, says tribal chairwoman Jo Ann Jones. Allegations that the Genna Corporation has bought off half of the Winnebagos' tribal council in lieu of sharing the profits has so riven the tribe that members have been unable to meet and approve applications for government programs. Since June 1, 1990, all their federal grants for housing, education, and other social services have ceased.

So are the Genna Corporation and those other management companies corrupt? No one—neither the tribes nor the government—has taken the trouble to find out. While in Nevada and New Jersey the mere scent of ill repute will get one barred from even the lower echelons of casino management, aspiring Indian casino managers are currently disqualified only if the FBI—which runs fingerprint checks on request—discovers a felony conviction. The NIGC is supposed to be doing more sophisticated background checks, sniffing out the mafia and making sure tribes are getting a fair count from their management companies. But the commission is clearly not doing enough homework. Wayne Newton Enterprises' only other experience in Indian gaming, with the Santa Ynez of California, ended in bankruptcy. Emmet Munley was unable to get a gambling license through the Nevada Gaming Control Board on two occasions because he associated "with persons of questionable and unsavory character." (The NIGC's colleague, the Bureau of Indian Affairs [BIA], which must approve any contract between a management company and a tribe, has also been less than vigilant in sifting out undesirables. Indeed, it was a BIA agent, Thomas Burden, who originally recommended Emmet Munley when the Mohawks were searching for investors.)

What has the NIGC been doing since it was written into existence in 1988? Mostly finding office space; it wasn't until February 1991 that it settled on permanent quarters, and even then it needed an additional eight months to publish its first set of regulations. It has yet to hire field operatives and has no legal apparatus to make and enforce its decisions. The man Bush appointed to run the commission, Tony Hope (adopted son of entertainer Bob Hope), plans to have the commission up and running by this spring. In the meantime, most Indian casinos proliferate and run in a regulatory vacuum. "When we started having problems with our management company," says the Winnebagos' Jo Ann Jones, "we didn't even think of calling [the NIGC]."

Slow motion is a standard feature of federal bureaucracies, but the commission has also been hindered by the combined resistance of Indian leaders—many of whom see the commission as patronizing and unnecessary—and the states, which have their own interest in making sure the halls are functioning responsibly. Adjudicating between two sovereign entities makes painstaking debate on the commission's every move inevitable. A set of revised regulations on what types of electronic machines will be allowed in bingo halls was heatedly debated for months in hearings in five cities across the country.

Even after it publishes all its regulations, the commission will probably remain ineffective. For one, it is woefully underfunded. Today the New Jersey Casino Control Commission employs 400 people and spends $23 million per year to keep an eye on Atlantic City's 12 casinos. The Indian Gaming Commission will hire 25 people and spend $3 million per year to oversee more than 150 halls. And what the NIGC lacks in financial way, it won't be making up with regulatory will. Hope intends to preside over a relatively hands-off commission. "There will be no micromanagement from D.C.," he insists.

The style is the legacy of a Republican policy, initiated by Nixon in

1970 and expanded upon by Reagan and Bush, to encourage Indian self-determination by allowing tribes to make their own decisions wherever possible. When James Watt headed the Department of the Interior, he instructed BIA to review contracts between Indians and bingo hall managers only when tribes requested it, even though long-standing law requires that all such contracts get BIA approval. The NIGC is headed for a similarly minimalist approach in its role as watchdog.

That the growth of Indian gaming coincides with this new governmental disinterest is a historical accident and not a very fortunate one. Washington's libertarian impulses may arguably be long overdue in other realms of Indian life, but they are misplaced in gambling, an industry that constantly tempts those involved with large sums of immediately available cash and easily fudged ledgers. What is true for the owners and managers of casinos in Atlantic City and Las Vegas is true for the Indians: Without strong, vigilant, and impartial oversight, they are easy marks for the mob and all types of hustlers.

Tribes Collaborate with Gambling Entrepreneurs

The most recent opportunists have been Nevada entrepreneurs. The legitimate gambling industry, after years of casting an alarmed and disapproving eye on its down-market competitors and pressing Congress to legislate the Indians out of its domain, appears ready to adopt an if-you-can't-beat-'em-join-'em strategy. The first proposal was perhaps the most audacious. It came from Harvey's Wagon Wheel Inc., a Lake Tahoe resort hotel and casino that caters to 2.5 million visitors annually.

Harvey's and the Santee Sioux, a small and impoverished tribe in northeast Nebraska, hatched a plan to petition the federal government to take into trust three acres of land in Council Bluffs, Iowa, a small town just across the river from the 600,000 residents of Omaha. When the petition is approved by the BIA, the land will become sovereign territory, allowing the Indians to permit Harvey's to build a casino on it. Then Harvey's will buy 47 surrounding acres to build a $67 million hotel and convention center, cutting the Indians in on the action once the dollars roll in.

Sound dubious? Not to the tiny Kickapoo nation of Horton, Kansas, which is currently negotiating a similar deal with the massive Mirage Hotel and Casino. Since the Las Vegas-based company approached tribal leaders back in August 1991, the project has gotten a lot of popular support (the governor included) and made the tribe of barely 1,500 members some new friends. "We used to be 'those Indians,'" says Verna Finch, the tribal vice-chair. "People would not even use our name. Now we have a lot of folks acting like they've always been our buddies."

The Mirage deal is clearly good for the Kickapoo leaders' egos. Less clear is whether it is good for the Kickapoo rank and file, who suffer from a 60 percent unemployment rate. Although the nearby town of Hiawatha has offered to donate 70 acres of land within the tribe's ancestral boundaries to build the casino locally, the Mirage has made it clear that it's no dice unless the land is near Kansas City, an hour and a half away.

Because many Indians currently rely on far-flung, low-paying migrant work to survive, the promise of jobs is often a major incentive to tribes considering gaming. But these Vegas-scale operations will not ease unemployment. They need to be located near or within easy access of major population centers; most reservations, however, are in the hinterlands.

Some Tribes Benefit from Gambling

The jobs issue is even more important than it first appears because it is most often those halls and casinos employing and involving tribe members that succeed. While the Winnebagos went broke and the Mohawks turned to gunplay in squabbles over outside control, several tribes have been quietly fulfilling the gaming act's promise of more jobs and social services by operating their own shops.

Before the Mille Lacs Chippewas of Minnesota opened their Grand Casino in April 1990, 60 percent of their families lived below the poverty line; 45 percent were unemployed. By December, only a handful lived in poverty, virtually none were unemployed (most had gotten jobs in the casino), and the tribe had become the county's biggest employer. A modern sewer system, school improvements, and a health clinic are on the way.

The Oneidas, also from Minnesota, watched their unemployment rate fall from 40 percent in 1976 to 17 percent in 1991, thanks to their gaming facility—which is run with no outside management help. "I can't imagine why so many tribes are willing to give away 40 percent," says Bobby Webster, part of the tribal management team. With proceeds from their bingo hall, they have built a $10.5 million hotel and convention center and an environmental testing lab that has won state and federal contracts. They've subsidized their own Head Start program and built their own K-8 grade school. A high school is now in the works. While most reservations have been losing members, the Oneidas have seen their numbers swell by a third in the past 15 years.

The NIGC Should Be More Active

Still, even when it works this well, gambling is no panacea for deep social ills that could be billions of dollars and decades away from a cure. Even among the Oneidas unemployment is still high, and drug and alcohol problems persist. But if a few tribes can make a little progress through gaming, perhaps more can. And in the absence of other sources of funding, it means a few more Indian kids educated and employed and fewer houses with trash-bag roofs.

Yet in their current hands-off mode, the NIGC and the legislators who created it are repeating the mistakes of previous would-be benefactors who threw plots of land, and then money, at tribes. By their passivity, they're effectively ensuring that good programs are flukes, not formulas—and that beggared but eager tribes like Eagle Bend's Kickapoos will be playing against the odds.

Keeping decent information about what works and what doesn't, and then providing technical assistance for start-ups, should be the minimal role of the slumbering NIGC. But it's not enough. While some Indians might paint any oversight effort as an infringement on their rights of sovereignty, this is the wrong moment for the government to be daunted by that charge. After a green light from the federal courts, program-slashing by successive administrations, and a reluctant thumbs-up from Congress, the government now has an obligation to tribes to make sure that gaming is run legally and in the interests of the people it was intended to help—in short, that gambling is the "means of promoting tribal economic development, self-sufficiency, and strong tribal governments" Congress declared it would be in the eighties. The last thing the Kicka-poos need, after all, is another broken promise.

VIII

BEYOND
THE SOUND
AND THE
FURY

INTRODUCTION TO PART VIII

We end this anthology with a piece taken from the first comprehensive study of commercial gambling since the legalization of Atlantic City Gaming and the rapid growth of state lotteries. The authors explain how discussions of gambling are often biased by the assumption that gambling plays a more important role in the ordinary person's life than it does. Although legal gambling opportunities have grown greatly in the last few decades, most Americans who gamble, according to the authors, are not obsessed with gambling. Nonetheless, even if there were no reckless gamblers, commercial gambling would still raise important questions because of its far-reaching consequences for American society.

Before creating gambling policy, we need, according to the authors, to understand gambling within a large social and historical context. Write the authors:

> If society is to avoid a disaster gambling must first be seen
> clearly, without bias or prejudice, for what it is: conventional
> behavior practiced by most Americans. Next must come a
> perspective that differentiates among gambling games within
> the general context of leisure and play. Finally gambling games
> and behavior must be located within historical processes that
> are transforming many areas of American life.

23. Misconceptions Abound in the Debate over Legalized Gambling

Vicki Abt, James F. Smith, Eugene Martin Christiansen

Vicki Abt, professor of sociology at Pennsylvania State University, James F. Smith, professor of English also at Penn State, and Eugene Martin Christiansen, Special Assistant to the New York City Off-Track Betting Corporation, all believe that most discussions of American gambling oversimplify their subject.

They assert that it is difficult for people to discuss gambling dispassionately, since many people most vocal about gambling either equate it with sin or view all gamblers as actually or potentially pathological. According to the authors, gambling, like other activities, can be engaged in with varying degrees of responsibility. Millions enjoy it in moderation while a small percentage of gamblers are irresponsible. Assert the authors:

> Both drunks and the temperance movement need alcohol to function; for the rest of us a drink is optional, something we can take or leave alone. Betting serves a similar diversity of purpose: its abuse by a minority has provided steady employment for reformers ever since Adam and Eve.

The authors argue that it is difficult to think objectively about gambling also because many people have a financial interest served by viewing it as harmful or harmless.

Excerpted from *The Business of Risk: Commercial Gambling in Mainstream America* (Lawrence, Kansas: University Press of Kansas, 1985). Used by permission.

Secular critics of gambling involved in the treatment of "junkie" gamblers are sometimes themselves reformed compulsive gamblers, and are in any case professionally exposed only to the most harmful effects of commercial gambling. The gambling industry and, perhaps more seriously, a growing number of state and local governments have large vested interests in further legalization. Neither operators nor their critics are disposed to an objective view of gambling.

They further argue that gambling policy must be based on sound sociological research to avoid all-too-common biases. Not all gamblers are alike. Nor are all forms of gambling. Gambling has evolved from largely clandestine activities to businesses run by public corporations and even governments. To understand gambling we must, according to them, see it within a large social and historical context.

The fact that we conclude with this stand-alone piece should definitely not be taken to suggest that we endorse its arguments. We hope that it will stimulate disagreement and new insights. It is not the final word.

Gambling is a universal cultural phenomenon: one of a relatively small number of activities that occur in nearly all societies and every period. People have been playing risky games for at least 4,000 years, and virtually every culture has evolved ways of letting its members stake something of value on an event of uncertain outcome. Gambling might be said to have had a determining role in the antecedents of American society: the Old Testament God created man with a natural propensity to bet, and the Biblical account of the genesis of Western civilization begins with Adam and Eve wagering a stake, their innocence, in the hope of adding knowledge to that stake. The theology is obscure: like gambling since, the social value and moral consequences of Adam and Eve's wager are matters of debate. To many, man's fall from grace and subsequent history are proof it was immoral, or a sucker bet, the first step down the road to ruin that is the anti-gambling reformers' contribution to cartography. To others, the wager was an act of self-actualization: with knowledge Adam and Eve acquired humanity, and from the human interdependence created by the loss of Paradise society began.

This metaphor illustrates the human experience with gambling: thousands of years later mainstream America is still playing the game, but both the stakes and the social significance of the activity have changed. A lot of modern gambling is no longer play. Fairly late in the history separating the Devil's Tree of Knowledge from the neighborhood lottery agent gambling was commercialized. Today it is a business: the business of risk. It is a big business, $163 billion in gross wagering in 1983, with gross revenues (or losses) amounting to roughly 10 percent of that figure, or about $16.8 billion. And for the most part the business of risk is legal. Illegal wagering—mostly on the old American games of bookmaking and numbers—totaled some $28.9 billion, with gross revenues of about $5 billion, giving the Mob only about a 17 percent share of the market. This intelligence will be disturbing to much of the law enforcement establishment, which has made a practice of justifying part of its taxpayer-funded budgets with the specter of fantastic Mafia earnings from illegal numbers and sports betting. The truth will also be disappointing to the media and to a lot of ordinary people who may never make a bet but enjoy reading lurid tales about violent men with guns catering to America's appetite for cards and dice and horses. Organized crime's participation in the business of risk is a fact, but *Godfather*-like stories obscure the historic changes now transforming gambling in America. The characteristics of gambling games and how they influence (and are influenced by) players and society in general are fundamentally more important than the legal status of the supplier. The real story is the expansion of commercial gambling in the last twenty years and the concentration of this business into increasingly powerful corporate and governmental operations. Because of these events American life may never be quite the same again.

Paradoxically, the knowledge for which Paradise was lost has notably scanted the game at which it was won. Fear and fascination—the knee-jerk reactions when the subject of gambling is raised—are poor substitutes for understanding. Gambling is not some mysterious monolith. There are subtle but significant distinctions among commercial gambling games. Similarly, gamblers are not all the same. Their motivations, their play, and the outcomes of their gambling vary according to the individual and the surrounding, or containing, culture.

This blind determination to keep gambling games and behaviors beyond the pale of "normal" life has made it impossible to see the true relationship of the business of risk to the state and to society. In large measure this is because the focus has been on the wrong things. Earlier studies tended to deal with gambling in monolithic terms and to consider all gamblers as if they were already—or had the potential to become—pathological gamblers. These two ideas inform most of the enormous popular and professional literature on the subject. Unfortunately, these concepts have served only to divert attention from more substantial issues and keep our knowledge of gambling behavior and the business of risk at rudimentary levels. . . .

Most Writing on Gambling Is Dogmatic and Unhelpful

Gambling is an enduring controversy. Despite the fact that it is something most people do, Americans have a great deal of difficulty in talking about it, or writing about it, dispassionately. Although the literature is enormous most of it consists of superficial romanticizing or moral preaching or hysterical anti-gambling tracts.[1] Histories of the subject acquire lurid titles with a remarkable consistency: *Fools of Fortune*, *Sucker's Progress*, *Play the Devil*.[2] Even serious discussions of the psychology of gambling usually fail to consider gambling's relationship to specific situations and the historical context that give meaning to the activity. Psychologists' concern with individual behavior causes most studies of the psychology of gambling to focus narrowly on individual actions and decisionmaking processes rather than the larger issues these behaviors raise.[3] Popular as well as professional writing about gambling generally reads like the result of a particularly long and difficult psychoanalysis: as if the collective American psyche, unable to deal rationally with the gambling proclivities of its id, has discharged the resulting psychological tensions in a marathon emotional writing jag. The product of this binge (which shows no sign of abating) is a fog of verbiage, a wordy miasma of

misconceptions, stereotypes, loaded buzzwords, and simple misinformation through which the reality of gambling situations and gambling
behavior has been almost wholly obscured. The rapid expansion of legal
commercial gambling following the institution of a State lottery by New
Hampshire in 1964 has intensified and further polarized the gambling
debate, which is increasingly taking on the rigid characteristics of ideological polemic. As a preliminary to a more reasoned and less emotional
perspective on gambling it may be useful to review the main points of this
controversy.

On one side, legal commercial gambling is condemned by religious
leaders who have historically equated all gambling with sin, and by secular
critics, including psychiatrists professionally concerned with the treatment
of "sick" or compulsive gamblers, moral reformers, and some elected
officials, notably a succession of congressional and senatorial committees
that in the last thirty years have established as doctrine the belief of many
law enforcement professionals that illegal gambling bankrolls organized
crime and is linked to various kinds of corruption.[4] Both secular and
clerical critics tend to argue their views with an emotional fervor that
recalls nineteenth-century revivalist preaching: they perceive a devil at
large in the land, in the form of organized, concerted, and well-financed
gambling industries, to which, in opposition, "there has developed in the
United States and Europe a compulsive [sic] gambling movement. It is a
moral crusade similar in theory and practice to the moral crusade that was
organized for the passage of the Volstead Act in 1919."[5] This call to
arms—not, as one might suppose, from a cleric but from a professor of
sociology—against the dangerous permissiveness of allowing people to
gamble as they chose has been sounded regularly over the centuries, and
not just by Americans; sermons on the evils of gambling are staples of the
literature. Here is a seventeenth-century English writer:

> Gaming is an enchanting witchery, gotten betwixt idleness and avarice: an
> itching disease, that makes some scratch the head, whilst others, as if they
> were bitten by a Tarantula, are laughing themselves to death: or lastly, it is
> a paralytical distemper, which seizing the arm that man cannot chuse but
> shake his elbow . . . it renders a man incapable of prosecuting any serious

action, and makes him always unsatisfied with his own condition . . . till he has lost sight of both sense and reason.[6]

Such statements reflect enduring attitudes in what might be called the moral economy of vice. Both drunks and the temperance movement need alcohol to function; for the rest of us a drink is optional, something we can take or leave alone. Betting serves a similar diversity of purpose: its abuse by a minority has provided steady employment for reformers ever since Adam and Eve.

On the other side of the gambling debate are those who believe that, in the words of the Federal Gambling Commission, "gambling is inevitable."[7] A variety of vested interests argue the positive values of commercial gambling and gambling behavior. These proponents include an increasing number of legitimate, publicly held corporations,[8] the significant fraction of American agribusiness engaged in horse breeding, and numerous State, county, and municipal governments that depend in part on gambling revenues. Even some professionals in the social sciences, attempting to be objective, go so far as to argue that gambling is no different from any other form of play or social game behavior. These social scientists apply value-free theories of decisionmaking and rational calculation developed by economists and psychologists to horse-race betting and casino gambling.[9]

Caught between these two opposing forces is the American public, along with the police and the courts. In an era of unprecedented violent crime we are reluctant to assign high priority to the enforcement of anti-gambling laws that at best proscribe activities which may be legal in neighboring jurisdictions and are in any case directed at victimless, and very popular, crimes. Sustained opposition to gambling itself has lacked broad public support,[10] and people often condone the lax enforcement of anti-gambling laws, an attitude reflected in a 1982 Gallup Poll showing that 80 percent of those surveyed favored at least some legal opportunities to gamble.

For all the vehemence with which it is being conducted, the public debate over gambling has remained for the most part remarkably uninformed. Both sides vastly oversimplify the complexities of gambling behavior and the operations of modern commercial gambling. Secular critics of gambling involved in the treatment of "junkie" gamblers are sometimes themselves reformed compulsive gamblers, and are in any case professionally exposed only to the most harmful effects of commercial gambling. The gambling industry and, perhaps more seriously, a growing number of State and local governments have large vested interests in further legalization. Neither operators nor their critics are disposed to an objective view of gambling. Both sides have failed to develop a perspective permitting a reasoned analysis of the interrelationships among gambling games, situations, structures, and participants. This failure would be of purely academic interest were it not for the fact that this debate is not confined to an ivory tower. In large measure, it has determined the country's gambling policies and laws.

The reception of English law into American judicial processes by separate acts of the original thirteen States between 1776 and 1784 had the practical effect of making gambling statutes enacted by Parliament prior to Independence the basis for American gambling law. This law was then applied to American circumstances in American courts by American judges who for the most part reflected basically Puritan views towards gambling. Overwhelmingly, their opinions articulated an anti-gambling rationale, and so an anti-gambling bias was introduced into the American legal system.[11] Gambling has generally remained a matter of State jurisdiction, and in spite of sporadic relaxations anti-gambling law and enforcement grew progressively more rigorous, until by 1900 gambling prohibitions were firmly embedded in State constitutions and statute law.

Gambling Is Big Business

This complex legal edifice contained a serious structural defect: the American propensity to gamble. Puritan and clerical prejudice had succeeded in making gambling illegal but failed to alter American gambling behavior. From colonial times the statutory treatment of gambling had been marked by ambivalence: legal proscriptions alternated with gambling authorizations, usually for specific games and purposes. Economically weakened by the mercantilistic policies of England and lacking adequate systems of banking and taxation the colonies turned to lotteries as a method of public and private finance.[12] Public works of all kinds—highways, bridges, dams, fortifications, sewers and so forth—as well as schools, colleges, hospitals, and even churches were all funded by channeling the American demand for opportunities to bet through lotteries. This method of public finance was continued by the States following 1776 in the form of State-franchised private lottery companies, and their success in generating revenues is convincing evidence that gambling, at least at lotteries, enjoyed a considerable measure of social approval regardless of its legal status. As the nineteenth century progressed horse-race betting in the East and casino gaming at eastern spas and along the frontier became firmly established even while gambling proscriptions were being tightened, and, with the turn of the century, Americans' irrepressible propensity to gamble began to erode the States' gambling prohibitions. In 1931 Nevada legalized casino gaming along with most other forms of gambling,[13] and during the next decade pari-mutuel racing was legalized along the eastern seaboard and in parts of the Middle West. For a generation following World War II legal commercial gambling was confined to racetracks and Nevada casinos, but in 1964, with the start of the first State lottery in New Hampshire, a second wave of legalizations began that shows no sign of abating.[14] In the next twenty years twenty-two jurisdictions authorized lotteries; New York and Connecticut authorized government-operated off-track betting (OTB); pari-mutuel *jai-alai* spread from Florida to Connecticut, Rhode Island, and Nevada; and New Jersey legalized casino gambling in Atlantic City.

Today American commercial gambling is an industry of enormous dimensions. Thirty-six States allow some form of pari-mutuel betting; twenty-one States and the District of Columbia have authorized State-operated lotteries, of which eighteen are currently operating and four are in various stages of implementation; eight States allow card rooms; two States allow casino gambling; and one State (Nevada) allows bookmaking on team sports such as National Football League (NFL) games. Approximately 80 percent of the population has ready access to some form of legal commercial gambling. In 1983 Americans lost some $11.8 billion to legal gambling businesses. Another $5 billion was lost to illegal operations, principally numbers games and bookmakers, for a total expenditure of $16.8 billion.[15]

The issue of whether to allow gambling is moot. It is allowed. The debate should therefore be how to devise meaningful policies and effective laws and regulation for commercial gambling. Meaningful policies and effective laws and regulation cannot be created from the assumption that gambling is a sin and inherently evil. Yet most studies of gambling continue to be marred by an anti-gambling bias. In large measure this bias derives from an obsessive focus on "problem," or compulsive, gambling. It is important, therefore, to evaluate compulsive gambling and its relation to the availability of legal opportunities to gamble.

Most Gamblers Are Not Obsessed with Gambling

Nearly all observers who see gambling as evil and gamblers as actual or potential social problems grossly overestimate the importance of gambling for most people. While gambling is indeed a growing phenomenon in the United States, there is no reason to assume that it is a preoccupation for every American or even for every gambler. Gambling is the central fact only in the lives of problem or compulsive gamblers. Indeed, involvement with gambling to the exclusion of other things, the *compulsion* to play, are among the usual criteria for determining that an individual has a gambling problem.[16] For everyone else gambling is just one of many interests. An idea of the relative importance of gambling in American lives can be formed from calculating per capita losses: the $16.8 billion lost in 1983 works out to about $101 for every adult American. The survey of American gambling behavior conducted for the Federal Gambling Commission in 1975 estimated average per capita annual wagering at $150 for all adults and $387 for adults who bet, and average annual losses of about $30 per person over 18.[17] Even allowing for the possible understatement of losses inherent in any survey results there has been a massive increase in gambling expenditures since 1974.

A problem with gambling, or alcohol or narcotics or video games, can certainly have unpleasant or even tragic consequences. But many Americans gamble, drink, play Pac-Man, and indulge in other potentially addictive activities without becoming obsessed with them. Most Americans, including compulsive gamblers, are going to gamble regardless of the presence or absence of legal opportunities to do so. The failure of gambling prohibitions, enacted and enforced at every level of government over a period of two hundred years, to "reform" or even markedly to alter the American propensity to gamble is ample testimony to this fundamental fact. In focusing their attention on compulsive gamblers and their ire on the suppliers of gambling services, the critics of legal gambling ignore the overriding cause of our present dilemma: the demand for opportunities to gamble is deeply rooted in American society.

The extent of compulsive gambling behavior is critical to the rational discussion of gambling. How frequently does this behavior occur in the unstimulated population? Does the mere availability of legal but unpromoted commercial gambling significantly increase the incidence of compulsive gambling? Does the unrestricted advertisement of gambling by private or government operators create compulsive gambling that otherwise would not exist or stimulate latent compulsive gambling?

Compulsive Gamblers Are a Small Proportion of All Gamblers

The answers to these questions have important public policy and legislative implications. There have been numerous estimates of the incidence of compulsive gambling.[18] The most serious attempt to date to answer this question is the 1975 survey of American gambling behavior conducted by the Survey Research Center (SRC), whose findings regarding compulsive gambling have, by virtue of their comprehensive nature, a claim to be authoritative.[19] Relying on this survey, the Federal Gambling Commission concluded that 0.77 percent of the national population (or about 1.1 million persons over 18) were "probable" compulsive gamblers and another 2.33 percent were "potential" compulsive gamblers. The former statistic was much higher for Nevada residents, who are more exposed to legal commercial gambling: 2.62 percent "probable" compulsive gamblers and 2.35 percent—virtually the same as the percentage nationally— "potential" compulsive gamblers.[20] This finding led the commission to conclude that when widely available, legal commercial gambling leads to significant increases in compulsive gambling behavior:

> Not only is the incidence of compulsive gambling higher in Nevada than in the national sample, but the ratio of probables to potentials is as well. This is consistent with the hypothesis that widespread availability of gambling in a legal form leads a portion of those classified as potential compulsive gamblers to actualize their potential compulsion. This effect is more pronounced for women than for men and is also consistent with the observation that women are more easily accepted into legal gambling environments than into illegal operations, where the player frequently has to establish a credit rating; this may be a difficult matter for women who are dependent on their husbands financially.[21]

The commission concluded that in 1974 approximately 1.1 million Americans were compulsive gamblers. The numerous subsequent legalizations and apparent growth of illegal sports betting since 1974, when taken together with the commission's hypothesis that availability of legal gambling leads to increased compulsive gambling behavior, suggest that the number of Americans who gamble compulsively is higher today. Compulsive gamblers constitute a social problem of major proportions. The certainty that further legalization will occur means that the already large number of compulsive gamblers will grow. What is to be done about this?

Many religious and secular critics of decriminalization have a simple solution: return to prohibition. Make all gambling once again illegal, these critics say, rigorously enforce anti-gambling laws, and compulsive gambling will cease to be a problem. This has a certain plausibility. It seems reasonable, for example, that without legal opportunities to gamble susceptible individuals will not develop into compulsive gamblers. The realities of gambling and gambling behavior are, however, more complex than anti-gambling reformers are willing to admit, and the dilemma created by the presence of significant numbers of potential compulsive gamblers in the general population unfortunately resists such simple solutions.

Compulsive gambling presents policymakers with a complex set of choices. In deciding whether to allow a given form of commercial gambling, legislators and citizens must weigh the potential benefits—tax revenues, economic contributions, the provision of legal, honest, effectively regulated outlets for an already existing demand for gambling opportunities—against the social ills that may result from legalization. They should also consider the needs and preferences of the vast majority who are not potential compulsive gamblers.

A general principle of social policy is at stake here. If a society prohibits activities or substances because they are abused by a minority it often creates situations in which the majority suffers, either by being deprived of legal access to something it enjoys or because the resulting market for illegal suppliers leads to the rise of an organized criminal underworld. Legal proscriptions of selected behaviors have historically created as many problems as they have solved. Prohibition is the classic American example. The massive illegal bookmaking on team sports that pervades American life is another case in point: the United States is one of the few Western industrialized countries that do not allow sports betting and the only one to tax legal winnings as income,[22] policies that have combined to create perhaps the world's largest market for illegal bookmaking. Like the organized crime that supplied Americans with bootleg whiskey in the 1920s, our present illegal gambling problem is a self-inflicted wound.

Such "reform" involves a fundamental consideration of social policy: in whose interest are such policies to be made? If the solution to abuse by a minority—of activities or substances or even freedoms—is prohibition for everyone *anything* can become "wrong," and society is faced with a kind of tyranny. It is a basic tenet of democracy that in a free society people live the way they want to live, not the way some reformers, however well-intentioned, think they should. If large-scale gambling raises a number of intractable social issues—and it certainly does—turning "gambling" into a buzzword like "communism" or "homosexuality" only makes it more and not less difficult to resolve these issues. Devil-theories of gambling may have their place in church, but they are disastrous public policy.

To view gambling as inherently evil is a kind of scapegoating. Complex social problems generally have complex causes: blaming only one and overlooking all the others is unlikely to improve matters. It is easy and often emotionally satisfying for social reformers to argue that if society can only rid itself of a particular harmful activity all will be well. The fallacy in such arguments is that nothing—be it gambling, alcohol, or nuclear energy—is always in all circumstances bad. Value in this sense is a complex function of control, situation, regulation, and use. Like fire, gambling can lead to tragedy if it gets out of control, but like fire it can serve useful purposes. It is not inherently evil because of its potential negative effects.

A multitude of devils plague modern life. Gambling is one, perhaps, to some people but not to the majority and is by no means the source of all evil. In the context of a basically healthy society the question of whether to allow commercial gambling should not, as many clinical researchers and social critics argue, be decided solely in terms of the potential risk of increased compulsive gambling. Compulsive gambling is only one of the factors that should weigh in the decision to legalize. Without in any way minimizing the problem of compulsive gambling for affected individuals, it does not seem to us to constitute an unacceptable social risk of legalizing activities most Americans clearly approve of and enjoy without incurring unaffordable losses.

This more balanced evaluation of the medical implications of legalization for society as a whole derives from extensive study of gamblers in actual gambling situations, as opposed to clinical observations of advanced stages of compulsive gambling in isolation from the real-world gambling scene. Explanations of gambling behavior based on a pathological model invariably focus on the gambler to the exclusion of the gambling event. Such studies almost always emphasize the end result of long-term heavy betting, which usually involves serious economic and social loss. Moreover, many clinical researchers misunderstand the nature of gambling. The unfairness of all commercial games, which by definition have an advantage or edge that ensures revenues for the operator and losses for players, is used as the basis for a narrowly economic argument against the rationality of gambling: since gamblers voluntarily engage in activities that must *a priori* result in financial loss they are irrational and, if regular gamblers, "sick" because they are preoccupied with activities that almost inevitably lead to ruin.

Gamblers Behave Rationally

This argument has several defects. First, there is much evidence to suggest that gamblers behave rationally even in narrow economic terms. Observations in a wide variety of times and places have shown that gamblers are realistically aware of their chances of winning and conduct their wagering with deliberation and disciplined concentration.[23] Casino patrons tend to take the best odds,[24] and horseplayers tend to bet favorites[25] and make rational use of information concerning the prospects of each horse or betting interest.[26] In the short term most gamblers are economically rational; each gamble is evaluated according to odds, expected return, alternative betting opportunities, and a number of other structural characteristics.[27] It is only over extended series of gambles that the built-in edge of commercial games grinds away the players' bankrolls. A gambler who believes he will lose any particular gamble, and that his loss would outweigh any possible reward in terms of recreation or status, might, arguably, be judged irrational in this narrow economic sense. But no gambler loses every bet: there are inevitable streaks of good and bad fortune. It is in fact this unpredictable alternation of loss and gain that is one of the satisfactions of gambling; loss, in other words, far from being evidence of irrationality, is intrinsic to the utility of gambling activities. To say that every gambling situation demands irrational behavior is roughly equivalent to saying that every cocktail party leads to drunkenness or, worse, to alcoholism.

Financial Gain Is Not the Main Motive for Gambling

A second and more serious fallacy with the pathological model becomes apparent when it is used to explain gambling motivations and the dynamics of play. The inadequacy of the argument from narrow economic rationality derives from its assumption that the only measure of the utilities of gambling consumption is monetary—that gambling can be valued solely in terms of gain or loss. This assumption is clearly at odds with reality. Few racetrack and casino gamblers we questioned mentioned the possibility of monetary gain as their primary reason for gambling.[28] Most said they gambled because they liked the excitement, the escape from everyday routine, or the company of gambling cronies.[29] Gamblers who seek these satisfactions exercise rational choice in deciding to spend (or lose) money at gambling. Reductive economic theories of behavioral motivation were too simplistic when they were proposed by Karl Marx as explanations of social conflict in history and such an approach is equally misleading as an explanation of gambling behavior. The confusion arises from the fact that in gambling money is used as the stake and payoff. Money is the agreed-upon measure of worth in our society, and as such it is the obvious and appropriate medium for gambling. It is not, for most gamblers, the end. Money heightens player involvement and provides an easy measure of outcomes, but gain or loss is not always or even usually the primary motivation. Players gamble *with* but not always *for* money.

Nor is it necessarily true that compulsive gamblers gamble in order to lose. There is a psychological fallacy underlying this common assertion. It is all too emotionally satisfying to adopt a "just desserts" model of causality—to make causal links between motivations, intentions, and results. Compulsive gambling is pathetically a bad result, and it is very tempting to conclude that this behavior is prompted by self-destructive intent. Evil intentions, however, are not necessary to produce evil consequences, just as well-intentioned activity—like the "reform" embodied in the Volstead Act—does not always lead to social improvements. Much of sociology deals with the latent and unintended consequences of individual social actions. Many areas of modern life provide examples of persons reaping more or less than they sowed, and "just desserts" is often more a product of wishful thinking than a reflection of reality. For good or ill, this appears to be especially true of gambling. We do not agree that all compulsive gamblers "deserve" their destructive losses because by incurring them they are satisfying the demands of psychological traits.

So far we have been using the terms *compulsive* and *pathological* without defining them. As noted, researchers using the pathological model commonly assume elements of compulsion and self-destruction in gambling, because they know that in the long run gamblers will lose. Our own research makes us question both of these traditional notions. Perhaps because so much of the study of gambling has depended on observations of members of Gamblers Anonymous (G.A.), gambling is portrayed as out-of-control, painful, compulsive behavior. As with its counterpart, Alcoholics Anonymous (A.A.), membership in G.A. is voluntary. When the pain or economic consequences of compulsive gambling reach a crisis point the gambler joins G.A. in order to stop. Consequently, to use G.A. members as representative of the gambling population is a little like sampling traffic court to find representative drivers, or Alcoholics Anonymous to find typical drinkers.

It is clear to us from our research that even among the ranks of "problem" gamblers there are persons who because of their financial or emotional resources never reach a crisis point, who never experience the pain of gambling-induced self-doubt or self-loathing, and who do not wish to stop gambling. Indeed, most gamblers do stop intermittently, whenever they can no longer afford to stay in action. We can still label these heavy bettors "problem" gamblers, either because they assign gambling an inordinately high priority in their lives or because they have reached very high levels of wagering. Many of these heavy bettors are however more usefully characterized as *obsessive* rather than compulsive gamblers.

Obsessive behavior may be defined as any behavior that takes over an individual's life and becomes central, all-engrossing, and perhaps all-consuming within definable boundaries of control. There are religious obsessions, sexual obsessions, and work obsessions—in short, any imbalance from the Aristotelian dictum of moderation in all things. All obsessions can be difficult to live with, and to their families obsessive gamblers, like workaholics or alcoholics, can be disruptive and perhaps destructive. But unless the gambler himself makes his family a higher priority than his playing—and by definition the obsessive gambler does not—he will not feel the pain his absence from home causes and so will have no motivation to stop gambling until his financial resources are exhausted.

What differentiates the obsessive gambler from the compulsive gambler is not the effect his behavior has on those around him but how he handles his betting and its effect on his life and self-image. On the one hand, because of the one-dimensional focus of his life the obsessive gambler dare not give up gambling; on the other, his gambling is controlled: he will stop before reaching the limit of his resources. These individuals do not bet the mortgage payment or the assets of their businesses or write bad checks; if they did they could not return to the gambling scene and get back into action. Instead of losing everything, they go back to their jobs and families, save up some money, and reward themselves with more gambling at the next opportunity. They are controlled gamblers, even though they invest virtually all their leisure time and disposable income in gambling. Unlike compulsive gamblers, whose gambling may cross the boundaries of socially acceptable behavior, obsessive gamblers are unusual principally in the object of their obsession: sports fanatics, joggers, dedicated athletes, performers, and workaholics who give themselves wholly to their jobs or professions—all of whom are usually considered to be "normal"—are fundamentally similar personalities. The dimensions of the problem of compulsive gambling have been overstated by the inclusion in psychologically oriented studies of these obsessive, heavy, but controlled gamblers. The differentiation between obsessive and compulsive gamblers is a necessary prerequisite to an accurate evaluation of this problem and of the social risk of legal commercial gambling.

As the foregoing discussion demonstrates, simple solutions to the problems raised by legal commercial gambling are likely to prove ineffective in practice, for the reason that these solutions focus on the individual to the exclusion of the larger social context. Compulsive gamblers, perhaps because of the pathos of their predicament, have been especially cursed by the purveyors of simplistic nostrums. It is all too easy, in trying to help these unfortunate people to work off the resulting emotional involvement on some convenient villain—usually the nearest gambling business.

By failing to take into account the gambling propensities of the non-compulsive majority that gave rise to commercial gambling in the first place "reform" channeled in this direction will continue to fail to resolve our present dilemma. Even if there were no compulsive or obsessive gamblers commercial gambling would remain an enterprise with far-reaching consequences for American society. Gambling, on the scale it is presently being conducted in the United States, raises fundamental social issues. It poses serious questions for our democratic capitalist system, and it is modifying the socio-cultural values of Americans in ways only dimly understood. Only a few years ago, in a landmark study of the regulation of gaming in Nevada, Jerome Skolnick termed casinos a "pariah industry,"[30] a half-outlawed, half-legal multi-billion dollar business, alternately and inconsistently reviled and embraced by mainstream America, that because of its ambiguous legal, cultural, and sociological status has created unique and heretofore insoluble problems for society. Commercial gambling has continued to expand since Skolnick's study, but little progress towards resolving the dilemma he so thoroughly elucidated has been made. Gambling, though indulged in by many Americans, is still considered socially deviant behavior; but commercial gambling should no longer be considered a pariah.

Gambling Is Mainstream, Not Deviant

This comfortable hypocrisy, that gambling is deviant and pathological, is the root cause of our inability to deal rationally with gambling behavior and the commercial gambling industry. The point cannot be made too strongly: legal commercial gambling raises profound issues for our society and capitalist system precisely because it is so perfectly integrated into mainstream American life. If gambling were truly deviant, if racetracks and lotteries and casinos did not satisfy a widely and deeply rooted demand, the problems created by gambling would be trivial, and confined to the small segment of the population liable to become compulsive gamblers. Instead we find:

- that in just five years of some of the most explosive growth in the history of American business, Atlantic City casinos were (in 1983) generating gross revenues (or player losses) approaching $5 million a day, with single-day individual casino wins exceeding $1 million an increasingly routine experience;

- the rapid expansion of state lotteries and their transformation from "benign" weekly and monthly drawings to an aggressive form of gambling offering daily drawings, instant ("paper slot machine") games, player-active numbers games, and in 1984, on an experimental basis, player-active lottery video games that potentially can put the combined attractions of Pac-Man and "one-armed bandits" in the more than 100,000 outlets selling lottery tickets to some 56 percent of the U.S. population;

- the imminent expansion of off-track betting to Illinois, and then to other major pari-mutuel racing states;[31]

- the utilization of advanced communications technology to bring live televised horse racing ("simulcasting") into neighborhood OTB shops and to homes via closed-circuit television in conjunction with racetrack-operated telephone deposit-account betting;

- the continued rapid growth of bookmaking on team sports into an illegal commercial gambling business of massive proportions.[32]

The list could easily be extended. A historic confluence of forces— government's need for new, "painless" sources of revenue, private industry's ingenuity in supplying ever more attractive opportunities to gamble, changing public mores and attitudes, and above all the gambling propensities of mainstream America—has combined to make legal commercial gambling, with gross wagering estimated at nearly $135 billion in 1983,[33] one of the largest leisure industries in the United States.

Gambling is not, as we like to believe, some sort of "fringe" activity that isn't really competitive with the mainstream economy. Gambling competes too well. Some years ago, in the early morning hours at one of the restaurants in Caesars Palace in Las Vegas an old, successful, and respected gambler was musing on the business in which he'd spent his life. "Give me a dozen of these," the gambler said, indicating with a jeweled index finger the casino floor, "and permission to put them anywhere I choose, and with them I can destroy the economy of any city in the world." We have come to believe he had a point. To paraphrase another, fictional gambler, American commercial gambling today is bigger than U.S. Steel.[34]

The time is long past when taking refuge in the myth of gambling as deviance and relegating commercial gambling to the status of a pariah industry can pass for meaningful responses to the phenomenon of gambling. The difficulties that have been created by these shopworn attitudes should by now be apparent. Compulsive gamblers receive an excess of attention and far too little real help from authorities reluctant to assume responsibility for the problem. Consistent gambling policies are made impossible by contradictory gambling laws and public apathy. The federal tax treatment of legal winnings is an incentive to massive illegal gambling, while the task of supplying an enormous public demand for sports betting is left to the underworld. In all, regulation of the entire industry, legal and illicit, may accurately be characterized as too little and too late. If society is to avoid a disaster gambling must first be seen clearly, without bias or prejudice, for what it is: conventional behavior practiced by most Americans. Next must come a perspective that differentiates among gambling games within the general context of leisure and play. Finally gambling games and behaviors must be located within historical processes that are transforming many areas of American life.

Sociology Offers Help in
Understanding Gambling

No single perspective is adequate for an understanding of something as complex as gambling. In rejecting the psychological approach to an explanation of mainstream American gambling behavior we are not discounting the real contributions of psychology to the study of compulsive gambling, individual gambling careers, and individual risky decisionmaking. In all these areas psychologists have added to our knowledge. Gambling, however, is more than a series of individual risky decisions. It is an activity with specific structures and contexts that exist regardless of individual motivations. The psychological approach, with its focus on the individual, overemphasizes stability and consistency of personality as well as personal motives and judgments in explaining gambling behavior. At the same time it underestimates the significance of the games themselves, the other actors, and the gambling situation as an enclosed system offering many alternative behavior options. As we have noted, where compulsive gambling is concerned this emphasis produces useful results. Like other compulsions, uncontrollable gambling is a manifestation of individual psychological traits for which gambling situations are the occasion but not the cause. But, while it is certainly true that each gambler has his or her own psychological goals, perceptions, and interpretations of the gambling scene, the "worlds of reality" gamblers inhabit are largely situational—and not the autonomous creations of individual psyches. From buying lottery tickets to shooting craps the structure of their experience relies heavily on socially constructed systems of meaning: on norms and ideologies that define games, playing strategies, and what constitutes winning and losing. No analysis of individual gamblers, however complete or profound, can reveal these meanings. Gambling cannot profitably be studied in isolation from its social context.

Gambling and Symbolic Interactionism

What is needed is an overview, a perspective that takes in not only gamblers individually but the games themselves, within specific cultural contexts that are the product of particular historical processes. Sociology provides this perspective. Along with the steady accretion of clinical studies, a sociology of gambling has developed. This literature has sought to apply the sociology of leisure to the study of gambling as games and play.

In his landmark theory of games,[35] Roger Caillois, building on the seminal work of Johan Huizinga,[36] classifies lotteries, casinos, and parimutuel betting as (primarily) games of chance (*aléa*) located on the margins of the social order.[37] Gambling, however, is not asocial: play at games of chance[38] "presuppose[s] not solitude but company" and is fundamentally a social activity. Through this social aspect of play, games, including gambling games of chance, are involved in relationships that cross over all four of the categories into which Caillois analyzes play: chance (*aléa*), competition (*agon*), mimicry, and vertigo (*ilinx*). Horse racing, for example, is "typical *agon* for the jockeys [and] at the same time a spectacle which . . . stimulates *mimicry* and is also a pretext for betting, through which the competition [of the horses and jockeys] is a basis [or object] of *aléa*."[39] These relationships may have a psychological dimension: "In games of chance . . . a special kind of vertigo seizes both lucky and unlucky players. They are no longer aware of fatigue and are scarcely conscious of what is going on around them. They are entranced by the question of where the ball will stop or what card will turn up. They lose all objectivity and sometimes gamble more than they have."[40] The social activity of roulette—and not a psychological trait—produces vertigo that robs the player of his objectivity and may thereby stimulate excessive loss regardless of his motivation for playing roulette (which may, of course, include a conscious or unconscious desire to experience vertigo). This explanation of excessive—not compulsive—gambling requires, as we have said, a context and structure beyond the individual player's personality. It is, most certainly, not the same thing as individual decisionmaking. Gambling cannot exist without a social system in which to gamble; paradoxically, Caillois suggests that a society such as ours where "the entire social structure rests upon [*agon*, or competition]" may not be able to exist without the socialized chance of gambling: "*agon* and *aléa* no doubt represent the contradictory and complementary principles of a new social order. Moreover, they must fulfill parallel functions which are recognizably indispensable. . . ."[41] The kind of play that is gambling provides an escape from the discipline of work and from the boredom and routine it engenders. For Caillois and Huizinga, by reintroducing chance in the (socially constructed) forms of racetrack and lottery and casino games into societies ruled by competition, gambling frees us, if only temporarily, from the tyranny of rational order.

Erving Goffman extends the sociology of gambling to the prosaic world of "everyday" situations.[42] He argues that orderly social life at the most pragmatic levels is made possible by unspoken rules of social interaction, or rituals, that serve to sustain the action of society. Gambling games offer a particular kind of action: consequential, avoidable chance. All games, including gambling games, have as their rationale the game itself; observing players in action we do not have to know anything about their individual personalities to understand their moves and strategies. The gambler, in other words, does not autonomously generate gambling behavior from his own psyche. The games he plays are cultural in origin, social constructions of risk. A society, Goffman is saying, gets the games—and the gambling—it deserves. Our competitive and materialistic culture, where money is central to real and symbolic values, is as responsible for the game of *Monopoly* as is Parker Brothers. In *Monopoly* collecting money, buying symbolic properties, and building token houses are acceptable behavior toward the prescribed end of bankrupting other players. Outside the game these houses and deeds are valueless: the winner of a state lottery, for example, would be outraged if his payoff were in *Monopoly* money. The excitement of and motivation for *Monopoly* reside in the game, but its rules and roles, and its meaning, are conventional and derive not from the players but from their culture.

So with gambling. Goffman is less sure of the liberating qualities of gambling than Huizinga and Caillois: individuals, he argues, whatever their motives for engaging in this kind of action, are not free even in the gambling situation to create their own worlds of meaning. Like *Monopoly*, gambling is conventional: as with other social activities all gambling situations contain rules and roles; the meaning of betting, as distinct from the monetary value of a bet, can be arrived at only through subjective utilities that are by no means necessarily economic. A nickel pot is worth a nickel, but the value of gambling for a nickel pot to any particular individual is objectively incalculable. In Goffman's perspective the social valuation of gambling is likewise a subjective calculation. Gambling is not a pathology, but a specific form of social behavior that occurs only within a given system of internally consistent, culturally determined, and socially agreed-upon meanings. Action and its social context are inseparable.

One of Goffman's contributions to the sociology of gambling is the brief but cogent description of gambling games in the opening pages of "Where the Action Is," which provides a solid underpinning for his examination of interactive gambling behavior. As we have noted, the failure to look carefully at the games gamblers play is one of the principal shortcomings of the psychological literature. The structural analysis of games that is the subject of the next chapter [of the book by Abt et al.], while primarily an exercise in structural functionalism, derives its significance from one of the most basic theoretical approaches within the sociological perspective: symbolic interactionism.[43] The ideas of George Herbert Mead, presented in *Mind, Self, and Society*,[44] center on the importance of games for the development of society and the socialization of the child. It is through games that the child learns to play roles in society and, in the process, develops a sense of self and internalizes cultural meanings. These ideas underlie much of the work, by Howard Becker, David Matza,[45] and others, on "deviance"—including gambling—as conventional behavior. In these studies the complex question of how a person comes to define himself as a gambler, or any other "deviant," is addressed within the framework of symbolic interaction.

Becker's classic study of deviant careers, "Becoming a Marijuana User," offers a sociological explanation for social pathology: we can learn deviance just as, and just as easily as, we can learn "acceptable" behavior.[46] Rather than assuming users are motivated by happenstance or some personality disturbance, Becker argues that marijuana use is the result of several interrelated conditions: an available, secure supply, an appropriate time and place, and the example of other users. These conditions are met through a complex social interaction between the novice and more experienced marijuana smokers. Following his initiation the novice develops routines of secrecy, redefines his earlier (and of course culturally, and not psychologically, derived) notions regarding the morality of smoking marijuana, and associates regularly with other marijuana smokers. Becker concludes: "Instead of the deviant motives leading to the deviant behavior, it is the other way around; the deviant behavior in time produces the deviant motivations." The parallel with Goffman's findings is exact: The sensations produced by marijuana, like the satisfactions of *Monopoly* or the excitement of gambling, which are internal and intrinsic to the game or drug, not to the personality of the individual, become the motivation for the "deviance" of gambling or smoking marijuana. These sensations and satisfactions are sought and experienced through interactive social behaviors that only occur in the social contexts of gambling or marijuana-smoking situations; and over time elaborate interactive rituals develop in the gambling or drug subculture that transform individual actions into definite patterns of everyday social behavior.

A similar approach underlies Henry Lesieur's *The Chase*, a study of pathological gamblers seeking to repeat a big win they, or their gambling acquaintances, once experienced.[47] Jay Livingston and Igor Kusyszyn adopt a similar view in their description of the stages through which problem gamblers progress in learning the role of sick players.[48] The compulsive gambler may not have personality problems at the outset of his eventual downfall, but over time, through differential association and immersion in gambling situations and the resulting congruence of the gambler-role and his identity, he becomes a different individual and his behavior becomes pathological. In this view a "gambling personality" is not so much a cause of gambling as it is one of gambling's effects on the individual. Here, as in Goffman's analysis, the importance of socially and culturally constructed roles in determining gambling behavior emerges. On entering gambling situations individuals assume one of many possible gambler-roles, one of which is the role of compulsive gambler.

We can at this point summarize the insights into gambling and gambling behavior provided by symbolic interactionism. These are: 1) the importance of games; 2) the conventional nature of most behavior, even behavior usually considered deviant; and 3) an understanding of the process of socialization into deviant careers. Symbolic interaction is essentially biography rather than history. Its primary focus is on the individual within social situations. In order to arrive at a complete understanding of the social functions of gambling games, however, a second sociological approach is needed. This second approach is structural functionalism.

One of the functions of society is to provide mechanisms that enable people to deal with and control potentially dangerous situations. Many social rituals perform this function: for example, a funeral helps mourners adjust to the loss of a loved one. For the great majority of Americans who gamble without becoming compulsive, gambling, like other forms of play, performs analogous social functions. For most people gambling is a healthy recreation. It provides escape from both the uncertainty and the boring routine of modern life by reinforcing, in familiar and highly ritualized surroundings, conventions and roles that let gamblers feel, at least for the duration of the game, that they are the masters of their fates. Some of the more structured gambling situations, such as horse-race betting, allow gamblers to confront the probabilistic, chancy nature of existence within the comforting bounds of ritual order. Other games, of which craps is an example, give players the subjective (and in this case illusory) feeling of influence (by throwing the dice) over the outcome of the gambling event. State lotteries have the perhaps more dubious function of offering the hope, against astronomical odds, of striking it rich to people who in a capitalistic system have few realistic prospects of realizing the American dream. Games may vary in the satisfactions they offer, but all gambling, and many other games and sports as well, have in common the major social function of the disenchantment of chance by subjecting it to the rules of play. In the most ordered and technically proficient culture there remains an unpredictable and uncontrollable challenge to personal survival arising from the random nature of events. Gambling, with its predictable uncertainties, tames chance and turns it— for most people—to useful social purpose.[49]

Gambling and Structural Functionalism

In contrast to symbolic interactionism, structural functionalism does not focus attention on the biography of the individual or on the process by which he internalizes external social facts or rules. The structural functionalist assumes that order is "out there," created by society independently of the individuals living within it. Order is a social fact that functions to maintain the integrity of the system. Structural functionalism attempts to explain social forms and rituals not in terms of the psychological motives of individual participants, but rather in terms of the often latent functions these activities have for the survival of society itself. In this view society is a thing *sui generis*, and as such has its own survival mechanisms, or cultural subsystems, that perform different and specialized functions to get the job of society done. Each of these systems of action, or social institutions, can be conceptualized separately within its own boundaries, and yet each is interconnected with other systems, in much the same way as one's cardiovascular system is separate from but related to one's muscular system.[50] Most studies in the sociology of gambling have, at least implicitly, some underlying basis in structural functionalism. Gamblers and gambling are seen as fulfilling certain functions for society. Several structural functionalist studies also look at the various ways a gambling structure maintains itself. For example, Irving Kenneth Zola's "Gambling in a Lower Class Setting" shows how the role of a good gambler among fellow gamblers functions as a chance for individuals to practice a productive presentation of self: being a good winner or loser has positive functional value for the gambler and also helps to maintain the game.[51] Goffman similarly speaks of structural mechanisms that "cool out" the loser and keep him from disrupting the game.[52] Robert D. Herman, in his study of the racetrack, looks at the function of various structural aspects of gambling in the context of the gambling situation. Money, for example, functions to "verify the decisionmaking process" of betting a horse; it also "verifies the involvement of the bettor in the action."[53] All of these studies speak to those aspects of the gambling situation that facilitate the involvement and participation of gamblers. While maintaining the action, Herman suggests that these mechanisms of involvement—tote boards, for example, which "give prominence to the total amounts of money wagered and information concerning the odds"— also emphasize the importance of "weighing alternatives, making decisions, and signaling these decisions by attaching money to them." Further, through these system-maintaining devices players emulate traditional entrepreneurial roles—in this case the role of the investor watching the stock market ticker-tape—which are of course basic mainstream American cultural values: "Gambling, by this view, is less dysfunctional than it appears to be to those who judge it solely by standards linked to the production of goods."[54]

Gambling Is a Caricature of Capitalism

We argue that commercial gambling caricatures the nineteenth-century ideology of enterprise—sober individual risk-taking, thrift, effort, and self-denial—that legitimated investment capitalism in a democracy.[55] These values constituted what Max Weber called "the Protestant ethic,"[56] which is caricatured insofar as the gambler invests in the present—in a chance for immediate, materialistic rewards and payoffs in an atmosphere of self-indulgence. Gambling thus exemplifies a reversal of American values:[57] the ethic of saving, of self-denial and capital accumulation, has been replaced by an ideology of hedonistic consumerism, which Christopher Lasch has perceptively termed the culture of narcissism.[58] Today Americans eagerly consume disposable time and wealth. The accumulation of capital is no longer as important to most people as the search for ways to use money in pursuit of pleasure and status. This emphasis on consumption is quite functional in a modern capitalistic society. By embracing gambling and so enthusiastically caricaturing the work ethic of our parents, mainstream Americans truly mirror a historic cultural change.

The structural characteristics of gambling fit the times extremely well. Caillois observes that the lottery of heredity has always been resented by egalitarian societies;[59] for this injustice of biology, the unflinchingly democratic odds of casino games, which are the same for everyone whether the wager is large or small, is a measure of social compensation. From roulette to slot machines, these games of pure chance are equally accessible to anyone with the money for a minimum bet.[60] In contrast the odds at pari-mutuel horse racing are neither egalitarian nor stable,[61] but in their teasing fluctuations at once facilitate and stimulate and emphasize the consumer's decisionmaking process. As well as Zola's lower-class betting milieu, racetracks and casinos are prototypical arenas for the displays of money that in this country confer power and prestige.

The peculiar "fit" between gambling and capitalism was first suggested by Edward Devereux in an early functional analysis of gambling as a kind of safety valve for the unfulfilled hopes of the lower classes.[62] In Devereux's view modern capitalistic society contains a basic contradiction, between the ideal of equality of opportunity and the actual inequality of capitalistic economic institutions, that gambling, through its ability to provide an outlet for the frustrated hopes of less fortunate classes, has helped to obscure: "Upon gambling can be heaped the onus of responsibility for our collective guilts. Gambling must be tolerated, even allowed to flourish, in practice, since its elimination would leave the contradictions of capitalism untouched and over-exposed. The pretense that we aim to eliminate it must, however, be maintained."[63] We find a number of pleasing ironies, and more than a measure of truth, in Devereux's image of a capitalist system founded by anti-gambling Puritans held hostage to a roulette wheel.

One of the more recent and comprehensive studies of the sociology of gambling, by D.M. Downes et al., attempts to combine Caillois's sociology of games and play and Devereux's structural functionalist hypothesis with an effort to ascertain empirically the sociological functions of gambling considered as a game.[64] This attempt inadvertently points up several limitations common to all such studies. The literature to date on the sociology of gambling has failed to differentiate in any very thorough and rigorous way among the highly diverse structures of the games used in commercial gambling.[65] Devereux's thesis of the safety valve function of gambling may help explain the rapid institutionalization of State lotteries, but it is certainly less helpful in explaining the appeal of casino games like blackjack or baccarat, whose players come from the middle and upper strata of American society. A more general defect of these studies is that sociologists, while recognizing that gambling has social functions, have in their desire to generate quantifiable data (Downes) or make *in situ* observations (Herman and Zola) often fallen into precisely the methodological (if not conceptual) error they try to avoid: the trap of psychological reductionism.

One of the earliest sociologists, Emile Durkheim, pointed out in his classic study *Suicide*[66] that one cannot arrive at an understanding of social functions by studying individual intentions and actions. Durkheim concluded that the difference in suicide rates among countries could only be explained by variations in the mechanisms of social cohesion in different societies, not by the personalities of individuals living in these societies. In other words, suicide cannot be attributed to personality problems. Similarly, society is not reducible to the sum of its parts. The latent functions of social phenomena cannot be elucidated by questioning individuals about their motives or intentions or through personality studies. Psychology, in short, is an avenue of research into the individual personality; but it does not lead very far toward an understanding of social constructs and behaviors, such as gambling and gambling games, or of society.

A third defect in the literature is that it is ahistorical and, in a peculiar sense, acultural as well. Neither symbolic interactionists nor structural functionalists have taken sufficient account of the larger historical processes that are affecting games and gamblers, society, and the social meaning of gambling.

Gambling and Conflict Theory

There is a third approach within sociology, one that has not previously been applied to the sociological study of gambling.[67] This approach is conflict theory. Like gambling, conflict theory is not a homogeneous entity. Conflict theory recognizes that there may be important differences in the bases for social conflict, in how social conflicts are resolved, and in whose interest they are resolved. But conflict theory has the important advantage of being oriented toward a historical view of social phenomena. This approach seeks to explain social behavior as motivated by the quest for power among competing individuals or interest groups.[68] Conflict theory does not assume social consensus or functionally interrelated natural subsystems cooperating to maintain society. Instead, conflict theory assumes there is no single macro-entity or process called society. Rather, society is whatever the individual or group in power defines it to be. This approach would define the contemporary gambling scene as a result of a history of competing interests—one that would spread gambling opportunities, and one that would prohibit or severely constrain such opportunities.

Conflict theory explains relationships among a series of events dynamically related through history more effectively than does the structural approach, which posits a static, self-maintaining, perfect-state model of society in which norms exist virtually unchallenged. According to conflict theory, actors within any situation represent interests, and their actions are strategies. Conflict theory speaks of bargaining, staking new claims, and shifting alliances depending upon changing situations. No one has permanent, nonmaterialistic, nonspecific loyalties in a world defined by conflict theory. This conception clearly opposes a world of *a priori* values or unchanging social functions.

Conflict theory specifies conflict as the mechanism of historical change. Marx generally argued that the history of legal, political, and cultural "superstructures" is ultimately the product and reflection of underlying shifts in economic relationships. Values and norms are ideologies that serve to legitimate and maintain the position of those currently in control of the social structure. Weber, though also a conflict theorist, believed Marx was mistaken in making economic forces the sole determinants of history and the structure of society. For Weber ideas were not simply reflections of underlying interests. He was aware of the role ideas play in strengthening and guaranteeing the position of interests within a given social order. In Weber's view, people also have nonmaterial interests and beliefs about the world. These beliefs are not simply rationalizations of economic interests but exist in their own right. Both variations of conflict theory agree, however, that for a group to maintain power—regardless of its particular interest—it must eventually justify its position through cultural mechanisms of legitimacy and authority.[69] As we will show in Chapter 6 [of *The Business of Risk*], this relates directly to the history of commercial gambling in America.

Conflict theory explains a number of seeming contradictions within the gambling scene. For instance, a clergyman with a personal moral bias against gambling might allow his congregation to sponsor a weekly bingo game or raffle if he sees these activities as revenue producers for his parish.[70] Similarly, a State or locality that prohibits gambling in accordance with the expressed moral reservations of its citizens may be persuaded to legalize lotteries or racetracks or casinos in an attempt to raise revenues without direct taxation and justify the action with the arguments that gambling revenues are "painless" taxes, or will go to the arts or the elderly or the poor, or for some other especially deserving purpose.

Conflict theory may be applied to very specific gambling situations, including the actual playing of games. As Caillois notes, gambling contains elements of competition. Conflict theory can explain gambling as an attempt by players to beat each other (in pari-mutuel betting) or the house (at casino games) by adopting strategies to maximize their self-interests, whether that is winning money, having a good time, or just experiencing the excitement of action. Applications of conflict theory at this level need not be restricted to gambling behavior. When individuals responsible for regulating commercial gambling leave modestly salaried government posts for more highly paid positions in the gambling industry, they follow a time-honored precedent established by the government regulators of virtually every major industry in the United States: like gamblers, or casinos and racetracks, these people use gambling to maximize their self-interest.[71] Individual movements from one gambling interest to another are in fact common at every level, even among gamblers themselves. Bookmakers are frequently recruited from the ranks of serious bettors.[72] Ken Uston, a card-counter whose profession cast him and casinos in adversarial roles, capitalized on his experience by writing books on blackjack and eventually running blackjack seminars under the auspices of a casino.[73] Both Uston and the bettor-turned-bookmaker use gambling as a means to a rational end; the variations on similar shifts between roles and interests created by gambling are numerous.

Finally in this review of methodological approaches to the study of the sociology of gambling there is the importance of history. As one major form of commercial gambling after another enters mainstream America they do so as the result of historical processes that are unique and could not be predicted by any sociological or economic model. Conflict theory can explain how State lotteries have grown in just twenty years from an acknowledged failure to the second largest commercial gambling game in the United States. But it could not have predicted this surprising turn of events. Moreover, the anticipated introduction of a new technological contrivance, electronic video gaming devices, into State lottery operations while an enormously popular indigenous gambling activity like sports betting remains proscribed is explainable only in specific historical terms. As these examples show, commercial gambling is more than the sum of the motivations of individual gamblers. It is that sum and the product of diverse and complex historical factors as well. Gambling is not a single activity but a set of diverse activities that are related to the unique complex of structures and contexts that are particular to each game.

Thus, it is clear that a broader focus and a reframing of the issues are necessary to understand the business of risk. The nature of gambling has changed as it has evolved from sub rosa activities, run by individual entrepreneurs or springing up spontaneously among a group of players, to legitimate businesses run by public corporations and even governments. Society can no longer afford to focus almost exclusively on individuals and the problems some of them have with gambling. It can no longer take refuge in a moral crusade to prohibit behavior most Americans enjoy. And the relationship between Big Gambling and American society can no longer go unexamined. By analyzing the real differences among gambling games, by focusing on the major forms of legal commercial gambling, by taking a detailed look at the many types of gamblers, and by looking at the relationship of commercial gambling to our society and our culture, we offer an alternative view of issues that have been clouded by much sound and fury and suggest some more practical ways to deal with commercial gambling in mainstream America.

Notes

1. Examples of superficial romanticizing include Lucius Beebe, *The Big Spenders* (New York: Doubleday, 1966); Alexander Gardiner, *Canfield: The True Story of the Greatest Gambler* (Garden City, N.Y.: Doubleday, Doran, 1930); Will Irwin, *Confessions of a Con Man* (New York: B.W. Huebsch, 1909); Robert Irving Warshaw, *Bet-A-Million Gates: The Story of a Plunger* (New York: Greenberg, 1932). A recent representative hysterical anti-gambling tract is Tomás Martinez, *The Gambling Scene: Why People Gamble* (Springfield, Illinois: Charles C. Thomas, 1983). Moral preaching includes John Morris, *An Exposure of the Arts and Miseries of Gambling* (Cincinnati, Ohio, 1843); W.T. Stead, *Satan's Invisible World Displayed* (New York: World Publishing, 1972). For a sober, thorough, and excellent overview of American moral views of gambling see Raymond C. Bell, "Moral Views on Gambling Promulgated by Major American Religious Bodies," in *Gambling in America: Final Report of the Commission on the Review of the National Policy Toward Gambling* (Washington, D.C.: Government Printing Office [GPO], 1976), Appendix 1, pp. 161–239.
2. John Philip Quinn, *Fools of Fortune* (Chicago: G. Howe, 1890); Herbert Asbury, *Sucker's Progress: An Informal History of Gambling in America from the Colonies to Canfield* (New York: Dodd, Mead, 1938); Henry Chafetz, *Play the Devil: A History of Gambling in the United States from 1492 to 1955* (New York: Clarkson N. Potter, 1960).
3. The basic text on the psychology of gambling is Edmund Bergler, M.D., *The Psychology of Gambling* (New York: Hill and Wang, 1957). Representative examples of the literature include William E. Aubrey, "Altering the Gambler's Maladaptive Life

Goals," *International Journal of the Addictions* 10 (1975), pp. 29–33; Robert M. Lindner, "The Psychodynamics of Gambling," *Annals of the American Academy of Political and Social Science* 269 (May 1950), pp. 93–107; Robert Ladouceur and Marie Mayrand, "Evaluation of the 'Illusion of Control,'" in *The Gambling Papers: Proceedings of the Fifth National Conference on Gambling and Risk Taking*, vol. 4, *Studies in Gambling Behavior*, ed. William R. Eadington (Reno: University of Nevada, 1982), pp. 61–78; Jay Livingston, "Compulsive Gambling: A Culture of Losers," *Psychology Today* 7 (March 1974), pp. 51–55; Henry Lesieur, *The Chase: Career of the Compulsive Gambler* (Garden City, N.Y.: Anchor Press, 1977); Igor Kusyszyn, "Compulsive Gambling: The Problem of Definition," *International Journal of the Addictions* 13 (1978), pp. 1095–1101.

4.   Bell, "Moral Views on Gambling," is the best summary of American religious views concerning gambling. Protestant Christians have been the severest critics: Lycurgus M. Starkey, Jr., is representative: *The Christian Church and Gambling* (Washington, D.C.: General Board of Christian Social Concerns of the Methodist Church, n.d.); "Christians and the Gambling Mania," in *Gambling*, ed. Robert Herman (New York: Harper and Row, 1967); and *Money, Mania, and Morals: The Churches and Gambling* (New York: Abingdon Press, 1964). Moral reformers have often viewed gambling, legal or not, as an evil most effectively prevented by social institutions rather than law and enforcement measures: "Whether [anti-gambling] efforts will prevail over the vested gambling interests depends . . . upon the moral tone of our present and future citizenry. . . . Important in this molding process are the church, the home, the school, motion pictures, books, magazines, and newspapers. Courts and police are prosecuting rather than preventive agencies." Paul S. Deland (Managing editor of the *Christian Science Monitor*), "The Facilitation of Gambling," *Annals of the American Academy of Political and Social Science* 269 (May 1950), pp. 21–29. The development of the doctrine of organized crime's control of, and financial dependence on, illegal gambling is examined in Peter Reuter and Jonathan B. Rubinstein, "Fact, Fancy, and Organized Crime," *Public Interest* 53 (Fall 1978), pp. 45–67. The relationship of anti-gambling law enforcement and police corruption is examined in Jonathan Rubinstein, "Gambling Enforcement and Police Corruption," in *Gambling in America*, Appendix 1, pp. 600–632. Robert F. Kennedy, "The Baleful Influence of Gambling," in *Gambling*, ed. Herman, pp. 169–77, is a succinct statement of this doctrine. The Kefauver committee's *Report on Organized Crime: Report of the Special Senate Committee to Investigate Organized Crime in Interstate Commerce* (New York: Didier, 1951) and the McClellon committee's *Gambling and Organized Crime: Report of the Committee on Government Operations by its Permanent Subcommittee on Investigations*, 3 vols. (Washington, D.C.: GPO, 1962) are the most important statements of this doctrine by Congress. See also the discussion of illegal gambling in the Appendix.

5.   Martinez, *The Gambling Scene*, p. 152.

6. Charles Cotton, *Games and Gamesters of the Restoration: The Compleat Gamster* (1674; London: Kennikat Press, 1930). Compare Ernest E. Blanche, chief statistician for the United States Army general staff's logistics division: "The mathematical odds or probabilities in all gambling games are so determined that only the operator . . . can win during the continued conduct of the games. . . . The following summaries of the more popular ways of losing money may make each suggested game a loathsome, sickening purgative." "Gambling Odds are Gimmicked!" *Annals of the American Academy of Political and Social Science* 269 (May 1950), pp. 77–80.

7. *Gambling in America*, p. 1. The commission was created by Congress in the Organized Crime Control Act of 1970 (P.L. 91–452) for the purpose of conducting "a comprehensive legal and factual study of gambling in the United States and existing Federal, State, and local policy and practices with respect to legal prohibition and taxation of gambling activities and to formulate and propose such changes in those policies and practices as the Commission may deem appropriate." The commission's membership comprised four senators, four representatives, and nine other persons, including the chairman, Charles H. Morin, and executive director, James E. Ritchie. The commission handed up its final report in 1976.

8. A number of racetracks and vendors of pari-mutuel betting systems have been publicly traded for years. Prominent examples include Santa Anita Companies (NYSE, the operator of a major Southern California racetrack), Churchill Downs (OTC, the operator of the Kentucky racetrack holding the Kentucky Derby), General Instrument Corporation (NYSE, a vendor through its subsidiary American Totalizator of pari-mutuel betting systems), and many other companies. Since the enactment by the State of Nevada of corporate gaming acts in 1967 and 1969 publicly traded corporations have come to dominate casino gaming. Hilton Hotels (NYSE), Holiday Inns (NYSE), Caesars World (NYSE), Showboat (AMEX), Ramada Inns (NYSE), and MGM Grand Hotels (NYSE) are examples. State lottery games are supplied by private sector vendors that are for the most part publicly traded: Bally Manufacturing (NYSE, through its subsidiary Scientific Games), GTECH (OTC), Syntech International (OTC), and other companies.

9. Rational decisionmaking analyses include William J. Corney and William Theodore Cummings, "Information Processing Biases and Gambling Behavior," in *The Gambling Papers*, ed. Eadington, pp. 120–30; William R. Eadington, *The Economics of Gambling Behavior: A Qualitative Study of Nevada's Gambling Industry*, Bureau of Business and Economic Research Report no. 11 (Reno: University of Nevada, 1973); Terry J. Knapp, "A Functional Analysis of Gambling Behavior," in *Gambling and Society*, ed. Eadington, pp. 276–94; R.N. Rosett, "Gambling and Rationality," *Journal of Political Economy* 73 (December 1965), pp. 595–607; N. Kogan and M.A. Wallach, "Risk Taking as a Function of the Situation, the Person and the Group," in *New Directions in Psychology III*, eds. George Mandler, Paul Mussen, Nathan Kogan, and Michael A. Wellach (New York: Holt, Rinehart and Winston, 1967).

10. See Thomas W. Mangione et al., "Citizen Views of Gambling Enforcement," in *Gambling in America*, Appendix 1, pp. 240–300; Frederick Pratter and Floyd J. Fowler, Jr., "Police Perceptions About Gambling Enforcement," ibid., pp. 461–93; James M. Kretz and Carol H. Duncan, "Police Attitudes Toward Gambling Enforcement," ibid., pp. 565–73; Carol H. Duncan, "State and Local Gambling Enforcement: Arrest, Disposition, and Sentencing Statistics," ibid., pp. 679–744; and Peter Reuter, "Enforceability of Gambling Laws," ibid., pp. 551–64; Kathleen M. Joyce, "Public Opinion and the Politics of Gambling," *Journal of Social Issues* 35 (Summer 1979), pp. 144–65; Judge John M. Murtagh, "Gambling and Police Corruption," *Atlantic Monthly* 206 (November 1960), pp. 49–53.

11. Cornell Law School, G. Robert Blakey, supervisor, *The Development of the Law of Gambling: 1776–1976*, prepared for National Institute of Law Enforcement and Criminal Justice, Law Enforcement Assistance Administration, United States Department of Justice (Washington, D.C.: GPO, 1977), pp. 39ff., 59–61. This massive review of American gambling law is supplemented by G. Robert Blakey and Harold A. Kurland, "The Development of the Federal Law of Gambling," *Cornell Law Review* 63 (August 1978), pp. 923–1021. There is an excellent summary of federal gambling law and regulation in *Gambling in America*, pp. 11–33, with extensive, detailed, and accurate notes.

12. The best history of American lotteries is John Samuel Ezell, *Fortune's Merry Wheel: The Lottery in America* (Cambridge, Massachusetts: Harvard University Press, 1960). For lotteries in England see C. L'Estrange Ewen, *Lotteries and Sweepstakes: An Historical, Legal, and Ethical Survey of Their Introduction, Suppression, and Reestablishment in the British Isles* (London: Heath Cranton, 1932; New York: Benjamin Blom, 1972). Ewen provides extensive selections from original source materials and is the best history of English and colonial lotteries. John Ashton, *A History of English Lotteries* (1893; reprint, Detroit, Michigan: Singing Tree Press, 1969), provides source materials of an anecdotal nature. Chafetz, *Play the Devil*, pp. 20–28, provides useful anecdotal material. See also Asbury, *Sucker's Progress*; Eric J. Bender, *Tickets to Fortune: The Story of Sweepstakes, Lotteries, and Contests* (New York: Modern Age Books, 1938); Harry Bischoff Weiss and Grace M. Weiss, *The Early Lotteries of New Jersey* (Trenton, N.J.: Past Times Press, 1966); Francis Emmett Williams, *Lotteries, Laws, and Morals* (New York: Vantage Press, 1958); George Sullivan, *By Chance a Winner: The History of Lotteries* (New York: Dodd, Mead, 1972).

13. Lotteries, except keno, and pari-mutuel betting remained prohibited.

14. The evolution of legal commercial gambling has been on a State-by-State basis and can best be followed in *The Development of the Law of Gambling*. Aspects of this evolution are summarized in Fact Research, Inc., "Gambling in Perspective," in *Gambling in America*, Appendix 1, pp. 1–101. Chafetz, *Play the Devil*, is a good general history of American gambling. See as well Mark H. Haller, "The Changing Structure of American Gambling in the Twentieth Century," *Journal of Social Issues* 35 (Summer

1979), pp. 87–114.

15. See the Appendix [of *The Business of Risk*] for a summary accounting of legal commercial gambling losses and a discussion of various estimates of illegal gambling.

16. There is an enormous literature on the definition of compulsive or pathological gambling. A recent, brief summary of this literature is Nancy Ashton, "Gamblers: Disturbed or Healthy?" in *Gambling Today*, ed. David Lester (Springfield, Illinois: Charles C. Thomas, 1979), pp. 53–70.

17. Maureen Kallick, Daniel Suits, Ted Dielman, and Judith Hybels, Survey Research Center, Institute for Social Research, University of Michigan, "Survey of American Gambling Attitudes and Behavior," in *Gambling in America*, Appendix 2, pp. 93–95. The estimates of gambling expenditures given in this survey are discussed in the Appendix.

18. The most widely quoted estimates range from 2 percent to about 6 percent of the U.S. population. For the 2 percent figure, see Robert L. Custer, "Description of Compulsive Gambling" (paper prepared for the American Psychiatric Association Task Force on Nomenclature for Inclusion in its Diagnostic Statistical Manual III, 1976); and for the 6 percent figure, see *Gamblers Anonymous* (Los Angeles: G.A. Publishing, n.d.).

19. Kallick, "Survey of American Gambling," in *Gambling in America*, Appendix 1, pp. 417–54.

20. *Gambling in America*, pp. 73–74.

21. Ibid., p. 74.

22. For the federal tax treatment of winnings see John L. Kellogg, "The Federal Tax Treatment of Winnings, Losses, and Expenses of the Sports and Casino Bettor," in *The Gambling Papers*, ed. Eadington, 5:1–25; and *Gambling in America*, pp. 14–18. Citing the stimulus to illegal gambling and interference with State gambling policies created by the inclusion of legal winnings in taxable income as reasons, the commission recommended "that winnings derived from legal gambling entities be excluded from gross income, with the affirmative burden being placed upon the taxpayer to declare the income and prove the legality of the source" (p. 15). Successive administrations have declined the commission's recommendation, even to the limited extent of repealing withholding from legal payouts. In 1982, Assistant Secretary of the Treasury for Tax Policy John E. Chapoton testified against bills to repeal or limit withholding on the grounds that the argument "that the imposition of withholding . . . creates an incentive for patrons to wager with illegal bookmakers . . . proves too much. . . . One must ask . . . why . . . bettors prefer to place their bets with illegal bookmakers. One natural conclusions is that some, if not a substantial portion, of these bettors must be attempting to avoid the reporting and withholding requirements of current law. . . . Reduced to its essential points, this argument asks us to condone implicitly a failure to report income by making it easier to win at legalized establishments and not report winnings. . . . Treasury simply cannot stand by and acquiesce in a change which will encourage, rather than discourage, the failure to report income accurately." In other

words, Treasury recognizes the inclusion of legal winnings in taxable income is an incentive to illegal gambling, further recognizes that withholding from legal payouts is a further stimulus to illegal gambling, and wants to continue both policies. John E. Chapoton, statement, House Committee on Ways and Means, 97th Cong., 2d sess., Hearings Before the Subcommittee on Select Revenue Measures, March 16, 1982. Chapoton's solution to the problem of the diversion of legal wagering to illegal operators, caused by withholding requirements is "increased enforcement of the withholding laws" (Chapoton, letter to Sen. Paul Laxalt, May 21, 1982).

23. See, for example, Erving Goffman, "Where the Action is," in *Interaction Ritual: Essays on Face-to-Face Behavior* (New York: Pantheon Books, 1967, 1982); Robert D. Herman, "Gambling as Work: A Sociological Study of the Racetrack," in *Gambling*, ed. Herman; Otto Newman, *Gambling: Hazard and Reward* (London: Athlone Press, University of London, 1977); Irving Kenneth Zola, "Observations on Gambling in a Lower Class Setting," in *Gambling*, ed. Herman, pp. 19–31.

24. The fact that craps, which offers bets with house advantages ranging from 1.402 percent to 16.667 percent of handle has in practice an effective average edge of 2 percent to 3 percent is convincing evidence that most players choose the most favorable odds. See the Appendix [of *The Business of Risk*] for a fuller discussion.

25. In horse racing, favorites are established by the subjective opinions of published handicappers (the "morning line") and subsequently by the process of pari-mutuel betting, which establishes the *odds paid*, or return on investment, for each betting interest. In 1981, for example, favorites won 32 percent of U.S. thoroughbred races. *The American Racing Manual* (Hightstown, N.J.: Daily Racing Form, 1982), p. 234.

26. That this is the case is most persuasively demonstrated by the weak efficiency of pari-mutuel betting markets. See the discussion of pari-mutuel betting in Chapter 3.

27. These structural characteristics are discussed in Chapter 2. Economic rationality in risky decisionmaking is analyzed by Theodore Tsukahara, Jr., and Harold J. Brumm, Jr., "Economic Rationality, Psychology and Decision-Making under Uncertainty," in *Gambling and Society*, ed. Eadington, pp. 92–107.

28. Since the opening of Resorts International in Atlantic City in 1978, we have been conducting an on-site study of gambling at racetracks in New Jersey, New York, and Pennsylvania and casinos in Atlantic City and Nevada. In the course of this study we have interviewed persons at all levels of commercial gambling, including most especially racetrack and casino executives and employees. We have also been conducting extensive interviews with gamblers at these establishments, and designed a detailed questionnaire that has been administered to more than one hundred casino patrons and horseplayers. These interviews have employed forced-choice and open-ended questions that, among other things, elicit information about the kinds of games preferred, the kind and location of gambling establishments patronized, the reasons for this patronage, perceptions of success or failure at gambling, levels of wagering, and reactions of friends and relations to gambling. We also explored gamblers' careers

or histories, including questions relating to initial introductions to gambling. Data collection and analysis are on-going, but preliminary findings have been presented in several papers. Final study results will include a comparison of respondents to a control group of nongamblers from a randomly distributed questionnaire. We are especially interested in comparisons of socioeconomic status, leisure interests, marital and occupational stability, social networks, and attitudes about "luck," "fate," and the gamblers and nongamblers themselves. Data to date do not support the accepted psychological stereotypes of compulsive gamblers, nor do gamblers appear to differ significantly from the control group. Unlike Ted E. Dielman, "Gambling: A Social Problem?" *Journal of Social Issues* 35 (1979), pp. 36–42, we have found no indications of social or personal disorganization among racetrack and casino gamblers, who on the contrary are quite *conventional*. It was this finding that prompted us to rethink the issue of gambling as deviance/pathology and/or related to general social disorganization.

29. Compare the findings of the University of Michigan's Survey Research Center survey: 86 percent of trackgoers and 78 percent of casino patrons gave "to have a good time" as their reason for gambling, with "to make money" the reason of 33 percent and 36 percent of these respective groups. "Excitement" (the primary reason given by 51 percent of trackgoers and 46 percent of casino patrons) and "challenge" (40 percent and 41 percent, respectively) were also more common motivations than making money. Kallick, "Survey of American Gambling," in *Gambling in America*, Appendix 2, pp. 45–48.

30. Jerome H. Skolnick, *House of Cards: Legalization and Control of Casino Gambling* (Boston: Little, Brown, 1978). This classic study is usefully supplemented by John Dennis Dombrink, "Outlaw Businessmen: Organized Crime and the Legalization of Casino Gambling" (Ph.D. diss., University of California, Berkeley, 1981), with much valuable material on Atlantic City.

31. Off-track betting has been an issue in California since the early 1970s. Prior to 1983 the various interests that comprise the State's racing industry were unable to agree on a format for OTB; during the summer of that year, however, an industry accord was reached on an off-track betting proposal embodied in Assembly Bill 1517, which despite considerable support failed to pass the legislature due to opposition from the State's attorney general and governor, who threatened to veto the bill. The legislation's prospects for enactment in 1984 are unclear at the time of writing; there is, however, widespread expectation that off-track betting is an inevitable development in the majority of racing States. As of 1984, Illinois is the State most likely to legalize off-track betting.

32. For a discussion of illegal sports betting and other forms of illegal gambling, see the Appendix.

33. For the derivation of this estimate see the Appendix.

34. Mario Puzo, *The Godfather* (New York: Putnam, 1969).

35. Roger Caillois, *Man, Play, and Games*, trans. from *Les jeus et les hommes* (Paris: Gallimard, 1958) by Meyer Barash (New York: Schocken Books, 1979).

36. Johan Huizinga, *Homo Ludens: A Study of the Play-Element in Culture* (Boston: Beacon Press, 1955).

37. Caillois, *Men, Play, and Games*, pp. 41, 54.

38. And, in fact, all four of Caillois's categories of play: *aléa*, competition (*agon*), mimicry, and vertigo (*ilinx*). Ibid., p. 40.

39. Ibid., p. 72.

40. Ibid., p. 73.

41. Ibid., p. 157.

42. Goffman, "Where the Action Is," pp. 149–270.

43. For a general discussion of symbolic interactionism see Jerome Manis and Bernard Meltzer, eds., *Symbolic Interaction: A Reader in Social Psychology* (Boston: Allyn and Bacon, 1972); Anselm Straus, *George Herbert Mead on Social Psychology* (Chicago: University of Chicago Press, 1964); Don Martindale, *The Nature and Types of Sociological Theory* (Boston: Houghton Mifflin, 1960); Ruth Wallace and Alison Wolf, *Contemporary Sociological Theory* (New York: Prentice Hall, 1980).

44. George Herbert Mead, *Mind, Self and Society* (Chicago: University of Chicago Press, 1934).

45. Howard Becker, *Outsiders: Studies in the Sociology of Deviance* (New York: Free Press, 1963); David Matza, *Delinquency and Drift* (New York: Wiley, 1964).

46. Becker, "Becoming a Marijuana User," *American Journal of Sociology* 59 (November 1953), pp. 235–42.

47. Lesieur, *The Chase*.

48. Livingston, "Compulsive Gambling: A Culture of Losers," pp. 51–55; Kusyszyn, "Compulsive Gambling," pp. 95–101.

49. This theme is developed by Mary Douglas and Aaron Wildavsky, *Culture and Risk* (New York: Random House, 1982).

50. For a discussion of Durkheim and modern sociological structural functionalism see Robert K. Merton, *Social Theory and Social Science* (Glencoe, Illinois: Free Press, 1957); Talcott Parsons and Edward Shills, eds., *Toward a General Theory of Action* (New York: Harper, 1951); George Simpson, *Emile Durkheim* (New York: Thomas Y. Crowell, 1963); Wallace and Wolf, *Contemporary Sociological Theory*.

51. Zola, "Observations on Gambling in a Lower-Class Setting," pp. 353–61.

52. Goffman, "Where the Action Is."

53. Herman, "Gambling as Work," p. 101.

54. Ibid., p. 107.

55. Vicki Abt and James Smith, "Playing the Game in Mainstream America," in *World of Play*, ed. Frank E. Manning (West Point, N.Y.: Leisure Press, 1983).

56. Max Weber, *The Protestant Ethic and the Spirit of Capitalism* (New York: Charles Scribner, 1930).

57. Not coincidentally, at a time when real investment opportunities are largely foreclosed within the economic system, at least for the lower classes. For many of the multi-million dollar lottery prizewinners whose rags-to-riches biographies are regularly reported in the press investments in the local State lottery may indeed be the most likely chance of exchanging their rags for a piece of the American dream.

58. Christopher Lasch, *The Culture of Narcissism: American Life in an Age of Diminishing Expectations* (New York: Warner Books, 1979).

59. Caillois, *Man, Play, and Games*, p. 158.

60. Games of mixed chance and skill (e.g., poker, baccarat, and blackjack) are not as democratic: skill, which is a function of biology to the extent that intelligence and stamina are factors in its development and exercise, partially determines the odds at which these games are played.

61. Here also skill is a factor, in that considerable expertise is required to use the information reflected in the constantly shifting pari-mutuel odds to best advantage.

62. Edward C. Devereux, Jr., "Gambling and the Social Structure: A Sociological Study of Lotteries and Horseracing in Contemporary America" (Ph.D. diss., Harvard University, 1949).

63. Devereux, quoted in D.M. Downes, B.P. Davies, M.E. David, and P. Stone, *Gambling, Work and Leisure: A Study across Three Areas* (London: Routledge and Kegan Paul, 1976), p. 79.

64. Ibid.

65. Goffman, as has been noted, is an exception, but the essay form of "Where the Action Is" did not lend itself to an exhaustive treatment.

66. Emile Durkheim, *Suicide* (1897; Glencoe, Illinois: Free Press, 1964).

67. A notable exception is Skolnick's *House of Cards*.

68. For a good overview of sociological conflict theories see Reinhard Bendix and Seymour M. Lipset, eds., *Class, Status and Power* (Glencoe, Illinois: Free Press, 1953); Percy S. Cohen, *Modern Social Theory* (New York: Basic Books, 1968); Irving Louis Horowitz, ed., *The New Sociology: Essays in Social Science and Social Theory in Honor of C. Wright Mills* (New York: Oxford University Press, 1964); Graham C. Kinloch, *Ideology and Contemporary Sociological Theory* (New York: Prentice Hall, 1981); Wallace and Wolf, *Contemporary Sociological Theory*.

69. A detailed comparison of various conflict theories can be found in H.H. Gerth and C. Wright Mills, trans. and eds., *From Max Weber: Essays in Sociology* (New York: Oxford University Press, 1958); Reinhard Bendix, *Max Weber: An Intellectual Portrait* (New York: Anchor Books, 1962); Julien Freund, *The Sociology of Max Weber* (New York: Vintage Books, 1969); T.B. Bottomore, "Marxist Sociology," in *International Encyclopedia of the Social Sciences*, ed. David L. Sills (New York: Free Press, 1968), 10:46–53; Robert Friedman, *Marxist Social Thought* (New York: Harcourt, Brace and World, 1968); Claus Offe, "Political Authority and Class Structures: An Analysis of Late Capitalist Societies," *International Journal of Sociology* 2 (Spring 1972), pp. 73–108; and Robert Alford, "Paradigms of Relations Between State and Society," in *Stress and*

Contradiction in Modern Capitalism, ed. L. Lindberg (Lexington, Massachusetts: Heath, 1977), pp. 145–59.

70. Many clergymen do see gambling as an acceptable revenue producer, at least for religious institutions. Charitable gambling is allowed in nearly every State, and, if charitable bingo is included, generates several hundred million dollars in revenues annually.

71. This is not to beg the important and difficult questions of public policy that are raised by the movement of regulators and other persons who by virtue of public office are in positions to influence gambling policies or businesses, from government to the gambling industry. Conflict of interest *while the individual still exercises regulatory power* is an ever-present and serious problem. Government's ability to compete with the gambling industry for talented personnel is also questionable in many States: it is clearly in the public interest to have regulators of the highest caliber, but when middle-level gambling industry executives are more highly paid than the highest elected officials, as is very often the case, it may be impossible to attract qualified persons to regulatory agencies or keep them from moving into the industry.

72. The best account of bookmaking careers is Peter Reuter, *Disorganized Crime: The Economics of the Visible Hand* (Cambridge, Massachusetts: MIT Press, 1983), pp. 26–29.

73. See for example Ken Uston, *Million Dollar Blackjack* (Hollywood, Calif.: Scientific Research Services, 1981). This is the most recent of three books Uston has written on blackjack. The Treasury Casino in Las Vegas sponsored Ken Uston's blackjack seminars, at which counters were allowed to play under certain time and betting limitations.

Bibliography

Abt Associates, Inc., *Income from Illegal Gambling* (Cambridge, Massachusetts, 1982).

Abt, Vicki, and Martin C. McGurrin, "Commercial Gambling and Values in American Society: The Social Construction of Risk," *Journal of Gambling Studies* 8, no. 4 (Winter 1992).

Abt, Vicki, James F. Smith, and Eugene Martin Christiansen, *The Business of Risk: Commercial Gambling in Mainstream America* (Lawrence, Kansas, University Press of Kansas, 1985). The first comprehensive study of gambling since the legalization of Atlantic City gaming and the rapid growth of state lotteries.

Acuri, A.F., D. Lester, and F.O. Smith, "Shaping Adolescent Gambling Behavior," *Adolescence* 20 (1985).

Albanese, Jay S., "The Effect of Casino Gambling on Crime," *Federal Probation* 49, no. 2 (June 1985), pp. 39–44.

Ali, Mukhtar, "Some Evidence of the Efficiency of a Speculative Market," *Econometrica* 47, no. 2 (March 1979), pp. 387–392.

Allmone, Carolyn I., and Mary Pope, *The Economic Impact of the Horse Racing and Breeding Industry* (Bloomington, Minnesota: Minnesota Racing Commission, April 1991).

Alsop, Ronald, "Casino Glut in Atlantic City Brings Intense Competition," *Wall Street Journal*, January 14, 1981.

Barr, Stephen, "Video Gambling: Help for State Budget or Just Another Game?" *New York Times*, February 17, 1991.

Barthelemy, Sidney J., "A Review of Studies on Casino Gambling in New Orleans," report by the Mayor, New Orleans, Louisiana, May 8, 1989.

Bell, Raymond C., "Moral Views on Gambling Promulgated by Major American Religious Bodies," in *Gambling in America: Final Report of the Commission on the Review of the National Policy Toward Gambling* (Washington, D.C.: GPO, 1976), Appendix 1, pp. 161–239.

Better Government Association, *Staff White Paper: Casino Gambling in Chicago* (Chicago, Illinois, October 1992).

Blakey, G. Robert, "State Conducted Lotteries: History, Problems, and Promises," *Journal of Social Issues* 35, no. 3 (Summer 1979), pp. 62–86.

Bloomberg, Jeffrey L., Testimony at Hearing on the National Impact of Casino Gambling Proliferation, Committee on Small Business, U.S. House of Representatives, Washington, D.C., September 21, 1994.

Borg, Mary O., Paul M. Mason, and Stephen L. Shapiro, "The Incidence of Taxes on Casino Gambling: Exploiting the Tribal and Poor," *American Journal of Economics and Sociology* 50, no. 3 (July 1991).

Branch, Taylor, "What's Wrong with the Lottery?" *New England Monthly* (January 1990).

Brenner, Reuven, and Gabrielle A. Brenner, *Gambling and Speculation: A Theory, a History, and a Future of Some Human Decisions* (Cambridge, Massachusetts: Cambridge University Press, 1990). An important work on gambling by an economist who argues that gambling prohibitions tend to produce more harm than good.

Campbell, Felicia, "Gambling: A Positive View," chapter 13 in *Gambling and Society, Interdisciplinary Studies on the Subject of Gambling*, ed. William R. Eadington (Springfield, Illinois: Charles C. Thomas Publishers, 1976).

Center for State Policy Research, *State Gambling Issues* (Washington, D.C.: Center for State Policy Research, 1992).

Center for State Policy Research, *Gaming Issues Report: An Industry Matures* (Washington, D.C.: Center for State Policy Research, 1994).

Chafetz, Henry. *Play the Devil: A History of Gambling in the United States from 1492 to 1955* (New York: Clarkson N. Potter, 1960). A highly readable general gambling history.

Christiansen, Eugene Martin. "The New Jersey Experience and the Financial Condition of Atlantic City," newsletter of the Institute for the Study of Gambling and Commercial Gaming, April 1991.

Citizen's Research Education Network (CREN), *The Other Side of the Coin: A Casino's Impact in Hartford* (Hartford, Connecticut: CREN, December 1992).

City of Chicago Gaming Commission, Report to the Mayor (Chicago, Illinois), June 10, 1992.

Clotfelter, Charles T., and Philip J. Cook, *Selling Hope: State Lotteries in America* (Cambridge, Massachusetts: Harvard University Press, 1989).

Commission on the Review of the National Policy Toward Gambling, *Gambling in America, Appendix 1: Stafford Consultant Papers, Model Statutes, Bibliography, Correspondence* (Washington, D.C.: Government Printing Office, October 1976).

———, *Gambling in America, Appendix 2: Survey of American Gambling Attitudes and Behavior* (Washington, D.C.: Government Printing Office, October 1976).

———, *Gambling in America, Appendix 3: Summaries of Commission Hearings* (Washington, D.C.: Government Printing Office, October 1976).

Cook, James, "Lottomania," *Forbes*, March 6, 1994, p. 94.

Cooke, Robert Allan, and Sandeep Mangalmurti, *State Lotteries: Seducing the Less Fortunate?* (Chicago, Illinois: The Heartland Institute, 1991).

Cornelius, Judy, and William R. Eadington (eds.), *Gambling and Public Policy: International Perspectives* (Reno: University of Nevada Press, 1991).

Custer, Robert L., and Harry Milt, *When Luck Runs Out* (New York: Facts on File, 1985).

Dao, James, "Casino Issue Divides Mohawk Reservation in New York" *New York Times*, March 21, 1993, p. 33.

Dombrink, John, and William N. Thompson, *The Last Resort: Success and Failure in Campaigns for Casinos* (Las Vegas: University of Nevada Press, 1990).

Ezell, John Samuel, *Fortune's Mercy Wheel: The Lottery in America* (Cambridge, Massachusetts: Harvard University Press, 1960). An excellent history of American lotteries.

Findlay, John M., *People of Chance: Gambling in American Society from Jamestown to Las Vegas* (New York: Oxford University Press, 1986).

Florida Department of Law Enforcement, *The Question of Casinos in Florida—Increased Crime: Is it Worth the Gamble?* (Tallahassee, Florida: Florida Department of Law Enforcement, August 15, 1994).

Fox, Candace E., *Fiscal Impact Analysis—Casino Gambling and the Public Sector* (Reno: University of Nevada Press, 1990). Presented at the Eighth International Conference on Risk and Gambling, London, England, August 1990.

Goodman, Robert, *Legalized Gambling as a Strategy for Economic Development* (Northampton, Massachusetts: United States Gambling Study, March 1994).

———, *The Luck Business: The Devastating Consequences and Broken Promises of America's Gambling Explosion* (New York: Free Press, 1995). An important book by a leading gambling policy analyst who argues that state governments have created gambling policies that tend to hurt rather than protect the poor.

———, Testimony at Hearing on the National Impact of Gambling Proliferation, U.S. House of Representatives, Committee on Small Business, Washington, D.C., September 21, 1994.

Governor's Advisory Commission of Gambling. *Report and Recommendations of the Governor's Advisory Commission of Gambling* (Trenton, N.J., June 30, 1988).

Governor's Office of Planning and Research, *California and Nevada: Subsidy, Monopoly, and Competitive Effects of Legalized Gambling* (Sacramento, California: Governor's Office of Planning and Research, December 1992).

James, Raymond and Associates, *The Dramatic Growth of Legalized Gambling in North America* (St. Petersburg, Florida: Research Report, September 3, 1991).

Kindt, John W., "The Economic Impacts of Legalized Gambling Activities," *Drake Law Review* 43, no. 1 (1994).

———, "Increased Crime and Legalizing Operations: The Impact on the Socio-Economics of Business and Government," *Criminal Law Bulletin* (November-December 1994).

———, "U.S. National Security and the Strategic Economic Base: The Business/Economic Impacts of the Legalization of Gambling Activities," *St. Louis University Law Journal* 39, no. 2 (Winter 1995).

King, Rufus, John J. Congressional Representative, Statement at Hearing on the National Impact of Casino Gambling Proliferation, U.S. House of Representatives, Committee on Small Business, Washington, D.C., September 21, 1994.

Lehne, Richard, "A Contemporary Review of Legalized Gambling," in *Report and Recommendations of the New Jersey Governor's Advisory Commission on Gambling* (Trenton, N.J., June 30, 1988).

Lesieur, Henry R., *The Chase: Career of the Compulsive Gambler* (Cambridge, Massachusetts: Schenkman Books, 1984). A discussion of the mindset of compulsive gamblers by a leading expert.

———, "Compulsive Gambling," *Society* (May/June 1992).

———, "Report on Pathological Gambling in New Jersey," in *Report and Recommendations of the Governor's Advisory Commission on Gambling* (Trenton, N.J., June 30, 1988).

Lowenstein, Roger, "Video Lottery Stock Has Been a Winning Bet, but the Odds Aren't All in the House's Favor," *Wall Street Journal*, October 9, 1991.

Marcum, Jess, and Henry Rowen, "How Many Games in Town? The Pros and Cons of Legalized Gambling," *The Public Interest* 36 (Summer 1974).

Massachusetts Attorney General's Office, "Attorneys General from Five N.E. States and N.Y. Speak Out Against Expanded Gambling," press release, November 22, 1993.

Meier, Barry, "Casinos Putting Tribes at Odds," *New York Times*, January 13, 1994, p. D1.

Minnesota Indian Gaming Association, "Economic Benefits of Tribal Gaming in Minnesota," March 1992.

Minnesota Planning, *High Stakes: Gambling in Minnesota* (St. Paul, Minnesota: Minnesota State Planning Agency, March 1992).

Mobilia, Pamela, "A Little Bit More Evidence of Lottery Regressivity: The Kansas State Lottery," *Journal of Gambling Studies* 8, no. 4 (Winter 1992).

Morin, Charles H. *Gambling in America: Final Report of the Commission on the Review of the National Policy Toward Gambling* (Washington, D.C.: Government Printing Office, 1976).

National Indian Gaming Association, *Speaking the Truth About Indian Gaming* (Washington, D.C., 1993).

New Orleans District Attorney's Office, *The Impact of Casino Gambling on the City of New Orleans* (New Orleans, Louisiana, June 1986).

Office of Planning and Budgeting, *Casinos in Florida: An Analysis of the Economic and Social Impacts* (Tallahassee, Florida: Executive Office of the Governor, Office of Planning and Budgeting, 1994).

Pannell, Kerr, and Forster, *Gambling Impact: An Overview of the Effect of Legalized Gambling in the City of New Orleans* (New Orleans, Louisiana: Prepared for the Gaming Committee of the Greater New Orleans Tourist and Convention Commission, April 1986).

Passell, Peter, "Lotto Is Financed by the Poor and Won by the States," *New York Times*, May 21, 1989, p. E6.

Public Affairs Research Council of Louisiana, Inc., "Legalized Gambling in Louisiana: A Review of the Issues," February 13, 1986.

Reuter, Peter, *Disorganized Crime: The Economics of the Visible Hand* (Cambridge, Massachusetts: MIT Press, 1983). Contains an excellent account of bookmaking careers.

Rose, I. Nelson, "Gambling and the Law," *Indian Gaming* (January 1992), p. 12.

Rosett, R.N., "Gambling and Rationality," *Journal of Political Economy* 73, no. 6 (December 1965).

Sasuly, Richard, *Bookies and Bettors: 200 Years of Gambling* (New York: Holt, Rinehart and Winston, 1982).

Scott, L., and Earl Ryan, *The Economics of Casino Gambling* (Baton Rouge, Louisiana: Louisiana State University Press, 1987).

Senate (New York State) Finance Subcommittee on Racing, Gaming, and Wagering, *Staff Report on Casino Gambling Legislation* (Albany, N.Y.: New York State Senate, June 23, 1994).

Shaffer, Howard J., "The Emergence of Youthful Addiction: The Prevalence of Underage Lottery Use and the Impact of Gambling," Technical Report No. 011394–100 (Boston, Massachusetts: Massachusetts Council on Compulsive Gambling, January 13, 1994).

———, Sharon A. Stein, Blase Gambino, and Thomas A Cummings, *Compulsive Gambling: Theory, Research and Practice* (Lexington Books, 1989).

Sifakis, Carl, *The Encyclopedia of Gambling* (New York: Facts on File, 1990).

Skolnick, Jerome H., *House of Cards: Legalization and the Control of Casino Gambling* (Boston, Massachusetts: Little, Brown, 1978). This classic study is highly recommended.

Thompson, William et al., *The Economic Impact of Native American Gaming in Wisconsin* (Milwaukee, Wisconsin: Wisconsin Policy Research Institute, April 1995).

Thompson, William N., *Legalized Gambling* (Santa Barbara, California: ABC-CLIO, Inc., 1994).

Todd, Nancy, "Legalizing Gambling and Doing It Right," *Campaigns and Elections* (April 1984).

Vizenor, Gerald, *The People Named the Chippewa: Narrative Histories* (Minneapolis: University of Minnesota Press, 1984).

Walker, Michael B., *The Psychology of Gambling* (Oxford, England: Pergammon Press, 1992).

Weinstein, David, and Lilian Deitch, *The Impact of Legalized Gambling: The Socioeconomic Consequences of Lotteries and Off-Track Betting* (New York: Praeger, 1974).

Wolf, Frank R., Congressional Representative, Introductory Statement on National Gambling Impact and Policy Commission (Washington, D.C.: Office of Representative Frank R. Wolf, January 11, 1995) (in conjunction with 104th Congress, H.R. 497, A Bill to Create the National Gambling Impact and Policy Commission, submitted January 11, 1995).

Reprint Acknowledgments

"Quick Draw McGraws," by R. Emmett Tyrell, Jr. Reprinted from *The American Spectator*, February 1966. Reprinted by permission of Creators Syndicate. "The Wagers of Sin," by Nick Gillespie. Reprinted, with permission, from the June 1996 issue of *Reason* magazine. © 1996 by the Reason Foundation, 3415 S. Sepulveda Blvd., Suite 400, Los Angeles, CA 90034. "Against All Odds," by John Zipperer. Originally printed in *Christianity Today*, November 14, 1994. Reprinted by permission of the author. © 1994 John Zipperer. "Gambling's Advocates are Right–But for the Wrong Reasons," by Gary S. Becker. Reprinted from March 31, 1995, issue of *Business Week* by special permission. © 1995 by the McGraw-Hill Companies, Inc. "Compulsive Gambling," by Henry Lesieur. Reprinted from *Society*, May–June, 1992. © 1992 Transaction Publishers. Reprinted by permission of Transaction Publishers of Rutgers University, the State University of New Jersey. "Refuting the Myths of Compulsive Gambling," by Richard E. Vatz and Lee S. Weinberg. Reprinted from *USA Today Magazine*, 1993. Reprinted by permission of the authors and *USA Today Magazine*. "Casinos and the Compulsive Gambler: Is There a Duty to Monitor the Gambler's Wagers?" by Joy Wolfe. Reprinted by permission of the University of Mississippi Law School. "America's House of Cards," by Marc Cooper. Reprinted with permission from the February 19, 1996 issue of *The Nation*. "Lotto Fever, We All Lose," by Peter Keating. Reprinted from *Money*, May, 1996. © 1996 Time-Warner Inc. Reprinted by permission of Time-Warner Inc. "The Negative Impacts of Legalized Gambling on Businesses," by John Warren Kindt. Reprinted by permission of the author and the University of Miami Business Law School. "Government, Taxation, and the Impact of Prohibitions," by Reuven Brenner. From *Gambling and Speculation: A*

Theory, a History . . . by Gabrielle A. and Reuven Brenner. © 1990 Cambridge University Press. Reprinted with the permission of Cambridge University Press. "The Explosive Growth of Gambling in the United States." Reprinted by permission of Senator Paul Simon. "Address to the National Coalition Against Legalized Gambling," by Senator Richard Lugar. Reprinted by permission of NCALG. "Yes, Gambling Is Productive and Rational," by David Ramsay Steele. Reprinted by permission from the September 1997 issue of *Liberty*, published by R.W. Bradford, P.O. Box 1181, Port Townsend, WA 98368. "The Promises and Perils of Legalized Gambling for Local Governments: Who Decides How to Stack the Deck"? by Paul D. Delva. Reprinted by permission of the author and Temple University School of Law. "State Rights, Tribal Sovereignty, and the 'White Man's Firewater': State Prohibition of Gambling on New Indian Lands," by Leah Lorber. Reprinted by permission of the Indiana University School of Law. "The Good Gamble." Reprinted from *The Luck Business* by Robert Goodman. © 1995 The Free Press, a division of Simon and Schuster. Reprinted by permission of Simon and Schuster. "Tribal Gaming: Myths and Facts." Reprinted by permission of the National Indian Gaming Association. "Casino Wars–Ethics and Economics in Indian Country," by Jon Magnuson. Reprinted from the February 16, 1994 issue of the *Christian Century*. © 1994 Christian Century Foundation. Reprinted by permission from the Christian Century Foundation. "On the Indianness of Bingo: Gambling and the Native American Community," by Paul Pasquaretta. From *Critical Inquiry* 20, no. 4 (1994), pp. 694–714. © 1994 University of Chicago Press. Reprinted by permission of University of Chicago Press. "Dances with Sharks," by David Segal. Reprinted with permission from *The Washington Monthly*. © The Washington Monthly Company, 1611 Connecticut Ave., N.W., Washington, D.C. 20009 (202) 462-0128. "Misconceptions About Legalized Gambling." From *The Business of Risk* by Vicki Abt, James F. Smith, and Eugene Martin Christiansen. Reprinted by permission of University Press of Kansas. ©

Index